Remade in China

Remade in China

Foreign Investors and Institutional Change in China

Scott Wilson

OXFORD
UNIVERSITY PRESS

2009

OXFORD
UNIVERSITY PRESS

Oxford University Press, Inc., publishes works that further
Oxford University's objective of excellence
in research, scholarship, and education.

Oxford   New York
Auckland   Cape Town   Dar es Salaam   Hong Kong   Karachi
Kuala Lumpur   Madrid   Melbourne   Mexico City   Nairobi
New Delhi   Shanghai   Taipei   Toronto

With offices in
Argentina   Austria   Brazil   Chile   Czech Republic   France   Greece
Guatemala   Hungary   Italy   Japan   Poland   Portugal   Singapore
South Korea   Switzerland   Thailand   Turkey   Ukraine   Vietnam

Published by Oxford University Press, Inc.
198 Madison Avenue, New York, New York 10016

www.oup.com

Oxford is a registered trademark of Oxford University Press

Library of Congress Cataloging-in-Publication Data

Wilson, Scott Howard.
Remade in China : foreign investors and institutional change in China /
Scott Wilson.
    p. cm.
Includes bibliographical references and index.
ISBN 978-0-19-538831-2
1.   China—Foreign economic relations—1976– 2.   Investments, Japanese—China.
3.   Investments, American—China.   4.   China—Economic policy.
5.   China—Social policy. I. Title.
HF1604.W55 2009
330.951—dc22   2008051383

9 8 7 6 5 4 3 2 1

Printed in the United States of America
on acid-free paper

Acknowledgments

The course of writing this book has been long and winding, including three trips to Shanghai and one to Tokyo for interviews as well as documentary research at libraries in Shanghai, Tokyo, and the Washington, D.C., area. Consequently, there are many people to thank. In Shanghai, the Shanghai Academy of Social Sciences provided a welcome research environment and help translating a number of interviews from Japanese to Chinese. At SASS, Professor Xie Kang helped to arrange contacts with local labor leaders, and Li Yihai, director of the International Affairs Office, as well as other members of his staff, including Zhao Nianguo and Xu Jia, facilitated my research affiliation, helped translate interviews from Japanese, renewed my family's visas, and even took me to the Shanghai Circus. In Tokyo, Kazuo Kato of Sophia University made possible an extensive visit to his institution, provided encouragement, helped to arrange several interviews, and warmly welcomed me to Tokyo, including accompanying me to watch sumo wrestling and a Tokyo Giants game, two unforgettable experiences.

The bulk of the research presented here was conducted in 2000, with trips to Tokyo in 2001 and Shanghai in 2005. Additionally, I conducted phone interviews with human resource specialists during 2003 and with human resources and legal professionals in 2007. During the course of the research, it was a pleasure to interview over 100 business managers, business organization representatives, attorneys, and staff for this book. Although I guard their anonymity here, I am deeply indebted to their time spent answering my questions. Without them, the writing of this book would have been impossible. The research also could not have proceeded without several substantial grants. The research was launched with a yearlong grant from the Committee for Scholarly Communication with China in 2000. My round of interviews in Tokyo was generously supported by funds from the Japan-U.S. Friendship Committee, administered by the Social Science Research Council. I was able to make shorter visits to Shanghai and Washington, D.C., thanks to the University Grants Committee at the University of the South, chaired by Deans Tom Kazee and Rita Kipp.

During the seven years of researching and writing, I received encouragement and feedback from George Farmer, Jacques deLisle, Peter Katzenstein, Vivienne Shue, David Wank, Andrew Cortell, and members of a Salzburg Seminar titled, "China and the Global Economy." Dave McBride at Oxford University Press provided timely feedback on the review process and shepherded the manuscript to eventual adoption. Dorothy Bauhoff greatly improved the readability of the manuscript with her copy-editing skills. Colleagues at my home institution, including Charles Brockett, Gayle McKeen, Paige Schneider, Safia Swimelar, Elwood Dunn, Jim Peterman, Richard O'Connor, Yasmeen Mohiuddin, and Harold Goldberg encouraged my work on the manuscript and were good friends and colleagues over the years. Additionally, Woody Register, Julie Berebitsky, Nancy Berner, David Coe, Steve Raulston, and Jenny Raulston deserve special thanks for their support of the project and the understanding that friends extend during difficult times in the writing process. I am deeply indebted to their friendship and intellectual nourishment.

Marc Blecher, who taught and inspired me at Oberlin College, continues to mentor me and serves as a model of a scholar who is equally dedicated to his family life. I have long strived to follow in his footsteps, but I have never been able to keep up with him or to fill his shoes. He is too modest to acknowledge the profound influence that he has had on me and so many other young scholars in the China field. He also read the entire manuscript and conveyed his enthusiasm for the project. Additionally, my parents, Hugh and Barbara Wilson, showed constant interest in this project and its progress. Thanks to them for not blinking when I first discussed studying in China in 1985 as an undergraduate, which turned out to be the starting point of my relationship with Chinese studies. Of course, all errors and omissions are my responsibility and not the fault of the many people who lent a hand in the final version of the book.

Finally, I am most deeply indebted to my family for their patience and support over the long course of completing this manuscript. My daughters, Marisa and Kyra, offered ample and welcome distractions from my teaching and writing. I only regret that I did not have more time for coaching their soccer and baseball teams. My deepest gratitude goes to my wife, Sherri Bergman, without whom this project would not have been possible. Not only did she take on the role of single parent during several of my research trips to Shanghai and Tokyo, but she also showed confidence in my writing, even when mine began to flag. To her with love, I dedicate this book.

Contents

List of Figures

List of Tables

List of Abbreviations

ACFTU	All-China Federation of Trade Unions
CCP	Chinese Communist Party
CIETAC	Chinese International Economy and Trade Arbitration Commission
CJV	Cooperative Joint Venture
CSR	Corporate Social Responsibility
EJV	Equity Joint Venture
FBIS	Foreign Broadcast Information Service
FDI	Foreign Direct Investment
FESCO	Foreign Employment Services Company
FIE	Foreign-Invested Enterprise
GNI	Gross National Income
HR	Human Resources
IMF	International Monetary Fund
JPRS	Joint Publications Research Service
JV	Joint Venture
MBO	Management by Objective
MFN	Most Favored Nation
MNC	Multinational Corporation
MOFCOM	Ministry of Commerce
MOFTEC	Ministry of Foreign Trade and Economic Cooperation
NPC	National People's Congress
SEZ	Special Economic Zone

SFAIC	Shanghai Far East Aero-Technology Import and Export Corporation
SOE	State-Owned Enterprise
TRIPS	Trade-Related aspects of Intellectual Property
UN	United Nations
UNCITRAL	United Nations Commission on International Trade Law
USCBC	United States-China Business Council
WFOE	Wholly Foreign-Owned Enterprise
WTO	World Trade Organization

Remade in China

Introduction: China and Globalization

China's opening to foreign investment, trade, and culture generated consternation among Chinese leaders and citizens. When China opened its doors to foreigners in 1979, many Chinese citizens and leaders expressed concern about a return to foreign domination over China. A common analogy offered up by critics of the policy was China's futile efforts to resist imperialism during the Opium Wars (1839–1842 and 1856–1860) and the subsequent concessions to open China's ports to foreigners. China, a very poor country at that time, was carved up by imperialists, causing a steep decline of social, economic, and political standards. In 1981, just two years after China opened up to foreign investment and trade, *Renmin Ribao,* China's leading state-run newspaper, ran an article that addressed the role of Lin Zexu, the Chinese general who, in 1839, led a group of Chinese to destroy a shipment of British opium by dumping the drug into ponds mixed with lime and salt—an act akin to the Boston Tea Party—igniting the First Opium War against British imperialism. According to the article, China should view General Lin as a hero for leading the fight against the British and, more importantly, for his efforts to import Western weapons to be turned against imperialists. General Lin had the insight to use foreign technology in order to advance Chinese national interests, thus, "open[ing] up an unprecedented vista for the ignorant and blindly xenophobic society of his time and enlighten[ing] some patriotic and progressive senior officials to the reality of the day."[1]

The publication of this odd account must be understood against the backdrop of China's political debates about its contemporary open door policy. Just as Lin Zexu tried to rouse China out of its insular and superstitious

3

slumber to fight foreign aggressors, preeminent leader Deng Xiaoping, who led China to adopt a policy of global engagement, found himself in a battle on two fronts: to convince the Chinese Communist Party (CCP) not to be blinded by socialist ideology but to use empirical analysis in the process of formulating policies, even if that meant borrowing or learning institutions from the West; and to guide the foreign actors to help strengthen China.[2] Although China lost the Opium Wars and endured a "century of humiliation," the article lauds Lin Zexu's efforts to import Western guns to strengthen China and to fend off western powers.[3] In 1839 and in the context of China's 1979 open door policy, Chinese leaders struggled to determine how to integrate with and to learn from foreign countries while maintaining Chinese sovereignty and control. By analogy, post-Mao Chinese reformers were being patriotic by arguing that China had to absorb Western technology, capital, and business practices in order to advance China's Four Modernizations, in the fields of agriculture, industry, science and technology, and defense.

In 1979, the Chinese state began to guide China's opening to foreign trade, investment, and cultural flows in order to promote national advancement without sacrificing China's economic and political sovereignty. The question that China faced in 1981 and still faces today is: Can China absorb foreign investors and their institutions while directing those organizations and institutions toward national goals? Alternatively, will opening China to foreign firms and models unleash influences that China's leadership cannot tame? As China moved from a period of economic closure in 1976 to the world's largest recipient of foreign direct investment (hereafter, FDI) in 2003, the issue of how to manage the transplantation of foreign corporations and their business institutions became increasingly acute.

Foreign Investors and Institutional Change

Since 1978, when China began to permit foreign investment, it has climbed to be the world's leading recipient of FDI, receiving over $60 billion worth of investment annually since 2004. China's massive inflow of foreign investment raises two questions that animate the discussion in the rest of this book. First, has the presence of a growing number of foreign investors affected the course of local business and legal institutional reforms? Some scholars contend that global actors such as multinational corporations (MNCs) can alter a host country's institutions through competition or bargaining.[4] Host governments may adjust their laws, regulations, and tax codes to attract or to keep foreign investors.[5] MNCs also demonstrate alternative institutional designs, which local firms in host environments may emulate.[6] Accordingly, globalization has pressured China to converge on international economic, political, legal, and cultural institutions. Another group of scholars writing in path dependency, varieties of capitalism, and historical institutionalist veins claims that it is difficult for people—even reformers—fundamentally to change economic and political institutions.[7] Instead, reformers tend incrementally to alter existing institutions rather than creating new institutions from scratch.[8] Hence, many scholars contend that economic, legal, and political institutions are likely to remain distinct, rooted in national contexts, rather than to converge on some rational international model.[9] Shah M. Tarzi, however, contends that the relative bargaining power of particular host states and foreign investors determines the concessions made by host countries.[10] China is not a typical host economy because its population, strategic importance, military power, and legacy of socialist planning institutions enhance its bargaining power with foreign investors and international organizations. China has been well positioned to guard its institutions from foreign pressure, and Chinese leaders have used their bargaining strength to manage its relations with globalizing forces such as MNCs, making China an excellent case study for analyzing globalization and the dynamics of institutional change.

A second question that shapes the analysis of this book is: How have investors from different countries approached operating in China, and what distinct effects have they had on China's host environment? China has attracted investment from firms based in countries with widely varying economic institutions, including Japan, Hong Kong, Taiwan, France, Sweden, and the United States. Based on their home-country practices, firms have brought to China varying approaches to industrial relations,[11] management,[12] and legal dispute resolution.[13] How have the diverse institutions transplanted to China, combined with local institutions, and affected reform of local institutions? Addressing such questions from the vantage point of different investors helps to specify which ideas and institutions matter and the types of human agents who shape institutional change.

The interplay of foreign firms and China's domestic reform process is both dynamic and multifaceted. I contend that foreign investors and other foreign actors are providing models for China to emulate as Chinese officials attempt to craft new business, labor, and legal practices. Foreign companies that have moved to China have proved useful to the state by implementing new rules on labor and managerial practices that Chinese officials have sought to push through against the opposition of state-owned enterprises (hereafter, SOEs). Foreign actors have contributed to the modeling and implementation of China's domestic institutional reform process.[14] Though China's state is guiding its reforms and integration with the global economy, foreign firms and international actors are playing an increasingly important role in helping China to alter its economic practices and rules of the game. Foreign and domestic actors are not inherently opposed, but they can and do find mutual accommodation and act to achieve common goals. China is a crucible in which economic and legal institutions brought by foreign investors are challenging and are being combined with existing institutions and practices in China. In that sense, business and legal institutions in China should bear the label, "remade in China."

Early studies of foreign investment in China chronicled the tight strictures placed on foreign businesses operating in China, including regulations placed on management of foreign-invested enterprises (FIEs),[15] monitoring and control of foreign investors through the joint venture (hereafter, JV) partnerships with local SOEs,[16] and the creation of special economic zones (hereafter, SEZs) to isolate foreign businesses physically from domestic firms. By the late 1990s, China had loosened many of its controls over foreign investors (and foreign researchers), and researchers began to document foreign investors' contribution to China's domestic reforms, especially in the areas of management and labor practices.[17] The latest wave of scholarship on FDI in China establishes a critical linkage between China's creeping globalization and its domestic institutional reforms. For example, Doug Guthrie has argued that foreign investors have provided managerial and labor relations models for state owned enterprises to mimic. According to Guthrie, SOEs with JV partners were more likely to adopt western style management structures than SOEs without JV partners.[18] Mary Gallagher provides a more generalized understanding of the influence of foreign direct investment on labor and legal reforms in China. She asserts that SEZs served as "laboratories for reform" in which state officials and SOEs could learn new managerial techniques, and that foreign enterprises introduced new models for SOEs to mimic.[19] David Zweig contends that leading Chinese reforms such as Zhu Rongji used China's internationalization policy as "a cudgel with which to force through the reform of state-owned enterprises and to decrease corruption."[20] In addition, he argues that internationalization unleashed a domestic dynamic that pressed for further openness to international forces.[21] This book contributes to the growing scholarship on the process of institutional change in China, especially the diffusion of foreign institutions to China.

One shortcoming of most existing works on China's open door policy is a tendency to treat foreign direct investors as a unified group with similar interests and influence in China. In fact, firms from Japan, Europe, Hong Kong, and the United States, for example, brought starkly different expectations and institutions from their home countries, which shaped their experiences in China. While foreign investors have offered alternative institutional models for the Chinese to emulate and have introduced new ideas into China's economy, not all of the models and ideas have had the same effect on China. Some institutions have floundered in China or have come under critical scrutiny by Chinese and foreign observers alike, while others have flourished and received official praise. Moreover, the plurality of new models introduced by foreign investors created opportunities for Chinese reformers and firms to select which institutions they might wish to adopt. In the following chapters, I distinguish how foreign investors from different home countries have interacted with China's host business and legal environment, noting both the difficulties of transplanting foreign practices to China and China's selective adoption of foreign models for their domestic reforms. The study makes an important contribution to the study of China's globalization by answering key questions, such as: Which foreign models and institutions matter, and why? What roles do various domestic and foreign actors play in transferring such models to China?

To explore foreign investors' varieties of experience in China, I compare Japanese and U.S. corporations that have moved to Shanghai. Japanese and U.S. firms have brought to China contrasting approaches to management, labor relations, and legal issues, making them excellent cases with which to analyze how firms with different institutional backgrounds operate in and affect China's business and legal environment. Moreover, Chinese officials have, at various times, pointed to Japanese and U.S. institutions for analysis and emulation. In addition, Japan and the United States are two of the top investors (by volume of investment), so they are important cases to analyze.

Few scholars of foreign investment have undertaken systematic comparisons of the experience and influence of Japanese and U.S. investors in China. Of the few existing studies on Japanese and U.S. firms' labor practices in China, most scholars suggest that the Japanese model is better suited to China's host environment.[22] These authors contend that China is adopting a corporatist labor bargaining arrangement with weak labor organizations, a model similar to that employed in Japan. In the legal realm, Japanese legal traditions and practices borrowed heavily from Chinese legal institutions, so one might expect Japanese firms to operate well in China's legal framework, but that has not been the case. In contrast, I argue that U.S. investors, at least since the mid-1990s, have had greater influence on Chinese labor, managerial, and legal institutions. Japanese firms in China have encountered many problems implementing their business and legal approaches in China. Somewhat surprisingly, Chinese workers, especially white-collar staff, have responded favorably to U.S. business institutions, which sharply contrast to the egalitarianism and long-term employment commitments that, at least until recently, characterized the labor practices in large Chinese and Japanese firms. Similarly, China's growing legal contentiousness, evinced by a ballooning number of legal cases and lawyers, hints that China's legal culture and institutions are dynamic and are moving in the direction of an American rather than a Japanese pattern of legal practice.

Although I argue that China's business and legal institutions are following aspects of American practice, China is far from falling under the spell of U.S. hegemony. To the contrary, top Chinese officials repeatedly have asserted China's independence and the need to be selective in the adoption of foreign institutions. At the inception of its opening to the world in 1978, China exercised firm control over foreign actors entering their shores. China's autarkic development under Maoist leadership (1949–1978) positioned China well to manage its relations with the rest of the world and to limit foreign actors' influence over China's institutions. Yet, over the reform period, China has adopted many aspects of foreign business and legal institutions. As China approaches its fourth decade of international engagement, it is important to reflect on how investment and trade flows and China's growing participation in international organizations are affecting Chinese political, economic, and legal development.

Foreign Capital and China's State-Guided Globalization

The above discussion of China's opening to foreign capital emphasized the impact of foreign investors on China's domestic reforms, but such an understanding threatens to overshadow the role of domestic actors in the process. At the center of China's reforms is the state, and any analysis of China's reforms and globalization must take account of it. Much of the process of institutional change has taken place at the level of formal rules and regulations, which state officials construct and apply. More broadly, officials pursued the open-door policy in order to achieve state-defined goals, namely technology transfer and infusion of capital, as part of a grand strategy of national development. The open-door policy was initially devised to limit the power of foreign actors over the Chinese economy and to secure state control over global integration. In the transition from a planned to a market economy, the state was well-positioned to manage the process of surrendering or off-loading, depending on one's perspective, some of its economic functions. With international engagement, however, China has significantly loosened its control over foreign investors and has found itself deeply embedded in international organizations and global economy. Has the Chinese state lost control over the forces that it invited to China and sought to harness for national purposes?

Foreign actors have brought significant pressure to bear on Chinese officials and non-state actors to revise policies and to alter its institutional makeup, yet China has enjoyed a context that allowed it to resist such pressure. As one interviewee commented, "For sure, there has been some protest of Chinese policies by foreign businesses, but that pressure alone would not cause the Chinese government to change its policies. The Chinese government would not have changed the rules if it was not interested in doing so."[23] Indeed, much of the story of China's institutional reform recounts how China's interests and preferences developed and were influenced by foreign actors.

I contend that foreign actors have helped China's state to reform its institutions in four ways. First, international actors have introduced new models of institutions, particularly in the area of industrial-labor relations and legal institutions. By introducing new institutional models and indicating where Chinese standards and rules have fallen short of international expectations, foreign parties have encouraged China to move toward international norms of conduct or to adopt their home-country practices. Foreign investors have brought distinct institutions and expectations for how to organize business and legal practice, which have combined with China's own institutions in unique ways and have offered Chinese reformers a menu of models with which to experiment. Second, international actors, especially foreign investors and international law firms, have trained Chinese actors who are forming a policy community, a group of professionals with policy-related expertise. These policy communities—bridging public and private sectors—are open to and advocate for China adopting foreign or hybrid legal and business institutions. Chinese trained in this way can spread knowledge of foreign-inspired institutions by taking their knowledge to Chinese organizations—both state organs and firms. For example, Chinese staff who work in foreign enterprises learn about foreign industrial relations and hiring practices, which they can transfer to their new firms if they change jobs. Third, through competition with local firms, foreign firms create pressure on local firms to adopt foreign institutions.[24] To the extent that foreign investors can produce more efficiently than local producers, local producers will face a choice of potential bankruptcy (a real possibility for many Chinese SOEs) or institutional reform. The fact that many of the firms imperiled by the entry of foreign investors are state-owned, again underscores the centrality of the state in the process of institutional change. Yet, domestic enterprises may emulate the institutions of successful foreign enterprises without a deep understanding of the institutions that they are adopting. In other words, institutional change should not be confused with self-conscious attempts to promote efficiency; rather, it can result from actors wanting to appear legitimate in the eyes of others.[25] Fourth, international organizations, non-governmental organizations, investors, and others in international society provide Chinese leaders and domestic institutional reformers with information on international legal and business norms and practices. China's leaders, although they bristle at foreign actors' attempts to erode their sovereignty in their rhetoric and in some of their actions, have shown increasing concern for world opinion. In some cases, foreign actors convince domestic reformers that adopting international institutions will raise a country's legitimacy in the eyes of the international community.[26] As long as such adoptions do not unduly harm their government's domestic legitimacy, China's leaders may choose to adopt international institutions. To develop their status as a country that respects rule of law in international society, China has joined a growing list of treaties such as the New York Convention and international organizations such as the World Trade Organization (hereafter, WTO).[27]

Outline of the Book

The remainder of the book focuses on the dynamics of institutional change in China by analyzing the interaction of foreign and domestic actors in the process of negotiating the diffusion of foreign institutions to China, especially those related to China's foreign investment regime, labor practices, and commercial dispute resolution. In chapter 1, I review previous works on institutional change and globalization, and I develop a heuristic model to explain the roles of states and MNCs in the process of path dependent institutional change. Many works on institutional change focus exclusively on endogenous dynamics that reproduce institutions or exogenous "shocks" such as warfare and economic depression that cause radical institutional change. I elaborate a theory of how states guide globalization that links endogenous dynamics (values and legitimacy, local policy communities of lawyers and business consultants, and the actions of firms and individuals in markets) to exogenous dynamics (international norms, international organizations, and foreign investors). Additionally, I analyze the interaction of domestic and international ideas and actors at three levels of analysis: the macro-, meso-, and micro-levels. In the process of state-guided globalization, Chinese officials have attempted to harness globalization to advance its reform agenda, although it finds itself increasingly bound by international norms and rules in the process. Chapter 2 provides a historical overview of China's approach to its post-1979 open door policy. Over the course of four periods (1979–1983, 1984–1992, 1993–2001, and 2001–present) China has moved from a position of tight control and segregation of foreign investors to a policy of deep integration, allowing foreign investors to establish subsidiaries without Chinese partners and participating in international organizations such as the WTO. Chapter 3 details shifts in China's foreign investment policies and the flow of investment into China. Most works on foreign investment in China focus on the period when JVs predominated, but beginning in 1988, foreign investors rapidly shifted toward a new investment vehicle, the wholly foreign-owned enterprise (hereafter, WFOE). I explore the causes for the shift as well as the ramifications for Chinese economic control over foreign investors and their institutions.

In chapter 4, I examine how U.S. and Japanese companies affected China's legal development, especially international commercial dispute resolution. It also considers how the prevalence of *guanxi*, or "social ties," an informal Chinese practice of handling conflict and interaction with the state, has shaped foreign investors' behavior. In that chapter, I contend that Chinese officials who were interested in legal development adopted norms on international commercial arbitration and (partially) responded to foreign actors' complaints regarding the Chinese International Economic and Trade Arbitration Committee (hereafter, CIETAC), the main legal body used by foreign businesses to settle disputes. While China has made significant progress in developing new legal forms, domestic legal fissures between center and locality and between the arbitration bodies and courts have limited the effectiveness of China's legal reforms. In addition, foreign businesses' reliance on *guanxi* undermined their calls for "rule of law."

Chapters 5 and 6 analyze labor practices in foreign invested enterprises and their interplay with domestic labor reforms. Chapter 5 examines Japanese and U.S. firms' approaches to transplanting their wage and bonus systems to China. As with labor market reforms, China began to introduce wage and bonus reforms in the late 1970s, but such efforts were limited by the persistence of intra-firm egalitarian norms in SOEs. By the late 1990s, after the shift toward the WFOE investment structure, foreign firms enjoyed greater flexibility in devising their pay schemes. Japanese firms transplanted wage systems that were much more egalitarian than U.S. firms, and therefore, closer to China's existing employment practices. Yet, Japanese employment institutions did not engender a strong work ethic in Chinese workers and dissatisfied employees and managers. American firms encountered some problems with labor turnover in their subsidiaries, but their strong "pay-for-performance" schemes appealed to many Chinese workers. Thus, U.S. firms became a model for Chinese SOEs and even some Japanese subsidiaries in Shanghai. In chapter 6, I focus on how firms hire, promote, and dismiss employees. The chapter traces early Chinese reform efforts to move from the "iron rice bowl" model of lifelong job security to greater flexibility in managing SOE workforces, and how those efforts encountered political obstacles from employees and from local officials who faced protests from laid-off workers. Over the course of the reform period, foreign firms were given increasing leeway to dismiss surplus or unwanted workers in their enterprises, which helped to break through the deadlock on domestic labor reforms. The chapter details the construction of a key economic institution, a functioning domestic labor market.

Finally, the Conclusion (chapter 7) takes up the issue of economic engagement and China's evolving relationship to international institutions. It addresses the following questions: Has thirty years of foreign engagement altered China's relationship to international norms and made it a less threatening country? What kind of country is emerging out of China's reforms—one that is growing into a member of international society that respects international rules and norms or one that seeks to revise international institutions? In probing those issues, I sketch China's record on security, human rights, and legal norms. I find that engagement has benefited China's movement toward compliance with international rules and norms by deepening its interdependence with international economy, through the diffusion of international norms to China's meso- and micro-level actors, and by giving rise to a group of domestic actors who understand and advocate for Chinese adoption of international norms. The conclusion also analyzes why China's state has successfully guided its globalization process by comparing China's management of foreign capital, especially loans versus foreign investment, to that of Argentina, Mexico, Brazil, Thailand, and Indonesia. In Latin America, high levels of borrowing from the IMF and foreign commercial lenders, dependency on U.S. trade and investment, and states controlled by economic elites have forced many Latin American countries to swallow harsh neoliberal policy prescriptions. At the start of China's reforms, the state was not compromised because of the absence of foreign debt and investment, and because of the relatively egalitarian nature of China's society, although during the early reform period China relied more on foreign borrowing over foreign direct investment.[28] China receives significant investment from firms based in Hong Kong, Taiwan, South Korea, Japan, the United States, and Europe, presenting Chinese organizations and officials with a menu of institutional models from which it can adopt and diffuse. With so many distinct institutions and practices introduced by foreign investors, China's institutional reform path allowed for shifts toward different models, underscoring the state's ability to guide globalization.

The book makes three principal contributions to the analysis of China and its political economy. First, the work lays out a theoretical argument about the process of path dependent institutional change. I argue that human actors in multinational corporations, state organizations, law offices, and human resource consultancy firms provide information and examples of foreign and international institutions, which Chinese actors combine with domestic institutions in the process of institutional change. As the state guides the globalization process, these new institutional models can form an institutional sub-regime that competes with the dominant institutional regime. The proposed theory contributes to our understanding of the roles of state officials and international actors in China's institutional change. Second, works on globalization in general, and on China in particular, have tended to treat globalization in terms of "global" vs. "local" forces, usually lumping together actors from advanced capitalist economies as working in unison.[29] Consequently, Japan and the United States have distinctly affected China's institutional reform efforts. Furthermore, I contend that global and local forces selectively worked together to reform Chinese business and legal institutions. Third, the research presented here goes beyond existing scholarship on foreign investment in China, which typically focuses on the period when JVs predominated to include the shift to investment in WFOEs.[30] The shift in investment models deeply affected the Chinese authorities' ability to control foreign investors, and the present research helps to sketch the ramifications for China's state.

The book draws from two main types of sources: relevant laws and policies in China and data collected from interviews about foreign business operations, Chinese reactions to foreign businesses, and foreign and Chinese understandings of the process of transplanting institutions to China. Chinese laws and policies detail reforms of existing institutions and development of new institutions to manage China's changing economy, but a simple examination of policies and laws does not reveal how and why foreign and Chinese actors interacted in the process of institutional change. To examine those dynamics, one must rely on interview material. For this project, I conducted 91 interviews in China and Japan over the period 2000–2007. In 2000, I interviewed managers in 59 Japanese, Hong Kong, and U.S. firms in Shanghai (42 of the firms were randomly selected) as well as nine attorneys, union leaders, and business organization representatives.[31] In 2001, I conducted 15 interviews in Tokyo. In 2003, 2005, and 2008, I returned to Shanghai for follow-up rounds of interviews with fourteen lawyers, consultants, and managers of foreign enterprises. Personal interviews conducted over seven years, supplemented by readings from the Chinese press, shed light on the process of institutional transplantation and reform. Interviews reveal the problems encountered by foreign businesses operating in China and the difficulties that Chinese have faced in working for Japanese and U.S. businesses. The interviews also highlight the interests and approaches taken by various foreign and domestic actors in the reform period and during China's opening to the outside world.

1

Globalization and Path-Dependent Institutional Change

As their name implies, institutions are resilient; yet, institutions can and do change. The combination of institutional continuity and change has compelled scholars and practitioners to puzzle over the agents and causes of institutional reproduction and reform. The debate has led people to focus on actors and dynamics along the following two axes: domestic versus international spheres, and macro-level versus micro-level. Generally speaking, studies of domestic politics and organizations are skeptical of the prospects for institutional change, while scholars of international relations are more likely to claim that global forces can compel domestic institutional change.[1] Varieties of capitalism and path dependency theories, two of the most robust explanations of endogenous institutional development, claim that national institutions tend to resist reform, even in the face of globalization, because institutions are embedded in the normative, social, and political fabric of a country, which are slow to change.[2] Path dependency theorists claim that initial institutional designs establish a path for future institutional development[3] and that even small institutional decisions early on can have significant long-term development consequences.[4]

International relations theorists and other proponents of exogenous explanations of institutional change focus on how international crises such as warfare and economic depression can jar domestic leaders to revise institutions. According to Steven Krasner, institutions do not evolve incrementally in response to slow shifts in domestic or international contexts because actors fear the high costs and unpredictable results of institutional change; only structural crises can compel populations and leaders to alter institutional designs, and then the reforms are likely to be significant.[5] Yet, a number of studies on institutional change have underscored the very difficulty, if not improbability, of radical institutional reform, instead predicting incremental shifts to be the norm.[6] For example, in the 1990s, despite negative feedback from prolonged economic slumps, embedded economies such as Germany, Sweden, and Japan have cleaved to existing institutional arrangements, raising questions about political and business leaders' ability and willingness to recognize poor performance of existing institutions, and of citizens' and leaders' willingness to alter institutional designs.[7] Alternatively, financial crises may open the door to international economic organizations such as the International Monetary Fund (IMF) and World Bank (WB) to require structural adjustments and institutional changes of economies that need financial bailouts.

A second point of disagreement is the role of actors at the macro- and micro levels in the process of institutional change. Most authors focus on macro-level institutions such as national regulations as the starting point for understanding institutional dynamics, and multilateral organizations such as the WTO and IMF have concentrated on macro-level reforms in member states. A minority of authors have examined the role of firms and micro-level organizations in the process of institutional change. Due to their small size and their competitive context, firms are theorized to adjust their behavior and firm-level institutions more readily than states can act at the macro-level. Economies function well when macro-level institutions are compatible with the practices and institutions at the micro level, and firms can create pressure on states to adjust national institutions to conform with and to support institutional changes taking place at the micro level. In the China field, Doug Guthrie has argued that foreign investors have facilitated Chinese institutional change by introducing micro-level changes.[8] Institutional change imposed on governments by multilateral organizations is likely to encounter resistance from state officials at the macro level and economic organizations at the micro level. Without support from domestic actors at one or both levels, the prospects of coerced institutional change being effective are poor.

Examining these two axes of institutional dynamics (domestic-international and macro-micro linkages) helps us to develop a thorough understanding of globalization and institutional change. Globalization affects both sets of axes because it entails the circulation of institutional forms, norms, and ideas through economic, political, cultural, and social networks across nation-state borders, thus eroding the coherence of national institutions. Additionally, globalization opens economies to the involvement of international actors at the macro- and micro levels. Globalization threatens to "disembed" political economy from its national roots by transforming domestic firms into global actors with weak commitments to any particular nation-state and by introducing new actors such as MNCs and new ideas.[9] Actors bearing new models can change the balance of domestic coalitions that support existing institutions and can disrupt the positive

feedback loop that, according to path dependency theory, helps reproduce existing institutional arrangements. Unlike exogenous theories of
institutional change that focus on crises as trigger mechanisms, globalization opens up a new set of dynamics because it occurs in ebbs and flows
rather than in grand exogenous shocks. International goods, services, and
capital—important measures of globalization—flow incrementally and
reversibly, a sharp contrast to external shocks. Globalization also introduces
new points of pressure at the macro- and micro levels of political economy.
International actors such as the WTO, non-governmental organizations,
and MNCs transmit ideas, norms, and institutional forms to state leaders
and their constituencies, which simultaneously foment new lines of criticism of existing institutions and introduce new institutional models to
adopt. These dynamics can induce national leaders to adjust macro-level
institutions to mesh with international and foreign models.

Although studies of institutional change tend to focus on the pressure
that international actors bring to bear on national level leaders to alter
institutions, globalization also opens an economy to pressure from MNCs
and other actors at the micro level. MNCs transmit and model foreign institutions in a host economy. As the new institutional models take root and
some enjoy success, local organizations may opt to replicate them. To be
most effective, firms operating under such models often require adjustments of national institutions such as new regulations on labor, intellectual
property, and marketing, to bring them in line with foreign or international
practices. In other words, the introduction of MNCs can recast domestic
institutional dynamics, fostering micro-level pressure to adjust macro-level
institutions.

The introduction of new ideas and institutional designs may transform
domestic institutions, but that fails to address the following question: Which
ideas matter, that is, can affect another country's institutional change?
Existing studies of globalization and institutional reform ignore the variety of
institutions and interests that international actors such as MNCs from different countries bring to a host economy. Following the "varieties of capitalism"
approach, MNCs bear institutions shaped by their home-country practices,
so they present distinct models for reformers and firms in host countries to
examine, to select, and to emulate. Arguments that globalization compels
countries to adopt a particular model of economic and political institutions
ignore the plurality of models that exist, as well as host actors' power to select
new institutional designs for adoption. To the extent that MNCs and domestic firms offer a plurality of institutional models, state leaders and firms are
presented with a menu of models to emulate or to graft onto existing institutional forms. Even though multilateral organizations such as the WTO and
the United Nations may have more concrete institutional mandates embedded in their rules, a number of specific models may satisfy these mandates.
This combination of external and domestic pressure and interests focuses
our attention on the state's role in managing institutional dynamics.

Exogenous explanations of institutional change have contributed greatly to our understanding of dynamics at the micro level or the macro level, but they downplay important connections between the two levels. Indeed, foreign actors' attempts to alter a country's institutions by creating pressure at the macro level or at the micro level are likely to have limited success. Research on endogenous institutional reform suggests that domestic agents of institutional reform often meet intense opposition to reform efforts,[10] that actors may reform formal institutions without altering the cognitive maps or scripts of people in organizations,[11] and that domestic reformers ignore negative feedback, such as economic recessions, rather than undertaking institutional change.[12] International actors such as treaty organizations can devise formal rules and institutions for member states to adopt and procedures for compelling compliance, but even international organizations may be helpless in securing more than states' superficial adoption of institutional forms without adhering to the spirit and substance of the rules and institutions.[13] A more promising path to institutional reform entails linking international and domestic forces with ideas about institutional designs.[14] The state plays a crucial role in mediating these two levels, and a thorough account of globalization and institutional change must take stock of state agents, their interests, political pressures, and actions.

To address these issues and to explain the integration of both endogenous and exogenous and macro- and micro-level dynamics in the process of globalization, I adopt the term, "state-guided globalization." The concept conveys state attempts to interact with global actors at the macro- and micro-levels in order to advance its interests and to achieve state policy goals. Yet, states cannot fully control global actors who stretch the boundaries of state policy reforms, add their criticism to feedback from existing domestic actors in the assessment of existing institutional models, and model possible institutional reforms. I analyze institutional dynamics at three (macro, meso, and micro) levels, with the state mediating interactions at each level. At the macro level, states develop a legal and regulatory environment in which domestic actors (individuals and organizations, including foreign investors) operate, comply with mandates from international organizations and other states, and act within the parameters of domestic normative structures and political conditions. At the micro level, the following processes occur: (i) organizations establish or transfer firm-level institutions that shape their operations; (ii) firms compete with one another for business and for hiring staff, creating pressure to improve institutional designs; (iii) informal institutions such as workers' social norms shape intra-firm behavior; and (iv) individuals provide feedback on firms by choosing for whom they want to work. At the micro level, firms and individuals generate a great deal of information and feedback on the performance of firm-level institutions and on macro-level institutions that create a context in which firms operate.

At the meso level, an understudied level of analysis, actors such as consultants, business organizations, and policy communities study trends and feedback from micro-level organizations with distinct institutional designs, extracting advice and models for diffusion. At this level of analysis, institutional regimes and sub-regimes take shape, contend, and are diffused to state reformers above and organizations below. Typically, a dominant institutional regime forms through interactions of individual firms, the state's regulatory environment (formal institutions), and social norms (informal institutions).[15] Through the work of firms (especially foreign firms that fall outside domestic production and exchange networks in a host economy) and policy communities at the meso level, alternative practices and sub-regimes can emerge that compete with and challenge the dominant institutional regime. State agents exercise some indirect control over the emergence of sub-regimes through their policies and licensing of firms, but they exercise more direct guidance over the maintenance of dominant regimes through the creation of regulations and with controls over state-owned (or state-subsidized) enterprises, an important legacy in post-socialist economies. At the meso-level, the balance of power between regimes and sub-regimes shifts, based on the action and success of firms and laborers at the micro level and state intervention at the macro level. When organizations prove relatively successful under sub-regimes, compared to their performance under the dominant regime, or when the sub-regimes help states to achieve reform goals, they may enjoy state backing, thus diffusing institutional change.

The chapter begins with a brief discussion of the definition of institutions and the domestic and international factors that limit and compel institutional change. Next, I analyze institutional dynamics at three tiers—macro, meso, and micro levels—with the state mediating the interplay of actors at the three levels. Finally, I conclude with a discussion of some of China's particular features that affect how international and domestic agents influence institutional change. I integrate dynamics at the three levels by examining the state's role in mediating the interplay of domestic dominant regimes with emerging sub-regimes that are shaped by various international institutions carried and diffused by MNCs, business organizations, and legal and management consultants. The study advances our understanding of the institutional change in three ways, by: (i) identifying how the interaction of exogenous and endogenous institutions affects change and the roles that various actors play in that process; (ii) highlighting the state's role in guiding globalization at the three levels of analysis; and (iii) revealing the varieties of institutional models that foreign investors potentially present to host economies and the process of selecting new alternative institutions to adopt or to layer onto existing institutions.

The above issues are of more than mere theoretical concern; they directly touch upon prominent and practical issues regarding national development and international relations. The book sheds light upon how foreign countries, international organizations, and other members of international society interact with countries that wish to enter international society. Mapping China's approach to state-guided globalization directs our attention to how rising states' attempt to balance protecting their interests and autonomy with undertaking institutional reforms that realize long-term goals and deepen their relations with international economy and society. China's approach to globalization also reveals how existing members of international society devise strategies to protect their status and to socialize emerging powers to international norms in a context of interdependence and globalization. Such considerations are salient for post-socialist countries and rapidly developing economies, two sets of countries that include China.

Domestic and International Dynamics of Institutional Change

No single, accepted definition of institutions exists because of the many disciplines and theories involved in the study of institutions. Drawing from Douglass North's work, Peter Hall and David Soskice define institutions as follows: "a set of rules, formal or informal, that actors generally follow, whether for normative, cognitive, or material reasons."[16] The definition is sufficiently broad to encompass both the detailed rules of constitutions and laws, on the one hand, and unwritten norms of behavior within communities and firms, on the other. Typically, political reformers seek to alter formal institutions such as laws and policies at the macro level, but informal institutions are equally important in determining behavior at the micro level. The above definition leaves actors' motivations unspecified, allowing various theoretical approaches to employ the definition without violating their core assumptions. Before elaborating a theory of state-guided globalization, I briefly review existing works on endogenous and exogenous theories of institutional development.

Domestic (Endogenous) Dynamics of Institutional Reproduction and Incremental Change

Studies of endogenous institutional development, especially path dependency theory, often focus on the tendency to reproduce existing national institutions and the persistence of variation across countries. Early institutional theorists such as Thorsten Veblen, Karl Polanyi, and Mark Granovetter have claimed that economic action and decision making are embedded in webs of social relations and their accompanying informal rules of behavior.[17] Social considerations such as equity, justice, and identities are strongest in communities where social networks are dense and norms of behavior are enforced through face-to-face encounters, but actors, including firms, also follow the logic of appropriate socioeconomic behavior in exchanges at the national level. A country's social, political, and economic organizations and competition span national borders, but most economic transactions are embedded in and reproduce a national normative framework. Within these networks of exchange and cooperation, such as supplier relations, informal national institutions are diffused and reproduced.[18] Richard Whitley asserts that a given firm (even an MNC) within an economy primarily competes with other national firms, and such competition causes firms to improve upon national institutions, a form of bounded innovation.[19] The effect of cooperation and competition among national firms is to lock-in a path of institutional development on which actors tend to reproduce and to improve upon existing national institutions rather than reject them. Whitley's approach provides an important link between micro-level firm behavior and national institutions and regimes.

If actors are embedded in social networks and social organizations, then behavior should differ in distinct social contexts. Building on path dependent analyses, authors in the varieties of capitalism school contend that early institutional choices shape a country's development pattern and deter convergence.[20] Empirically, national distinctions have been pronounced, and many scholars distinguish societies along the axis of "embedded" versus "neoliberal" economies. Even within the broad categories of "embedded" capitalism that characterize many Asian economies[21] and Anglo-American "neo-liberal" capitalism,[22] scholars note important and enduring institutional distinctions based on national patterns of state action, industrial relations, intra-firm organization, and inter-firm relations. According to path dependency, distinctions among countries persist due to the following factors, each of which is elaborated below: (i) cost of shifting paths; (ii) stability of normative frameworks; (iii) cognitive limitations; and (iv) coalitions of institutional supporters.

Cost of Shifting Paths

Paul Pierson has employed the concept of "increasing returns" to explain how political institutions, much like economic institutions, tend to resist change. Drawing on Brian Arthur's work on technology, Pierson identifies four mechanisms that generate increasing returns: "set-up or fixed costs" (returns brought by high costs of establishing an institution); "learning effects" (returns from knowledge gained by working with an institution); "coordination effects" (returns from multiple people adopting a particular institution); and "adaptive expectations" (returns from perceived pressure to adopt a good institution at the start).[23] The four mechanisms help ensure that people will sustain institutions by attracting people to follow the institutions. The longer institutions persist, the more positive feedback the institutions receive and the greater the cost of institutional change.[24]

Increasing returns to institutions also accrue due to synergistic interaction between institutions. For example, in several Asian countries including Japan, business networks (*keiretsu*) took advantage of the high levels of trust and social obligations among the population to develop relational contracting.[25] Synergistic interaction among institutions underscores the way in which institutions cohere and make sense in a national context. Changing one institution without altering the institutions around it may destroy the synergy, in addition to increasing costs by developing new institutions. Globalization can erode the effect of increasing returns to existing institutional designs, which apply more to changes of existing institutions than the introduction of exogenous institutional designs. While it may be difficult for an economy to produce its own new institutions, global actors such as MNCs can introduce new institutional designs and values, in addition to forming new networks of firms to coordinate behavior. Given their size, efficiency, and bargaining power, MNCs can attract domestic firms to engage in new forms of behavior and to adopt new institutional designs. When a number of MNCs enter a host economy with similar institutions that are distinct from local designs, the new institutions can coordinate behavior of firms around new principles, forming an institutional sub-regime.

Stability of Normative Frameworks

In a mutually constitutive fashion, values and ideology shape institutions, and institutions reinforce values and belief structures. Actors design institutions to conform to popular values and ideas, and people judge institutions by those values and beliefs. When institutions conform to popular values and norms, the institutions enjoy legitimacy, and a type of equilibrium exists. Conversely, institutions will lack stability if they stray too far from popularly held norms and ideals, causing people to view them and their designers as illegitimate. Values and norms in a society can change, but they tend to change very slowly; hence, the normative framework for judging the legitimacy of institutions and reformers is also relatively stable. According to Krasner, institutional change typically lags behind drifts in popular opinion, and institutional change occurs to close the gap between institutions and values.[26]

Although leaders may change national laws at the macro level or an organization's rules at the micro level, people can drag their feet and persist in following informal norms of behavior rooted in popular values. Sociological institutionalists have shown that norms and values shape everyday behavior, which, through repetition, becomes an unconscious "cognitive map" or "script" to follow in everyday practice.[27] Through repeated action in accordance with institutions, people internalize norms and no longer focus on why they behave that way but uncritically follow their cognitive script. Thus, people reproduce informal institutions at the micro level, which act as a weight against formal institutional change. By extension, people are not likely to be receptive to attempts to substitute new scripts or negative feedback on existing institutions from the outside, nor are there any guarantees that foreign scripts will function well when introduced to a new cast.[28] For example, attempts to raise productivity by introducing performance-based pay in Japanese companies and Chinese state-owned enterprises have met with much resistance from workers and middle-level managers, who are accustomed to egalitarian labor markets.[29] Globalization destabilizes a country's normative framework by introducing new ideas and values to a host country. When people accept the new values, pluralism and new lines of criticism can emerge. MNCs may transplant new values and cognitive scripts, and as people work in the MNCs, they adjust their everyday understanding of the world.

Cognitive Limitations

Institutional theorists have asserted that human cognition is imperfect and prone to positive evaluation of existing institutions. Due to subjective interpretations of feedback on institutions caused by imperfect information flows and personal ideological commitments, people are predisposed to interpret feedback positively and, thus, to find that their institutions succeed at achieving ends.[30] Institutional analysts assert that imperfect human perception helps sub-optimal institutions to persist over time.[31] People fail to recognize negative feedback on the performance of institutions, creating a positive feedback loop. Such cognitive limitations explain both why institutions are likely to persist and why institutional convergence on "best practice" is unlikely.[32] Actors want to believe that their institutions function well, and, indeed, they might function well according to criteria rooted in national values or company cultures, even though an outsider might judge the national institutions less favorably against some abstract, universal (or foreign) model of efficiency. One might apply such a line of argument to all organizations, including firms,[33] but states and their agents are more prone to ideological limitations on reading feedback than are people in other organizations.[34] Hence, state leaders are less responsive to changing environmental conditions and feedback than are organizations and firms.[35] Stephen Krasner asserts that there are certain to be costs associated with institutional change, in terms of dismantling existing institutions and creating new ones, but any benefits are uncertain, while the cost-benefit analysis of maintaining existing institutions is relatively clear because of the flow of information on existing institutions.[36] Except in times of crises, when institutions are reconsidered, Krasner concludes, "even if there is widespread societal dissatisfaction with a particular set of institutions, it may be irrational to change them."[37] Globalization does not change cognitive processes, but, to the extent that ideological commitments cloud reason, globalization can improve cognition by breaking down or challenging existing ideologies.

Coalitions of Institutional Supporters

A fourth impediment to institutional change is that some actors benefit from existing arrangements. In economies with states that coordinate market activities, firms depend on regulatory frameworks for protection and their survival.[38] States and firms find it difficult or undesirable to abandon institutions because institutions have distributive consequences, and political and economic actors who benefit from existing institutions form coalitions to keep the institutions in place. In countries with strong labor organizations that are included in political coalitions, for example, states may find it difficult to reduce welfare commitments and to deregulate labor movements. Relative "losers" may become proponents of institutional reform because they enjoy fewer benefits from the institutions and, hence, have less to lose and more to gain in changing them.[39] Richard Deeg claims that "losers" in institutional struggles may opt to form alternative institutional models called "subregimes," which potentially give rise to significant institutional reform.[40] The struggle between "winners" and "losers" in state institutional arrangements might be a source of endogenously produced institutional change, but there are two obstacles to relative losers propelling institutional change. First, winners tend to have more resources than losers in such struggles and, therefore, are better positioned to win future struggles over institutions. Second, the outcome of struggles between relative winners and losers of institutional arrangements is not likely to be a fundamental revision of existing institutions but rather an incremental revision of institutions and policies or, as Krasner calls it, "allocation within a given set of rules" rather than "a struggle over the basic rules of the game."[41] Even countries undertaking purposeful and holistic reforms such as post-socialist economies find themselves following paths set up by their preceding institutions, in part, because of the legacy of power brokers from previous regimes who shape institutional reforms.[42] Globalization introduces MNCs with significant resources but with weak political and social ties to the host environment. Thus, MNCs may disturb coalitions that support existing institutions.

External Factors

While path dependency theorists tend to focus on domestic dynamics that shape institutional design and limit institutional change to incremental reform, exogenous factors—including mandates from international organizations and "shocks" such as warfare and economic depression—can give rise to discontinuous institutional change. International crises can generate negative feedback, causing leaders to reconsider the design of their national institutions[43] and altering domestic leaders' calculations, especially in countries directly imperiled by warfare or depression, about the viability of their institutions and the desirability of institutional change. Economic depressions constitute prolonged and acute negative feedback on economic institutions, which can rouse leaders to reexamine their ideological commitments and institutional designs.[44] In crises, the insecurity and imagined perils of "standing pat" rise in comparison to the uncertainty and potential benefits of reform. International shocks or crises create structural conditions conducive to institutional change, but they do not explain the direction of institutional change other than modernizing property rights, taxation, and war-making capacity.[45]

By disrupting domestic institutions' positive feedback loop, external shocks generate "forks in the road" that allow leaders to reconsider the course of their institutional designs.[46] External shocks can serve as trigger events that crystallize nascent trends or lay transparent subtle shifts in values that previously had gone unnoticed, and institutional shifts help to realign institutions with current functional needs or values of society.[47] Yet, as path dependence theorists claim, political leaders may either ignore shocks and other forms of negative feedback or interpret such information through their ideological lenses. State officials may respond slowly (or not at all) for the following reasons: (i) they do not interpret shocks and even prolonged economic slumps as such; (ii) they are at a loss as to how to respond to such negative feedback; (iii) they face political pressure from coalitions that oppose reform (winners of current institutional designs); and (iv) reforms violate their strategic goals or ideology. In other words, leaders do not read feedback in a neutral fashion but view it against the backdrop of ideology, power structures, and their interest or goals. Even non-state actors such as large firms may be slow to react to negative feedback to their firm-level institutions or may find it difficult to alter behavior of actors who follow informal institutions even after the firms adopt formal institutional changes. For example, as Steven Vogel points out, the prolonged economic slump experienced by Japan in the 1990s did not generate significant institutional reforms in that country.[48]

International actors such as regional and international organizations devise rules and regulations for members to follow, many of which compel member states to alter domestic political and economic institutions,[49] and non-governmental organizations and nation-states help to diffuse the norms and practices of international society.[50] International economic organizations have defined policy recommendations for countries to adopt. In dispensing loans, the IMF and the World Bank may include structural adjustment requirements, mandating states to alter business and political institutions. The IMF and the World Bank have used their leverage to force borrowers to increase the distance between government officials and businesses, to open up trade and investment regulations, to undertake banking reform, and to otherwise accept neoliberal models of economy and legal-regulatory transparency. Membership in regional and international organizations and structural adjustment loans from the IMF or the World Bank are examples of what Paul Dimaggio and Walter Powell call "coercive isomorphism,"[51] in which, through pressure or dictate (even under voluntary membership), countries are compelled to bring their institutions in line with the standards of another organization. Nevertheless, the prescriptions of international organizations and non-governmental organizations (NGOs) are often broadly framed, allowing states to fit different institutional models under such dictates, which leaves open the specific models of institutional reform that leaders select.

Moreover, pressure and information flows from international or regional organizations primarily aim at affecting institutional adjustments at the macro level, but those organizations face difficulties in diffusing institutional change down to micro-level organizations. Despite requirements to alter national level institutions and the regulatory environment, micro-level organizations and individuals may persist in early forms of behavior, following informal norms or firm-level institutions. In other words, international organizations affect state institutions (mainly, regulatory policies) at the macro level but lack power to ensure compliance down to the micro level. As I argue below, MNCs and other micro-level international actors can deepen the level of monitoring of economies and enhance pressure for compliance on the ground. Macro-level pressure may not result in state-led reforms, but the presence of foreign firms at the micro level can add force to proponents of institutional reform and demonstrate models that may prove more effective during crises.

In sum, globalization can bring pressure to bear on national institutions at the macro and micro levels. At the macro level, international organizations,[52] regional organizations,[53] and states such as the United States, through bilateral relations, can pressure states to revise their national institutions.[54] States must balance these exogenous pressures from global actors against the interests of domestic constituents, firms, and state agents. In countries that are shifting from embedded to liberal economies, the role of the state and its interactions with firms at the micro level are crucial areas to observe and to monitor. Pressure and institutional changes at the macro-level are important but may be insufficient to guarantee the diffusion of new institutions to the micro level. The presence of micro-level actors, especially MNCs, who are critical of existing institutional arrangements in a host economy can help to sustain institutional change from below. Globalization can compel and catalyze institutional change through the following four processes: (i) enhancing information flows and creating new feedback mechanisms; (ii) disrupting coalitions in support of existing institutions at the micro level through the entry of MNCs; (iii) bringing macro-level pressure for institutional change from integration with international economic and treaty organizations; and (iv) fostering a general structure of competition that heightens the importance of reading feedback correctly, both at the macro and micro levels.

State-Guided Globalization

Here, this book develops a theory of state-guided globalization that conceptualizes the state as an active agent in guiding the process of integration with global political economy at both the macro and micro levels. At the macro-level, states guide globalization by determining which international organizations to join and which treaties to sign. States can affect international actors at the micro level by establishing regulatory environments for businesses and professional services, including the establishment of special rules on foreign investment sites. Finally, states guide the articulation of foreign and domestic spheres at the micro level by encouraging adoption of particular institutional models through administrative guidance and incentives and at the macro level by adjusting national institutions to conform to international norms and models.

Of the actors involved in the globalization process, only host states have the capacity to mediate institutional dynamics at all three levels (macro, meso, and micro) of analysis, which also makes them subject to political pressures from multilateral and international organizations, foreign states, MNCs, business associations, attorneys, and business consultants. The conflicting pressures from international and domestic actors, the state's ideological orientation, and the state's international commitments complicate the process of institutional reform. International actors may work with a transitional economy, such as that of China, not just based on economic interest but also to socialize the country to international business and legal norms. Domestic actors may attempt to thwart institutional changes, even when their host state is instigating the reforms. In this way, institutions become a point of potential conflict between domestic and international actors over the direction of a country's development. State leaders are constricted by globalization, but they can also use globalization to help meet state reform goals.

Officials find radical institutional change difficult because citizens judge the legitimacy of institutions (and institutional designers) according to the extent that they embody national values, protect citizens' interests, and reflect citizens' identities, all of which are slow to change.[55] International society judges a country's legitimacy by the domestic institutions—democratic rule, human rights, free trade, and property rights, to name a few—that it adopts.[56] Although international pressure to adopt particular institutional designs can spur domestic institutional change, considerations of domestic legitimacy often trump international concerns because leaders recognize the importance of domestic political support. The potential contradictory pressure from international organizations seeking to diffuse international norms and domestic forces opposed to radical institutional change underscores the mediating role played by state agents in the process of pushing through reforms, opposing institutional change, and/or selectively adopting new models.

While dual considerations of legitimacy may hem in reformers' actions, especially when international and domestic actors work in concert, leaders can also exploit differences between international and domestic demands to enhance state autonomy. Reformers who face opposition from domestic actors may use foreign pressure to adhere to international models and norms in order to push through domestic institutional changes. For example, the rules of the European Union have allowed domestic officials to put through neoliberal institutional reforms such as privatization and anti-inflationary measures against societal opposition, claiming that they must do so in order to meet international dictates.[57] In China's case, reformers have used the slogan, "getting on track with international practices (*jiegui guoji*)" to add force, luster, and legitimacy to difficult-to-accept reforms, including rolling back social welfare commitments for urban workers and reducing protection for agricultural and manufactured goods.[58] Membership in international and treaty organizations is one method that present leaders can use to lock in domestic institutions on a reform path so that later leaders cannot undo institutional changes.[59] Appeals to international norms and practices add powerful external logic and legitimacy to the institutional reform process, supplementing and possibly overriding domestic political considerations. Officials and domestic business leaders can exercise some discretion over the appropriation and mobilization of international norms and models, particularly when domestic actors enjoy relative autonomy from international organizations and foreign investors. Menus of institutional models enhance reformers' power to affect the path of institutional reform. Conversely, officials and domestic business leaders may use local pressure as an explanation for non-compliance with international institutions. States, located at the interface of domestic and international actors, may play the two off against one another in order to enhance their autonomy and to negotiate their way between two sets of criteria by which they are judged.

In all economies, states shape the behavior of micro-level actors through their creation of laws, regulations, and policies. Such guidance is more pronounced in economies with legacies of state intervention because they have a history of direct control over (former) SOEs. In guiding globalization and institutional change, states employ several techniques: (i) management of dominant regimes (and, in some instances, permissiveness towards subregimes);[60] (ii) layering new institutional designs onto or alongside existing institutional models;[61] and (iii) applying pressure on organizations to adopt new norms and cognitive scripts.[62] Through its reciprocal interactions with international organizations at the macro level and organizations at the micro-level, states play a pivotal role in evaluating feedback, matching reform models with state interests and societal values, formalizing institutional changes, and encouraging organizations to alter their practices.

MNCs and Globalization

Many actors contribute to the process of institutional change in this study, but here the focus is on the interaction of multinational corporations (and their accompanying legal and business services) and state agents. Important but secondary roles are assigned to international organizations, such as the WTO, who define parameters of acceptable institutional models, policy communities that provide information on business and legal models to firms and to state agents, and average citizens who make decisions on which firms and, by extension, what kinds of institutional models they wish to work under. Scholars have documented the role of international organizations and NGOs in shaping domestic reforms, but the contribution of MNCs, related legal and consulting services, and business organizations in diffusing international institutions has not been very well spelled out and has provoked disagreement. Various works on MNCs have advanced the following incompatible claims: (i) that MNCs carry their home-country institutions with them;[63] (ii) that MNCs transform local business environments; (iii) that MNCs encounter opposition to their firm-level institutions in new environments;[64] and (iv) that MNCs tailor production and marketing either to function in a new environment or to improve their products' appeal.[65] In sum, theorists disagree on the degree to which MNCs cleave to parent-company institutions and act as agents of change in host economies, or whether MNCs are shaped by institutions of their host environment.

Organizational learning theorists and several recent studies of institutional change in China have analyzed firm-level dynamics involving foreign investment. In their analyses of foreign investment, organizational learning theorists tend to focus on JVs as an organizational model that pools knowledge between foreign and local firms, thus facilitating foreign partners' adjustment to the host environment. Studies of Chinese JVs, the dominant form of investment in the early period of China's open-door policy, have shown that, through JV partnerships, foreign firms have diffused international norms and foreign firms' institutions to Chinese firms.[66] These studies reveal the importance of human and organizational linkages in the diffusion of information. Others have emphasized competition among foreign and local firms at the micro level to explain how less-successful firms are compelled to adopt new organizational models.[67]

While much of the argument presented in the following chapters complements the above lines of analysis, a focus on joint ventures and organizational learning suffers from four points in application to the study of foreign investment in China. First, early foreign investment flows to China used a JV model, but those early investments have been dwarfed by the more recent use of the WFOE investment vehicle. Concomitantly, WFOEs have come to dominate during the period of the heaviest investment, while JVs were in ascendance during a period of relatively slow investment flows. A focus on JVs overstates their importance in China, and it mistakes such a model as a preference when, in fact, many foreign investors were pressed by the Chinese government to use such an investment vehicle.[68] Organizational learning, with its rather rosy view of compatibility of JV partnerships, provides a better explanation for the initial establishment of JVs than it does for their failure to adjust and to overcome problems embedded in the model.[69] Second, foreign investors abandoned the JV model because partners lacked trust, and the model facilitated misinformation in many cases. In many JVs, partners learned that they did not share goals, information, or knowledge to advance the JV's goals. Third, many firms do not adjust well to information flows. Although some organizational theorists argue that learning is a social process and therefore subject to imperfections of human interaction,[70] the term "learning" (and more so, "evolution") implies a rationalizing process,[71] while the theory offered here claims that ideology and norms color the interpretation of information.[72] In other words, institutional theory underscores the subjectivity of processing information and feedback, which limits learning and the capacity of information flows to generate institutional change. Even though subsidiaries may encounter difficulties operating in a host economy, which their managers may recognize as institutional problems, MNCs' headquarters may discourage managers in subsidiaries from attempting to adjust company institutions. Similarly, some Chinese SOE managers sought to undertake reforms, but state leaders and policies provided disincentives to do so, and managers thus failed to act on their new knowledge. Conversely, host country firms in China have demonstrated that they may resist change unless compelled to do so by the leaders of the organization or by the state. Finally, institutional change at the macro and micro levels has been characterized as much by bargaining and negotiating as by cooperation. Rather than use the term, "learning," I use "selection" to explain how organizations adopt institutional designs because the latter is neutral with regard to objectivity and, I assert, better explains the roles of ideology, interests, and political pressures in the reform process than "learning" does.

From the above lines of criticism, institutional legacies and organizational ties weigh down firms, reducing their responsiveness to environmental changes and information flows. According to this institutionalist approach, subsidiaries of MNCs are readily recognizable by their parent-company and/ or home-country practices when abroad, which affects their relationship to institutional change in a given host environment. Subsidiaries are unlikely to stray far from their parent company institutions, but they can serve as models for emulation by other firms (if the firms can respond flexibly to new information). Although firm-level analysis is not the primary concern of this book, in the chapters that follow, anecdotal evidence suggests that firms have limited capacity to learn, and, to the extent that firms adapt, they do so based on their existing institutions and company culture. Here, the focus is more on the institutional models that firms put into competition at the micro-level, from which models for diffusion emerge at the meso level.

Richard Whitley, who is generally skeptical of the ability of multinational corporations to shape the business institutions of host environments, offers a set of conditions under which foreign investors might affect their host environment, including high thresholds of foreign investment from a particular country and a high degree of institutional unity among foreign investors. [73] The greater the concentration of foreign direct investment and the greater the institutional coherence among investors, the more influence foreign investors can exercise over host environments. Whitley views the dynamics of institutional pressure primarily in terms of conflict and competition between MNC and host-environment firms, and he asserts that institutional variance among foreign investors weakens investors' bargaining position against host economies and states. While competition can generate pressure for incremental improvement on institutions, more radical institutional change is likely when new information flows through cooperative networks of human actors rather than abstract market competition. Networks that link up MNCs and host-country firms can diffuse new institutions to the host environment.[74] Such information flows can be achieved through JV partnerships or through third parties such as business consulting firms who advise on how to transplant and localize new institutional models. In cases in which reformers recognize that foreign investors transfer technology and business models that can improve upon local firms' institutions, institutional transplantation is more likely to succeed. The key for reformers is to select aspects of such models that help to achieve state goals or conform to its ideology rather than being overrun by foreign investors.

The likelihood and thoroughness of institutional diffusion throughout a country increases when MNCs operating at the micro level work in concert with international actors at the macro level to contribute to domestic institutional change. MNCs, as bearers of home-country and international institutions, can contribute to the process of institutional change in host economies in the following four ways. First, while international organizations supply general institutional models for adoption at the macro level, foreign investors help to identify discrepancies between host-country institutions and international norms and models, or provide negative feedback on domestic institutions at the micro level. International organizations help to define broad rules and norms of appropriate conduct and institutional forms at the macro level, but the international business and legal communities help transmit detailed information about such rules and norms at the meso level, as well as supplying feedback about institutional designs through the operation of businesses at the micro level. Second, multinational corporations from various home countries offer a "menu" of institutional forms, from which domestic reformers may selectively adopt and which fit the less-specific advice on institutional designs offered by international organizations.

Third, MNCs provide feedback on host economies' institutional designs, adding to the legitimacy of institutional reformers. The international community judges domestic leaders' legitimacy according to external criteria, which are framed by international institutions and organizations.[75] Finally, MNCs and legal and business consulting services train and educate domestic actors in the norms, practices, and logic of international institutions at the meso and micro levels. The domestic actors, as part of a policy community that spans international and domestic boundaries, internalize international institutions and bring domestic pressure to bear on host reformers in addition to diffusing models to organizations at the micro level. When alternative models to dominant regimes gain force, policy communities and firms contribute to the rise of institutional sub-regimes.

Macro-level Processes

At the macro level, the central state guides the process of globalization in two ways: by joining international economic organizations and treaty organizations; and by establishing a regulatory environment through laws and policies. For example, accession to the WTO requires states to adhere to the principle of "national treatment" (providing foreign firms and goods with the same type of protections as national producers enjoy), to remove barriers to trade, to follow TRIPS (trade-related aspects of intellectual property) and TRIMS (trade-related investment measures) agreements, and to compel the legal system to abide by and to enforce decisions of the WTO dispute settlement mechanism. Such mandates may force states to adjust their national institutions, but some states comply at the national level by adjusting laws and regulations without fully complying at the sub-national level. For example, states may lower tariff rates on imports, but sub-national organizations sometimes persist with non-tariff barriers to trade, which the WTO bans but are much harder to detect and to remove. When states violate the rules of regional economic organizations or those of the WTO, states may enter into negotiations to improve compliance, or the states may go through a dispute-settlement mechanism to resolve their differences. Moreover, states initially guide globalization by choosing whether or not they wish to accede to international organizations such as the WTO or to receive loans from the IMF.

In terms of global integration, states develop regimes to regulate trade, investment, taxation, property rights (including intellectual property rights), environmental pollution, and employment—all of which affect the level and type of foreign trade and investment flows. Advanced capitalist states have quite formalized rules and regulations in such areas, although they differ significantly in the particular institutional designs. Often, transitional economies and newly industrializing economies either have less formalized, opaque institutions or lack national institutions that meet international standards in some of these areas. The contours of state regulations shape globalization in a host economy. For example, a decentralized investment-approval process allows sub-national leaders to compete with one another for foreign investment, whereas centralized control allows states to control the type and level of investment flows. The specific attributes of the tax regimes and guidelines on approval can facilitate the entry of labor-intensive firms or firms that bring advanced technology. Additionally, states create enforcement mechanisms for policies and laws, which vary in orientation, such as adversarial vs. non-adversarial, and litigious courts vs. alternative dispute-resolution mechanisms, as well as in their level of decentralization and overall adherence to rule of law principles. States that develop legal systems that guarantee intellectual property and that are transparent are more likely to attract large-scale foreign investment projects with advanced technology than states with poor and opaque legal systems for securing property rights. Institutional legacies and pressures from domestic and international actors structure state choices, but states guide their interactions with the global economy and affect their development potential.

Foreign actors often focus their pressure on domestic states to adjust national institutions to create a general environment hospitable to business activity, but they do not necessarily specify the shape or form of organizations that implement institutions. For example, signatories to the New York Convention on enforcement of commercial arbitration decisions (see chapter 4) agree to abide by and enforce commercial arbitration decisions in other signatory states, but the convention does not specify how countries will do so. Even more general is the concept of "rule of law," which many international actors evoke but few specify in detail. Rule of law clarifies the role that law should play in governance and dispute resolution, but it leaves open the specific character of judicial organizations, such as whether they should be adversarial or inquisitorial, reliant on litigation or alternate dispute-settlement mechanisms. In the business realm, national treatment leaves open how each state treats its own national firms, so long as states harmonize treatment of all firms—local and foreign. At the macro level, then, international actors press countries to define business and legal environments that fall into the parameters acceptable to international society, but states and sub-national organizations have a great deal of room to define institutions within such parameters. Moreover, MNCs and foreign states may provide information on, and pressure host states to reform institutions along the lines of, their home-country practices because these are familiar to them. A focus on macro-level processes leaves open the specific direction of institutional change, and current theories offer little help in addressing such a matter.

Micro-level Processes

At the micro level, domestic and foreign firms are the main actors, but average citizens in the labor market also contribute to institutional change. Firms model distinct institutions, generate information on how different firm-level models perform in a country's institutional environment (laws, regulations, and normative structure), provide feedback on national institutions, and train staff in institutional models that are diffused to other firms. Domestic firms tend to follow a dominant institutional form due to their embeddedness in the national institutional structure for the reasons offered above by the varieties of capitalism literature; therefore, they supply limited information on alternative institutional models. Foreign investors who are not as rooted in the host economy can draw on experience in other countries to model alternative institutions in a host economy. Competition among firms generates feedback on how the firm-level institutions perform in comparison with one another. Such feedback may be slanted, however, because, in comparison to domestic firms in developing and transitional economies, foreign firms often have superior technology, which confounds comparisons among firm-level institutional models. Comparing the performance of domestic and foreign firms may measure technological development rather than the quality of the institutions used by the firms.

Organizations in the host economy also may compare feedback from institutional models with different home-country practices. A large economy such as China hosts foreign investors from several countries with a variety of institutional formations, creating what Paul Pierson calls a "menu" of institutional models. From the menu, institutional reformers can consider and select institutional designs.[76] A variety of investors with distinct institutional models may benefit domestic reformers by: (i) increasing the range of information on alternative institutional designs; (ii) allowing experimentation with distinct institutional designs; and (iii) increasing the perception of the host country's choice in institutional reform rather than being forced to accept a particular design from a dominant foreign actor.

The most important process at the micro level is the flow of information on institutional models and feedback on existing models, which can take several forms. First, foreign investors with different home-country institutions provide feedback on the functioning of distinct kinds of institutions and practices in the host environment, including both the shortcomings of existing institutional models and the potential benefits and pitfalls of newly transplanted models from abroad. Such feedback provides crucial information to state agents and local firms who seek to push through institutional reforms but who do not know what kinds of reform models are likely to succeed or, more likely, to meet state goals. The popularity of new institutional models, too, affects institutional reforms. For example, a foreign investor's stratified wage policy might appeal to a sub-population seeking greater rewards in a host environment with a dominant egalitarian ethos. Foreign investors, by introducing institutions founded on alternative values and norms, and individuals voting with their feet in the labor market can all indicate to institutional reformers previously unregistered shifts in popular values or subsets of values to which reformers might appeal. Allowing MNCs to establish such models reduces the uncertainty and anxiety associated with institutional change, a concern that Steven Krasner has identified as an impediment to incremental institutional change.[77] Without investing financial and political capital on potentially poor performing institutional models, domestic actors can examine the performance of new models on their menu and choose ones that help solve institutional problems that they have identified.

More significantly, firms generate feedback on institutional models through an analysis of the difficulties that they encounter and through the domestic institutional problems that they help to solve, such as poor labor productivity or slow technological development. Foreign investors can compare their results to the operators of their parent-company subsidiaries in other locations to draw conclusions on how their institutions mesh with their new host environment. In contrast, few domestic firms have ties to subsidiaries outside their locale, limiting their capacity to judge institutional performance except against company values, expectations, and profitability.

Firms can observe and compare the performance of other firms at the micro-level, although the flow of information depends on the degree of openness of the communications environment and the number of ties among organizations. In China's context, state control over channels of communication limits information flows among firms, a problem that was severe through the mid-1990s. Thus, direct ties between domestic and foreign firms, which facilitate information flows, have been a subject of great interest and importance to researchers.[78]

Within foreign firms (including JVs), managers diffuse technical information on institutions and socialize staff to work within the foreign institutional models through staff training. Such training in the forms and practice of foreign business institutions is particularly important to local managerial staff. When hired away by other companies or when they establish their own companies, local staff can take the technical and practical information on company culture and institutions to their new organizations. In this way, institutional models are diffused through human agents who negotiate between foreign business forms (and their logic) and domestic organizations with their institutions.

At the micro level, actors also generate feedback on host economies' level of compliance with international institutions. International organizations help to transmit international norms and institutional forms for states and businesses to emulate, but they are limited in their capacity to monitor and affect institutional diffusion beyond the level of formal state institutional reforms. Supplementing the monitoring done by international organizations, foreign investors, non-governmental organizations, and legal and business policy communities operating at the meso and micro levels provide feedback on the functioning of national institutions and their relationship to international practices. International actors that operate in a host country can see how the institutions function in practice, allowing them to compare such institutions and practice in the host economy to what they have encountered in other countries. Foreign investors draw on their experience in advanced capitalist economies and expertise where rule of law tends to be well developed and where economic institutions are rooted in neoliberal ideology to press host leaders to adopt similar kinds of practices. For example, WTO membership forces states to extend national treatment, but investors may discover informal barriers to market access or biases in registration procedures that fall outside the legal forms adopted by the state. When local institutions and the operation of local firms seem out of step with international practice(s), then foreign investors—individually, through foreign government agents, or through international business organizations—pressure local and/or national officials to adjust host institutions and practices to come into compliance. Thus, MNCs and related business organizations help to monitor economic and legal institutions in practice, to clarify the substance of international institutions for their hosts, and to point out gaps between international models and actual practice.

Individuals in the labor market provide feedback on the degree to which various institutional designs of firms match the values of national populations, including sub-populations in the country. By voting with their feet and selecting the firms for which they wish to work, individuals indicate what types of firm-level institutions appeal to different segments of the workforce. In contrast to images of rather homogeneous national populations and their values and institutions, as depicted by authors in the varieties of capitalism vein, I assert that pockets of populations hold alternative values and that firms with institutions that do not conform to the dominant institutional regime may appeal to such people. High-quality staff moving to firms with alternative institutional models can create pressure on other firms to emulate alternative institutional models in order to hire and retain scarce highly trained personnel. While new or reformed institutional models can emerge from endogenous dynamics, foreign entrants to a host economy can provide more radical alternatives to dominant institutions, thus spurring competition for workers and offering plural models for local laborers to select as potential employers.

Meso-level Processes

Firms dominate the activity at the micro level, and state agents lead the institutional dynamics at the macro level, but a great deal of activity and interaction between the two levels occurs at the meso level. While information and feedback on state-level institutions and firm-level institutions is produced at the micro level, at the meso level, information about the institutions of particular firms is aggregated into models for diffusion and emulation. Slightly above the fray of firm-level competition, but not at the level of state policy making, policy communities, consultants, and the legal community synthesize and abstract institutional models for policy makers (above) and firms (below) to adopt. They provide information to the state and firms about the performance of specific and composite models at the micro level as well as information about models from outside the host economy. Typically, dominant institutional regimes form around the interaction of state regulations and national values and norms (including business norms) at the meso level, but potentially, sub-regimes can emerge to challenge dominant regimes.

Foreign firms that differ from dominant business practices in a host environment can give rise to "sub-regimes"—alternative patterns of organizations, values, and institutions—that emerge next to the dominant institutional model but that can lead economies to shift to new institutional paths.[79] As firms (often foreign-invested enterprises) are allowed to transplant new business institutions to a host economy, new managerial and labor models emerge in the form of alternative sub-regimes to dominant national institutional regimes. Within a sub-regime, a plurality of models may exist, based on the distinct institutions brought to a host economy by FIEs with different home-country practices. Gradually, local actors may adopt the sub-regime's institutions because they perform better, they enjoy a lofty reputation among the local population, or they satisfy the functional needs of a group whose interests were not well served by dominant institutional designs.

The introduction and presence of foreign investors can weaken existing linkages among firms and between firms and officials. In embedded capitalist host environments, foreign firms are less likely to have close ties to government officials than local firms, although some foreign investors in China have attempted to develop relations with officials to secure preferential treatment. Foreign firms also enter a host environment with a weak network of local firms for relational contracting. Foreign firms that follow arms-length contracting practices in a host environment contribute to the marginalization of embedded capitalism and reward (through contracts and new business opportunities) those who work in the new institutional pattern or sub-regime. Unlike local firms who primarily rely upon local markets and suppliers, foreign firms trade with and maintain supplier relations with firms outside the host economy. Such external ties give foreign firms some flexibility to act outside the local dominant institutional regime. Slowly, foreign investors erode coalitions that support embedded capitalism by creating an alternative institutional sub-regime. Over time, sub-regimes can grow in scope to create institutional pluralism in a country, even challenging the hold of dominant institutions. Institutional reformers may also adapt to the introduction of new institutional models by layering elements of the new models onto existing institutional models and adding state pressure to undertake firm-level reforms.

The introduction of new paradigms, ideas, and institutional models can break the lock-in effect of path dependence and can spur institutional reform, but, as Thomas Risse-Kappen notes, ideas do not travel on their own but are transmitted by human agents.[80] Policy communities and networks located at the meso level and that have linkages beyond national boundaries help to compile and disseminate information about institutional designs and create pressure for reform.[81] Foreign companies, legal firms, and consultants provide technical training to domestic actors in international legal, business, and political models, as well as how they function in practice. MNCs hire local managers, introduce them to company institutions, and even send them abroad for direct observation of the firms' home-country operations in order to train them in the foreign firm's institutional logic and to act as agents of the firm. Thus trained, MNCs can substitute local managers for their more expensive expatriate counterparts in the management structure without greatly diminishing parent company operating norms in foreign subsidiaries. Law firms, which tend to follow their home-country MNCs abroad to provide legal services that bridge state and regulatory boundaries, typically recruit, train, and work with local legal personnel. International law firms, thereby, provide opportunities for local legal professionals to learn international legal forms and to deepen their understanding of the logic and application of such forms. Consulting firms provide information on foreign managerial and business practices not just to foreign firms but also to local businesses and their professional staff. Business organizations and NGOs provide organizational and lobbying models that local actors emulate. Such policy communities, consultants, and business organizations can have a significant effect on institutional change, in part, because the hiring of consultants indicates an organization's receptiveness to institutional reform.

Global integration provides a set of strong incentives to local actors to acquire skills that would be attractive to firms, policy makers, and law firms that work with foreign actors. International engagement, through the economic incentives that it creates, entices citizens to study abroad in order to learn about international legal and business norms and practices. Training and education on international norms and institutions brings local actors into transnational policy communities, promoting diffusion of international norms. Within a developing economy, a corps of trained specialists can become powerful advocates of institutional change toward internationally accepted norms and institutional models. Rather than accepting the received "scripts" or logic of existing institutional configurations, professionals who study abroad or work for foreign professional organizations learn foreign scripts, which they tend to follow and use to judge domestic institutions and to advocate for institutional change. For example, Judith Teichman has shown that Latin American policy makers who studied abroad (especially in the U.S.) became leading proponents of neoliberal economic policies such as privatization in their countries.[82] When combined with economic crises and/or pressure from international organizations, Latin American policy communities propelled and shaped domestic institutional reform. In general, the pressure that domestic policy communities bring to bear on officials is very important and, perhaps, of longer duration than the direct pressure applied by MNCs and other international actors. "Localizing" pressure and institutional models from foreign actors can increase the legitimacy of institutional reforms in the eyes of citizens and policy makers who may have nationalistic reactions to external pressure for reform. The development of a local policy community helps to transmit important technical information, and such communities can become important agents of institutional change.[83] Once such a policy community forms, it can advocate institutional change at the macro and micro levels, working with state agents and firms.

Depending on the attributes and functions of specific states, officials exercise a mixture of indirect and direct controls over the influence of policy communities. States create a regulatory environment for legal professionals by establishing qualifications, court procedures, and licensing of professional firms. The state may allow non-governmental agencies such as bar associations to administer many of these functions with varying degrees of autonomy. Some states, such as China, strictly control the approval of civil society organizations, including business and professional associations that provide platforms for the gathering of policy communities. More generally, states can establish patterns of interaction with policy communities, choosing formally to include them in policy discussions through special committees, to consult with them less formally, or to exclude them from policy discussions. Moreover, state agents can guide the process of policy diffusion by selecting which professional groups or particular members of a policy community to consult. Such controls allow states to guide their process of globalization and to limit the pressure from domestic and foreign actors on them.

Even professionals who do not work with officials to alter formal institutions such as laws and policies can contribute to changing business and legal practices through their personal endeavors. Business consultants, business managers, and attorneys who have cooperated with foreign parties advise other local businesses on firm-level institutional change, thus diffusing institutional designs to third parties. Local professionals who are ambitious enough to study abroad and to work with foreign law firms, consulting firms, or businesses often aspire to run their own business. Drawing on their technical training from abroad and their knowledge of local institutions, such professionals can navigate between dominant local institutions and sub-regimes of institutions inspired by foreign actors, establishing hybrid institutional models that layer elements of foreign institutions onto local practices, or simply diffusing foreign practices to local businesses. The newly formed businesses based on their new institutional models elaborate and build sub-regimes that encroach upon and compete with dominant institutions. Armed with technical expertise and personal wealth, professionals help to diffuse international practices learned from transnational policy communities to policy makers and to local organizations (see Figure 1.1).

Institutional Change—But in What Direction?

This chapter has emphasized the state's role in selecting institutional models while still bounded by domestic constraints such as ideological commitments, political coalitions, and institutional legacies. A yet unanswered key issue in the literature on institutional change is the following: What determines the type of institutional models that a country selects for adoption? To the extent that authors have taken up such an issue, they tend to rely on economic success of particular models in abstract market competition. While competition can be an incentive to emulate particular institutional forms and models, it does not explain what types of institutional changes a firm will adopt and how the reforms are selected. Even more so, it is difficult to determine how states will respond to new institutional designs because of the ideological and political cultural influences on their decision making. I posit that organizational leaders select institutional reform models, taking into account the following three factors: (i) the type of feedback on institutional models (a term that is both more specific and neutral than "success" in markets); (ii) the strength of policy communities associated with particular institutional models; and (iii) the meshing of state leaders' interests with the feedback on particular institutional models.

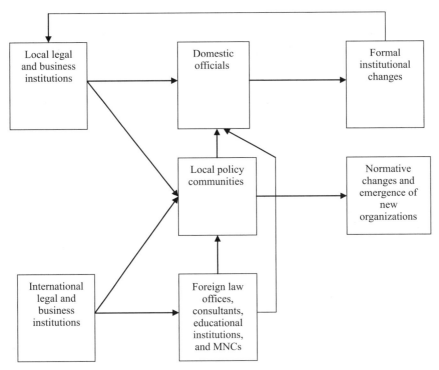

Figure 1.1   Model of Local Policy Community Formation and Institutional Change

Policy communities serve as informed analysts and advocates of particular institutional designs, and countries associated with some institutional models have developed more influential policy networks than others. In this study, the United States has developed more robust, externally oriented business and legal communities than Japan, which gives U.S. organizations a strong position from which to advocate and to diffuse their institutions. In comparison to U.S. and European firms, Japanese firms tend to focus inward on their company operations and to guard information about their firm-level institutions. The prevalence of internal labor markets (promoting employees from within rather than hiring from a labor market for mid-level positions) is just one manifestation of the inward orientation of Japanese firms. Additionally, many large Japanese manufacturers that invest abroad ask their Japanese suppliers to set up factories in the host economy, thus limiting contact between Japanese foreign investors and local suppliers.[84] The paucity of Japanese attorneys and the small number of legal cases tried in Japan are also suggestive of the limited capacity of the Japanese legal community to influence other countries' legal institutions.

Finally, state agents look to alternative models to meet particular reform goals and political interests, including retaining their own power. Reformers' adoption of alternative models based on some objective measure of institutional performance is by no means guaranteed because leaders hold ideological positions and face coalitions of supporters and opponents. While state reformers have a number of potentially conflicting interests and the order of importance of the various interests may shift, leaders will consider feedback on dominant institutional regimes and sub-regimes in determining the appropriateness of models for emulation. Reformers in non-democratic regimes do not face periodic evaluation by citizens, which can limit institutional reform by shortening the time frame for judging leaders' legitimacy. Leaders in a country such as China can lengthen their time horizons and opt for institutional models that address long-term problems. Hence, Chinese central officials look to models that help to solve strategic problems in the area of technological development, labor reform, managerial reforms, and property rights protection, without creating significant social, political, and economic instability.

Toward a Model of Globalization and Path-Dependent Development

This chapter has contended that the literature on globalization and institutional change has two problems: (i) previous studies of institutional change cleaved to a rather rigid bifurcation of exogenous dynamics acting on states at the macro level and endogenous dynamics at the micro level of society, rendering a relatively weak understanding of how international pressures at the macro level interact with inter-firm dynamics (including the role of MNCs) at the micro level in the process of institutional change; and (ii) the literature provides little guidance on direction of institutional reform and the process by which organizations and states select new institutional models. The theory of state-guided globalization helps to address these issues by focusing on the interaction between international and domestic actors at the macro, meso, and micro levels: mainly, host economy officials, MNCs and their staff, international law firms, and business consultants. To host economies, exogenous actors supply information about alternative institutional designs, provide feedback on domestic institutions, offer new criteria by which to evaluate institutions, and train professional practitioners in the form and logic of foreign institutions. A focus on international business and legal actors is worthwhile because: (i) they establish an ongoing presence in host economies; (ii) investment is a more common occurrence than warfare, depression, or other exogenous shocks; and (iii) they provide feedback on institutions at both the macro and micro levels.

In addition to exogenous shocks and dictates from international organizations, foreign actors play both negative and positive roles in institutional change. Foreign actors disrupt the positive self-reinforcing mechanism of path dependency by altering the terms of evaluating existing institutions and by indicating discrepancies between international and local institutions. Foreign actors contribute to the construction of institutional sub-regimes at the meso level and compete with organizations under dominant institutional regimes for staff and contracts at the micro level. In addition, actors in international society help to define the terms of legitimate institutions and of responsible members, thereby encouraging states and reformers to take on new identities and institutional designs. When domestic actors accept new institutional forms, adopt new scripts for behavior, and judge institutions by

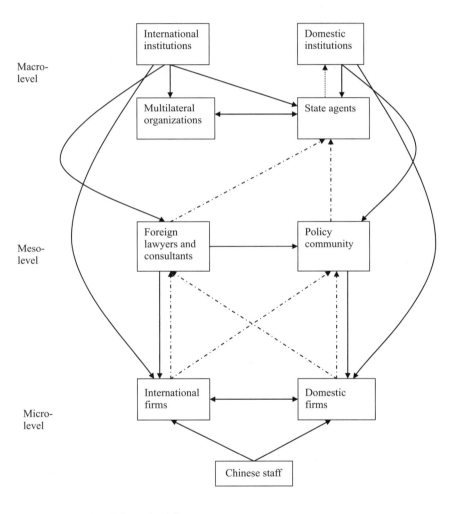

Figure 1.2   Model of Institutional Change

new criteria, then significant institutional change can occur incrementally. Essentially, exogenous pressure for institutional change is localized, increasing the probability that it will be sustained. Figure 1.2 depicts the flow of information, feedback, and institutional reform at three levels of analysis.

Particular Features of the Chinese Case

Applying such a model of international integration and institutional change to China requires consideration of the country's particular features. Most of the literature on institutional change and nearly all of the varieties of capitalism authors develop arguments based on cases of democratic, advanced capitalist countries. In democracies, leaders clearly are embedded in the population's normative framework; are subject to pressure from domestic political constituencies through periodic elections, protests, and lobbying; face constitutional rules that weigh against rapid institutional change; and, in most cases, are active participants in international society and adhere to international norms. One-party states, in contrast, do not face the periodic electoral competition that checks officials' actions and that provides feedback on the legitimacy of state institutions; such states generally lack constitutional balances of power that create "veto points" against institutional change.[85] Chinese state officials' relative autonomy from society and from constitutional constraints simultaneously makes them more selective in how they respond to civil society pressures and lobbying and more able to enact significant reforms, at least at the macro level.[86] Similarly, one-party states such as China are less susceptible to international pressure and, at times, have flouted international opinion of their actions. Yet, China's interest in becoming a great power requires it to take note of international norms and standards of conduct.[87] China's state-guided globalization, which has entailed high levels of foreign investment and trade, joining many treaty and multilateral organizations, and a mixed record of acceptance of international norms on human rights and rule of law make it difficult to determine the direction of China's institutional change and its intentions. Chinese leaders' interest in institutional improvement compels them to listen to advice from international and domestic actors, but their relative autonomy increases their ability to select which groups, ideas, and models to heed.

Domestic leaders act in accordance with international institutions and in response to international pressure due to a mixture of concerns over their identities and material interests. Officials in countries that desire international power, such as China, pay some attention to international norms of behavior in order to improve their ability to get along with other powerful states and to enhance their leadership in international society.[88] Leadership in international society requires a country to take on some of the attributes and values of international society; even a country intent on revising some of the norms and rules of international society typically will play to the rhetoric and principles of international society.[89] In particular, creating a comfortable environment in which MNCs operate, including adoption of familiar international legal and business institutions, brings the additional benefit of attracting foreign capital flows. It may also be the case that a country like China will adopt institutional forms such as tariff rates or dispute-resolution mechanisms that mimic international institutions while maintaining informal non-tariff barriers or protectionist means to undermine legal principles. On this point, the international business and legal communities play a crucial role in monitoring implementation. Nevertheless, enjoying a good international reputation and "getting on-line with international rules" pays.

A second important Chinese distinction at the start of the reform period was China's legacy of state socialism, which entailed extensive state controls over many aspects of the economy and society. China has loosened many of its economic controls during its transition from a planned to a mixed economy, but it still regulates enterprises (at least SOEs) and coordinates many aspects of economy. Under such institutional arrangements, officials have a great deal of autonomy to revise institutions, yet face numerous institutional and financial commitments that limit their capacity radically to alter institutions. For example, China has sought to reform and even privatize elements of its economy, but reformers also must maneuver through a minefield of entrenched bureaucratic interests in state ministries and recalcitrant local officials, while avoiding a financial collapse of its strained state-owned banks and state-owned enterprises, both of which carry a massive debt load. Further complicating reform by administrative fiat, state agents face workers in SOEs who cleave to many of the egalitarian principles embedded in socialism.[90] Additionally, the Chinese party-state has been reluctant to relinquish the considerable power it exercises over civil society, but despite such controls, Chinese citizens increasingly engage in protests, strikes, unofficial NGO activity, and lobbying.[91]

China, then, is an excellent case of an autonomous, sovereign state that wields enormous power and regulates its interaction with domestic and international actors as well as between domestic and international actors. It is also a state and economy that is of great interest and concern to international organizations, foreign governments, and MNCs and, therefore, is subject to strong pressure from international agents at the macro and micro levels. Of course, given the legacy of state socialism and China's Communist Party, one would expect state officials to figure prominently in any analysis of institutional change. The variety of investors coming to China strengthens officials' hand in directing institutional reform. Yet, Chinese officials cannot fully control the actions of foreign investors, local actors, and international organizations that bring pressure to bear on reformers. In this sense, China is best described as pursuing *state-guided globalization,* a term that reflects state efforts to harness global forces that it cannot fully control in order to advance its long-term development strategy and short-term goals. The following chapters examine the process and direction of institutional change in China. By following macro-, meso-, and micro-level dynamics, the book traces the gradual adoption of many aspects of U.S. institutions. The outcome of China's globalization has been a significant shift in the direction of concern with international institutions in general and U.S. and European models in particular.

Part I

Macro-level Dynamics and
Institutional Change

Typically, authors who analyze globalization and institutional change focus on state regulations, laws, and policies at the national level. The interaction of international norms and institutional models with domestic institutions is an important aspect of global integration. Analyzing macro-level changes necessitates the interaction of domestic and international actors, the diffusion of international and foreign institutional forms, and the development of national-level regulations and laws to facilitate international economic exchanges.

In the following three chapters, I focus on changes in macro-level policies and legal institutions. The chapters highlight how China's government has guided the process of globalization by constructing and adjusting national policies in pursuit of particular strategic goals and interests. Chapter 2 analyzes the development of China's changing orientation to globalization and its concomitant evolving interests. The chapter reveals how Chinese reformers have shifted over time from a stance of marginalizing and controlling foreign engagement in China to a position of deep global integration that encompasses foreign investment opportunities throughout China, lifting many strictures on the form of investment and fields in which investment can take place, along with increased participation in international organizations that condition Chinese institutional change, the most effective being China's accession to the WTO. China's desire to enter the WTO became an underlying logic for reform, and WTO rules and principles framed many of its specific decisions on the direction of institutional reforms, even prior to detailed negotiations over accession in the late 1990s.

Chapter 3 addresses the shifting investment pattern in China from the overwhelming prevalence of joint ventures to the dominance of the wholly foreign-owned enterprise investment vehicle, a previously understudied topic. The early pattern of joint ventures maximized state organizational control over foreign investors; allowing wholly foreign-owned enterprises, on the other hand, granted foreign firms maximum control over firm-level practices. The account of this quite surprising alteration of policy details the shifts in the order of state reformers' interests brought on by the acute financial pressures of the late 1980s and early 1990s, feedback on investment policies, and necessary institutional changes in preparation for China's WTO entry. China's government balanced its competing goals and interests, but ultimately shifted in the direction of greater leeway for foreign investors to meet its long-term strategic goals and in response to problems encountered by foreign and domestic partners in joint ventures.

In chapter 4, I focus on national-level institutional reforms to meet the norms of international society and of foreign countries on international commercial arbitration and enforcement of arbitration judgments. Multilateral organizations and foreign organizations define the parameters of acceptable international commercial arbitration and, more broadly, rule of law, but Chinese leaders and organizations selectively adopt those practices in order to help China to meet other reform goals, such as developing a society based on rule of law and securing high-tech investment projects. FIEs at the micro-level and legal policy communities at the meso level contribute to the reform process by supplying information on institutional forms and the shortcomings of Chinese practices. American firms and law offices, more so than Japanese, have contributed to the diffusion of international legal practices by providing training programs and rule of law initiatives and by openly contesting the actions of Chinese arbitration organizations and courts for their occasional non-compliance with international norms. From the micro and meso levels, foreign actors have helped to create pressure and to provide information to bring Chinese national legal institutions into closer compliance with international legal norms. The process of legal reform, however, has been a top-down exercise of power, as China's government has sought to select arbitration procedures and enforcement mechanisms that balance domestic institutional legacies and the demands of foreign businesses, as well as to compel local courts to follow central dictates on legal reforms.

In this section, actors at the macro, meso, and micro levels all interact, exchange ideas, and contend over institutional forms and practice, but the emphasis is on the actors at the macro level. In each chapter, national-level actors initiate institutional change to come into compliance with international norms and practices. Once open to the influence of foreign and international actors, however, national leaders revise and refine their goals to advance further reforms and/or to maximize economic benefits from the open-door policy. Collectively, the chapters reveal: (i) the process by which China's state guides the process of globalization; and (ii) the way that initial modest institutional reforms necessitate later deeper institutional reforms. Over the course of the reform period, China has incrementally shifted from a country that segregated and minimized exchanges of goods and ideas with foreign economic actors to an economy that has opened almost all aspects of its economy to globalization and one in which international legal principles are beginning to gain traction.

2

China's Opening and Institutional Change

Before proceeding with detailed analyses of the interaction of foreign invest-ment and Chinese labor and legal reforms in later chapters, the following account outlines the shifting Chinese attitudes toward foreign investors and the development of international actors' influence in China. How did China's relationship to foreign capital and foreign institutions evolve over the course of the reform period? And, how did the interaction of foreign and domestic actors transform China's interest in institutional change and help to chart China's movement toward greater compliance with international norms of behavior? This chapter analyzes shifts in interests and policy expressions such as laws and regulations to detail shifts in the Chinese state's approach to guiding its globalization course. Most of the account focuses on central policies and debates about how to harness foreign investors' contributions in China to meet policy makers' goals. Additionally, China's grand strategic goal of becoming an international power led it to push for WTO membership and to join other multilateral organizations, which, in turn, gave China a set of guideposts for their institutional reforms, including how to open their economy to trade and investment.

In late 1978 China began to integrate with international economy, under its "open door" policy, in order to meet domestic goals, especially the "Four Modernizations" program.[1] China hoped foreign investors would: (i) invest much-needed capital; (ii) transfer technology that could help to upgrade Chinese industry; (iii) expand China's export markets; and (iv) introduce new managerial and production techniques.[2] At the inception of the pol-icy, China used foreign investors as an isolated supplement to the domestic economy rather than as a key component. Concomitantly, China pursued another set of domestic reform goals, including a return to family-based farming, development of private firms, introduction of incentives and markets for labor, reinvigoration of state-owned enterprises (SOEs), and development of rule of law.

Since 1979, China has moved in fits and starts from a position of limiting and isolating foreign investors and their business institutions to a stance of using foreign investors to model domestic reforms.[3] As the reform period progressed, foreign investment has become more integrated into China's national economy, has provided a growing share of employment in manufacturing and services, and has become the leading source of Chinese exports. According to Sarah Tong, exports from foreign investors in China accounted for 13 percent of all exports leaving China in 1990; the figure soared to 55 percent of all exports in 2003.[4] In 1990, the ratio of Chinese urban workers employed by SOEs to those employed by FIEs was approximately 157:1; by 2006, the decline of SOEs and expansion of FIEs changed the ratio to 4.6:1.[5] Such statistics indicate one of the structural shifts in the relative bargaining power of foreign investors and China's state. The below account sketches how China's initially narrow open-door policy has been widened, and how foreign investment has interacted with domestic reforms, especially managerial, labor, and legal reforms. I contend that foreign investment has contributed to the reform process in at least three ways. First, foreign investors helped China's state to implement some of its domestic reform goals by putting into practice difficult policies that Chinese actors were reluctant to adopt. Second, foreign investors pressed for a broadening and deepening of reforms, thus stretching reformers' initial conception of the boundaries of institutional reform. Third, foreign investors introduced alternative models that Chinese officials and firms could emulate or combine with their own institutions.

1978–1983: An Uncertain Beginning

Deng Xiaoping and China's reformers inherited from Mao an autarkic development model that eschewed foreign technology, investment, and trade with all countries save socialist ones. Due to its isolation, misguided economic initiatives such as the Great Leap Forward, and political movements against intellectuals such as during the Cultural Revolution, China fell further behind other economies in terms of technology and levels of development. Through the decades of isolation, China's industries had failed to keep up with international technological development, and their economic institutions remained mired in out-dated, inefficient forms of socialist organization.

In late 1978, Deng Xiaoping and Chinese reformers made a calculated gamble to open China's door to foreign trade and foreign direct investment as a means to acquire foreign technology and to jump-start national development. The 1978–1983 period of China's integration with the global economy was characterized by debates over how and whether to induce foreign direct investment and how to shelter the rest of the economy from foreign influence.[6] Leery of a return of Western imperialism, leftist and nationalist members of the CCP complained that foreign investment and foreign trade compromised China's sovereignty and independence and laid China open to exploitation by MNCs.[7] Opponents of China's opening feared that globalization was tantamount to Westernization.[8] Even editorials advocating the open door policy called for patriotic loyalty to China and cautioned against "worshipping foreign things and fawning on foreign powers."[9] Opponents also claimed that China's opening imperiled China's scant hard currency reserves because either foreign investors would sell their products to China (rather than exporting them) and would repatriate profits, or advanced capitalist countries would enjoy a trade surplus with China.[10] Chinese leaders' concern that their hard currency would flow to foreign countries—a fear steeped in memories of China's experience with Western imperialism after the Opium Wars—led reformers to construct a mercantilist model of foreign economic engagement. Under such a model, Chinese leaders sought to manage foreign engagement in order to guard against foreign exploitation of Chinese resources, including laborers.

Proponents of the open-door policy urged that China needed to quicken its development and that foreign investment and trade would help to rationalize production and resource allocation.[11] Others noted that foreign investors contributed capital, technology, and managerial know-how to China's Four Modernizations program, and that China should take a flexible approach without compromising its sovereignty.[12] Correctly, proponents of China's opening urged that, unlike its position during the "century of humiliation" (from the Opium Wars in 1839 to the founding of the People's Republic of China in 1949), China was in a strong position to guard its sovereignty against incursions by Western imperialism.[13]

A second area of debate among Chinese leaders concerned whether China should imitate the practice of foreign (especially Western) investors. China's leaders wavered on whether to limit the transplantation of foreign business institutions or to emulate such institutions.[14] Initially, China was reticent to follow other countries' paths, especially those of advanced capitalist countries, but Deng Xiaoping advanced a theoretical position that allowed for greater receptivity to institutions from other countries. In 1978, Deng called for China to "seek truth from facts," a Maoist methodological position, which Deng used to focus on empirical results rather than ideological determinism ("politics in command"), even possibly learning from the West.[15] In 1978, official journal articles called on China to learn from the experience of a set of moderately reformist socialist countries, including Romania, Hungary, and Yugoslavia about economic openness—hardly a leap into deep international integration.[16]

More ardent reformers sought to learn managerial techniques from foreign investors, which required the state to loosen restrictions on foreign investors to introduce their institutions in FIEs.[17] Foreign investors, especially those from advanced capitalist countries, brought new patterns of industrial organization, labor relations, and expectations of the legal system with them to China. Displaying their distrust of U.S. and Japanese investors, China's press called for favoring investment from Hong Kong and overseas Chinese rather than from Western countries and Japan. According to Zhao Yuanhao, overseas Chinese investors were "in a better position to understand their homeland (China)" and "can bring with them at least a patriotic heart."[18] Early Hong Kong and Taiwanese investment was concentrated in hotels, real estate, and light-industrial, labor-intensive manufacturing, so China's preference for Hong Kong and overseas investment undermined other strategic goals such as transfer of technology and learning advanced management techniques.

Competing goals—the desire to attract and learn from foreign investors and the need to limit foreign investors' control over China—generated tension between Chinese leaders and foreign investors, as well as within China's officialdom. By 1981, Chinese journal articles (such as the one cited here), called for cautiously learning from foreign models "for the purpose of learning advanced science, technology and managerial experiences," but warned against "blind worship of foreign things."[19] By advocating the learning of foreign science, technology, and management techniques, China sought to limit dependence on foreign investors and the scope of contact with foreign business and culture.

As a compromise strategy, China adopted policies to confine the geographical scope and managerial autonomy of foreign investment and to limit competition among foreign investors and domestic firms. In 1979, China designated four special economic zones (SEZs) in southern China at Shenzhen, Shantou, Xiamen, and Zhuhai as open to foreign direct investment, and the state poured money into developing those sites' port facilities, roads, and other "hard" infrastructure. The SEZs effectively established a parallel economy for foreign investors by quarantining foreign investors, thereby marking off FIEs' geographic range of influence. The SEZs' placement opposite Taiwan and near Hong Kong was meant to attract foreign investors from the overseas Chinese community, who China considered less threatening than western investors.[20] China even developed a separate currency (*waihuiquan*, or "foreign exchange certificates") to be used by foreign investors, which enjoyed, unlike the local (People's) currency (*renminbi*), limited convertibility into hard currencies.[21] China constrained foreign firms' managerial and functional autonomy by: emphasizing exports by foreign firms out of the SEZs, applying strict rules on pay in foreign enterprises, and pushing foreign investors to link up with Chinese enterprises in JVs.[22] Officials designed rules on exports and exchange of Chinese currency for foreign currency to limit FIEs' access to China's market and to regulate the outflow of capital, as part of a mercantilist strategy. Foreign investors' access to the domestic market was strictly limited, likely due to the concerns of Chen Yun, China's leading economist of the time, who sought to balance foreign currency and to protect state industries.[23] Although not officially favored, in practice, officials encouraged JVs, usually with majority Chinese ownership,[24] while officials privately discouraged WFOEs.[25] China favored JVs over WFOEs because the former helped secure mutual benefit for Chinese and foreign partners in the form of shared profits while securing for the Chinese side the training of managerial personnel and Chinese control over operations.[26] Additionally, China used regulations to guide investors into targeted industries that would help to achieve the following domestic goals: (i) upgrade technology; (ii) increase exports to promote balanced trade and new trading partners; and (iii) expand employment opportunities to ease China's massive underemployment problem.

China's numerous restrictions and the uncertainty of China's commitment to a long-term open-door policy slowed the takeoff of foreign investment. During the period 1979–1983, foreign direct investment into China approximately amounted to $1 billion, a figure dwarfed by foreign investment flows in later periods (see Figure 2.1). In addition, China faced other structural problems in its effort to attract investors: underdeveloped port facilities and transportation networks; lax work standards among Chinese employees, especially those trained in SOEs that became JV partners with foreign investors; an inadequate corpus of business law; and ineffective legal organizations to secure property rights in contracts.

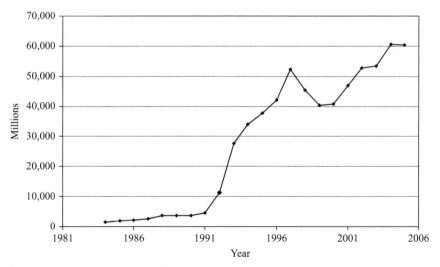

Figure 2.1   Annual In-flow of Foreign Direct Investment to China in Current U.S. Dollars. Source: Chinese Economic Statistical Yearbook Editorial Committee, *Chinese Economic Yearbook* (Beijing: Chinese Economic Yearbook Publishers, various years).

China mainly was exposed to Hong Kong and Taiwanese investors during this period. Although China did not disaggregate investment flows by country for this early period, in 1985, shortly after this period ended, Hong Kong accounted for approximately 49 percent of all foreign investment into China[27] (see Table 2.1). In light of Chinese leaders' stated preference for investors from Hong Kong and Taiwan and the proximity of the SEZs to Hong Kong and Taiwan, it is reasonable to assume that such overseas Chinese firms dominated early investment in China's SEZs. Few Japanese, U.S., or western European firms established companies in the SEZs, which thwarted China's ability selectively to learn advanced production and managerial techniques from foreign investors. Undoubtedly, the predominance of Hong Kong and Taiwanese investors in China's SEZs was helped by overseas Chinese investors' familiarity with the host culture and language, as well as Chinese officials' fear of Japanese and Western investors.[28] Chinese leaders sought to use FIEs, especially labor practices of FIEs in Shenzhen, as models for reforming SOEs.

Table 2.1
Chinese Annual Realized FDI by Source (Selected Countries) (Millions of Current U.S.$)

Year	Hong Kong	Taiwan	Japan	US	FDI Total
1979–84				274	3,060
1985	956		315	357	1,658
1988	2,428		319	236	3,194
1989	2,342		339	284	3,392
1990	1,913	222	349	456	3,487
1991	2,487	466	437	323	4,366
1992	7,706	1,053	1,101	511	11,008
1993	17,445	3,139	2,751	2,063	27,515
1994	19,823	3,391	3,377	2,491	33,767
1995	20,185	3,165	3,752	3,083	37,521
1997	20,632	3,289	4,526	3,239	45,257
1998	18,508	2,915	4,546	3,898	45,463
1999	16,363	2,599	4,032	4,216	40,319
2000	15,500	2,297	4,071	4,384	40,714
2001	16,717	2,980	4,688	4,433	46,878
2002	17,861	3,970	5,274	5,424	52,743
2003	17,700	3,377	5,054	4,199	53,505
2004	18,998	3,117	5,452	3,941	60,630
2005	17,949	2,152	6,530	3,061	60,325

Source: Chinese Economic Statistical Yearbook Editorial Committee, *Chinese Economic Yearbook* (Beijing: Chinese Economic Yearbook Publishers, various years).

During this early period of the open-door policy, Chinese leaders set out to revise their legal institutions and to develop a limited version of rule of law, mainly to prevent Chinese leaders from exercising personal, arbitrary power (rule of man), typified by mass movements such as the Cultural Revolution during the Mao era.[29] Some Chinese even recognized the necessity of constructing a set of legal institutions that would be "in keeping with current provisions in the world and acceptable to foreign capital" in order to attract investment.[30] Similar to the quarantine model of SEZs, China elaborated a parallel set of legal institutions, including regulations and arbitration bodies to govern the behavior of foreign investors in China. During this initial period of opening, China did little to elaborate or improve legal organizations that enforce such laws and regulations, leaving foreign investors to rely on personal relations with Chinese officials to manage most administrative and legal matters.[31]

Even after China opened to foreign investment, debate among the leadership roiled over the role of foreign direct investment in China's economy, manifested in the form of a critique of Chinese cultural trends. By 1983, leading opponents of the open-door policy blamed foreign influence for several worrisome domestic phenomena such as the reemergence of prostitution, drugs, and political protest. Opponents of the reforms attacked foreign investment and market reforms under the guise of a campaign against "spiritual pollution."[32] Although the campaign was short-lived and had little effect, it did indicate continuing political division over transplanting foreign institutions to China's environment.

1984–1991: Opening the Door Wider and a Failed Attempt to Slam It Shut

The mid- and late 1980s included cycles of China's relative opening and closure to foreign influence. During the period 1984–1989, local and central state reformers pushed for further opening to foreign investment, in terms of geographical scope, lines of industry open to investors, and managerial control over their business operations in China.[33] The period of opening was punctuated by the Tiananmen Square demonstrations of June 4, 1989, and their violent suppression, which stalled significant domestic reforms for two years while conservative leaders held sway. In the immediate aftermath of the June 4, 1989 massacre—and to address an overheated economy in the late 1980s—Chinese leaders cooled their heels on domestic reforms but simultaneously tried to assuage foreign firms' fears that China was closing its economy to foreign investment.

At the start of the period, Chinese leaders remained divided over how receptive China should be to foreign, especially Western ideas and institutions. Clearly, reformers were emboldened by some of the reform program's early success, such that they called for deeper integration with Western economies. By 1984, *Renmin Ribao,* China's leading state-run newspaper, ran articles that advocated a much deeper form of integration and borrowed from the experience, technology, and managerial skills of capitalist economies. [34] Such articles were significant not only for their overt advocacy of learning from capitalist countries but also their linkage of economic openness to China's domestic reforms such as advancing "science and technology" and "management."

The first geographic expansion of the open-door policy came in 1984, when China opened Hainan Island and fourteen more cities to foreign direct investment. In 1985, China opened the Pearl, Yangzi, and Min river deltas for foreign direct investment. Still, reformers intended to keep China's open-door policy distinct and isolated from domestic labor and legal reforms, for instance. Although China shifted toward greater receptivity to Western institutions, opponents of the open-door policy took two approaches to limiting foreign influence in China. First, conservative leaders pointed to the return of unsavory cultural phenomena such as the re-emergence of drug usage and prostitution as evidence that foreigners were encouraging decadence in China. In 1986, conservative leaders helped to launch a campaign against "bourgeois liberalization," which targeted such social problems and foreign influence. Second, conservatives called for a critical appraisal of the SEZ policy, which, they contended, had failed in many respects. [35]

Liberal reformers such as Zhao Ziyang overcame conservative opponents to expand further investment opportunities during the period 1986–1988. To improve the investment environment and to induce foreign investment flows, China's State Council in 1986 began to clarify its regulations and procedures related to foreign investment and to grant preferential tax treatment to investors who helped to meet policy goals. [36] Although the rules and procedures were far from transparent, the "Provisions of the State Council on the Encouragement of Foreign Investment" (1986) clarified preferred types of investors (Article 2), gave priority access to scarce water and electricity to preferred types of investors (Article 5), and allowed targeted FIEs to remit profits without paying income tax (Article 7). [37] New regulations enhanced FIEs' managerial control over labor, including the right to hire directly from the labor market, [38] to exercise discretion on which employees to retain in the process of forming a JV, [39] and to raise salaries for employees by removing a previous cap. [40]

In addition, China softened its stance on domestic market access and foreign currency exchange. In the previous period, Chen Yun had succeeded in establishing a strong mercantilist orientation, but China came to realize that such an approach discouraged foreign investment and technology transfer. Export requirements were better suited to "sunset industries" such as labor-intensive textile producers from Hong Kong than auto manufacturers, for example. [41] To attract investors with more advanced technology, China revised its rules to allow investors to produce goods that substituted for imports or that transferred desired technology.[42] Firms with domestic market access needed to convert their domestic currency to foreign exchange, and China slowly liberalized its foreign exchange controls.[43]

In 1988, General Secretary Zhao Ziyang announced the "coastal development strategy," which both expanded the geographical scope of foreign investment along the entire coast and selected interior cities and devolved approval procedures for foreign investment proposals. The coastal development strategy allowed foreign investors to explore multiple investment sites, thus generating competition among local officials to attract foreign firms.[44] In the competition to attract investment, local officials extended to foreign firms special privileges and greater autonomy, even in violation of national regulations.[45] The increased number of Chinese actors involved in attracting foreign capital improved investors' relative bargaining position, which helped investors to press for looser regulations and greater managerial control.[46]

As a consequence of the improving investment regime, China's inflow of FDI grew steadily from US$1.419 billion in 1984, to US$4.661 billion in 1991, an increase of 228 percent over the period.[47] Throughout the 1980s, Hong Kong and Taiwanese firms continued to dominate foreign direct investment flows to China.[48] In 1985, Hong Kong investment alone accounted for roughly 49 percent of all FDI in China, and in 1990, the combination of Taiwanese and Hong Kong investment amounted to 57 percent of total FDI flows.[49] Through the late 1980s, investment from the U.S. and Japanese firms remained relatively flat. In 1989, U.S. and Japanese investment flows to China grew in real terms and accounted for 18.3 percent of foreign direct investment flows, but the June 4, 1989, Tiananmen Square massacre temporarily reined in enthusiasm for new investment projects.

Firms' home-country origins shaped their interests and the expectations of foreign investors and, therefore, their impact on Chinese institutional reforms. Hong Kong and Taiwanese investors were willing to go around rules and to rely on personal relations (*guanxi*) in arranging and managing foreign investment.[50] Moreover, overseas Chinese investors tended to transfer low-tech, labor-intensive forms of production to China, thus presenting a rather exploitative model of labor management to Chinese reformers.[51] The prevalence of Hong Kong and Taiwanese investors did little to improve rule of law or otherwise to alter China's business institutions, for three reasons: (i) at the time, low technology was readily available in China and did not require heightened legal protection; (ii) labor-intensive production tends to squeeze labor rather than to improve efficiency; and (iii) the use of social ties to get around rules undermined rule of law initiatives.[52] Later, the growth of capital-intensive and technologically sophisticated forms of productive investment from Japan, the United States, and other advanced capitalist economies contributed to Chinese efforts to build greater respect for rule of law, to protect intellectual property rights, and to improve on China's production and managerial model.

Shifts in the legal realm demonstrated China's growing consciousness of and concern for foreign legal norms, even if such consciousness did not alter Chinese legal behavior on the ground. In 1987, China's accession to the New York Convention on International Economic Arbitration,[53] which bound China's courts to enforce international arbitration decisions rendered in other signatory countries, marked the beginning of a shift in its legal reform process from isolating the domestic legal system from international legal norms to engaging with international legal norms. After signing the New York Convention, China sought to address inadequacies in its legal forms and organizations that serviced foreigners through a series of legal and arbitration reforms, such as those to the Chinese International Economic and Trade Arbitration Commission (CIETAC), the body that hears most cases involving foreign investors and traders in China. The rule changes indicated a heightened concern for legal protection of foreign parties' interests. Chinese law allowed foreign investors to enter the Chinese court system, but most investors were loathe to have local courts hear their cases because of the poor training and potential bias of judges, and so, foreign firms persisted in segregating themselves into cases heard by CIETAC, which provided a higher standard of justice than the local courts. Throughout the period, too, China maintained distinct rules and regulations for foreign and domestic enterprises.

Beginning in the last quarter of 1987, even prior to the June 4, 1989, massacre, conservatives in the CCP attempted to slow China's overheated economy by tightening access to credit, but after June 4, 1989, conservative politicians struck out against China's (mainly domestic) reforms and reformers associated with the recently deposed General Secretary Zhao Ziyang. Despite the political retrenchment, Chinese officials (especially at the provincial level) used reassuring language or created new preferential policies to try to assuage the fears of foreign investors who were shaken by the protest's violent suppression.[54] Central officials attempted to attract foreign investment by further liberalizing China's investment climate. In 1990, China issued clarifying regulations on investment in the form of WFOEs.[55] In the same year, China authorized Pudong, Shanghai, to become the latest and largest SEZ in China. Unlike earlier SEZs, Pudong was targeted for high-tech investment, an attempt to upgrade foreign investment flows to China. The Pudong SEZ continued a policy to expand the number of high-tech development zones, which began with the 1988 Torch Program.[56] Local officials, especially in Shanghai, personally appealed to foreign investors to enter China.[57] Moreover, facing tightened access to Chinese credit but still needing capital to fuel development, local officials relaxed restrictions on WFOEs, which required no capital commitment from Chinese sources. The period ended with foreign direct investment flows remaining basically level during 1988–1990, followed by a modest upturn in 1991. Throughout the period, China endeavored to maintain barriers between foreign investors and domestic institutions, but China demonstrated growing interest in foreign legal and business models.

1992–2001: A Flurry of Investment and Deepening of Integration

In the spring 1992, Deng Xiaoping's "Southern Tour" reaffirmed the course of further economic reform and China's open-door policy. Deng's statements brought a tidal wave of foreign investment to China, much of it from advanced capitalist countries such as the United States and Japan. Aggregate FDI flows into China more than doubled, from US$4.666 billion in 1991 to US$11.291 billion in 1992. FDI flows spiked in 1997 to US$52.387 billion and finished off this period at US$46.878 billion in 2001 (see above Figure 2.1). In particular, U.S. and Japanese firms greatly expanded their investment in China after 1993 (see Figure 2.2). In 1992, U.S. firms invested $511 million in China, but their investment soared to $4.433 billion in 2001; during the same period, Japanese investment jumped from $1.101 billion to $4.688 billion. Foreign trade flourished as well, in part due to: (i) foreign pressure on China to remove trade barriers; (ii) increased trade by FIEs operating in China; and (iii) China's interest in joining the General Agreement on Tariffs and Trade (GATT), predecessor to the World Trade Organization (WTO). In

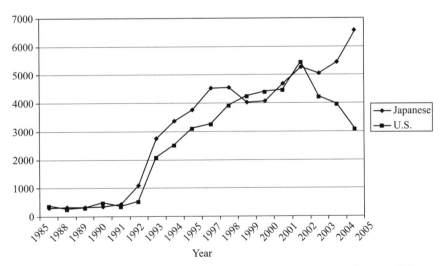

Figure 2.2   Japanese and U.S. Annual Foreign Direct Investment Flows to China (in tens of millions of current U.S. Dollars). Source: Chinese Economic Statistical Yearbook Editorial Committee, *Chinese Economic Yearbook* (Beijing: Chinese Economic Yearbook Publishers, various years).

1992, China also signed an agreement with the United States that eased or removed trade restrictions.[58] All of the above indicators signal that China's global economic engagement and concern with international institutions were intensifying.

According to Susan Shirk, in 1992 domestic political rivalries and competition for foreign investment flows among provincial and local leaders led China's central government to authorize 21 additional cities to receive foreign capital flows.[59] With more areas open to investment, foreign investors could pit officials in different cities against one another to extract concessions in investment opportunities, further improving the relative bargaining strength of foreign firms. To attract foreign investors, local officials promised tax breaks and created special investment zones without approval of the central state.[60] Consequently, central officials lost some of their control over the approval process and over foreign investors in China.

Changes in the structure of FDI, too, contributed to the state's eroding control over foreign investors. In the 1990s, foreign investors shifted from using primarily JVs to WFOEs as an investment structure (discussed in greater detail in chapter 3). Until 1988, WFOEs accounted for a scant one percent of FDI flows to China, but, beginning in 1992, foreign investors' interest in establishing WFOEs soared. In 1992, 22 percent of all FDI flows took the form of WFOEs, and 73 percent formed equity JVs (hereafter, EJVs) or cooperative JVs (hereafter, CJVs) (see Figure 2.3). By 2001, WFOEs accounted for 51 percent of all FDI flows and EJVs and CJVs combined for just 47 percent. The ascendance of the WFOE investment structure had profound

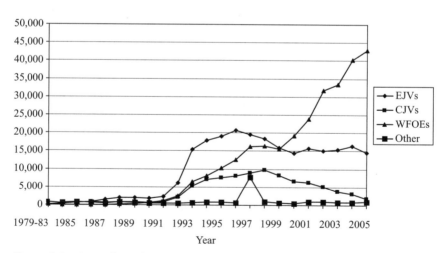

Figure 2.3   Annual Foreign Direct Investment Flows by Investment Vehicle (in millions of current U.S. Dollars). Source: Chinese Economic Statistical Yearbook Editorial Committee, *Chinese Economic Yearbook* (Beijing: Chinese Economic Yearbook Publishers, various years).

implications for Chinese control over foreign investors. Without Chinese JV partners to influence boardroom decisions, WFOE managers enjoyed greater freedom to transplant their home country business institutions.[61] Local and central officials could still monitor the activities of WFOEs, but in such firms, foreign investors enjoyed wide discretion over operations. WFOE managers resisted attempts to establish trade union (and Communist Party) branches in their firms, which undermined the principal organizational tools to control foreign investors' actions.[62] Even WFOEs that allowed trade unions to be established in their factories found that the unions played little or no role in the firm's operations. Increasingly, foreign investors used WFOEs to transfer their home-country institutions such as labor practices, management style, and company culture to China.

Foreign business practices affected China's reforms in SOEs and in the legal-regulatory field. During the period 1992–2001, surging foreign direct investment flows synergistically interacted with China's domestic reforms, evinced by the many significant reform laws and regulations issued by China. The 1994 Labor Law (discussed extensively in chapters 5 and 6) defined new guidelines for employment relations that provided clearer rules for workers' benefits and the right to organize trade union affiliates while also ushering in more conflict-laden industrial relations due to the law's sections on dismissal and labor arbitration. Such legislation met the needs of many foreign investors who clamored for greater leeway in managing their workforce and presaged dismissals and layoffs in the SOE sector. The Labor Law also helped Chinese leaders to press through changes that finally altered the ethos of SOEs but angered workers who faced layoffs in the process. While SOEs initially sidestepped labor reforms aimed at creating more incentives and less security, competition from foreign firms for top SOE personnel and new entrants to the Chinese workforce compelled SOEs finally to break their egalitarian ways and to offer their top employees highly lucrative contracts. Significantly, the 1994 Labor Law fused rules for foreign and domestic enterprises in China, which simultaneously stretched the boundaries of SOE labor reforms and extended new controls to FIEs.[63]

In the legal realm, foreign actors raised concerns about many aspects of China's legal system, including piracy, bias against foreign parties in arbitration and in courts, and the courts' failure to enforce decisions in favor of foreign parties. During the period 1992–2001, China's leaders four times (in 1994, 1995, 1998, and 2000) revised the rules of China's International Economic and Trade Arbitration Committee (CIETAC). Some of the revisions responded to complaints from foreign parties and CIETAC panelists, while other changes in 1995 and 1998 sought to make CIETAC rules consistent with China's recently revised Arbitration Law, which applied to domestic and international cases.[64] In 1998, China authorized CIETAC to hear cases involving all parties—foreign and domestic, which further broke down the barriers between the legal environment for foreign and domestic parties. China also tightened its control over the lower courts in attempt to improve compliance with CIETAC verdicts. Although legal reforms left many investors dissatisfied, the reforms aimed to assuage some foreign investors' concerns about secure property rights. It is worthwhile to note, too, that harmonization of legal procedures could have been achieved by bringing the justice system for foreign interests down to the level of protection for domestic parties, but the Chinese government attempted to harmonize upward, essentially improving the procedures for domestic parties by allowing them to use the same institutions as foreign investors.

More broadly, China opened itself to institutional transplantation by increasing the opportunities for advanced capitalist countries to train Chinese in the legal and business fields. For example, China's state worked with foreign organizations, including the US-China Business Council (USCBC) to implement a rule of law initiative.[65] Initiated in 1994, the USCBC program provides modest funding for a variety of rule of law initiatives such as training Chinese defense lawyers, assisting in China's rewriting of its Civil Procedure Code, and training Chinese judges in the areas of intellectual property law and WTO law. In 1994, the Ministry of Foreign Trade and Economic Cooperation signed an agreement with the European Commission to establish a JV business school in Shanghai, called Chinese European International Business School, which trains mainly Chinese managers in advanced capitalist management techniques.

China's interest in joining the WTO structured the country's interaction with foreign actors and receptiveness to foreign institutions. China began its quest to join the WTO in 1986 (then called the GATT), but domestic and international events sidetracked their progress toward entry until the mid-1990s.[66] WTO principles, especially the concept of "national treatment," which calls for WTO member states to provide the same regulatory treatment to goods from foreign and domestic firms, further tore down the regulatory wall between domestic and foreign institutions. Moreover, the anticipated heightened competition with foreign firms led China to reinvigorate SOE reforms, in particular to learn from foreign models of management and labor institutions.

During this period (1992–2001) of intense global engagement, Chinese leaders made great strides in advancing their domestic reform agenda, deepening China's relations with foreign actors, and harmonizing the regulatory frameworks for domestic and international firms. They marginalized opponents of globalization, revised and introduced new legislation that committed domestic firms to adopt reforms and allowed foreign firms to institute market-oriented practices, and engaged foreign parties to help in the process of transplanting business and legal institutions. Foreign firms continued to identify weaknesses in China's evolving regulatory and legal environments, and Chinese officials at least responded to many such concerns with partial remedies. Moreover, China's leaders used foreign firms' practices as models for SOEs to emulate and used international norms and legal institutions as guideposts for domestic legal reforms.

2001–Present: WTO Accession and Forced Institutional Reform

The final period under discussion began with China's accession to the World Trade Organization (WTO) in September 2001 and continues through the present. As David Zweig convincingly argues, Chinese reformers used WTO accession to lock China into a path of further reform and global integration.[67] The WTO accession agreement created a schedule for China to open new sectors to trade and/or to foreign investment, which provides foreign financial services and agricultural products (among other goods and services) greater access to China's market.[68] The WTO gave detailed prescriptions, including "national treatment" of foreign goods and companies, harmonizing tax codes, and protecting intellectual property, which continued earlier trends toward convergence with the international trade regime.[69] Furthermore, the WTO dispute settlement mechanism demands that national courts enforce its decisions, which presses China to improve the transparency and predictability of its court system. Although China's compliance with WTO provisions is imperfect, China is moving in a direction of greater adherence to international standards of liberal political economy.[70]

Improved regulations and the economic prospects of China's WTO accession induced high levels of FDI. Foreign investment flows to China peaked in the mid-1990s, slightly declined in the late 1990s, and rose again after 2000. For the period 2001–2005, annual FDI flows to China increased from US$46.9 billion to US$60.3 billion. The earlier pattern of growing high-tech investment and the shift from JVs to WFOEs persisted during the post-2001 period. By 2005, approximately 71 percent of all foreign direct investment flows took the form of WFOEs. Foreign investment continued an earlier trend of decreasing investment from Hong Kong and Taiwan as a share of overall investment flows, while the share from the United States and Japan stayed relatively flat. In 1992, investment from Hong Kong and Taiwan accounted for approximately 80 percent of all foreign direct investment flows to China, but in 2004, only 35 percent. Technical upgrading of investment and the introduction of Western and Japanese models of labor relations and management went hand-in-hand with declining shares of overseas Chinese investment and growing reliance on the WFOE investment structure. During this period, China also responded to foreign actors' criticism of China's legal system with more revisions to CIETAC's rules and tightening of enforcement mechanisms for CIETAC decisions. The rapid proliferation of Chinese civil court cases, too, suggests that using the legal system to settle disputes began to penetrate the consciousness of average citizens.[71]

To prepare for heightened competition brought on by WTO accession, Chinese officials guided domestic firms to use foreign investors as models for economic reforms. Chinese private and state-owned firms alike have turned to foreign actors to learn advanced management techniques. Some domestic firms have hired away Chinese human resource managers from FIEs, while others have hired foreign (and some domestic) consulting firms. According to a Chinese human resource manager working for a U.S.-based global consulting company, the Chinese government produced an internal document that called for SOEs to adopt Western management practices, especially pay-for-performance schemes.[72] Essentially, foreign pressure and foreign examples helped Chinese reformers to achieve their long-standing goal of "breaking the iron rice bowl." SOEs are adopting pay schemes that mimic income stratification patterns of foreign firms, especially those from the United States, thus breaking down their egalitarian ethos.

Conclusion: Globalization and Dynamic Development of China's Open-Door Policy

Since 1978, ideas, strategies, models, and political coalitions changed over the course of the post-Mao era, all of which shaped the interaction of foreign actors and Chinese institutional change. Table 2.2 summarizes the institutional and policy changes with regard to foreign investment, as well as shifts in the patterns of foreign direct investment flows. At the start of the reform period, China sought to isolate foreign investors to limit their influence over domestic institutions. By the current period of reforms, China used foreign investors, international organizations, and treaties as catlysts of domestic institutional change. What accounts for the dynamism?

Changing Political Coalitions

In 1978, Deng Xiaoping returned to leadership over a deeply divided CCP, and significant segments of the party opposed the open-door policy. Initially, concern over China's potential return to a pattern of imperial dependency, erosion of control over capital, and unhealthy social trends led to a compromise between reformers and conservatives: to quarantine foreign investors and to foster state control over foreign investors. As the open-door policy developed in the 1980s and 1990s, local officials allied themselves with national reformers to press for greater openness, forming a coalition that conservative leaders could not suppress. Even the political challenge of the June 4, 1989, movement, which momentarily galvanized conservatives and economic reformers who sought to cleave to one-party dominance, slowed domestic economic reforms but could not stop the coalition of local and national officials who continued to press for greater openness to foreign investors. Since Deng Xiaoping's southern tour in 1992, conservative leaders have been marginalized and China has further opened its door to foreign investment and trade. Moreover, China has fused foreign investors and their institutional models to the process of domestic institutional change. Accession to the WTO laid the future path of China's open-door policy so that leaders cannot reverse the course of institutional change.

Table 2.2
Summary of Strategic, Institutional, and Investment Flows by Period

Period	Major Institutional and Policy Changes Changes in FDI Flows
1979–1983	• Strategy: guard Chinese sovereignty, isolate investors from the rest of the economy, culture, and politics, develop exports • Policy and institutional developments: Equity Joint Venture Law (1979), creation of SEZs (1980), separate currency (Foreign Exchange Certificates) from the People's Currency (*renminbi*) created for foreigners and investors (1980) • FDI: slow takeoff, dominated by JVs, majority from Hong Kong and Taiwan
1984–1991	• Strategy: shift from export-led growth to technological upgrading • Policy and institutional developments: Hainan Island and fourteen cities opened to FDI (1984); opening of Yangzi, Pearl, and Min river deltas to foreign direct investment (1985); WFOE Law (1986); accession to the New York Convention on foreign commercial arbitration awards (1987); loosening of some restrictions (including limited market access) for JVs; loosening of some restrictions on WFOEs; and coastal development strategy (1984–1992); CJV Law (1988); and revision of CIETAC Rules (1988) • FDI: slight increase of FDI, leveling off at the end of the period and increase in WFOE investment after 1988
1992–2001	• Strategy: harmonization of Chinese and international institutions • Policy and institutional developments: twenty-one additional cities opened for FDI (1992); Labor Law harmonizes labor regulations for domestic and foreign firms (1994); Foreign Exchange Certificates phased out (beginning in 1994); revisions of CIETAC rules including allowing domestic firms to file cases at CIETAC (1994, 1995, 1998, 2000); negotiations to enter the WTO • FDI: takeoff of FDI flows; more investment in WFOEs; increase in Japanese and U.S. investment; growth of high-tech investment
2001–present	• Strategy: implementing plans for harmonization with international institutions and full participation in international society • Policy and institutional developments: China accedes to the WTO (2001); New Implementing Rules for WFOEs opens up domestic market to goods from FIEs (2001); revision of CIETAC rules (2005); China develops the Shanghai Cooperation Organization (2001) • FDI: increase in FDI flows, WFOEs dominate new FDI flows by the end of the period

Changed Strategies and Reordering of China's Interests

While at the start of the reform, China was desperate for cash, technology, and training in new managerial techniques, China's concern with guarding its sovereignty and avoiding dependencies on foreign actors was paramount. The cautious approach resulted in China's quarantining foreign investors in SEZs and emphasizing export-led growth. Yet, pursuit of that model limited technology transfer and discouraged foreign investment from Japan and Western countries. In the late 1980s, China shifted the focus of its foreign investment strategy to increase the transfer of technology and to introduce advanced managerial techniques. To pursue the reordered priorities, reform-minded Chinese officials altered China's regulations and policies on foreign direct investment by enhancing foreign managerial control over JVs and by loosening restrictions over investment in WFOEs.

Foreign Ideas and Actors

Over the course of the reform period, China became more receptive to foreign ideas and foreign investors held an increasingly important position in China's economy. Foreign investors contributed a growing share of China's fixed capital investment and exports, which increased the importance of foreign investors' interests in policy discussions without formally making foreign actors a part of China's governing coalition. Through a mixture of struggle and cooperation, foreign actors (multinational corporations, non-governmental organizations, and international organizations) diffused new business and legal models to China's economy. Over the course of the open-door policy, officials added Japanese and Western institutional models to their menu of options, which was earlier dominated by overseas Chinese such as Hong Kong. The shift occurred, in part, because critical appraisal of the SEZs led to reconsideration of overseas Chinese investors' practices, and because Japanese, U.S., and European firms demonstrated alternative models to address Chinese business problems. Japanese and U.S. investors transmitted their institutions to China by training local personnel in the operation of their business and legal institutions and by working with host officials to diffuse their institutions throughout China. Such actions by U.S. and Japanese organizations and investors helped to shape popular attitudes toward their institutions and the pressure—both foreign and domestic—brought to bear on reformers. Receptivity to Japanese and U.S. institutions increased by seeing such institutions at work in China; Chinese officials' relative preference for the two different institutional models changed with feedback on the institutional models' operation in China and the long recession in Japan in the 1990s.

In sum, domestic leaders and their strategies worked in tandem with foreign ideas and actors to alter the course of China's open-door policy. Increasingly, China has been receptive to foreign ideas and institutional models, which have shaped the direction of institutional reform. The particular foreign and domestic actors involved in various stages of the reform process affected which ideas and institutional models mattered in China's reforms. Over the course of the reform period, foreign investors enjoyed greater leeway to establish purer versions of their institutional designs in China and the types of investors expanded to include capital-intensive investors from the United States and Japan. Slowly, a menu of institutional models developed for Chinese reformers to weigh. Chapters 3–6 will analyze particular examples of this dynamic process at work in the areas of foreign investment vehicles, labor reforms, and international commercial arbitration.

3

The Shift Toward the Wholly Foreign Owned Enterprise Structure

After China opened its economy, foreign investors raised several significant policy issues, including the following: (i) access to China's market; and (ii) foreign investors' freedom to choose their investment vehicle. These two macro-level issues initially pitted China's cautious approach to surrendering sovereign control over foreign economic actors against international norms of economic openness on trade and investment, codified in the GATT and replaced by the WTO. The chapter details how and why China's interest in greater openness to trade and to new investment vehicles became more closely aligned with international norms and institutional designs. In addition to micro-level pressure from foreign investors for greater openness to trade and greater control over their investment, Chinese policy makers also were influenced by macro-level institutional requirements for WTO accession and by their need to upgrade the technological level of foreign investment.

Lost in most analyses of the mercurial rise in foreign direct investment flows to China during the 1990s is a fundamental change in investment vehicles from JVs to WFOEs. During the period 1979–1999, the most popular investment vehicle for new FDI to China was the JV model but, beginning in 1988, investment in WFOEs began to take off and eclipsed annual investment in JVs beginning in 2000 (see Figure 3.1). By 2001, a slight majority of all new foreign direct investment in China took the form of WFOEs, and the share has continued to rise. During the period 1988–1991, a complex set of factors combined to compel China to alter its approach to foreign investment, which allowed foreign investors to gravitate toward the WFOE model.

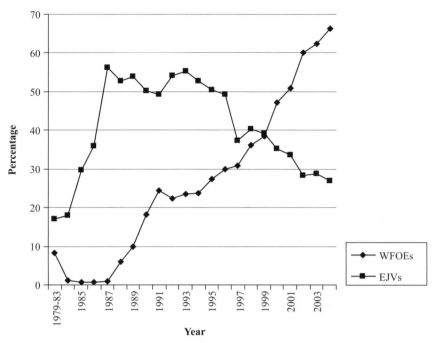

Figure 3.1   Percentage of Total FDI in WFOEs and EJVs by Year. Source: Chinese Economic Statistical Yearbook Editorial Committee, *Chinese Economic Yearbook* (Beijing: Chinese Economic Yearbook Publishers, various years).

JVs require foreign investors to work with one or more Chinese part-ners—usually SOEs—by pooling capital and/or other resources such as technology and fixed assets (machinery, factory buildings, and land) to form a newly registered business. Thus, the JV model allowed the Chinese state to have some direct control over the operation of foreign invested enterprises within its borders through state-owned Chinese partners. As subsidiaries of foreign companies, WFOEs include no local investment, share no corporate control with local firms such as voting on the board of directors, and, conse-quently, receive their cues from the firm's home office. The WFOE investment structure allows the foreign investor complete control over the operation of the foreign subsidiary, thus stripping away some of the Chinese government's ability to affect the actions of foreign investors, except through its regulatory framework for such enterprises. The choice of investment vehicles, then, sig-nificantly affects the balance of Chinese and foreign control over the result-ing companies.

The type of investment vehicles used by foreign firms is a significant mat-ter. First, the rise of WFOEs has undermined China's state control over for-eign investors, an issue that was paramount at the inception of the open-door policy in 1979. Second and related, the move toward WFOEs indicates broad changes in China's foreign investment regime and its goals of international economic engagement. Few authors have analyzed the shift,[1] but several early works noted foreign investors' frustration with the JV model, thus presaging the rise of the WFOEs.[2] Existing works on the problems encountered by JVs in China have focused on cultural difference or lack of trust,[3] struggle for operational control over the corporations, and poor profitability.[4] In light of the importance attached to the issue, the shift in investment policy and practice has received surprisingly little scholarly attention.

This chapter addresses two questions. First, what accounts for the rapid shift from the JV to the WFOE model by foreign investors? Existing works have explained the shift in terms of the problems encountered by foreign investors in JVs, decentralization of decision making on foreign investment approvals, and changing rules on foreign investment in China. Such accounts emphasize alterations in foreign firms' strategies, but they fail to account for changes on the Chinese side of the approval process. Why did China shift its approach to managing foreign investment, giving more opportunity to foreign investors to start up WFOEs? Mary Gallagher's analysis of the decentralization of approval of foreign investment as a consequence of the coastal development strategy comes closest to analyzing the rise of WFOEs from China's vantage point,[5] but it essentially contends that the growing number of WFOE approvals was an unexpected consequence of the coastal development strategy, that is, local officials more readily approved WFOE proposals than central officials would have liked. While such an analysis is insightful, it downplays the changes in the central government's approach to WFOEs. Rather than being an unintended consequence of the coastal development strategy, I contend that the rise of WFOEs indicated a revised approach to managing foreign investment. In addition to conflicting interests that drove many JV partners apart, the shift toward WFOEs was spurred by the following set of factors: (i) central officials' evolving goals for foreign investment policy; (ii) changes in investment rules; (iii) tightening financial constraints in China during the period 1987–1991; (iv) foreign concerns over protection of intellectual property rights (IPR); and (v) foreign investors' growing knowledge of China's investment environment.

Second, how does the shift to the WFOE investment structure affect the process of Chinese institutional change? The shift toward investment in WFOEs has marked a decline in state control over foreign investors' operations, but the shift in investment vehicles evinces a reordering of China's interests with regard to foreign investment. Specifically, China has surrendered some state control over foreign investors in order to guide investors to transfer desirable advanced technology, contributing to industrial upgrading in China. With operational control gained through investment in WFOEs, foreign firms have introduced new managerial models that China can emulate, meeting another long-standing goal of China's open-door policy. Foreign firms enjoy greater autonomy in WFOEs, which has helped them to diffuse firm-level institutions to Chinese firms and has even altered the institutional makeup of some JVs. In WFOEs, foreign investors could introduce new institutions, including new cognitive scripts with little or no resistance from local employees because of the absence of a Chinese partner. WFOEs exercise full control over hiring, so managers can attract and keep only those employees who perform well under the foreign institutions.

To analyze the shift toward investment in WFOEs, the discussion begins with the heyday of the JV model, 1979–1988, and explains why foreign investors relied on the JV model, as well as why foreign and Chinese parties became disenchanted with it. Next, I examine the shift toward the WFOE model, which began in the period 1988–1991. The gradual rise of investment in WFOEs out of the shoals of the 1989 political demonstrations and their violent suppression is puzzling. Typically, political economists have bracketed the period 1989–1991 from the rest of the economic reform era, arguing that reforms stalled due to financial crises and the brief ascendance of octogenarian conservatives in the CCP.[6] To the extent that China's foreign economic regime during that period has been analyzed, authors have focused on the temporary reconsideration of Zhao Ziyang's coastal development strategy.[7] This chapter chronicles China's subtle but significant changes in the policy on investment in WFOEs, which led to the takeoff of WFOEs in the 1990s. Finally, I address how the shift to the WFOE model has influenced the Chinese state's ability to control foreign investment and the changing capacity of foreign investors to affect Chinese business institutions.

The Dominance (and Inadequacy) of the JV Model, 1979–1988

Although China began the open-door policy with many competing interests such as attracting capital flows, transferring technology, learning advanced management techniques, promoting exports, and expanding employment, China subordinated the developmental goals of foreign economic engagement to protecting its sovereignty.[8] Such an approach led China to try to maximize its control over foreign investors and to promote a mercantilist model that emphasized exports and limited foreign access to China's market. While some foreign investors sought cheap Chinese labor to lower the cost of their exported goods, many foreign firms desired access to China's domestic market to sell products. Concomitantly, foreign investors wanted the same control over the operations of their enterprises and protection of their technology that they enjoyed in other international operations.[9] Foreign investors and China's state held conflicting interests, but such differences were initially overlooked because of foreign investors' dearth of knowledge about China's investment environment. During this early period of the open-door policy, foreign investors were uncertain of how to proceed for the following reasons: (i) many of China's economic institutions bore the imprint of socialism; (ii) the Chinese language—to most Western and Japanese investors—was incomprehensible; and (iii) China's legal and regulatory fields were opaque. Foreign investors sought out partners to serve as local guides to navigate their way in China's newly opened economic frontier, which bore little resemblance to the host environments encountered by investors in other economies. Chinese and foreign interests and the above structural conditions pushed partners to form Sino-foreign JVs.

State Control and JVs

When China began to accept foreign investment in 1979, officials sought to moderate foreign investors' power by devising rules and procedures for foreign investment that preserved Chinese control over its economy, even over the new foreign investment projects. In addition to isolating foreign companies in special economic zones, China's investment regime pressed foreign investors to select JVs rather than WFOEs as an investment vehicle. For example, China passed the Law of the People's Republic of China on Chinese-Foreign Equity Joint Ventures (hereafter, EJV Law) in 1979, seven years before it adopted the Law of the People's Republic of China on Wholly Foreign Owned Enterprises, 1986 (hereafter, WFOE Law). Falling quickly on the heels of the establishment of the SEZs in 1979, the EJV Law facilitated the creation of EJVs, while WFOEs and CJVs only could be established by analogy. The Chinese government sought to stem foreign investors' control over their economy by limiting competition with Chinese firms, by securing Chinese managerial control over FIEs, and by limiting market access.[10]

The approval process for foreign invested enterprises gave central state officials power over the types of foreign enterprises that could form. Through the Ministry of Commerce (hereafter, MOFCOM, the successor to MOFTEC and MOFERT), the central government played an important role in brokering "marriages" of JV partners.[11] In the negotiation process, MOFCOM pressed for favorable terms with foreign investors who were anxious to gain a share of the Chinese market. For example, MOFCOM pressured foreign investors to accept large numbers of SOE employees, Chinese majority ownership, and inflated Chinese in-kind contributions to the project such as land, facilities, and antiquated machinery at high dollar values, thus boosting the Chinese side's share of investment and income. Especially in the 1980s, such JV negotiations usually were protracted. Officially, the partners of a prospective JV were responsible for negotiating their contract, but Chinese partners feared moving ahead without MOFCOM's guidance and/or MOFCOM demanded constant reporting on the progress of negotiations. In the case of negotiations between Beijing Auto Works and AMC Jeep to form Beijing Jeep, a Sino-U.S. JV, the negotiations took four years (May 1979–May 1983), during which Beijing Auto Works had to report to central ministries over 300 times.[12]

The JV model ensured that Chinese authorities could extend their organizational tentacles to monitor and to control foreign business operations in their borders. For example, initially JVs had to establish party cells and trade union organizations, which were transferred into the JV by the Chinese partner.[13] Party cells gave China's officials direct access to information about the activities and decisions of the JVs and created a pressure point on the leadership of the JVs, with which to shape the practice of foreign investors. Establishing branch organizations of the All-China Federation of Trade Unions, which is a mass organization attached to the Chinese Communist Party, ostensibly helped Chinese authorities to protect the rights of workers.

Until China's State Council revised the EJV Law in 1990, the regulatory framework created by the EJV Law of 1979 and subsequent regulations enhanced state control over JVs. Regulations allowed foreign investors to invest 25–99 percent of a JV's capital, but through the late 1980s the Chinese state was reluctant to approve majority foreign ownership. Even if foreign parties gained a majority share of a JV, the 1979 rules granted the Chinese side the position of chair of the board of directors,[14] which ceded to the Chinese partner power to set the agenda within the JV. China's highly restrictive investment regime proved a deterrent to foreign direct investment, so, beginning in 1986, China loosened some of the mechanisms of control over foreign operations, such as easing restrictions on foreign exchange (1986)[15] and on local market access for import substitution products (1986 and 1987).[16] China's state continued to make concessions on its control over the operations of JVs during the transitional period (1988–1991) when foreign investors shifted to the WFOE structure. For example, in 1990, the State Council amended the EJV Law to allow foreign parties to hold the position of the chair of the board of directors and to secure for the board of directors the right to make all major decisions concerning the venture, thus reducing the legal scope of official interference in the operation of JVs.[17]

Encouraging foreign investors to use the JV model, then, reflected a conscious effort by China's state to control foreign investors' operations, thereby protecting China's sovereignty and financial interests. Moreover, shared management in JVs, Chinese officials believed, would facilitate the diffusion of managerial techniques and working knowledge of technology. Using such a model, Chinese officials hoped to maximize their control over foreign investors and enjoy the developmental benefits of cooperation.

Chinese Partners as Guides and Marketers

Foreign firms sought out Chinese partners to help navigate China's investment environment. At the inception of the open-door policy in 1979, foreign investors—at least those who were not from Hong Kong and Taiwan—had little idea of how to operate a business in China's socialist economy with non-transparent rules and procedures on foreign direct investment and without reliable market information. Complicating information flows, China relied on internal (*neibu*) documents to communicate unannounced official policies on regulating JVs to CCP members without informing foreigners.[18] In such a context, local officials and foreign publications emphasized that foreign investors must have extensive Chinese contacts (*guanxi*), primarily gained through Chinese business partners, to get things done.[19] Investors perceived that *guanxi* was important in receiving government approval for investment projects, gaining access to scarce materials such as land, managing relations with workers, and marketing products in China. According to Hongying Wang, investors in the mid 1990s still contended that *guanxi* was instrumental in gathering information and gaining approval for projects.[20]

A president of the China-based operations of a U.S. company with several factories in China explained how *guanxi* came to be emphasized, "The closed nature of China for almost sixty years led to a mysteriousness of China. When China began to slowly open itself, some people were allowed to come in and others not. People wanted to understand why, and they decided it was *guanxi*. People decided it was who you know and not what you know that mattered."[21] In the early 1980s, complex administrative lines and opaque rules on foreign direct investment approval baffled investors. Without a clear legal framework for investment, foreign investors sought guarantees for their investment through personal contacts with officials up and down the administrative ladder.[22]

To establish contacts with administrators in China's vast bureaucracy, foreign investors needed Chinese partners with strong social networks. Foreign investors assumed that the staff of the SOEs had appropriate contacts and the knowledge of how to get things done in China's administrative and business environment. After all, many managers in SOEs who transferred into JVs had decades of experience dealing with Chinese bureaucrats and had built up significant social networks with officials. Among foreign investors, Japanese and U.S. investors were interested in developing social networks to smooth the operation of their firms.[23]

When foreign investment regulations loosened in the late 1980s, local governments took the initiative to develop special investment zones, many of which lacked central government approval or which violated central policies, to compete for investment projects.[24] Chinese partners emphasized that their connections to local or high-ranking officials would protect foreign partners from government reprisals. Foreign investors were highly dependent on people who could navigate the Chinese approval and administrative structures and who could differentiate legitimate opportunities from chimera or at least help to protect the foreign firms from officials who sought to enforce the law. Some foreign investors cemented such ties to local officials by forming JV partnerships with local governments participating as investors. As long as the regulatory environment remained opaque, newly arriving foreign investors sought out local partners to help them navigate the Chinese economy. Thus, at the inception of the reforms, Chinese and foreign sides sought each other out for partnerships, but the two sides quickly discovered that their interests were often incompatible.

Dissatisfaction with the JV Model

To explain the souring of the JV model in China, several works used the analogy of a Chinese expression, "same bed, different dreams" (*tongchuang yimeng*) and the metaphor of "divorce."[25] According to those works, Chinese and foreign partners simply came from different cultures and approached business with different interests. While cultural and linguistic difference may have deterred effective communication, conflicts of interest drove partners apart. According to general managers of fruitful JVs in China, their success was due to both partners acting on behalf of the JV rather than each guarding its particular interest.[26] Most managers of JVs, however, emphasized the sharp conflict of interests among partners, which often were present at the founding of the partnership. In the late 1980s, Chinese authors began openly to document JV partners' diverging interests.[27] Even a general manager of a successful JV complained about relations among partners: "Most JV managers say, 'we have good relations with our JV partner.' What does that mean? When JVs make money, everyone is happy. Ask the foreign partner what the Chinese side contributed. In most cases, they did not contribute a thing."[28] JV partners were susceptible to distrust, lack of mutual respect, communication problems, and conflicts of interests. Both sides perceived their JV partners as deficient in many ways.[29]

Foreign and Chinese partners often disagreed on the most basic issue: the purpose of the JV enterprise. The Chinese side sought an infusion of cash from the foreign investor and from export earnings, while many foreign investors sought access to China's market. State owned enterprises needed new cash sources to relieve some of their mounting financial burdens. As an indicator of the degree of losses suffered by state owned enterprises, in 1985, China subsidized loss-making enterprises with over 50 billion Chinese *yuan* (approximately, US$17 billion).[30] SOEs were saddled with many welfare functions, such as providing goods, subsidies, services, and income to employees. Consequently, SOE partners in JVs were more concerned with generating short-term income to distribute than long-term profit making.[31] Once JVs were up and running, Chinese managers assumed that they would produce revenue to be split between the two partners. A consultant to foreign investors in China for over two decades suggested that the Chinese side viewed JVs as "a big bag of money," which led to a "zero-sum game" over controlling cash flow.[32]

A Sino-U.S. JV manager recalled clashes with his Chinese partners over the JV's failure to produce profits. The Chinese side had entered into the venture as a means of providing financial relief to its ailing state-owned enterprise, while the U.S. company sought to use the JV to provide technical support for the rest of its firm's operations in China. These positions pitted the partners in opposition over pricing of goods and services. The Chinese side sought to raise the JV's prices to increase revenue flows and profits, while the U.S. side sought to keep prices low to serve its other China-based companies that used the Shanghai JV's goods. For the U.S. side, the prices on goods and services coming out of the JV were an intra-company matter, and the U.S. partner had no interest in raising its prices, thereby robbing Peter to pay Paul. According to the U.S. general manager of the JV, "Board meetings here are painful. The two sides have completely different agendas."[33]

Additionally, foreign investment offered an opportunity for SOEs to off-load many of their staff onto JVs, which eased the SOEs' payroll expenses and reduced their future retirement burdens.[34] Chinese SOEs employed many workers at low pay to provide social welfare to workers, but foreign enterprises sought to pay higher wages to a smaller staff in order to promote worker productivity.[35] The different perspectives on the function of enterprises pitted Chinese against their foreign partners. The overstaffing of JVs not only added to JVs' payroll expenses but also transferred poor work habits into JVs by underemploying large numbers of redundant workers.[36]

Chinese officials' intervention in negotiations and indirect control over JVs exacerbated the potential for conflict within JV partnerships. A Chinese author noted that the Chinese preferred foreign management to joint management and joint management to Chinese management because Chinese managers cannot act independently of their state bosses who guide their actions.[37] According to a long-term advisor to foreign investors in China, "In the mid and late 1980s, JV marriages were often ordained in Beijing" but these marriages often ended in "divorce" such as one of Caterpillar's operations.[38] After pairing JV partners together, state officials persisted in intervening in their everyday operations. In 1989, Chinese newspaper and journal articles began to criticize state officials for their frequent intervention in the operations of the JVs[39] and called for Chinese officials to grant foreign investors more managerial authority.[40] In coastal cities, where most foreign investors established operations, state officials began to back away from interference in JV negotiations at the end of the 1980s, the same time that China shifted toward greater acceptance of WFOEs. Nevertheless, according to a regional manager of a U.S. company's investments in China, state officials continued to intervene in JV negotiations in the interior of China.[41]

Importantly, Chinese authorities' and foreign investors' interests diverged over access to China's market. Taking a long-term view of investment in China, foreign (especially Japanese, U.S., and European) investors were interested in establishing a strong market share in China, even if it required running at a loss in the short term, in order to turn bring profits in the future.[42] Chinese authorities, however, hoped to: (i) make money quickly by expanding export markets; and (ii) protect SOEs from competing with foreign investors' goods.[43] The export-led approach fused China's mercantilism with its desire to gain capital quickly in order to meet the financial needs of SOEs through JVs. Foreign investors were willing to sacrifice profits in the short term in order to gain long-term market share in China, while their Chinese partners tended to sacrifice long-term profits to achieve short-term financial goals.

Initial regulations "encouraged" JVs to market products overseas and could only gain limited access to China's market by selling products "that China urgently need[ed] or import[ed]"[44] to the Chinese market. Such language gave Chinese authorities broad latitude to block JV products on the Chinese market, which nearly ruined several JVs.[45] The 1986 Provisions of the State Council for the Encouragement of Foreign Investment noted that foreign investors introducing technology or technologically advanced products could sell their products on the market as well as receive tax credits and preferential access to electricity and water from the state.[46] Yet, in the same year, China's state called for JVs to "maximize the export of their products and the generation of foreign exchange in order to achieve a balance in foreign exchange income and expenditure."[47] Foreign enterprises had to apply to the government to secure import-substitution status. To make matters worse, the regulations on JVs (and WFOEs) required FIEs to give preferential treatment to Chinese suppliers of inputs over foreign ones.[48] Local inputs, especially in the 1980s, were not up to international standards, which undermined the foreign investors' ability to export goods and to meet internal quality standards.[49] During the 1980s, the rules on exports were even more stringent on WFOEs than on JVs, so foreign investors who wanted even limited market access in China had little choice but to form JVs.

Despite the cultural conflict in JVs, foreign investors would have retained their partnerships had the Chinese side been able to make good on its promises to help with domestic marketing. Foreign investors believed that Chinese partners would help the JV to gain a strong market share in China's rapidly developing economy,[50] but marketing goods in China was no mean feat. Before acceding to the WTO in 2001, China's internal market was carved up into small provincial markets, which were protected by local officials from outside products, including Chinese products from other provinces. Local officials charged excessive fees on outside products, refused to sell imported goods in local stores, and even charged high transportation user fees for shipping goods through their provinces, counties, townships, and villages.[51] These idiosyncratic rules (and violations of central regulations) greatly complicated the development of foreign investors' sales strategy for all of China.

Foreign investors were confident that their Chinese partners knew the domestic market, so they typically left the marketing department in Chinese hands. Foreign investors believed that the Chinese partners' marketing teams would bring with them knowledge of how to gain market share in China, especially across provincial borders.[52] As it turned out, Chinese partners, who mainly came from SOEs, knew far less about marketing in China than they claimed or than foreign investors anticipated.[53] Marketing teams in SOEs had operated primarily under state plans and, to the extent that they sought out market transactions, tended to rely upon personal connections (*guanxi*). In the 1980s, reliance upon personal connections may have been particularly important, but as price and marketing reforms advanced and as foreign investment poured into China through the 1990s, personal connections for sales began to lose some of their salience. More importantly, the Chinese marketers' connections bore little fruit.[54]

A manager in a Sino-U.S. high-tech JV had to reorganize the firm's marketing strategy. He complained, "The marketing division is still in the hands of a Chinese, but a new person with no connection to the partner's old operation. The employees from the old company have been no help. We thought that we could use their marketing connections, but we could not. They did not have that many customers, and the ones that they did bring could not pay bills."[55] Another Sino-U.S. JV that manufactured small- and medium-sized engines initially allowed the Chinese side to take control over marketing, but the U.S. manager soon found himself forced to conduct all marketing research. Eventually, the general manager moved marketing out of the JV and opened a representative office fully under the control of the foreign investor to manage marketing.[56] Additionally, Chinese marketers from state-owned enterprises were accustomed to using kickbacks and other schemes to sell their goods, rather than developing a steady clientele based on transparent prices and quality products. Foreign firms often tried to use their corporation's standards on sales, but Chinese staff had difficulty operating under such rules.[57]

In the 1980s and early 1990s, prospective Chinese partners greatly inflated the demand for goods produced by JVs to induce foreign firms to invest in JVs. A U.S. manager lamented that his company had been deceived when it set up a Sino-U.S. JV in 1995, "When we opened our JV, we relied on the local government for market information. They told us figures for sales, but they were apples to our oranges. We greatly miscalculated our market potential here, partly because of government misinformation."[58] Much of the predicted demand turned out to be guesswork, and JVs found less demand for their goods than they expected.

Faced with such marketing difficulties, foreign investors had several options. Foreign partners in existing JVs could either take control over their firm's marketing functions or spin off the marketing to an independent unit under the foreign firm's control. Alternatively, new investors might opt for a WOFE structure, under whose rules the firm would fully control marketing, albeit with more limited access to China's market. In all cases, foreign parties asserted greater operational control over the marketing functions of FIEs. Through the 1980s, Chinese regulations on local market access presented foreign investors with a dilemma: enjoy control over functions in WFOEs but have very limited Chinese market access, or surrender partial control to Chinese partners in JVs in order to gain some local marketing privileges.

Ultimately, the above competing interests were irreconcilable. After a disappointing number of foreign investors had entered China in the early and mid 1980s, China softened its position on domestic market access by permitting, for example, manufacturers of import-substituting goods. In the 1990s, China's desire to enter the WTO forced officials to lower its tariffs and to remove many other trade barriers, including granting domestic market access for many goods and services offered by foreign investors. The loosened restrictions on market access, however, came too late to stem the shift toward the WFOE investment model.

The Rise of WFOEs

While the above analysis of the JV model explains partners' potential lines of criticism of JVs, two things require explanation. First, why did Chinese officials become more willing to approve applications for WFOEs? Second, why did foreign investors use the WFOE model to remedy their concerns rather than staying with the JV model? Unlike existing studies of the rise of WFOEs that have focused on the interests of foreign investors, I account for shifts in Chinese officials' goals, too. Foreign investors moved toward the WFOE model for the following reasons: changes in WFOE regulations, Chinese officials' evolving interests, China's tightened financial constraints, foreign investors' desire to protect intellectual property, and foreign firms' growing knowledge of China's investment environment.

Chinese Reformers' Shifting Interests

At the outset of China's open-door policy, officials sought to balance several competing goals: (i) to attract foreign capital in order to spur development;[59] (ii) to transfer technology;[60] (iii) to increase exports, thereby maintaining a positive trade balance;[61] (iv) to expand employment opportunities while avoiding exploitation of China's workers;[62] (v) to guard China's sovereignty, especially limiting access to China's marketplace; and (vi) to learn foreign managerial techniques.[63] In the early 1980s, China emphasized guarding sovereignty and enhancing its exports over the other goals, but in the mid- and late-1980s, Chinese leaders began to reassess the open-door and the SEZ policies, which led to several adjustments of regulations and some reordering of priorities. China shifted its emphasis from control over foreign investors to using foreign investors in order to promote technological upgrading, learn foreign management techniques, and spur manufacturing. During the period 1988–1991, Chinese publications called for—and provincial and central authorities developed—new policies and approaches to foreign investment that gave rise to investment in WFOEs. Newspaper and journal articles identified shortcomings of the JV model (such as excessive state management of foreign investors), praised WFOEs, and called for shifts in China's foreign investment regime.

In addition to the heavy-handed intervention in foreign investors' operations, the Chinese press identified several related problems with China's foreign investment regime, including: foreign investment was concentrated in the area of services, real estate, and natural resources rather than in manufacturing;[64] the JV model thwarted learning advanced managerial

techniques from foreign investors; and few investors transferred significantly high levels of technology because China's push for exports attracted
low-tech manufacturers and conversely, high-tech investors were interested
in access to China's market, which China's state denied them.[65] The location
of China's first SEZs and early statements on the open-door policy targeted
investors from Hong Kong and Taiwan,[66] but such firms were primarily in
service industries such as hotels or in "sunset" industries such as textiles and
electronics assembly that sought cheap labor to extend the profitability of
exports. Indeed, the special economic zones emphasized exports and balancing payments over technology transfer.[67] The early pattern of investment
helped to meet the goal of promoting exports, but it fell short of other goals
such as introducing advanced technology and upgrading management techniques.[68] Moreover, investors from Taiwan and Hong Kong (among investors
from other countries) tended to introduce harsh, if not, exploitative labor
practices in such export-led labor-intensive manufacturing.[69]

In the early 1990s, a Chinese survey found that only 13 percent of the
production equipment in major Chinese firms was up to or near international standards for quality.[70] In 1990, Gu Ming of the National People's
Congress complained that only 3 percent of Chinese JVs (over 10,000 existed
at that time) had transferred advanced technology.[71] To attract investors who
would introduce technology, high-tech manufacturing, and advanced management techniques, China had to loosen its regulations on foreign investors
and, otherwise, improve its investment climate. In 1988, China commenced
the "Torch Program" to develop the technological capacity of its industrial
base, which, hitherto, the state found woefully underdeveloped. As part of
the Torch Program, China set up over 36 technological investment zones
throughout China in the first three years of the program.[72] In Shanghai
alone, the state opened three high-tech investment zones (Caohejing,
Hongqiao, and Minhang) in 1986 and 1988.[73] The zones sought to attract
foreign investors who would help China to raise the technological capacity of its industrial base. The shift away from low-tech export-processing
zones to high-tech development zones demonstrated a practical alteration
of policy goals, while, in general, China evinced greater openness to emu-
lating international models on managing foreign investment. For instance,
on the management of technological development zones, one author boldly
suggested that China learn from Taiwan's Hsinchu Scientific and Industrial
Park, as well as from similar technological zones in Singapore and South
Korea.[74]

To meet the goals of technology transfer, introducing new managerial methods, and expanding China's manufacturing base, critics of the
early pattern of foreign investment claimed that China should attract funds
from the United States, Japan, and Europe more than from Hong Kong and
Taiwan, and should allow more WFOES to form.[75] Li Xiangyang succinctly
wrote, "the two chief objectives in attracting direct foreign investment—the

advanced technology it brings, and earning foreign exchange through exports—are in mutual conflict."[76] Other authors went further to complain that Chinese partners and personnel in JVs were limited in their capacity "to digest and absorb many advanced technologies."[77] If China wished to upgrade its technological capacity through foreign investment, it would have to relax its restrictions on investment in WFOEs.

Chinese press and academic accounts of the open-door policy also noted the need to soften China's mercantilist trade policies, surrendering access to part of the domestic market in order to attract investors and to encourage WFOEs.[78] Similarly, He Ying asserted that WFOEs, which play a positive role in China's development, should have greater market access, especially when China cannot produce the same goods alone.[79] Such assertions reflected a changing discourse if not reordering of priorities with regard to the open-door policy, the role of mercantilist export promotion (and limited domestic market access), and the scope for WFOEs to operate.

Finally, the critical assessment of China's open-door policy in the period 1988–1991 identified the failure of the earlier period to diffuse advanced management techniques to China. Chinese analysts noted that under the early model of foreign investment, the state tended to intervene excessively in JVs and to overregulate WFOEs.[80] In response, the state, as indicated by the new rules on JVs in 1990, attempted to reassert the right of JVs to operate independently, without interference from outsiders, and the right of the JVs' boards of directors to run their enterprises.[81] Critics, however, found the problem of state intervention and conflicts of interest rooted in partners' distinct ownership structures endemic to the JV investment model.[82] Such a position led authors to argue for greater opportunities for foreign firms to establish WFOEs. *Renmin Ribao*, the leading newspaper in China, advocated greater reliance on foreign investment in order to "achieve advanced technologies and management skills."[83]

Changes to Investment Rules

One long-time consultant to foreign investors in Shanghai claimed that "ninety-nine percent of the shift to investment in WFOEs has occurred because of changes in the rules on investment."[84] While the consultant may have overstated the impact of rules changes, he did point to the important alterations taking place in China's investment regime. China passed the *WFOE Law* in 1986, seven years after passing the *EJV Law,* although some firms established WFOEs before 1986. During the period 1986–1988, Shanghai authorities approved just one WFOE application; they slowly began to approve such WFOE applications—in real terms and as a percentage of all approvals—in 1989 (see Table 3.1). The 1986 *WFOE Law* resulted in no immediate increase in investment in WFOEs as a percentage of FDI flows because the regulations in the 1986 *WFOE Law* were stringent and unclear

Table 3.1

Number of Foreign Investment Proposals Approved by the Shanghai Government by Type of Proposal (percentage of total approvals in parentheses)

Year	WFOEs	EJVs	CJVs	Total
1985	0 (0)	62 (66)	32 (34)	94
1986	1 (2)	46 (74)	15 (24)	62
1987	0 (0)	60 (79)	16 (21)	76
1988	0 (0)	205 (94)	14 (6)	219
1989	9 (5)	175 (88)	15 (8)	199
1990	30 (15)	159 (79)	12 (6)	201
1991	50 (14)	292 (80)	23 (6)	365
1992	169 (8)	1,592 (79)	241 (12)	2,012
1993	511 (14)	2,445 (67)	691 (19)	3,650
1994	760 (20)	2,067 (54)	961 (25)	3,802
1995	799 (28)	1,373 (48)	664 (23)	2,845
1996	815 (39)	808 (38)	483 (23)	2,106
1997	845 (47)	565 (31)	392 (22)	1,802
1998	833 (56)	378 (25)	278 (19)	1,490
1999	817 (56)	399 (25)	255 (19)	1,472
2000	1,146 (63)	441 (24)	226 (12)	1,814
2001	1,740 (71)	506 (21)	210 (9)	2,458
2002	2,302 (76)	530 (18)	175 (6)	3,012
2003	3,367 (78)	818 (19)	132 (3)	4,321
2004	3,422 (79)	811 (19)	95 (2)	4,334

Sources: *Shanghai Shi Duiwai Jingji Maoyi Tongji Nianjian* (various years), *Shanghai Shi Duiwai Jingji Tongji Nianjian, 1978–1995, Shanghai Duiwai Jingji Maoyi Tongji Nianjian* (various years).

on the business fields open to investment in WFOEs.[85] Article 3 of the 1986 *WFOE Law* states the following:

> Enterprises to be established exclusively with foreign capital shall be conducive to the development of China's national economy. Such enterprises shall use advanced technology and equipment or market all or most of their products outside China. Provisions regarding the lines of business which the State forbids wholly-owned foreign enterprises to engage in or on which it places certain restriction will be made by the State Council.[86]

The article's language was ambiguous and open-ended, leaving much discretion to officials on whether or not to approve applications for WFOEs. Foreign firms were reluctant to take the cumbersome steps to apply for approval to establish a WFOE when the process was opaque and the outcome uncertain or worse, likely to result in denial of approval. In addition to problems with meeting the rule on balancing foreign exchange, the requirement, in most instances, of exporting "all or most" WFOE products directly conflicted with many investors' interests.[87]

In 1990 the State Council issued *Detailed Rules for Implementing the Law of the People's Republic of China on Enterprises Operated Exclusively with Foreign Capital,* which clarified investment guidelines. Specifically, China could approve applications for WFOEs that benefit China and that transfer advanced technology, which help China to meet environmental or other goals, or proposals that entail exporting 50 percent or more of the final product.[88] More importantly, Article 4 of the regulations stipulated business sectors in which WFOE investments are prohibited, and Article 5 listed business sectors in which WFOE investments are restricted.[89] Such restrictions and prohibitions increased investors' use of the WFOE structure by clarifying the criteria for acceptance or denial.

During the period 1988–1991, sub-national officials were given freedom to alter their approach to WFOEs. Proliferation of technological and other development zones created intense competition among officials in the various zones to attract investors.[90] In the process, local officials offered preferential treatment for foreign investors,[91] and leaders from the original SEZs (Zhuhai, Xiamen, Shenzhen, and Shantou) sought out investors for WFOEs.[92] In 1989 investment in WFOEs accounted for less than 10 percent of national foreign direct investment flows, but in Xiamen, during the first eight months of the year, 65 percent of contracted invested projects were for WFOEs.[93] A delegation from Shantou visited Hong Kong in 1989 to attract investors and signed 45 investment contracts, 60 percent of which were for WFOEs.[94] Clearly, SEZ leaders were given approval to attract WFOEs, in what amounted to a fundamental policy shift. SEZs' leadership in contracting WFOE investment projects portended a broader shift in China's approach to WFOEs.

Finally, China's drive to join the WTO in the 1990s and its WTO accession agreement, signed in 2001, affected the regulations on WFOEs and, therefore, the shift toward investment in WFOEs, in two ways. First, China altered its trade regulations on WFOEs. In 2001, the State Council issued new implementing rules governing WFOEs that moved toward national treatment, in line with WTO guidelines.[95] In particular, the 2001 Implementing Rules abandoned export requirements for WFOEs, and granted WFOEs the right to sell their products in China.[96] Moreover, China granted WFOEs the right directly to market products in China without going through Chinese organizations[97] and relaxed rules on sourcing of materials and components for production.[98] Negotiations for China's entry into the WTO hastened foreign investors' abandonment of the JV model by greatly reducing the dilemma of choosing between exercising control over WFOES with minimal domestic market access or shared control over JVs with some domestic market access.[99] Second, the WTO accession agreement created a time frame for opening about one-third of the business areas that were restricted to JVs to investment by WFOEs such as the financial, transportation, and advertising sectors.[100] Companies such as Price, Waterhouse, Cooper moved into China to offer their accounting, labor, and market research services to foreign investors, which rendered foreign investors less dependent on Chinese partners for information. Cumulatively, such changes to the regulations on WFOEs improved the clarity of the approval process and helped foreign investors to gain confidence in the application process for WFOEs.

Fiscal Constraints

The push to attract WFOEs corresponded to a period of tightening of control over Chinese investment funds by the central government. In the mid- and late 1980s, China encountered two financial concerns: mounting foreign debt and double-digit inflation. For the period 1986–1990, China borrowed approximately US$6 billion per year, equivalent to 65 percent of all foreign capital inflow.[101] Although China's FDI flows have attracted a great deal of attention, Figure 3.2 shows China's heavy reliance on foreign borrowing through the 1980s, which was used to purchase equipment and technology for Chinese industry as part of China's limited open-door policy. In 1988, the amount of foreign capital that China borrowed was greater than FDI flows by a factor of 2:1. Financial problems, growing debt repayment obligations, and mismanagement of loans caused officials and analysts to reverse their preference for loans over foreign direct investment.[102] Explicit in the critique of foreign borrowing was a view that Chinese firms were ill-equipped to make good use of borrowed funds.[103] Foreign direct investment, however, brought improved management and working knowledge of technology to aid China's

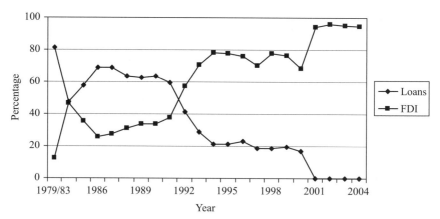

Figure 3.2   Shares of Foreign Capital Flows. Source: Chinese Economic Statistical Yearbook Editorial Committee, *Chinese Economic Yearbook* (Beijing: Chinese Economic Yearbook Publishers, 1995 and 2006).

development. Consequently, in the late 1980s, China shifted from reliance on borrowing capital to foreign direct investment flows.

From the fourth quarter of 1987 through August 1988, Chinese officials, especially conservative leaders, tightened credit to rein in inflation and to cool China's overheated economy, a policy that would not be relaxed until 1990.[104] After 1988, local officials still faced pressure to provide employment and social services to workers by expanding local industry,[105] but they had less access to credit for investment. Concomitantly, officials and SOE partners in JVs had begun to realize that JV partnerships required more capital infusions from the Chinese side and produced less revenue and profit than initially expected.[106] One author estimated that nearly one-third of JVs lost money in 1988,[107] which required further capital infusions by the partners to cover operating expenses. Compounding this problem, press reports complained that foreign partners in JVs were slow to contribute capital to JVs and were financing a declining share of the registered capital to such firms.[108]

In an interview with the *China Business Review,* Liu Chu, a former deputy director at MOFERT succinctly summarized how changing fiscal policy affected officials' attitudes toward WFOEs:

> It's true that in the mid-1980s WFOEs were not the favored form of foreign investment by Chinese officials. But since retrenchment began in 1988, China has had little money to invest in JVs. WFOEs seemed better than nothing, so more approvals were granted. Since then, it has become clear that WFOEs do have benefits for China—they employ local workers, buy local materials, pay taxes, and export their output to earn foreign exchange. Furthermore, they do all of this at no risk to China.[109]

Rather than allow planned JV investments to be cancelled due to a shortage of Chinese funds, officials permitted the projects to proceed in the form of WFOEs.[110] Under tighter financial constraints, outside sources of investment became increasingly important for local governments, and local officials thought that WFOEs provided a viable option.[111] At the time, journal articles called for greater reliance on WFOE investment because of China's tightening credit.[112]

China's tight credit policy also led existing JVs to be converted to WFOEs. After several years of financial losses in the 1990s, Chinese investors grew frustrated with JVs' need for cash infusions. After all, Chinese partners sought financial relief through JV investment.[113] Chinese partners could not afford to put more money into their JVs, and foreign partners took advantage to raise their stakes in the venture. A Chinese deputy general manager in a FIE describes how, piecemeal, foreign investors bought out Chinese investors' shares in JVs: "Usually, EJVs begin with 60–40 foreign majority ownership. After a period, the firm is losing money, and the foreign side looks to buy out part of the Chinese investment. That is how the process starts. The Chinese side sees this as a defeat. They look at an 80–20 or a 90–10 split of investment as having no interest for the Chinese side. Rather than accept such a split, they back out and a WFOE forms."[114] Some local partners allowed their foreign partners to convert their JVs to WFOEs, taking a lump sum payment for their struggling SOEs and relinquishing their greatly diminished authority, which had become a source of humiliation.

The June 4, 1989, demonstrations and their violent suppression exacerbated China's financial problems by causing many foreign investors to put their planned projects on hold. Conservatives reacted to the demonstrations, which were spurred, in part, by high inflation, declining economic security among urban residents, and popular anger at official corruption, by further tightening reins on finances and cracking down on local officials' corruption. Corruption associated with SEZs was an important object of conservative officials' criticism in the mid-1980s, threatening the coastal development policy that Zhao Ziyang had launched in 1988.[115] Conservative leaders quickly discovered, however, that China needed to maintain foreign capital infusions and foreign trade to meet its foreign debt payments and to spur economic growth necessary to provide jobs.[116] Rather than closing the open-door policy, central leaders widened the investment regime, especially by loosening control over WFOEs.

In 1989 and 1990, the central government gave legal and moral encouragement to investment in WFOEs.[117] On May 8, 1989, the leading Chinese newspaper, noting the shortage of Chinese funds for investment, called on China to "lay more stress on establishment of more ventures solely owned by foreign investors," adding that such investment "will not only enable us to achieve advanced technologies and management skills, but will also effectively promote the formation of the market mechanism and promote the development of in-depth reforms."[118] In December 1989, Zeng Defeng, vice mayor of Zhuhai (one of the original SEZs) said, "We should attract more wholly foreign-owned enterprises to compensate for the lack of funds on our side."[119] Foreign investors were interested in that investment option but were concerned with political instability after June 4, 1989, forcing Chinese officials to appeal directly to would-be investors and to loosen restrictions on FDI.[120] During the period of tight credit policy, 1988–1991, Chinese officials made overtures to foreign firms, including offers to approve WFOE applications in order to lure investors with high technology.[121] As foreign investors grew confident in the stability of politics and the leaders' commitment to foreign investment, firms increased their investment flows into China, growing more reliant on the WFOE investment vehicle. Deng Xiaoping's 1992 "southern tour," during which he affirmed the importance of economic development and the open-door policy with the statement, "development is the core principle" (*fazhan shi ying daoli*), was particularly important in regaining investors' confidence.

The period 1988–1992 produced few significant domestic reforms and was associated with political and economic retrenchment; nevertheless, it marked a shift in the relative bargaining positions of foreign investors and China's state.[122] Foreign investors who were less starry-eyed about China's investment environment were anxious to move toward a WFOE investment structure but faced some resistance from Chinese officials. When the June 4, 1989, demonstrations and repression occurred in the context of financial austerity measures, Chinese officials found themselves between a rock and a hard place. In order to ease the financial tensions in the economy and to attract U.S. and Japanese investors, Chinese officials compromised their opposition to WFOEs. Consequently, FDI flows to China picked up again in 1990[123] and 1991, and investment in WFOEs as a share of all FDI continued its upward trend that began in 1988.

Protecting Intellectual Property

While Chinese officials sought transfers of advanced technology, foreign investors were reluctant to agree to do so because of their concern over illegal technology transfer, a persistent problem.[124] The weak protection for intellectual property became a point of contention for foreign investors in China, especially those investing in JV partnerships. A former manager in a Sino-U.S. JV recalled his company's problems protecting its intellectual property:

> We had problems with a potential Chinese JV partner. Our vacuum cleaner division was negotiating with the Chinese. In the midst of the negotiations, our negotiator gave the Chinese a copy of our vacuum cleaner design. Later, the negotiations fell apart. A year later, I found that the company was producing a mock version of our product by themselves.[125]

Adding to the sting of fake copies of foreign products is the role that some Chinese partners play in piracy.[126] Detrimental to China's development, such cases of piracy have discouraged legitimate technology transfer to China.

Most foreign investors believed that attempts to use China's International Economic and Trade Arbitration Commission (CIETAC) and the courts to protect intellectual property were futile, leading them to conclude that JVs were prone to intellectual property problems.[127] One Japanese manager of a JV that converted to a WFOE noted that his firm, generally speaking, did not believe that Chinese factories could use advanced technology and replicate FIEs' high-quality products because of the antiquated machinery used by many Chinese manufacturers.[128] Yet, Chinese factories excelled at producing inexpensive but poor-quality imitations under copied labels, which undermined the legitimate product's standing in the local market.[129] Foreign investors mainly feared piracy of technology because it undermined Chinese perception of their products.

China's pursuit of technology transfer was a particularly nettlesome issue that required a shift toward the WFOE investment vehicle. A manager in a U.S. corporation that started up in 2000 explained the company's decision to opt for a WFOE structure:

> This plant will bring in new advanced technology. For reasons of
> protecting intellectual property rights, we chose a WOFE structure.
> If we had decided to bring in old technology, we probably would
> have formed a JV. We would have done so to gain access to the
> Chinese market. We decided to bring cutting-edge technology that is
> environmentally friendly. We are basically trading market access for
> use of advanced technology and a WFOE structure.[130]

Although another manager of a U.S. WFOE admitted that he could not
"completely control that a person can walk over to the Xerox machine and
copy blueprints," his firm opted to invest in a WFOE in order to take special
precautions to protect technology. For instance, his firm subcontracted shipping of goods to trusted firms and brought in foreign engineers to work on
technological projects, which minimized the potential for unwanted technology leakage.[131] China needed foreign investors to improve the technological level of its products and to introduce products that would better protect
its natural environment, but foreign investors lacked confidence in the ability to protect intellectual property in JVs. WFOEs helped both sides to meet
these goals by enhancing foreign managerial control and eliminating organizational linkage to SOEs.

Foreign Investors' Growing Knowledge of China's Investment Environment

The shift from JVs to WFOEs reflected foreign investors' growing knowledge
of China's investment rules and sources of inefficiency in China. A manager
in a Sino-Japanese JV explained, "Investors who do not understand China
want to form JVs because a Chinese partner can help to clarify administrative rules and get business going. If a foreign investor has been in China for a
while, they find the rules are not so badly defined, the laws are respected, and
the system is stable. Under those circumstances, they do not need a Chinese
partner."[132] Many companies that invested in WFOEs already operated JVs in
China and, therefore, had a good grasp of the investment environment. After
managers became familiar with China's investment rules, the bureaucrats
who oversee business operations, the market for goods, and appropriate ways
to manage Chinese personnel,[133] foreign investors began to view Chinese
partners as superfluous and wanted to operate WFOEs. In the words of a pair
of business consultants, "In some cases, the JV could have just outlived its
useful purpose."[134]

Experience also made foreign investors view their Chinese partners as a
source of inefficiency. A manager in a profitable Sino-U.S. JV bluntly criticized the JV model and his Chinese partner:

> I would never suggest a JV model to someone investing in China. I
> suppose if you are brand new to China, it could be helpful to have a JV,

but I would still recommend finding a Chinese partner to work with in a WFOE.... The Chinese partner brings absolutely nothing to this JV. We have been in China for a long time and we no longer need help filling out the business forms.[135]

Business experience in China thus substitutes for a Chinese partner in a FIE.

Foreign investors also learned that JVs were inefficient due to the size and poor productivity of their staff. Once locked into the JV contracts, it was difficult for managers to trim redundant personnel.[136] For example, a manager in a U.S. telecommunications manufacturing facility complained that the JV was required to take on several deputy managers who "added nothing to the enterprise. If they were to disappear overnight, the enterprise would be better off."[137] Another U.S. manager complained that, even after discovering the overstaffing problems in a previous JV, the U.S. partner was unable to reduce the staff size.[138] More readily than JVs, WFOEs can limit the number of staff from the start and can reduce unwanted staff after the business is started. Investors in WFOEs, working with local labor departments, may hire all of their staff from the labor market.[139] By hiring all personnel from labor markets, WFOEs have been able to recruit younger, better trained staff than would likely have transferred from SOEs into JVs.

Although it may seem counterintuitive, WFOEs that rely more on foreign managers who fetch very high compensation packages may have lower human resource costs than JVs.[140] Many foreign investors moved to China to take advantage of inexpensive labor, and the same logic compelled foreign companies to "localize" all or most of their managerial staff. Yet, the bloated managerial staff of JVs sharply raised wage costs for foreign investors, even beyond payrolls in WFOEs. WFOEs reduced overall payroll costs by trimming the number of local middle-level managers. A director of a U.S. business organization put it this way:

> There are cost issues related to hiring in JVs. In JVs, there are often two managers for every position—one Chinese and one foreign. Sure, Chinese managers are less expensive to hire, but I have not seen any studies that show that a JV management payroll is less than in a WFOE. I suspect that a JV actually has a payroll that is 20–30 percent higher for its managers than for those in a WFOE because of the extra number of managers.[141]

Distrust of JV partners undermines attempts to localize management of staff; hence, WFOEs can employ fewer managers and localize management more quickly than JVs.

In addition to swollen personnel roles, SOE employees who transfer to JVs often bring their cognitive scripts for labor relations based on the "iron rice bowl" model to their new employer. Although JV managers have tried to improve the work culture of their firms, personnel matters were often left to Chinese partners, who did not share the foreign partner's business culture.

A Chinese human resources manager in a U.S. WFOE but who had worked in a Sino-U.S. JV noted that JVs always had two sets of competing values—Chinese and foreign—that the partners tried to institute, while in contrast, "a WFOE has the advantage of being able to focus on one set of values and goals."[142] Another Chinese manager in a Sino-U.S. JV noted the difficulty that expatriate managers face in transferring new management and work institutions to JVs: "In JVs, almost all of the workers are local; there are usually just one or two foreign managers. It is difficult to transfer foreign management practices under those conditions."[143] Several foreign managers noted that they found it much easier to establish their company culture in WFOEs than in JVs. For example, one manager of a U.S. WFOE said, "We have a strong corporate culture. A lot of JVs in China have had little say over hiring; they are forced to accept workers from their JV partner. We established a WFOE because we want to have more sway over our corporate culture and hiring."[144] Based on the difficulty of establishing new human resource models in JVs, many foreign managers believed it was imperative to establish a WFOE or majority ownership of a JV to secure control over human resources away from Chinese partners.[145]

Implications of the Shift Toward WFOEs

Foreign investors' shift to the WFOE investment structure raises two questions: How does the rising number of WFOEs affect China's capacity to control foreign investors? How does the shift to investment in WFOEs alter foreign investors' role in institutional diffusion to China? Previous studies of WFOEs have partially addressed the first question, but few have touched upon the latter.

Ramifications for Sovereignty

The JV model was constructed to maintain Chinese state control over foreign investors through the shared governance of corporate boards of directors and through party-state organizational mechanisms—party branches, trade union organizations, and state managers—transferred into JVs. Hence, the movement toward a WFOE model constitutes an erosion of Chinese control over foreign investors. Regulations on labor-management relations in FIEs consistently have protected the rights of workers to form (ACFTU) trade union branches, and CCP members secured the establishment of such organizations in the newly formed JVs.[146] In WFOEs, the Communist Party faced a greater challenge because of the foreign investors' freedom to hire from the labor market. The party cannot guarantee that WFOEs hire one or more party members, whereas they can guarantee the transfer of party members into JVs.

Anecdotal evidence and Chinese press reports suggest that the CCP failed to gain a foothold in WFOEs.[147] The regulations on the operations of foreign enterprises in China gave weak support at best to the formation and activities of party cells.[148] For example, the Provisional Regulations on the Political and Ideological Activities for Chinese Employees of Sino-Foreign and Contractual Joint Ventures, Article 7, calls for the founding of party cells in JVs, but it is silent on the issue of party cells in WFOEs.[149] Both the WFOE Law (1986) and the Detailed Regulations (1990) failed to mention party cells in their articles, which led party organizers to lament their inability to set up branch organizations in WFOEs.[150]

The dearth of trade union branches in WFOEs has resulted from a complex combination of factors. Many WFOE managers who were concerned with maintaining operational control over their enterprises were reluctant to share power with party or trade union branches. For example, a manager of a Japanese WFOE in Shanghai reported that his company chose a WFOE structure, in part, to avoid establishing a trade union branch.[151] Trade union organizers lacked resources, including support among workers with which to compel WFOE managers to allow them to organize union branches. Finally, local officials who are dependent on foreign investors to generate local jobs, production, and tax revenue are not always strong supporters of All-China Federation of Trade Unions (ACFTU) organizers who might scare off foreign investors.[152] Clearly, the party-state has fewer organizational tools to control operations and personnel in WFOEs than in JVs.

In the course of the shift from JVs to WFOEs, China's state lost direct control over foreign investors; nonetheless, the state guided the process of altering investment structures. China's state shifted from preferring JVs because they did not meet state goals, while the state opened to WFOEs to achieve state development targets. Through its regulatory framework, China's state guided foreign enterprises to establish export-oriented, high-tech, and environmentally sensitive subsidiaries. Only with China's accession to WTO did the national treatment ideal begin to chip away at the state's ability to guide WFOEs into targeted areas. China's experience indicates the necessity (and possibility) of releasing direct control to guide investment to meet higher strategic goals.

Implications for Institutional Change

One of the persistent goals of the open-door policy was to have Chinese firms learn managerial techniques from foreign investors, but by encouraging the formation of JVs, officials limited the learning of such techniques. Chinese officials assigned JVs dual roles: (i) to monitor the operations of foreign investors; and (ii) to facilitate learning of foreign management techniques. Certainly, the close working relations within JVs created an environment for direct observation and learning, and organizational linkages between JVs and SOE partners facilitated the spread of foreign business institutions.[153] The two goals, however, partially were contradictory; Chinese partners simultaneously were asked to limit the autonomy of their foreign partners and to emulate the techniques introduced by their foreign partners. In practice, JV partners negotiated the types of practices and institutions adopted by the newly created firms, which resulted in a set of mixed, often dysfunctional institutions. JV partners often divided operational controls by department, with little communication among departments and between the foreign and Chinese sides—examples hardly worthy of study and emulation by Chinese firms. Too often, in Sino-Foreign JVs, local managers were reluctant to adopt new managerial techniques from their foreign partners.[154]

The shift to the WFOE investment structure had a mixed effect on the recasting of Chinese business institutions. Freed from sharing operational control with Chinese partners, foreign investors in WFOEs could transfer a purer form of their home-company institutions than was possible in JVs. By eliminating Chinese partners, however, no organizational linkage existed between the foreign investor and Chinese firms, which made it more difficult to diffuse the foreign institutions. Hence, WFOEs introduced to China better approximations of foreign institutions, but they lacked the organizational capacity to spread their institutions. Nevertheless, WFOEs have contributed to institutional diffusion in two indirect ways. First, WFOEs have trained Chinese managers in international business practices, including human resources and accounting techniques, whom domestic firms have hired away.[155] Although this is a limited and individualized means of diffusing institutions, the Chinese managers take a better model of foreign business institutions with them to their domestic firms than they could have from JVs. Second, as China loosened restrictions on business areas open to WFOEs, foreign companies in the services sector such as Mercer, Hewitt, and Price, Waterhouse, Cooper were able to establish consulting agencies in China and to diffuse international business norms and practices. As I argue below in chapter 5, Chinese firms began to hire away foreign-trained managers and to employ international consultants to learn foreign—mainly, Western—business institutions. Increasingly, SOEs emulated foreign human resource practices as WFOEs rose in popularity in China, a process thwarted by China's attempts to control foreign institutional diffusion during the heyday of JVs.

Conclusion: A Perfect Storm Clears the Path for WFOEs

The above account demonstrates that the shift from reliance on the JV to the WFOE investment vehicle has resulted from a complex set of factors concerning Chinese and foreign interests, as well as shifts in those interests. Without an evolution of China's interests regarding the open-door policy, it is doubtful that foreign investors' preference for establishing WFOEs would have altered the foreign investment practices in China. The period 1988–1991 proved a "perfect storm" to reorder the interests of Chinese officials in a direction that gave rise to the dominance of the WFOE investment vehicle. During that period of high political drama and repression, most economic reform efforts stalled until 1992, when Deng Xiaoping made his much-vaunted "southern tour" of SEZs and reaffirmed the path of openness. The foreign investment regime is exceptional because of the fundamental, if subtle, shifts that took place at that time.

Three trends coincided in China's economy and politics that contributed to the shift toward greater lenience for WFOEs, despite the fact that WFOEs undermined Chinese controls over foreign investors. First, China's bouts with inflation and mounting foreign debt in the mid- and late 1980s led officials to introduce a tight credit policy at the end of 1987 and the beginning of 1988, which lasted several years. Tight credit left local officials with few resources to invest in JVs, which coincided with mounting evidence that many JVs were not profitable and were draining away resources from rather than providing financial relief for SOEs. Second, a critical assessment of the first decade of Chinese reforms and open-door policy led Chinese officials to reorient their priorities toward industrial upgrading. A decade after reforms, China found it still depended on importing high-tech equipment and finished goods. Finally, the violent quelling of the June 4, 1989, demonstrations shifted bargaining power in the direction of foreign investors. Many foreign investors cooled their heels on foreign investment projects in 1989 and 1990, just as China needed an inflow of capital and technology to provide jobs and dynamism to the economy. The combination of these three factors provided powerful impetus to Chinese officials to soften their stance on investment in the form of WFOEs. Against the background of the above three factors, China's desire to enter the GATT/WTO grew in the mid-1990s, compelling China to make further concessions to foreign investors, including WFOEs, on the crucial issue of access to China's market. China's shift toward greater acceptance of WFOEs occurred as foreign investors soured on the JV model, while their interest in using the WFOE investment vehicle grew.

The shift from Chinese pressure to form JVs to openness to the creation of WFOEs constitutes a fundamental shift in Chinese economic institutions and reflects the incremental nature of reform. Ultimately, WFOEs helped foreign investors and Chinese officials to realize some of their interests, which developed over the course of the reform period. China began with two grand principles guiding its approach to foreign investors—control and protection of sovereignty manifested in mercantilist management over domestic market access—but it first softened its control over foreign investors by shifting to majority foreign investor control in JVs, then to the creation of WFOEs, finally followed by a loosening of domestic market access, even for WFOEs. With the exception of sunset industries, such as textiles, that sought cheap labor to improve exports, foreign investors began with a strong interest in domestic market access. Foreign investors also sought control over their operations, but they were willing to compromise by taking on local partners who, foreign investors believed, would help them to gain local market access. Over time, however, foreign investors began to push for local market access and control, both by taking over majority control of JVs, which had limited market access, and by switching to WFOEs to maximize foreign control. As China loosened restrictions on WFOEs' access to domestic markets, the dilemma for foreign investors of which model to pursue dissipated. Rather than China introducing sweeping changes in its foreign investment regime, institutional reform was piecemeal and responded to the evolution and reprioritization of interests, as well as to new models introduced by foreign actors such as the WTO.

4

Law *Guanxi:* Chinese Law Goes International and Foreign Investors Go Local

Legal institutions are natural points of contention between domestic and international actors because they are subject to competing domestic and international considerations of legitimacy.[1] Domestic views of justice and desires to promote development may conflict with international conceptions of rule of law, human rights principles, and business norms and rules articulated by international organizations such as the WTO or the UN. In guiding the globalization process, Chinese state officials have faced strong and competing pressures for international legitimacy gained through compliance with international legal norms, for domestic legitimacy by protecting domestic economic actors from competition, and for economic development generated by providing a predictable legal system that protects property rights and spurs economic activity, especially technological development. This chapter demonstrates how both international organizations and foreign states define international legal norms for adoption by states at the macro level and how foreign investors and foreign law firms transmit information about international legal norms to China's micro and meso levels. Such pressure from below combined with macro-level institutional demands from international organizations above (such as human rights treaties and the WTO) and dovetailed with growing Chinese central state interests in achieving international legitimacy and improving foreign investment flows through better protection of property rights.

International norms on legal issues, however, are somewhat open-ended as to the specific organizational models and legal forms that states must adopt, leaving some space for states to construct legal institutions that meet the dictates of international society and to satisfy domestic expectations. To China, investors bring information on their various home-country legal practices. Foreign investors from Japan and the United States, for instance, brought distinct information and interests to China, and Chinese state officials were able to select aspects of the models that were appropriate for its population.

Since 1978, China has opened its economy to foreign trade and foreign direct investment, but officials have carefully guarded Chinese political sovereignty. Over the course of China's reform period, officials came to strive for great power status and, thus, have shown a growing interest in joining international treaties and organizations and bringing domestic legal institutions into compliance with international legal standards, especially in the area of international commercial arbitration, which has the added benefit of inducing foreign investment flows.[2] Chinese officials and scholars have shifted from limiting foreign influence on China's legal realm to using international standards as guideposts for reforms and to measure the quality of Chinese legal reforms.[3] Such a development raises the following key questions in the area of globalization and norm diffusion[4]: Do globalization and marketization cause legal convergence? What roles do international and domestic actors play in the adoption of international legal norms? Given the variety of legal models in advanced capitalist economies, how do investors from different countries affect legal reform in China?

China's Interest in Legal Reform

In the late 1970s, Deng Xiaoping's cohort of reformers, many of whom had suffered during Maoist political campaigns, averred to develop "rule of law" in order to replace "rule by man," a pattern of personalized rule, if not dictatorship, under Mao.[5] Even though the goals of this shift more aptly portended rule *by* law rather than rule *of* law—leaving officials less susceptible to legal limitation on their power than ordinary citizens—the rhetoric of rule of law helped put China on a track for legal reform. The ideal of rule of law gave rise to forces that spawned new Chinese laws, which hitherto were woefully underdeveloped, reinvigorated legal organizations, and allowed more open access to the legal system. Chinese officials soon discovered that improving China's legal system could help to attract foreign investment. Property rights protection, which was virtually absent during the Mao era, became an important concern for foreign investors and post-Mao leaders.

Foreign investors and international organizations pressed China to develop greater legal transparency and to adopt Western-style property rights. While foreign pressure helped the effort Chinese leaders who were committed to legal development and desired to attract foreign capital, conflict developed within China's officialdom over the degree of openness to foreign legal institutions, which, if adopted intact, would erode Chinese sovereignty and would require officials to be subject to legal principles in the same fashion as average citizens. Chinese leaders' early wariness of appearing to adopt wholesale foreign legal institutions was typified by a 1982 speech by Peng Zhen, then head of the Party's Legal Affairs Committee, who said, "It is necessary to draw on beneficial experiences—ancient or modern, Chinese or foreign—in studying the science of law....We study them in order to make the past serve the present and foreign things serve China."[6] Qiao Shi, former chief of the secret police, who became head of the National People's Congress (1993–1997), was an unlikely proponent of rule of law, even calling for legal reform along the lines of foreign practice,[7] but he, too, argued against "just copy[ing] blindly."[8] Deng Xiaoping, in his opening speech to the 12th CCP National Congress, argued that "we must pay attention to studying and absorbing foreign experience....However, we will never succeed if we mechanically copy the experiences and models of other countries."[9] In the mid-1980s, Zhao Ziyang displayed greater willingness to learn from foreigners on legal matters. In 1985, he formed an economic legislation work group under the leadership of the State Council to draft economic laws and regulations and invited foreign advisors to contribute.[10] In 2005, Xiao Yang, president of China's Supreme People's Court said in a speech, "Law is the basic language with which we communicate with the world. To build up the legal system in our country, we must learn from the experience of various countries and keep pace with the global legal development."[11] Over the course of the reform period, Chinese officials and scholars have moved from emphasizing China's unique conditions in the process of legal reform to judging China's legal reform by international standards, a self-reflexive move that indicates China's desire to improve its reputation.[12]

Although foreign investors' efforts dovetailed with Chinese authorities' interest in developing new legal organizations, reforming existing legal institutions, and improving the training of legal staff, foreign and Chinese actors held different legal models. The main lines of disagreement between foreign investors and Chinese officials were over the substance of Chinese laws, especially over the degree of congruence with international legal norms, and over enforcement of Chinese laws in the courts. Initially, Chinese reformers sought to address foreign investors' concerns about China's legal system by developing a special arbitration body to cater to foreign commercial disputes (called the China International Economic Trade and Arbitration Commission, or CIETAC) that would be distinct from the local legal system. Foreign parties could use the local legal system, but China sought to more closely approximate international legal norms of formalization in CIETAC than in the domestic legal system. Such a dual legal system mimicked the attempts to limit contact between foreign and domestic firms in SEZs, in this case with two sets of legal organizations and arbitration rules.

China's renewed interest in legal reform spawned a takeoff of legal activity. During the period 1978–1998, the National People's Congress enacted over 337 new laws and regulations, many in the area of economic law.[13] The

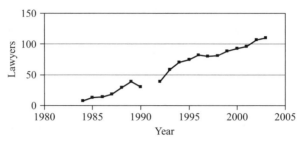

Figure 4.1   Number of Chinese Lawyers per One
Million Persons. Source: Chinese Economic Statistical
Yearbook Editorial Committee, *Chinese Economic
Yearbook* (Beijing: Chinese Economic Yearbook
Publishers, various years).

number of full-time Chinese lawyers ballooned from 8,330 (8 per one million persons) in 1984 to 136,684 (106 per one million persons) in 2002[14] (see
Figure 4.1). In 1984, Chinese courts heard 0.84 million first trial civil cases
(807 per one million persons), but in 2002, they heard 4.42 million cases
(3441 per one million persons)[15] (see Figure 4.2). China's proliferation of lawyers and civil cases approaches similar proxies for Japan but lags far behind
figures from the United States (see Table 4.1). The rising volume of Chinese
legal action, however, evinces a growing popular willingness to use the legal
system to settle disputes, but it is less clear whether Chinese legal institutions
are converging on international standards for rule of law.[16]
    International actors have had dichotomous effects upon Chinese legal
institutions. At the macro level, international organizations, such as the

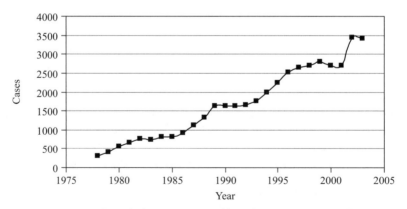

Figure 4.2   Number of Chinese First-Trial Civil Cases per One Million
Persons. Source: Chinese Economic Statistical Yearbook Editorial
Committee, *Chinese Economic Yearbook* (Beijing: Chinese Economic
Yearbook Publishers, various years).

Table 4.1

Key Legal Comparisons for China, Japan, and the United States
(for the year 2002, unless otherwise indicated)

	Number of Lawyers (per one million persons)	Number of First-Trial Civil Cases (per one million persons)
China	106.4	3,441
Japan	158.6 (2004)	3,664.6
United States	2,413	55,556.9

Calculated from: Chinese Economic Statistical Yearbook Editorial Committee, *Chinese Economic Yearbook* (Beijing: Chinese Economic Yearbook Publishers, various years); National Center for State Courts, Examining the Work of State Courts, 2003 http://www.ncsconline. org/D_Research/csp/2003_Files/2003_Civil.pdf; *Statistical Handbook of Japan*, 2004 http:// www.stat.go.jp/english/data/handbook/c02cont.htm#cha2_1; *Japan Statistical Yearbook*, 2005 http://www.stat.go.jp/data/nenkan/pdf/y2510000.pdf; U.S. Department of Labor, Bulletin of Labor Statistics http://www.bls.gov/oco/ocos053.htm.

WTO, and UN treaties have diffused particular legal principles and legal forms for adoption. These principles and forms constitute international legal norms with which members of international society are expected to comply. MNCs have helped Chinese officials to adopt formal procedures in international commercial arbitration, for example, that bring China into closer compliance with international norms. MNCs' efforts to promote rule of law partially are undercut, however, by their reliance upon personal relations, or *guanxi*,[17] a local institution that many actors use to guarantee economic transactions rather than formal contracts or, more subversively, to get around regulations and formal legal institutions. In other words, MNCs have contributed to Chinese legal development by providing feedback on gaps between Chinese legal institutions and international legal norms that call for formal legal procedures, but they have also reinforced local cognitive scripts (reliance on informal, personal relations) to avoid formal legal practices.

China's underdeveloped property rights and other legal guarantees encouraged corporations to rely on personal ties (*guanxi*) to secure their economic interests.[18] Recently, researchers have variously argued that *guanxi* has lost its importance in the increasingly market-oriented Chinese economy,[19] that foreign investment has flowed into China due to *guanxi*,[20] and that *guanxi* and market operations commingle.[21] More directly related to the issue of *guanxi* and the law, legal scholars contend that *guanxi* is compatible with capitalist development,[22] and that *guanxi* and the law can coexist.[23] This chapter argues that foreign firms and Chinese legal persons attempt to use personal relations to affect the outcomes of arbitration at CIETAC.[24] *Guanxi* is layered onto developing formal legal organizations,[25] for example CIETAC, thus affecting its operation and development. Legal development in China demonstrates the difficulties of diffusing new legal norms and cognitive scripts to the Chinese population. It also reveals subtle ways in which international legal norms and international organizations at the macro level and FIES and legal professionals at the micro and meso levels, respectively, helped to structure Chinese officials' interests and path of legal reform.

In order to focus the discussion of Chinese legal development, I analyze how Japanese and U.S. investors and lawyers approached arbitration at CIETAC and their attitudes toward and use of *guanxi*. I focus on arbitration because it is a more common means to settle international commercial disputes than recourse to courts and it is an area in which foreign investors have a strong interest in legal reform. The chapter begins with a theoretical discussion linking international norms, international actors, and Chinese officials to the process of Chinese legal development. Second, I trace the development of CIETAC, the Chinese dispute-resolution institution that is most frequently used by foreign investors to enforce property rights and to settle disputes. Next, I use interview data to analyze foreign investors' perception of the role that *guanxi,* an important aspect of China's legal culture, plays in administering their firms' affairs. I conclude with an account of China's legal development and the process of institutional change under path dependent development.

At first blush, analyzing the reform of commercial arbitration institutions may appear to be an "easy" case study because China's state and foreign investors each gain from improved protection of property rights and the economic development that it encourages. Yet, there are two complications to that viewpoint. First, to the extent that FIEs are more accustomed to and more likely to follow formal contracts, Chinese parties to international commercial arbitration suits were likely to lose their cases against foreign parties. Hence, improvements to CIETAC indirectly imperiled domestic firms who violated laws and relied on *guanxi* with local officials for protection from legal penalties. Second, as China's leaders discovered, it is difficult to develop one legal institution in isolation from the rest of the legal system. Legal development brings into play the writing of laws and regulations, training of legal professionals, and enforcement of laws. Conscientious efforts to develop an institution such as CIETAC: (i) served as a model of how legal reform should proceed, moving toward international institutional models; and (ii) had spillover effects on other parts of the legal system, especially in improving enforcement in the courts and raising standards for legal training and professionalism.

In the following pages, I contend that the Chinese state induced a pattern of globalization in which they adopted aspects of international dispute resolution organizational forms, patterned after the UNCITRAL Model Law on International Commercial Arbitration (1985) (hereafter, UNCITRAL Model).[26] To demonstrate the diffusion of such a legal form, I analyze CIETAC Rules changes to incorporate aspects of the UNCITRAL Model and to improve compliance with the New York Convention, which calls for reciprocal enforcement of international commercial arbitration decisions.[27] International actors, especially foreign investors and non-governmental organizations, played an important role in providing information on international legal institutions and in encouraging China to engage in domestic legal reform. Domestic reformers used the information from international actors to alter legal forms, but informal mechanisms that are a part of China's legal culture have proved resilient to alteration. Reforming CIETAC's formal organization proved easier to change than, initially, the substantive decisions of CIETAC, and later, the legal context in which CIETAC operated and in which its decisions were enforced. In China, foreign actors' reliance upon personal relations, or *guanxi*, to manage some aspects of administrative and exchange relations, allows informal legal practices to persist alongside legal formalization. In China's legal realm, informal local institutions such as *guanxi* persist alongside formal legal institutions that approximate international norms (at least in the area of commercial arbitration).

Culture, Law, and Globalization

International organizations and MNCs aid local adoption of international norms by compelling or encouraging economies to adopt particular legal forms and to adhere to general legal principles such as rule of law. For example, the IMF may require heavily indebted countries to adopt neoliberal regulations in order to attract foreign direct investment flows or to undertake structural adjustments.[28] At the micro level, MNCs press for adoption of international legal institutions to protect their property rights,[29] and at the meso level, non-governmental organizations (NGOs) and foreign law firms can provide information to and bring pressure to bear on officials to adopt international legal norms, for example in the area of human rights.[30] Policy networks composed of international and domestic actors, operating at the meso level, can supply information about international institutions to domestic policy makers in the diffusion of norms.[31] Domestic actors help to "localize" international norms to make them fit with existing local institutions, engage in "selective adaptation" to international legal practices, or "graft" international forms onto local institutions.[32]

MNCs face a dilemma with regard to their pursuit of profits and rule of law. On the one hand, MNCs desire a legal context that guarantees protection of their intellectual property and that provides fair, predictable, and impartial legal decisions. Such a legal system in a host environment can spur research and development and technology transfer by MNCs. On the other hand, MNCs seek opportunities to capture markets and to exclude competition by developing particularistic relations with local officials. The above two strategies work against one another; reliance on personal, pragmatic relations to gain special privileges undermines efforts to develop a formal, predictable system based on rule of law. Foreign investors with higher levels of technology seek stronger property rights protection than firms that rely more on labor-intensive production.

China's desire to become a great power and to gain the international respect that goes with such status has compelled China to improve its legal system.[33] Chinese officials have sought to improve their international reputation and to induce greater foreign investment flows by reforming their macro-level legal institutions, especially in the realm of international commercial arbitration, while international organizations and treaties have defined broad standards for Chinese officials, also at the macro level. The logic of appropriateness and international legitimacy are closely linked to material rewards gained from enhanced property rights protection. Foreign investors at the micro level and foreign law firms at the meso level have provided models that Chinese reformers selectively adopt and emulate, have given feedback on Chinese legal institutions, and have trained Chinese attorneys and business leaders who, in turn, demand greater legal transparency in China. Information and feedback from foreign actors has helped reform-minded officials to push through legal reforms and has given shape to some of China's legal reforms.

Yet, rule of law faces two main obstacles: (i) a culture that has not esteemed formal legal practices; and (ii) central-local tensions on the following central legal regulations and laws. Officials' interest in promoting their locale's development and foreign investors' interest in gaining market share at the expense of competitors act as a brake on efforts to reform China's legal system. The central state may define macro-level legal regulations and laws to follow, but local state agents may persist in following old scripts in order to protect local businesses. The central-local fissures in the Chinese legal system are caused by lower courts' reliance upon local government for funding and low levels of legal education among local legal professionals. Through their legal cases, MNCs and their attorneys have helped to identify the conflict between central and local officials' interests and legal norms, which, in turn, has spawned further systemic legal reform.

Sources of Legal Convergence and Distinction

International organizations and MNCs have pushed China to adopt formal, transparent legal institutions and law-making procedures, but China lacks a formal legal tradition from which to draw. Entering China's reform period, the combination of a Confucian legal tradition and socialism afforded private property little legitimacy and caused extensive reliance on informal legal practices. Weighing against foreign models of legal proceduralism is more than a millennium of Chinese reliance upon ethical conduct (*li*) in personal relations rather than formal law (*fa*) to create political order.[34] In general, Confucianism eschews reliance upon laws as a means of establishing order, instead asserting that moral exemplars, epitomized by the emperor, should inform citizens' behavior. Drawing on the Legalist school of thought, Chinese rulers have used the law as an instrument to extend state power rather than to define and protect individual rights.[35]

During the Mao era (1949–1978), the Chinese Communist Party did little to enhance legal formalism; they ruled more by official decree and policy directives than by adherence to legal proceduralism. The high tides of Maoist politics such as the Cultural Revolution allowed untrained mobs of activists to investigate and to decide the fates of people accused of "crimes" against policy lines.[36] Shying away from formal legal procedures in courts to settle conflict, Chinese traditionally have gravitated toward informal mechanisms of dispute resolution such as personal relations, mediation through third parties, or ideally, avoidance of conflict by following local norms of behavior and managing personal relations (*guanxi*) well. China continues to conceive of citizens' rights in the legal realm primarily in terms of socioeconomic rights, such as the right to subsistence, and as subordinate to collective interests, rather than individual human rights and political rights against the state. China's legal culture is increasingly dynamic, however, and foreign actors are deeply affecting the direction of legal thought in China. (see Figure 4.3.)

International society promotes formal and transparent legal institutions, and actors such as international and multilateral organizations and NGOs diffuse rule of law norms in order to ease friction among states and to promote human rights. International commercial arbitration is an important example of legal norm diffusion that is of particular interest to foreign investors. In recent decades, international norms have emerged in the area of international commercial arbitration, shaped by the New York Convention, which establishes reciprocal obligations for enforcement of arbitral awards among signatory countries, and by the UNCITRAL Model, which provides a flexible set of rules for arbitration that emphasizes the disputants' power to determine many aspects of the proceedings. At the end of 2005, 137 countries had signed the New York Convention (including the U.S., China, and Japan). In 2005, 45 countries (including Japan) and sub-national territories of three other countries, including Hong Kong and Macao in China; Scotland in the United Kingdom; and California, Connecticut, Illinois, Oregon, and Texas in the United States had adopted the UNCITRAL Model.[37] Additionally, the American Arbitration Association (AAA), which handles many commercial arbitration cases, and the International Chamber of Commerce, which provides international commercial arbitration services throughout the world, have adopted many elements of the UNCITRAL Model. Thus, the UNCITRAL Model has become a norm to measure the quality of commercial arbitration in a country.

To China, Japanese and U.S. actors bring distinct legal approaches and expectations. Since the writing of the Meiji Constitution in 1889, Japan has drawn from western legal traditions, especially from German and French legal models, but those efforts to develop formal legal institutions have been

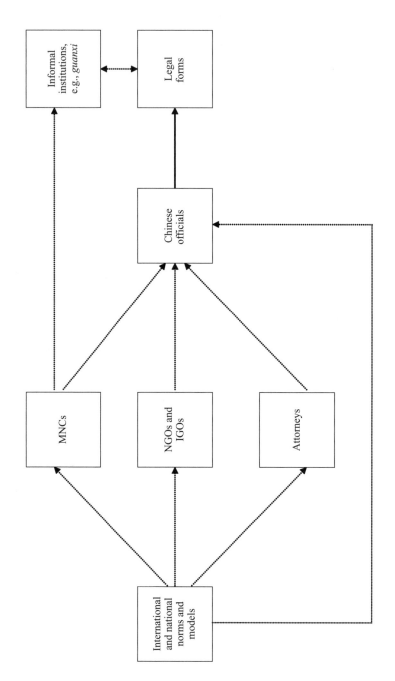

Dotted lines indicate information flows.
Solid lines indicate authority to make decisions.

Figure 4.3   Model of International Influences on CIETAC Reform.

layered onto Japanese norms and values.[38] Japanese actors are accustomed to working through non-adversarial means, including personal relations, to resolve conflict. Additionally, high court costs and bureaucratic assertiveness to address grievances in society have stemmed the growth of legal adversarialism. Japan's legal development has tended toward informal dispute settlement, bureaucratic intervention, and a reluctance to rely upon the courts.[39] Under the Japanese inquisitorial model, the goal of the courts is to gather relevant information and to determine the appropriate action rather than to choose sides between competing claims presented by opposing parties' attorneys.[40] The concept of personal relations (*giri*) plays an important role, and maintaining harmony of relations in proceedings is given greater weight than individual legal rights.[41] Cleaving to its pattern of international legal engagement, Japan follows the UNCITRAL Model on international commercial arbitration. An admixture of Confucian and civil law traditions has rendered a Japanese legal system that has formal, transparent legal institutions but a popular tendency to avoid the courts in favor of informal dispute resolution.

American actors mix reliance on formal, adversarial legal institutions to protect property rights with informal mechanisms to avoid legal conflict or to get special privileges. The United States has a formal legal apparatus that is rooted in the common law tradition of individual rights and that is widely regarded as adversarial.[42] In the last two decades, the United States has shown an increasing interest in alternative dispute resolution such as arbitration and mediation, which provides a non-adversarial and less expensive alternative to the courts, but international commercial arbitration rules lack uniformity in federal and state laws. In 1925, the federal government passed the *Federal Arbitration Act* (FAA)[43] and has amended it several times, but states have passed their own legislation to shore up the inadequacies of the Act. The United States has not passed national legislation that follows the arbitration procedures outlined in the UNCITRAL Model, but several states have done so.[44] In addition, the United States permits arbitration in the courts or on an ad hoc basis, and many organizations that provide arbitration services, such as the American Arbitration Association (AAA), arbitrate according to the UNCITRAL Model.

Actors Affecting Legal Reform

Neither international organizations that articulate norms for commercial arbitration at the macro level nor international actors such as MNCs at the micro level can directly shape Chinese legal institutions, but they can indirectly affect legal reform. International organizations affect domestic legal change in China (at least in the area of international commercial arbitration) by defining international legal standards—MNCs by bringing cases that highlight variation in the Chinese legal system from international standards, and foreign law firms and law schools by training actors in the Chinese legal system. Ultimately, Chinese actors reform CIETAC and Chinese legal forms,[45] but international actors help shape the ideational context in which Chinese reformers operate.

China's National People's Congress (hereafter, NPC) and the Supreme People's Court have emerged as the leading champions of rule of law. Although several "conservatives" within the CCP have headed the NPC, including Li Peng and Qiao Shi, they have taken up the mantle of legal development, producing an impressive array of laws, some of which are quite progressive.[46] The NPC also has opened the process of writing legislation to input from society by soliciting opinions on draft legislation, which has even included foreign actors. Xiao Yang, who held the position of president of the Supreme People's Court (1998–2008), made several contributions to the development of the courts as an institution, including strengthening higher courts' supervisory function within the hierarchy of courts and instituting a qualification examination system for judges.

Reluctantly, MNCs bring suits in courts and arbitration bodies, where they have discovered discrepancies between China's arbitration and enforcement mechanisms and international norms. In raising objections to the arbitration system, they indirectly have pressed China to reform its legal system so that it approximates foreign, formal legal models. Yet, pursuit of profits leads some MNCs to negotiate exclusive deals or special access to land permits or licenses through informal, particularistic relations with local officials who sell off "rents" in order to secure market share. MNCs seek formal legal rules to protect their property rights, but they also adopt informal local means to get insider deals that protect markets against competitors or that secure special production rights. The above competing principles render MNCs Janus-faced toward the issue of legal formalism. Firms from Hong Kong and Taiwan have relied heavily on *guanxi*,[47] while U.S. and Japanese firms have done so, but to a lesser extent.[48]

MNCs also pursue rule of law principles through business organizations such as the Keidanren (the Japan Federation of Economic Organizations), the American Chamber of Commerce in Shanghai, and the US-China Business Council, which operate at the meso level and help MNCs to overcome their private interests in building social relations and gaining insider deals. Both Japanese and U.S. business associations have called on China to comply with international standards of transparency, rule of law, and intellectual property protection.[49] The American Chamber of Commerce also has a committee that works specifically on legal issues with the Chinese government. After Presidents Jiang Zemin of China and Bill Clinton of the United States concluded a "Rule of Law" cooperative agreement in 1997, the US-China Business Council pooled corporate funds to support projects in its "Legal Cooperation" initiative, including the training of judges, assisting in revising China's Civil Procedure Law, and developing a handbook that contains a code of legal ethics for attorneys, among other projects.[50] Through their initiatives and complaints, NGOs simultaneously introduce models of foreign legal institutions and encourage China to adopt them.

American law firms abroad spread American legal practice by transplanting norms and fostering competition with local law firms, which encourages the latter to adopt American legal practices.[51] Until 1992, foreign law firms were excluded from operating in China except as consultants to foreign investors, but China has since loosened its restrictions such that during the period 1992–2001, 103 foreign law firms opened offices in China.[52] Even so, the Chinese government restricts foreign law offices, especially barring them from participating in Chinese court proceedings and representing clients in other legal matters.[53] Nonetheless, foreign law firms have significantly influenced China's legal development and work closely with FIEs. Once in China, foreign lawyers have called for transparent legal proceedings. Foreign attorneys provide advice to investors when evaluating investment proposals, in the signing of contracts, and during dispute settlement. In the early stages of reforms, those in the Chinese legal field lacked knowledge of the procedures, terminology, and forms that foreign actors introduced to China, but Chinese attorneys and judges increasingly are adopting a common international legal terminology and set of practices.[54]

Foreign law firms (especially in major cities such as Shanghai, Guangzhou, and Beijing) and foreign law schools contribute to the training of a rapidly growing number of Chinese lawyers. Foreign law firms that open offices in China hire local attorneys alongside foreign attorneys in their offices and work with local law firms to help represent foreign firms in legal proceedings. Within foreign law firms and foreign law schools, Chinese attorneys are introduced to international legal forms, legal ethics, and foreign approaches to adjudication, which they internalize. Thus trained, Chinese lawyers form a policy community with international attorneys, which advocates for legal reforms and provides technical information on international legal forms and practices as well as feedback on the shortcomings of China's existing institutions. For example, a Chinese lawyer who worked in Japan and who works closely with Japanese firms that do business in China has advised Chinese authorities on police reform and the handling of witnesses.[55] Another Chinese legal scholar, who studied environmental law while abroad, returned to China and authored a book on comparative environmental law. Subsequently, the Chinese government adopted many of the legal principles and forms that he analyzed in the book.[56]

China's state has used regulations on the licensing of lawyers to canalize foreign and domestic legal practitioners, it claims, to protect local law firms. At the end of 2001, China adopted regulations on foreign law firms' representative offices that banned Chinese attorneys from being employed in such offices.[57] Common practice in Shanghai allowed domestic attorneys to hold their Chinese license and to work as legal assistants in foreign law offices for up to two years. After two years, a Chinese lawyer may continue to work for a foreign law firm, but the lawyer would have to surrender his attorney's license.[58] In 2006, this modus operandi was threatened by a letter issued by the Shanghai Lawyers Association declaring that many foreign firms engaged in illegal practices, including hiring of Chinese attorneys.[59] This attempt to control interaction between foreign and domestic attorneys has only partially succeeded. Although Chinese law does not permit formal alliances or JVs between foreign and Chinese law firms, in 2007, a foreign law firm, McDermott Will and Emery, established an alliance with a newly founded Chinese law firm formed with over 20 lawyers who left one of Shanghai's top law offices, Allbright Legal Group.[60]

The emerging legal community at the meso level is growing in importance, but they must work with state officials who are the agents of Chinese legal reform and adoption of international commercial arbitration rules. For officials, legal reform has proven a nettlesome issue for two reasons. First, Chinese leaders have balanced commitments to protecting sovereignty with the desire to improve China's international reputation. By adopting legal forms that mimic international institutions and by participating in international organizations and treaties, Chinese leaders seek to raise their standing.[61] Yet, Peter Gries has shown that Chinese citizens will protest when they perceive that foreign actors are "pushing around" China.[62] Second, legal reform has divided officials along central-local and organizational lines.

Opening up China deepened fissures in the state, especially among central ministries and between levels of government. The China Council for the Promotion of International Trade (CCPIT) and Ministry of Foreign Trade and Economic Cooperation (MOFTEC) worked to convince MNCs that China was a secure legal investment environment. Central officials were divided on the scope of legal reforms, but Deng's 1992 "southern tour" reaffirmed the path of opening to foreign investment and trade and induced a wave of legal reform at the macro level in the rest of the 1990s. Local officials, however, violated central regulations (even establishing unauthorized investment zones) and told foreign investors that *guanxi* could substitute for formal legal protection in order to attract foreign direct investment to their locales.[63] For most of the reform period, within the court system, many local judges have lacked college degrees and formal legal training, which has limited their commitment to legal principles and their knowledge of international legal institutions. Paid by People's Congresses at the same level of government, local judges are ensconced in webs of personal relations that promote community development and protection, even in conflict with central directives. Local officials solicit the aid of judges in basic People's Courts to help protect businesses from lawsuits. In their haste to start up foreign investment projects, foreign investors and local Chinese officials often ignored regulations and laws on foreign investment.

In China's case, central leaders have put through a series of reforms to move domestic arbitration institutions toward greater compliance with norms on international commercial arbitration for a mixture of material and identity reasons. Materially, China's legal reforms help to attract foreign investors, while ideationally, China gains in reputation by improving its appearance in the eyes of the international community. MNCs have reinforced some existing local informal institutions by adopting local practices to manage in a foreign environment as much as they press for reforms to alter the local legal context. Such a pattern leads to dichotomous trends: adoption of formal legal institutions at the macro level and the persistence of informal legal institutions at the micro level. At the micro level, MNCs also have provided negative feedback on China's legal forms through their appeals to officials to improve rule of law and property rights protection.

CIETAC

As the institution most frequently used by foreign economic actors to resolve commercial disputes with Chinese parties, CIETAC has been exposed to a great deal of foreign scrutiny and to heavy doses of criticism for its failure to meet international standards of fairness and ethics. To secure foreign investment and to encourage higher levels of technology transfer through investment, Chinese officials have sought to advance CIETAC's movement towards compliance with international norms. In the aftermath of the June 4, 1989, suppression, Tang Houzhi, vice chairman of CIETAC, said that CIETAC was adopting international rules and sought a more important position in the world.[64] By the 1990s, leaders of the National People's Congress and the CCPIT, which oversees CIETAC, spoke freely about following international legal norms. In announcing the 1994 revisions to CIETAC Rules, Cheng Dejun, vice chairman of CIETAC, noted that China's arbitration practice "is moving nearer to the international standards,"[65] a clear indication of CIETAC's consciousness of international arbitral norms. Academic articles on topics such as arbitration have used international norms as standards to judge Chinese legal reforms.[66]

China has focused on creating national legal and arbitral institutions as well as a corpus of substantive law that could secure foreign investors' property and induce foreign capital inflow. CIETAC was a main target of reform and development because it is the primary site for resolving legal disputes involving foreign and Chinese firms. Initially, Chinese officials sought to develop CIETAC mainly in isolation from the rest of China's legal system. In that sense, China's central leaders tried to quarantine foreign firms' legal actions and their effect from the rest of China's legal system in the same way that special economic zones cordoned off foreign investors from the rest of the economy.

CIETAC is a centrally organized and administered arbitration body under the control of the CCPIT, a national organization. After 1980, leaders reformed CIETAC, which was designed in 1956 based on a Soviet model, to provide a legal framework for resolving disputes in the area of foreign economic activity (trade, technology transfer, and investment). CIETAC could hear cases involving international trade; relating to Hong Kong, Taiwan, and Macao; arising between two foreign-invested enterprises and between foreign-invested and Chinese enterprises; and concerning activities of Chinese legal persons related to foreign capital, technology, or service, among others.[67] During the period 1956–1979, CIETAC only arbitrated 38 cases,[68] but in recent years, CIETAC has carried the largest caseload of any international arbitration body (for example, in 1998 CIETAC accepted 678 new cases).[69] Partly in response to issues raised by foreign disputants and to improve the arbitration organ and procedures, the Chinese government revised CIETAC's Rules six times, in 1988, 1994, 1995, 1998, 2000, and 2005. With several of these reforms, CIETAC adopted more elements of the UNCITRAL Model on international commercial arbitration and rewrote judicial regulations to move toward more effective compliance with the New York Convention, which obligates signatories to mutual recognition and enforcement of international arbitration decisions reached in other countries that have signed the Convention. The UNCITRAL Model lays out several procedural recommendations for international commercial arbitration, and China incrementally reformed CIETAC Rules to move toward greater compliance with the UNCITRAL Model.

Appointing Panelists

Quality arbitration relies on unbiased selection of well-trained panelists who observe professional ethics. Unfortunately, CIETAC Rules and the performance of its panelists have not always met such standards. In the Mao era (1949–1978), China lacked specific training guidelines for its international arbitration panelists. Since 2000, China requires CIETAC arbitrators to have, among other qualifications, eight years of experience in arbitration or in the law (as a lawyer or judge), or similar legal training and experience.[70] Until 1988, CIETAC only allowed Chinese to serve as arbitrators, but to assuage foreign parties' concerns about the bias of Chinese panelists, CIETAC began to recruit a large number of arbitrators from Hong Kong and other countries and regions. In discussing the 1988 CIETAC reforms that would allow international panelists in CIETAC, Tang Houzhi, vice chairman of CIETAC, acknowledged foreign concerns about the fairness of Chinese panelists and the need to meet international standards of fairness.[71] CIETAC has picked high-profile international arbitrators—even occasional critics of CIETAC such as Jerome Cohen, Sally Harpole, and Michael Moser—as panelists to raise CIETAC's international credibility.[72] According to a recent count, CIETAC has 518 arbitrators, of whom 174 are from Hong Kong, Macao, Taiwan, or other countries.[73]

Until CIETAC changed its Rules for selecting panelists in 2005 (see below), each disputant selected one arbitrator from the panel of CIETAC arbitrators. The foreign party to the case typically selected a foreign arbitrator, and the Chinese party selected a Chinese arbitrator. If the two parties to the dispute could reach an agreement, they jointly appointed the third arbitrator; however, in most cases the two parties disagreed, so the chairman of CIETAC appointed the third arbitrator, typically a Chinese who served as the chair of the panel.[74] On this crucial point, CIETAC Rules mostly followed the letter of Article 11 of the UNCITRAL Model, which calls for the two designated arbitrators to determine the third arbitrator and, failing agreement, calls for the competent authority (CIETAC) to appoint a third panelist. CIETAC practice, however, departed from the substantive goal of the UNCITRAL Model to appoint someone from a third country to head the panel.[75] To win a case, one side needs a simple majority of the panelists' votes. The selection process potentially slanted the panel to decide in favor of the local party because of political pressure brought to bear on two of the three panelists who hear the case.[76] CIETAC officials have shown awareness of the norm of impartial justice in their admission that "arbitration should be independent from administrative organizations to ensure fairer judgments."[77]

In 2004, Jerome Cohen, one of the foremost experts on China's legal system and a former panelist of CIETAC, delivered a scathing speech on biases within the CIETAC system, including the selection of panelists, to a group in Xiamen, China. CIETAC removed Jerome Cohen from its list of panelists, but the 2005 CIETAC Rules took into account much of what he criticized regarding the selection of panelists.[78] First, the 2005 Rules provide for parties to arbitration to select arbitrators who are not listed as CIETAC panelists.[79] That rule change reduces the possibility that CIETAC leaders could exercise influence over Chinese panelists who hear a case.[80] Second, the reformed Rules give parties an expanded role in the selection of the crucial presiding arbitrator. Selecting a presiding arbitrator, the parties submit a list of potential candidates to serve that role. If the lists show agreement on one or more panelists to serve as presiding arbitrator, CIETAC will select one of the names on which the parties agree. If no agreement can be reached through this methodology, the head of CIETAC selects the presiding arbitrator from the list of CIETAC panelists.[81] Partially keeping with the spirit of the UNCITRAL Model, the 2005 selection method places more power in the disputants' hands. Table 4.2 summarizes the shift in CIETAC Rules toward greater compliance with the UNCITRAL Model's procedure for selecting panelists.

Interestingly, rules on the formation of CIETAC panels reinforce the importance of *guanxi* in arbitration procedures. Chinese attorneys, who often represent MNCs in CIETAC cases, sometimes select friends, coworkers, classmates, or other types of *guanxi* from the panel of eligible arbitrators. Although reluctant to admit that *guanxi* affects the outcome of arbitration cases, one Chinese attorney confided that he believed that he got a fair hearing from and felt more comfortable making his case in front of an arbitrator with whom he had *guanxi*.[82] International Bar Association and CIETAC Rules required arbitrators to recuse themselves from cases in which they had a personal interest and were appointed a panelist,[83] and, by the first

Table 4.2
CIETAC Rules Changes on Appointing Panelists

International Model	CIETAC Rules
UNCITRAL, Art. 11(2): "The parties are free to agree on a procedure of appointing the arbitrator or arbitrators, subject to the provision of paragraphs (4) and (5) of this article."	1988 CIETAC Rules, Arts. 14 and 15: Each party shall appoint one arbitrator from list of CIETAC panelists. The head of CIETAC appoints the third and presiding arbitrator.
	1995 CIETAC Rules, Art. 24: Each party shall appoint one arbitrator from the list of CIETAC panelists. The parties may jointly appoint the third, presiding panelist. If the parties fail to agree on the appointment of the presiding panelist, the head of CIETAC appoints the third panelist.
	2005 CIETAC Rules, Art. 21(1): "The parties shall appoint arbitrators from the Panel of Arbitrators provided by CIETAC."
	2005 CIETAC Rules, Art. 21(2): Upon agreement by the parties and with the consent of CIETAC, the parties may appoint arbitrators outside of the CIETAC Panel of Arbitrators to hear cases.

oral hearing, parties to a dispute could request removal of a panelist who appeared biased.[84] Interestingly, the U.S. FAA neither requires arbitrators to disclose personal interests in arbitration cases nor provides for parties to an arbitration case to challenge arbitrators.[85] Hence, U.S. firms' and attorneys' complaints about biases of CIETAC arbitrators are rooted more in international norms than in U.S. commercial arbitration practices.

CIETAC Rules permit foreign counsel to represent parties to arbitration hearings,[86] but foreign managers claim that bringing foreign attorneys to CIETAC proceedings is likely to enflame nationalist passions that work against foreign parties.[87] Japanese attorneys in Shanghai recognize the importance of *guanxi* to gain a fair hearing in arbitration and court cases. In selecting local counsel to represent a Japanese client in proceedings, a Japanese attorney asserted that, along with an attorney's qualifications, "[i]t is helpful to select a firm that is locally known and has good *guanxi*."[88] Another Japanese attorney, speaking with reference to labor arbitration, concluded, "It is most important to select the right attorney if you do go to arbitration....In every case, you want to have *guanxi*....If we select the wrong attorney, then the result could be bad, the worst."[89]

It is unclear how local attorneys' *guanxi* affects the outcome of arbitration cases. Several foreign attorneys and legal analysts have described CIETAC's proceedings as relatively fair. In 2000, some long-time consultants and managers in China noted that attorneys for their companies felt it worthwhile to take others to court or arbitration, a practice that was unthinkable to them as recently as a decade ago.[90] Still other attorneys, managers, and legal scholars (including CIETAC arbitrators) have described the Chinese arbitration process in highly negative terms.[91]

Rules for Procedures

The UNCITRAL Model allows parties to a dispute to follow their own procedures for arbitration as laid out in the arbitration clause of their contract. Based on fears of bias in CIETAC's procedures and experience abroad that allowed disputants sway over the construction of procedures, FIEs and foreign lawyers seek flexibility in stipulating dispute resolution procedures in their contracts. CIETAC Rules have not allowed much flexibility with regard to procedures for hearings. In 1988, CIETAC Rules were silent on the issue of alternative procedures, and it was implied that disputants would follow the rules of CIETAC hearings. The 1994 CIETAC Rules clarified that parties had to follow CIETAC hearing procedures. In the 1998 and 2000 versions of CIETAC Rules, disputants could follow their own rules for hearings with the permission of CIETAC. Finally, the 2005 CIETAC Rules permit the arbitration panel to determine the appropriate hearing procedures. The CIETAC Rules have moved in the direction of granting greater leeway for parties involved to determine hearing procedures, thus approximating the international standard on commercial arbitration as stipulated in the UNCITRAL Model, the AAA Rules, and the ICC Rules (see Table 4.3).

Table 4.3

CIETAC Rules Changes on Establishing Arbitration Hearing Procedures

International Model	CIETAC Rules
UNCITRAL 19(1): "Subject to the provision of this Law, the parties are free to agree on the procedure to be followed in conducting the proceedings."	1994 CIETAC Rules, Art. 7: "Once the parties agree to submit their disputes to the Arbitration Commission for arbitration, it shall be deemed that they have agreed to conduct the arbitration under these rules." 1998 and 2000 CIETAC Rules, Art. 7: Parties follow CIETAC procedures. "However, if the parties have agreed otherwise, and subject to the consent by the Arbitration Commission, the parties' agreement shall prevail." 2005 CIETAC Rules, Art. 29 (1): "The arbitral tribunal shall examine the case in any way that it deems appropriate unless otherwise agreed by the parties."

Expert Testimony

Drawing from their experience with adversarial dispute resolution models and relatively wide rules on discovery, U.S. observers have complained about the lack of transparency of CIETAC panels' handling of evidence. CIETAC panels may gather evidence independent of the parties to an arbitration case such as through the appointment of expert witnesses, an approach similar to Japanese arbitration rules and the UNCITRAL Model.[92] Until 1994, CIETAC Rules did not guarantee that attorneys representing parties to an arbitration case could examine and contest evidence or expert testimony gathered independently by a CIETAC panel. *Paklito Investment Ltd. v. Klochner East Asia Ltd.* (1993) highlights foreign opposition to CIETAC's approach to handling expert testimony. In that case the Supreme Court of Hong Kong overturned a CIETAC verdict for its failure to allow one of the parties to raise objections to expert testimony.[93] A year later, the State Council revised CIETAC Rules to guarantee each party the ability to examine and challenge evidence gathered by arbitration panels.[94] That shift brought CIETAC Rules in line with UNCITRAL Model's recommendation, and it underscores the influence of foreign legal feedback on the direction of Chinese legal reform (see Table 4.4).

Table 4.4
CIETAC Rules Changes on Examining Expert Testimony

International Model	CIETAC Rules
UNCITRAL Model, Art. 26(2): "Unless otherwise agreed by the parties, if a party so request. . . . the expert shall, after delivery of his written or oral report, participate in a hearing where the parties have the opportunity to put questions to him and to present expert witnesses in order to testify on the points at issue."	1988 CIETAC Rules, Art. 28: "The arbitration tribunal may consult experts or appoint appraisers for the clarification of special questions relating to the case."
UNCITRAL Notes on Organizing Arbitral Proceedings, Art. 72: "Arbitration rules that contain provisions on experts usually also have provisions on the right of a party to comment on the report of the expert appointed by the arbitral tribunal."	1994 (and after) CIETAC Rules, Art. 40: "The expert's report and the appraiser's report shall be copied to the parties so that they may have the opportunity to giver their opinion thereon. . . . [T]he expert and appraiser may be present at the hearing and give explanations of their reports . . ."

Enforcement of Verdicts

If a party receives a favorable judgment from a CIETAC panel, the party still faces the difficulty of enforcing the arbitral judgment. The New York Convention calls for courts in signatory countries to enforce international arbitration decisions reached in other signatory countries. Parties to a CIETAC case should voluntarily enforce a panel's verdict, but CIETAC lacks power to enforce its decisions. If a losing party fails to comply with an arbitration judgment, the 1991 Chinese Civil Procedure Law directs the winning party to request the people's intermediate court in the Chinese defendant's district to enforce CIETAC's decision, which the court is often loathe to do.[95] Chinese courts have failed to enforce international arbitral judgments, a breach of the Civil Procedure Law and the New York Convention. According to David Howell, "from 1990 to 1996 approximately 25 percent of the applications made for enforcement of arbitral awards were denied," but the figure may be significantly higher.[96] One U.S. attorney working in Shanghai charged, "Even if you receive a favorable hearing, it is difficult to enforce the ruling. The problem is systemic; local courts band together like a local mafia."[97]

China's 1991 Civil Procedure Law (CPL), which replaced the 1982 Civil Procedure Law (CPL), unintentionally facilitated local protectionism.[98] Under the 1982 version, winning parties who could not collect CIETAC judgments against recalcitrant losing parties had to turn to the intermediate court where the arbitration took place, usually Beijing, for help enforcing the decision. The 1991 CPL took the Beijing Intermediate Court out of the enforcement process, rendering winning parties dependent on local courts in the losing parties' backyards for help collecting compensation. Although the 1991 CPL ultimately marked a setback for enforcement procedures, the reform was adopted because the growing number of arbitration cases heard by CIETAC and domestic arbitration organs outstripped the Beijing Intermediate Court's enforcement capacity.

The 1991 CPL allows Chinese courts to declare a contract's arbitration clause null and void.[99] Local courts have used technicalities to set aside rulings by international arbitration bodies outside of China, a nationalist maneuver to protect Chinese firms but in violation of the New York Convention.[100] Article 260 of the 1991 CPL, which allows courts to deny enforcement of arbitration awards that "would be contrary to the social and public interests of the People's Republic of China…"[101] provides protectionist officials with another broad avenue to deny enforcement. The UNCITRAL Model and the New York Convention allow for non-enforcement when international arbitration decisions conflict with "public policy" in the losing party's country.[102] The Chinese terminology, "social and public interests," provides much more latitude for local courts' interpretation than the term "public policy" in the UNCITRAL Model and the New York Convention. Moreover, the term "social and public interests" is not transparent and, therefore, prone to use for political considerations.

In addition, Chinese courts exercise local protection by shielding Chinese firms' assets. Disputants can request that CIETAC have a court in the defendant's domicile freeze the assets of a Chinese defendant.[103] Nevertheless, Chinese courts have ignored such requests.[104] To thwart enforcement, Chinese defendants frequently claim insolvency, which local banks corroborate.[105] The opaque Chinese financial institutions, however, make it difficult to discern the veracity of such claims.[106] Refusal to freeze assets is a relatively simple method for local courts to help Chinese firms avoid financial settlements resulting from arbitration decisions.

One of the most notorious examples of local protectionism in the Chinese legal system involved a U.S. company, Revpower, operating out of Hong Kong, which in 1988 agreed to a compensation trade agreement with Shanghai Far East Aero-Technology Import and Export Corporation (hereafter, SFAIC) to produce batteries. In 1990, a dispute arose between the partners when the Chinese side unilaterally raised the selling price of the batteries 40–50 percent. Revpower investigated and disputed the Chinese side's claim that material prices of inputs had increased. Following the contract's arbitration clause, Revpower filed a complaint in Stockholm, where the case was heard and decided in favor of Revpower. During the hearing in Stockholm, the SFAIC filed suit in the Shanghai Intermediate People's Court, and that court accepted the case, claiming to have jurisdiction. As a signatory country to the New York Convention on international arbitration, Chinese courts should not have accepted the case and were obligated to enforce the Stockholm ruling.[107] The Shanghai Court demanded that the case be heard in China, but the Court, in turn, refused to accept Revpower's filing of briefs in the case.[108]

Robert Aronson, the president of Revpower, began mobilizing political allies in Washington and in China, for instance by twice testifying before a Congressional panel. Aronson's testimony called for a linking of improvement in China's compliance with the New York Convention to China's accession to the WTO and to continuation of most favored nation status from the United States.[109] Less than a year after Aronson's Congressional testimony in 1997, the Chinese authorities issued new rules that set time limits on enforcement of arbitral judgments.[110] The high-level pressure eventually contributed to legal reform in China, but by the time Revpower and its political backers convinced the Chinese government to reverse the court's decision, SFAIC had diverted its assets to its owner, the Ministry of Aeronautics and Astronauts in Shanghai. The Chinese courts failed to freeze SFAIC's or its subsidiaries' assets and did not enforce the arbitral decision.[111]

The Shanghai Intermediate Court's failure to abide by the New York Convention in the Revpower case pointed to a yawning chasm between CIETAC and the court system. The Chinese government has focused a great deal of attention on reforming CIETAC, a small centrally-organized body that primarily serves foreign parties and is under the control of central officials. In contrast, the court system is much larger, decentralized, and difficult to monitor and to reform. In addition, rivalries existed between courts at different levels and between local courts and CIETAC, which were manifested in local courts' refusal to enforce CIETAC rulings.[112] A local court has little interest in enforcing arbitral awards against local firms because doing so amounts to a loss of funds and jobs in the court's jurisdiction. Hence, below the provincial level, officials, businesses, and many judges do not always follow legal rules and regulations of the Supreme People's Court and have a limited understanding of Chinese commitments to international conventions.[113] To help improve local judges' commitment to legal norms, the US-China Business Council's legal cooperation fund has paid for training programs for local judges.[114] Cases such as *RevPower v. SFAIC* directed Chinese officials' attention to problems in the arbitration and enforcement process.

To improve compliance with the New York Convention and its own CPL, China had to address its courts as an enforcement mechanism. Since 1995, the Supreme People's Court has required lower courts that wish not to enforce a judgment to gain the approval of the area's High People's Court. If the High People's Court approves, it must forward the non-enforcement decision to the Supreme People's Court's for its approval.[115] Despite the 1995 guidelines, local non-enforcement remains a problem, which the Supreme People's Court addressed with more regulations issued in 2002. The 2002 regulations made Intermediate People's Courts in provincial capitals and designated cities or (basic) People's Courts in investment zones the courts of first instance for enforcing foreign arbitral awards rendered in China.[116] By restricting appeals for enforcement of awards mainly to Intermediate People's Courts and by reserving the right to revoke an intermediate court's jurisdiction, the Supreme People's Court sought to reduce the scope of local legal protectionism. The logic of this shift in enforcement appears to be that courts in SEZs and provincial cities have greater interest in serving the interests of foreign parties because the local economy is more dependent on foreign investment than other sites.

Three more recent cases, *TriNorth Capital, Inc. (Canada) v. Guilin South Rubber (Group) Corporation (China)* and two cases involving Zidell Valve Corporation and Chinese companies in Beijing and Taiyuan provide a mixture of optimism and frustration regarding court enforcement of CIETAC judgments. In 2001, CIETAC awarded TriNorth compensation of $4.2 million in its case, but the Guangxi People's Appeal Court refused to enforce the judgment. Ultimately, the Supreme Court upheld the CIETAC judgment and TriNorth received compensation at a lesser, settled amount ($2.5 million).[117] In 1999, CIETAC awarded Zidell damages against the Chinese companies in separate judgments. After many attempts by lower courts to avoid enforcement of the judgments, the Supreme Court ordered the lower courts to execute the awards. The Beijing defendant finally paid the principal and part of the interest on the award, but the Taiyuan defendant has dragged out any payment of the larger of the two awards.[118] The Supreme People's Court's 2002 Regulation may cut out the worst purveyors of local protectionism, but the Revpower case illustrates that Intermediate People's Courts, even in China's most modern city, can also produce poor, protectionist rulings. Still, the efforts of the Supreme People's Court should be read against a backdrop of efforts to centralize control over the lower courts.

The above examples demonstrate several facets of China's process of reforming commercial arbitration. First, at the macro level, international and multilateral organizations supplied models of international commercial arbitration, which China's state has used to guide its reforms of CIETAC. Second, at the meso and micro levels, foreign law firms and FIEs, respectively, helped to identify shortcomings of China's international commercial arbitration. Third, through training in foreign law firms and while abroad, Chinese lawyers have gained knowledge of international legal forms and adjudication procedures. Consequently, they have formed a policy community that provides information to the state as China reforms its legal system. The rhetoric of Chinese scholars and officials indicates a growing concern for meeting international legal standards such as the UNCITRAL Model. Finally, although China established CIETAC to handle cases involving foreign parties in isolation from the rest of the legal system, foreign parties uncovered tensions between China's courts and CIETAC. Efforts to reform CIETAC necessarily spilled over into the court system, requiring improved training of judges and better adherence to rule of law principles—both of which serve the general population.

Getting Around the Rules: Reliance on *Guanxi*

Although China has revised some of its formal legal institutions with an eye toward international models, China's legal culture, rooted in maintaining harmony through informal, personal bonds, has proved resilient. Moreover, through their interaction with officials, foreign investors have reinforced this emphasis on relations, or *guanxi,* variously translated as "connections," "social ties," and "relations." Since foreign investors began to arrive in Shanghai, they were told that maintaining *guanxi* with local officials was an important aspect of getting things done.[119] In order to attract foreign investors, local officials bent or broke central rules on foreign investment, claiming to have *guanxi* with higher officials to protect investors from reprisal.[120] Foreign investors, for their part, were tempted by claims that good "connections" could subvert the law or could substitute for formal legal protection. Based on the tendency to avoid legal disputes in Japan, Japanese investors and attorneys entered China prepared to rely on personal contacts to manage their relations with officials and with Chinese partners. Japanese attorneys noted that Japanese firms, at least initially, tended to rely too heavily on *guanxi* and not enough on detailed contracts to protect their interests:

> JV agreements between Chinese and western partners have many representation and guarantee articles. Our contracts do not include so many such clauses....We have no previous experience with such thick contracts. But in China, we find that the thicker the contract, the better. When Japanese firms came to China, they thought that they could bring their own culture with them. They were wrong. Many Japanese firms lost cases in courts. This has been a great embarrassment. Japanese firms made many mistakes in writing their contracts.[121]

The following comments from a Japanese general manager reveal how *guanxi* helped his business operate and to subvert formal law: "Sometimes we do things that legally are not possible, but we go to a restaurant with an official, and everything is okay. There are things that are illegal that can be papered over with personal relations. Chinese have commonsense that tells them where those boundaries are, but we as foreigners can never know."[122] The general manager explained that such *guanxi* helped his firm to handle a vehicle accident without going through formal police procedures. Local officials use their connections to help foreign investors, especially when the officials have invested in JVs. In fact, some foreign managers offered local officials the opportunity to invest a small share of a JV's total capital (often channeled through a local government-sponsored investment fund) in order to secure local state backing and protection from strict enforcement of regulations. Reliance on *guanxi* can also feed bribery and corruption. Japanese firms and lawyers relied on *guanxi* in the legal realm, but they also learned to write "thicker contracts" to protect their interests in the formal legal realm, where Chinese businesses have become adept.

The U.S. Foreign Corrupt Practices Act of 1977 forbids U.S. businesses from violating U.S. laws or codes of conduct when operating abroad, which discouraged U.S. firms from engaging in bribery. A U.S. commercial officer noted, "You know, bribery is a slippery slope. If you start early giving out bribes, then it will not stop. You will get a reputation for giving out bribes and more corrupt officials will continue to come."[123] A manager of a U.S.-invested WFOE noted that he receives no solicitations for bribes, but officials may drop hints about wanting gifts.[124] U.S. managers offer gifts to officials, take officials to lunch, and visit important officials in Beijing who can be instrumental in getting things done. One U.S. manager contended that developing relations with Chinese officials was crucial and said that she went "to kowtow to a long line of Buddhas" when she arrived in Shanghai.[125] Many U.S. managers acknowledged that analogous practices exist in the United States such as "old-boy networks" and that they were simply following a familiar pattern of conduct adapted to a new context. A U.S. manager in China said, "Personal relations are important everywhere. Chinese just have a name for it. In the U.S., we do not...well, maybe 'lobbyist.'"[126] A long-time U.S. manager in China described the role that *guanxi* continues to play, "Guanxi can open doors, but you must have a viable project that is within the regulations. *Guanxi* may quicken the process. We got a WFOE project approved in two months instead of the usual six or more months.... *Guanxi* helps you to understand the context of how to conduct business."[127]

U.S. attorneys and firms layer use of *guanxi* onto their practice of detailed formal contracts. U.S. attorneys in Shanghai who are accustomed to operating in a more formal legal environment raised the sharpest criticism of the Chinese practice of using personal relations in the legal realm. U.S. attorneys advise businesses on how to construct detailed contracts to limit the effect of *guanxi* in dispute settlement, for example by including statements in arbitration clauses that call for the head of CIETAC panels hearing their cases to come from a third country. Unlike Japanese firms that tend to substitute *guanxi* for formal legal protections, U.S. businesses and attorneys view reliance on relations as a necessary supplement to formal legal rules to succeed in China's business and legal environment. The pervasiveness in the business realm and applicability to the legal realm distinguish Chinese *guanxi* from the use of social relations in more formalized settings such as the United States.

Although foreign businesses seek formal legal protection for their investment, foreign managers' use of social ties in the Chinese legal system, an informal means of protecting property rights, undermines efforts to build a culture supportive of rule of law. Both local and home country operations bear some of the blame for the reliance on *guanxi* and its corrupting influence. Local officials and partners induce FIE managers to use *guanxi*, and some U.S. firms' headquarters pressure managers to extract insider deals. A long-time manager for an American company who had a leadership post in the Shanghai American Chamber of Commerce recalled the pressure that he felt from his home office to use inside connections illegally to engage in direct sales out of an office set up in Waigaoqiao, a bonded trading area in Pudong, Shanghai, that enjoyed special tax privileges but that bars marketing of products:

> My firm asks why we cannot have distribution in China like the Hong Kong and Taiwanese Chinese. Regulations forbid us to do domestic sales. The Taiwanese and Hong Kong Chinese create these businesses as fronts. They launder money for the mafia. They do not pay personal or firm income tax. The problem arises when you sell a product to someone and the person refuses to pay. You can go to court and the court will look at your contract and see that you do not have distribution rights. Then you are in trouble and will get kicked out. My company asks me why we cannot operate that way, and I ask them, "Do you want to take that chance?"[128]

A regional manager for a U.S. corporation with six factories in China was pressured by his home office to negotiate insider deals through *guanxi*, which he ultimately resisted.[129] Japanese firms replicated their penchant for informal legal affairs in their Chinese subsidiaries, while U.S. firms adapted their combination of legal formalism and "old-boy networks" to the Chinese context. Foreign managers' use of *guanxi* to get things done in China reproduces a culture of legal informality and limits their endeavors to foster rule of law.

Conclusion

The process of legal development in China and, specifically, reform of CIETAC highlights several key points about the dynamics of state-guided globalization. First, the impetus to develop rule of law rather than rule of man came from state officials in the early post-Mao period, but its initial conceptualization was quite narrow and was based on the interests of officials. Second, international organizations and treaties defined parameters of acceptable national legal forms that countries may adopt. Third, foreign investors at the micro level added pressure on China to improve its macro-level legal institutions to better protect investors' property rights. Central officials undertook meaningful reforms of CIETAC, but they initially kept the organization in isolation from other segments of China's legal system, which lagged behind in approaching compliance with international legal norms. Fourth, foreign investors and attorneys mobilized information about international legal norms, such as the UNCITRAL Model, and home-country legal models, such as the handling of expert testimony and adversarial proceedings, to indicate weak points in China's legal system. Over the course of the reform period, China's state moved to adopt many aspects of the international norm on commercial arbitration and provided a more flexible framework for parties to employ elements of an adversarial proceeding, if both parties agreed to such in the arbitration clause of their contract.

Finally, although China's state tried to isolate CIETAC from other areas of the legal system—another instance of dual institutions or a dominant institutional realm supplemented by an institutional sub-regime—the sub-regime had spillover effects into the dominant institutional sphere. The spillover effects have been limited, especially outside the business law realm, but they have all had a positive effect on other areas of the legal system.[130] The wall between domestic and international arbitration organs was formally torn down in 2000, when CIETAC permitted domestic parties to take their cases against other domestic parties to CIETAC for arbitration (earlier, foreign parties could take cases to domestic arbitration bodies). Over time, Chinese officials have made other areas of China's legal realm—including environmental, administrative, and, even, criminal law—open to international scrutiny and advice, some of which they have slowly adopted.[131]

In China, legal change involves the dynamic interaction of formal and informal, and international and domestic elements. China is piecing together a set of legal and arbitration institutions that combine elements of Chinese practice with those from the UNCITRAL Model. Chinese used information flows about international institutions gained from legal cases, complaints, and legal study to revise local legal institutions along the lines of international practice to assuage investors' fears and to garner legitimacy abroad. Many of the complaints raised by MNCs and foreign attorneys about the procedures and practices of CIETAC stemmed from comparisons to the UNCITRAL Model rather than to national law of the United States, an indication of the emergence of a norm on international commercial arbitration.[132] (Japanese arbitration conforms to the UNCITRAL Model, so there is no distinction between Japanese firms' comparisons of Chinese arbitration to the UNCITRAL Model and Japanese arbitration rules.) Chinese officials, especially those associated with CIETAC, draw from the language of international legal institutions to legitimate Chinese legal institutions and to raise China's international standing. In that sense, Chinese officials and scholars are increasingly defining their legitimacy in terms of identity with international institutions.

Part II

Micro- and Meso-level Dynamics and Institutional Change

The three previous chapters focused on how China's leaders adopted macro-level reforms to affect its path of global integration and to meet international norms on political economy as determined by international organizations, treaties, and states. In this section, I focus on micro- and meso-level dynamics in the process of institutional change, and, in particular, I highlight how Japanese and U.S. investors brought distinct institutional models to China. At the micro level, foreign investors form partnerships with local firms, compete with domestic firms and with each other for personnel and sales, and train staff in the practices of international business norms. Foreign firms also institute new institutional models for local firms and state agents to observe and to compare to local practices. At the meso level, policy communities such as managerial and human resources consultants and attorneys take shape, and they combine information on the performance of different institutional models at the micro level with their knowledge of foreign practices. These policy communities can disseminate such information and models to firms at the micro level and state agents at the macro level. Through their combined efforts, foreign firms and policy communities shape institutional sub-regimes. From the menu of models offered by different foreign investors that operate within the sub-regime, Chinese organizations and firms could select appropriate institutions to adopt and to graft onto domestic economic organizations.

Chapter 5 analyzes the above process as it applies to compensation practices. It details the difficulty that state agents faced altering the compensation practices in SOEs, as well as Japanese- and U.S.-invested firms' distinct experiences in applying their home-country practices to China's labor market. Japanese compensation practices, which are rooted in egalitarianism and long-term employment relations, tended to replicate many of the deficiencies of SOEs' "iron rice bowl" model, whereas U.S. compensation models, based on performance-based pay, better appealed to top performers in the Chinese labor market. Feedback from individuals in the labor market encouraged consultants to advocate particular kinds of models, namely those based on pay-for-performance models. State officials pressed SOEs to adopt pay-for-performance models because they helped to resolve readily identifiable problems in SOEs. Interestingly, Japanese firms gradually recognized the difficulties of applying their compensation models in China, but they were slow and resistant to adjust their compensation practices because of their well-defined parent-company rules and cultures.

In chapter 6, I examine how foreign investors from Japan and the United States have affected the development of China's labor market, especially hiring, promotion, and dismissal practices. Until China abandoned its state-unified allocation of labor in the early 1990s, China lacked a functioning free labor market and related basic practices such as job advertisements and job fairs. Foreign firms and consultants helped to transfer those practices to China. Foreign firms also adopted labor contracts and sought and used dismissal procedures against poor-performing employees earlier than SOEs. In these ways, FIEs helped Chinese reformers to institute practices at the micro-level that officials wished to adopt but that SOEs were reluctant to implement. As in the case of compensation practices, distinctions between Japanese and U.S. firms affected the contributions of the two sets of FIEs to this process. U.S. firms' reliance on market-based hiring practices, including mid-career hiring and headhunters, as well as evaluation and dismissal procedures, contrasted sharply to Japanese firms rules on internal (intra-firm) labor markets for promotion and penchant for retraining rather than dismissing poor performers. U.S. firm-level institutions better met identified goals of China's labor market reformers than did Japanese institutions. Hence, SOEs began to gravitate toward U.S. hiring, evaluation, and dismissal practices.

The chapters in this section illuminate several core elements of the process of institutional change: (i) the menu of institutional models that MNCs, business consultants, and lawyers offer based on their home-country origins; (ii) the generation of feedback on different institutional models by average citizens on the job market and firms in competition at the micro level; and (iii) the role of policy communities in aggregating information and feedback on models and the emergence of institutional sub-regimes. The account offered here links micro-processes to the actions of meso-level actors and pressures brought to bear on institutional reformers at the macro level. Ultimately, state officials guide the process of institutional reform and model selection, but they do so in the context of political coalitions, institutional legacies, and perceived feedback on various institutional models in play in the dominant regime and emergent sub-regimes.

5

The Diffusion of Pay-for-Performance Institutions

This chapter and the next address the dynamic interaction between micro-level institutional change and macro-level reforms of labor institutions. The current chapter focuses on compensation institutions, while chapter 6 examines hiring, retention, and dismissal. During the 1990s, by granting space to FIEs to institute their compensation schemes, the Chinese state gave increasing scope to a sub-regime of firm-level institutions that modeled pay-for-performance schemes. In the process of guiding globalization and adopting institutional change, the central state both gained information from foreign investors about alternative models for the reform of SOEs and pressured SOEs to undertake reform of their compensation systems. In other words, through an iterative process between macro- and micro-level actors, the Chinese state laid out basic principles for compensation reforms, gathered information about the functioning of firms with distinct models, reformed macro-level institutions, and combined with competition from micro-level FIEs to pressure SOEs to reform their compensation schemes.

Since China opened its door to foreign investment in 1978, labor practices in FIEs have been a point of concern and contention. Foreign investors have wanted to transplant labor institutions that are familiar to them and that have succeeded in their operations elsewhere, while the Chinese Communist Party has sought to limit the scope of foreign control over sensitive personnel matters such as the number of workers on firms' payrolls, wage rates, promotion, and hiring and firing. Compensation is a crucial and politically charged issue because it involves firms' efforts to motivate workers as well as Chinese and international conceptions of justice in the workplace. Some authors have claimed that foreign investors lower wages and labor standards in host countries, an argument challenged by wage data and empirical studies of China.[1] As the data in Table 5.1 show, average wages in FIEs and TFEs (territorially funded enterprises, including Hong Kong, Taiwan, and Macao) are significantly higher than in SOEs, which have the highest labor standards among Chinese firms. This chapter moves beyond the issue of wage levels in the aggregate to analyze the development of the models of compensation used by SOEs and FIEs and the role that foreign investors have played in China's ongoing compensation reforms. I argue that Chinese officials, frustrated by SOEs' slow progress on wage reforms, allowed foreign investors increasing leeway to introduce new compensation models. These models have enjoyed mixed success, and a sub-regime inspired by U.S. compensation practices has taken root in China and spread to SOEs.

Table 5.1

Average Annual Wages in Foreign-Funded, Territory-Funded, and State-Owned Enterprises (in Chinese *yuan*)

Year	China			Shanghai		
	FFEs	TFEs	SOEs	FFEs	TFEs	SOEs
1985	n.d.	n.d.	1,213	n.d.	n.d.	n.d.
1986	2,380	1,613	n.d.	n.d.	n.d.	n.d.
1987	2,826	1,830	n.d.	n.d.	n.d.	n.d.
1988	n.d.	2,966	1,853	n.d.	n.d.	n.d.
1989	3,567	2,995	2,055	n.d.	n.d.	n.d.
1990	3,411	3,687	2,284	n.d.	n.d.	n.d.
1991	3,918	n.d.	2,477	n.d.	n.d.	n.d.
1992	4,347	4,740	2,878	n.d.	n.d.	n.d.
1993	5,315	5,147	3,532	8,532	7,068	5,777
1994	6,533	6,376	4,797	11,445	9,597	7,534
1995	8,058	7,484	5,625	13,277	10,464	9,578
1996	9,383	8,334	6,280	15,696	12,743	11,015
1997	10,361	9,329	6,747	16,857	14,175	11,733
1998	11,767	10,027	7,668	n.d.	n.d.	13,746
1999	12,951	10,991	8,543	n.d.	n.d.	16,852
2000	14,372	11,914	9,552	23,525	17,232	18,865
2001	16,101	12,544	11,178	28,787	19,625	21,961
2002	17,892	13,756	12,869	30,192	19,583	24,719
2003	19,366	14,691	14,577	32,674	22,061	28,406

Source: Chinese Economic Statistical Yearbook Editorial Committee, *Chinese Economic Yearbook* (Beijing: Chinese Economic Yearbook Publishers, various years).

Chinese officials and foreign enterprise managers agreed that the legacy of Mao-era labor practices discouraged productivity and required change. Coming out of the Mao era, Chinese industrial work culture was aptly named the "iron rice bowl" because it provided extraordinary job security and equally rewarded workers for excellent and poor work habits.[2] The labor system thwarted initiative, rewarded seniority, and failed to punish poor performance. Moreover, the system encouraged managers to add staff to their work rolls, despite mounting economic losses for SOEs. In 1986, the *Renmin Ribao* estimated that 10 workers were often employed where five would have sufficed,[3] which fostered poor worker performance.[4] Beginning in 1978, Chinese authorities sought to crack the "iron rice bowl," thereby initiating reform of Mao-era labor institutions.

China's work culture impeded foreign investors' efforts to motivate local workers to meet international and company production standards, and they derided Chinese managers' resistance to attempts to reorganize the workplace.[5] The challenge for foreign investors and Chinese officials has been to redesign labor institutions to tap Chinese workers' latent productivity without unleashing social upheaval by workers. Complicating foreign investors' efforts, Chinese human resource and assistant general managers, who often had transferred in from SOEs and who were accustomed to the "iron rice bowl" model, typically sought to maintain control over labor institutions in the foreign-invested enterprises. Until recently, such Chinese human resources managers in JVs typically were party officials and who cleaved to egalitarian compensation institutions. Although Chinese authorities have sought to induce compensation reforms in Chinese firms, many leaders remained guarded about foreign capitalists leading the process.

In recent years, scholars have begun to analyze the interplay between labor reforms in state- and foreign-funded enterprises and have found that FIEs have affected SOEs' labor reforms in a number of ways.[6] Existing explanations for the interplay of foreign investment and labor reforms in China have emphasized officials' use of FIEs as "laboratories" for experimenting with reforms to be adopted in SOEs, mimicry of FIEs, competition between FIEs and SOEs forcing SOEs to adopt FIEs' labor models, and organizational linkages between SOEs and foreign firms in JVs.[7] Here, the focus is on distinct models that foreign investors brought to China, which shaped the process by which models for reform are selected and spread.

Previous studies of China's labor reforms have failed to explain what model(s) China has used for its reforms—and why. Too often, analyses of globalization depict the process as pitting foreign actors, usually international economic organizations, such as the IMF and multinational corporations (MNCs),[8] versus local actors such as local firms and/or labor. The chapter disaggregates how Japanese and U.S. investors interacted with China's workers and labor institutions. Japanese and U.S. investors' distinct compensation schemes, which formed a menu of institutional models that officials and firms could choose to adopt, generated different results and reactions from Chinese workers. The poor result of Japanese compensation schemes has caused Japanese firms to revise their models in China and has given pause to Chinese leaders who initially advocated adoption of Japanese labor practices. Wage reforms touch upon central themes of this book: a menu of FIEs' institutional models that China could emulate; FIEs' training of human resources personnel who formed a policy community and helped to diffuse institutions to Chinese organizations; and the emergence of sub-regimes of new institutional models for mimicry.

Japanese labor practices held out the possibility of inducing higher levels of productivity while maintaining a cooperative labor-management relation-ship.[9] U.S. firms tend to stratify wages and generate contentious industrial relations, which seem a poor fit for reformers who have feared social upheaval generated by SOE reforms. Comparing the human resources practices of Japanese and U.S. investors in China and the problems encountered by both clarifies why Chinese firms belatedly have shifted toward a U.S. model of labor practices. Japanese labor institutions have not motivated Chinese employees well, while U.S. firms' human resources practices have attracted ambitious staff. In practice, U.S. labor institutions have helped to overcome many of the problems of China's lingering "iron rice bowl" culture, while Japanese investors have tended to replicate such problems. Japanese firms, too, have begun to adopt U.S.-inspired labor institutions in the China-based subsidiaries and in their parent companies in Japan.

The chapter begins with an outline of the "iron rice bowl" and state compensation reforms, which demonstrate that state officials, early on in the reform period, had identified problems in the work culture as well as basic responses to those problems. Next, I analyze the efforts of foreign investors to transfer their compensation institutions to China, and, related, the com-parable success of those institutions in China. The sections on Japanese and U.S. compensation systems reveal the distinct approaches taken by foreign investors and the adjustment processes that each have undertaken in China. Finally, I analyze how foreign investors and Chinese actors have contributed to Chinese wage reforms.

The "Iron Rice Bowl" Model under Reform

In 1956, China adopted a Soviet-style wage system that lasted until 1976 with just modest reforms. The wage system assigned each worker a job clas-sification, which had 6–8 grades of pay, resulting in a quite flat wage scale. The system also minimized labor incentives, especially during the radical leftist periods under Mao. Officials and managers eliminated or restricted piece rates and bonuses because they were associated with capitalist mate-rial incentives.[10] Over the course of the Mao era, seniority in a firm largely determined workers' promotion and pay, rendering a highly egalitarian wage distribution within firms. Moreover, national policy rather than firm managers determined pay increases, which undermined efforts by managers to link individual workers' productivity to pay.[11] Under the "iron rice bowl" model, state officials assigned workers to jobs in SOEs and had to approve any transfer of workers to other jobs, a rare occurrence.[12] Equally important, managers in SOEs rarely fired workers, in part because they faced severe obstacles and had little financial incentive to do so.

In 1978, China set out to undermine the egalitarian principles that underlay the "iron rice bowl" and "eating from one pot." In 1978, the State Council passed a notice titled, "Implement the Socialist Principle of Distribution According to Work (*Anlao Fenpei*)." In a speech in support of the notice, Deng Xiaoping asserted, "distribution according to labor is socialist and not capitalist" and that rewards and punishments should be used to encourage workers' productivity.[13] "Distribution according to labor" became a general term for introducing incentives into the Chinese labor system and a guiding principle for Chinese wage and bonus reform. In 1979, the state announced a round of wage adjustments in SOEs, the intent of which was to reward workers' "merit and contributions."[14]

Editorials complained that the "iron rice bowl" led to overstaffing, poor worker productivity, and slack discipline.[15] The state authorities adopted several policies to devolve control over wages and bonuses to factory managers in an effort to unleash workers' productive potential. One of the first wage reforms was a revival of piece rates. Reformers claimed that piece rates embodied the principle of "distribution according to labor" (*anlao fenpei*) and reformers argued that the piece rate, although not universally applicable, helped to measure each worker's output and to establish a direct connection between wages and production.[16] The piece-rate wage system had the potential to upset the existing wage system, which allocated pay based on work norms, on seniority, and on position grades.

By 1980, firms experimented with "floating wages" and other performance-based pay schemes, specifically to improve labor productivity.[17] Floating wages, linked to output, contrasted to "fixed wages," which compensated for time worked. To advance Chinese modernization, reformers needed to establish clearer links between workers' output and pay. Typically, the floating wages linked either a component of individual's wages to his or her performance or a component of the enterprise's wage pool to enterprise profitability.[18] Similarly, the state linked bonus funds to the profits of enterprises, which fostered some differentiation of bonuses across enterprises, but within enterprises managers paid little attention to workers' individual productivity when handing out bonuses.[19] Some enterprises raised their floating wages faster than their productivity and profits rose, leading to an acceleration of wages and perpetuating the gulf between pay and performance. With soft budget constraints, SOEs had strong incentive to raise staff wages and bonuses, regardless of productivity. To limit enterprises' ability to indiscriminately raise wages, the state linked the firms' increase in their wage pools to their level of profit tax paid to the state.[20] If firms gave out wages above the targeted increases, they had to pay extra taxes.[21]

In 1985, SOEs adopted a "structural wage" system that consisted of three parts: basic or fixed wages (*jiben gongzi* or *guding gongzi*), positional wages (*gangwei gongzi*), and floating wages (*fudong gongzi*).[22] These rather modest reforms provided some linkage between workers' wages and performance. In SOEs, workers and some managers resisted piece rates and other performance-based pay schemes.[23] After 1985, despite receiving formal authority to introduce new differentiated pay schemes, many SOE managers persisted in slowly promoting workers based on seniority and raising workers' wages and bonuses in an egalitarian fashion.[24] State regulations linked enterprises' total wage funds to their economic performance. The June 4, 1989, demonstrations by students and workers highlighted the political tensions generated by inflation, reduction of subsidies, and inequality that reforms to SOEs and urban social services had begun to generate. The political climate that followed the suppression of the movement stalled most efforts to reform SOE labor institutions for several years.[25] Through the 1980s, wage and bonus reforms did not produce great changes in the "iron rice bowl" culture or practice in SOEs.[26] Changes in the composition of workers' total pay help to gauge the progress of SOE compensation reforms. Growth of variable components of total pay evinces SOEs' modest success at introducing pay-for-performance schemes. In 1978, bonuses and piece rates comprised a scant 2.4 percent of SOEs' total wage bill, but a decade later reached 19.5 percent, and fluctuated around the 19.5 percent mark for the period 1988–1995 (see Table 5.2). Growth of the bonus component of total wages was shaped by state policy, which allowed factories to offer the equivalent of up to four months pay to workers as a bonus.[27] The overall growth of bonuses as a share of total compensation masks managers' tendency to allocate bonuses in an egalitarian fashion. The variable component of pay increased without much differentiation in allocation.[28] In comparison to SOEs and Chinese collective enterprises, FIEs have relied more on flexible wage components such as piece rates and bonuses as a share of the total wage bill. During the period 1984–1995, foreign invested enterprises gave 19.6–25.5 percent of their total wage bill in the form of bonuses and piece rates. Excepting 1991 and 1992, the foreign invested enterprises' figures on bonuses and piece rates were higher than the same figures for SOEs (see Table 5.2). These figures give a rough indication of foreign firms' use of variable compensation components to induce hard work, while SOEs were tied down by their heavy subsidy burden.

Allowances and subsidies, on the other hand, continued to grow throughout the reform period. In SOEs, bonuses and piece rates never surpassed allowances and subsidies. Two factors contributed to the steady rise of allowances and subsidies. First, state officials and SOE managers were unwilling to abandon their commitments to subsidies because of the political turmoil that might ensue. The June 4, 1989, protest movement is an example of growing

Table 5.2

Bonuses and Piece Rates as a Percentage of Total Wage Bill by Enterprise Type

Year	SOEs	COEs	Joint Ownership and FIEs
1978	2.41	n.d.	n.d.
1980	9.70	6.50	n.d.
1984	16.43	16.18	22.22
1985	14.53	16.84	22.03
1988	19.53	18.01	20.00
1989	19.97	17.57	23.60
1990	19.09	14.56	20.87
1991	19.95	14.56	19.60
1992	22.21	15.06	20.83
1993	23.27	16.59	25.51
1994	17.89	15.29	24.19
1995	16.84	13.57	21.68

Source: Chinese Economic Statistical Yearbook Editorial Committee, *Chinese Economic Yearbook* (Beijing: Chinese Economic Yearbook Publishers, various years).

urban angst produced by eroding social guarantees and rising urban unemployment.[29] Second, urban inflation in general—and housing costs in particular—spiked during economic cycles, and the state had to raise subsidies to meet soaring prices. Commitment to such allowances and subsidies was partly to blame for SOEs' declining financial situation.

Even though state officials recognized the growing rate of subsidies and allowances as a financial problem, they did not seriously tackle the problem until the mid-1990s. The incremental reforms of the mid-1980s, in the long run, might have helped solve the problems of SOE subsidies and allowances, but the June 4, 1989, protest movement derailed any progress for a number of years. Worker participation in the 1989 protest movement (and in earlier protests of the 1980s) underscored the urban working class's disaffection over rising prices and their eroding living standard.[30] Political commitment to subsidies limited the capacity of SOE managers—some of whom were committed to wage reforms—to introduce pay-for-performance schemes.

Not until the 1990s (especially after the passage of the 1994 Labor Law), did the SOEs' wage system noticeably shift, at least for some workers and in selected industries. According to a study by Minghua Zhao and Theo Nichols, SOEs in the textile industry faced extremely harsh wage practices, such as docking workers' pay for poor performance, speeding up production, and increasing work hours.[31] Migrant contract workers who found jobs in SOEs (and FIEs) faced the harshest working conditions and had the most tenuous jobs.[32] The expansion of migrant labor hiring in SOEs, however, was merely layering a supplementary labor institution onto the dominant labor model to save SOEs, rather than a substantial reform of the "iron rice bowl."

In sum, through the mid-1990s, SOEs had made limited advances in meeting the substantive goals of their wage reforms, despite Chinese officials and academics having identified core problems and possible solutions to the "iron rice bowl" model as early as 1978. SOEs reintroduced bonuses, piece rates, and floating wages, but the actual distribution of the various forms of wages persisted down a path of egalitarianism. In practice, reformers found it difficult to get bureaucrats and SOE managers and employees to adopt new institutional models. Piecemeal reform occurred as incentive-laden wage institutions were layered onto egalitarian wage elements and informal normative expectations of workers. Hence, labor productivity did not rise significantly, but instead trailed behind wage growth.[33] The SOEs that did switch to radical wage reforms too often veered toward exploitative compensation systems in which reform measures were used to punish and fine workers rather than to provide inducements to raise productivity.

Foreign Investors and Shifts in Chinese Wage Institutions

At the forefront of some of China's wage reforms were overseas Chinese investors who set up factories in special economic zones, Shenzhen being the earliest success story.[34] Many reports praised the practices in Shenzhen FIEs, especially in the area of wage and labor reforms.[35] The Shenzhen wage system was based on workers receiving three forms of pay: (i) base wages; (ii) post or position wages; and (iii) floating pay.[36] In 1985, the same model was adopted by SOEs. Enterprises were allowed to emphasize the floating wage component to induce greater labor effort. In Shenzhen, the preponderance of firms was from Hong Kong, and authors noted that the Shenzhen labor model was developing along the lines of Hong Kong.[37] As early as 1983, Chinese papers acknowledged the punitive aspects of the Shenzhen firms' wage systems, though some of the early articles lauded such an approach. For example, the *Renmin Ribao* backed Shenzhen managers who reduced workers' floating wages for early departures from work or failure to show up for work,[38] which was lauded at the time.

Formally, regulations made special provision for the introduction of wage reforms in JVs, although officials limited FIEs' wage reforms in practice. In JVs, the boards of directors were allowed to determine their firms' wage, bonus, and subsidy systems.[39] At the time, Chinese regulations stipulated that the Chinese partner had the authority to appoint the chair of the board of directors,[40] which effectively ceded control over wage practices to the Chinese partner. Local authorities also maintained some regulatory control over the parameters of JVs' pay schemes by reviewing and approving the collective contracts signed by JVs and their workers.[41]

In the early stages of China's opening to foreign investment, Chinese officials carefully regulated foreign firms outside of the SEZs. Regulations prescribed that JVs pay workers 120–150 percent of the average wage for SOEs in the same industry in the locale—an attempt to squeeze higher wages out of foreign investors without creating wide disparities with workers' wages in SOEs.[42] Anecdotal evidence from early JVs outside of Shenzhen suggests that many SOE partners transplanted egalitarian labor practices into JVs.[43] Early JVs were known for chronic overstaffing, poor labor productivity, and egalitarianism, which were forced upon the foreign investors by Chinese managers, who typically controlled human resource functions.

The circumstances in Shenzhen allowed for greater wage experimentation than elsewhere in the country. First, as a rural area that was converted to an SEZ and that grew into a major city, Shenzhen had few SOEs and mainly young, non-unionized, rural employees who entered FIEs, a stark contrast to the older blue-collar workforce that transferred into many of the JVs established with large SOE partners in other parts of China.[44] Second, Guangdong Province was allowed to experiment with reforms, and Shenzhen was granted leeway to introduce labor reforms.

Although lauded for its early wage reforms, by the late 1980s, Shenzhen labor practices came under critical scrutiny. In Shenzhen, some firms violated national policies and laws by hiring child laborers,[45] refusing to allow workers to organize trade unions, requiring excessive overtime,[46] and failing to compensate for overtime.[47] The dilemma for state reformers—balancing tough reform measures with protection of workers' interests—was encapsulated by the following statement by Zhang Bai, office director of the Shenzhen Municipal Federation of Trade Unions: "The union had to accept that workers were being exploited...but it was their job to make sure they were not exploited too much."[48] During the period June 1989–December 1990, 69 strikes broke out in Shenzhen factories—including town-, county-, and foreign-funded enterprises.[49] That so many strikes, which are not legally guaranteed, broke out in the repressive climate of the period immediately following June 4, 1989, a time when "social stability" was the watchword, must have deeply concerned officials. In the early 1990s, a high level of labor disputes and strikes persisted in Shenzhen.[50] According to Anita Chan, Asian investors—mainly from Hong Kong, Taiwan, and South Korea—were the worst violators of Chinese labor laws in Shenzhen and other parts of Guangdong Province.[51] The rather harsh and exploitative labor regime in Shenzhen, which was heavily influenced by labor-intensive firms from Hong Kong (and Taiwan and South Korea), lost some of its luster.

Outside the SEZs, FIEs made little headway in transferring their pay schemes during the first decade of China's opening to foreign direct investment. One study of SOEs and JVs conducted in 1995–1996 showed that JVs had limited success in instituting "globalized" human resource practices.[52] Opposition from Chinese partners undermined JVs' efforts to transplant the labor practices of their foreign investors' parent companies. In brown-field investments such as JVs and with personnel who have taken on the norms of a workplace, managers find it very difficult to change the work culture and to substitute new cognitive scripts.[53] A close examination of U.S. and Japanese firms' experiences illustrate the process and the difficulty of institutional change and diffusion.

Japanese Firms and Shanghai Workers

In the early and mid-1990s two policy changes altered the ability of FIEs to transplant their human resource regimes to China: the easing of formal and informal restrictions on investment in WFOEs and passage of the 1994 Labor Law. Rooted in their home-country institutions, Japanese firms primarily introduced collectivist incentive programs that linked wages and bonuses to group performance and sought to institute loyalty to the firm, while U.S. firms tended to rely more on individualized, market-based mechanisms.[54] During the 1990s, Chinese policy makers looked favorably upon Japanese labor institutions and authors encouraged their adoption by Chinese firms.

Wages

In Japan, to encourage loyalty and the retention of trained workers, large corporations steadily increased workers' pay according to time spent with the company. Beginning in the 1950s, to improve upon the original seniority pay system, corporations began to consider workers' skill level in pay determination.[55] The outcome was the "seniority-plus-merit" system.[56] Accordingly, firms developed quite detailed wage tables to determine wages for workers, taking into account levels of education, skill, position, and seniority. After successful evaluations, workers may receive a step increase in wages based on the wage tables. In exceptional cases, a worker might receive a two-step increase in pay, a form of merit wage increase.[57] Workers who depart the firm for jobs in other corporations face a loss of accrued wages and benefits, which discourages mid-career job shifts.

The Japanese distribution of income is quite egalitarian in comparison to wages in U.S. firms.[58] Firms prevent income differentials from widening by limiting the remuneration differences for persons at the same level and rank and by avoiding gross inequities between production workers and management. A particularly egalitarian element of Japan's pay pattern is the rather narrow gap between blue-collar and white-collar workers, what Kazuo Koike has called the "white collarization" of Japanese blue-collar workers, which helps to foster a shared corporate identity.[59]

Approximately, 70 percent of the surveyed Japanese operations in Shanghai implemented a modified version of their seniority pay scheme in

Shanghai. One Japanese-invested representative office used a seniority pay scheme that included equal starting salaries for newly hired employees, gradual pay increases for the first 30 years of employment, small periodic bonuses, and across-the-board pay increases for employees.[60] Another Sino-Japanese electronics JV adapted a Chinese SOE pay system that was similar to the Japanese company's model, which emphasized seniority and large base salaries supplemented by small bonuses.[61] Many of these wage practices were analogous to Chinese wage institutions.

Japanese firms in Shanghai paid wages that compared favorably to domestic enterprises. In this sample, for the year 1999, the handful of U.S. and Hong Kong firms' trading offices paid on average, RMB 61,000 (US$7,376) per person, and Japanese trading offices paid RMB 47,750 (US$5,774) per person. American manufacturing enterprises in Shanghai paid their workers, on average RMB 39,436 (US$4,769), while Japanese manufacturers paid RMB 26,150 (US$3,169) per worker.[62] In part, the large differences in pay are explained by U.S. firms' greater degree of staff localization relative to Japanese firms. Expatriates take the most lucrative positions in firms, so high levels of localization raise the average local pay rate in a subsidiary. A Chinese human resources manager in a Japanese subsidiary in Shanghai claimed that, according to a study conducted by Japanese firms, Japanese companies paid more than Western firms to workers in similar jobs,[63] but the top positions were taken by expatriates in Japanese firms and were more likely to be localized in U.S. firms.

By 2000, nearly all interviewed managers of Japanese firms were dissatisfied with the operation of their wage and bonus schemes and had begun or planned to revise their compensation method. Specifically, Japanese managers complained that their compensation schemes led to poor worker motivation and high levels of labor turnover, especially among lower- and middle-level managers. Since China's opening to foreign investment in 1978, Japanese managers slowly realized that Chinese workers were motivated by different institutions than Japanese workers, and that attempts to transfer Japanese practices to Shanghai would not unleash the full potential of China's workforce.

The problem for Japanese companies is less the amount of pay than the method of determining pay. Interviewees agreed that Chinese workers prefer U.S. pay and promotion schemes to those offered by Japanese corporations.[64] Typical of the views held by expatriate managers, a Japanese office manager noted, "In general, Chinese, and especially people from Shanghai, are close to the U.S. way of thinking. I spent four years in Chicago, and people here act the same way. They want a higher salary, and they respond to incentives."[65] A Chinese human resources manager in a Japanese subsidiary in Shanghai claimed:

> For one group of Chinese workers, steady pay is important. For these workers, as long as they don't make any mistakes and work

well enough, then working at a Japanese company is a very good opportunity. They are not likely to leave the company. A new graduate who enters the company may feel that there is no space to advance. The person might think that his/her bonuses cannot grow, and s/he cannot advance in the company. Most people who want to leave are at the basic levels of management.[66]

Japanese managers recognized that the egalitarian Japanese model of wage distribution did not mesh well with China's workers, or at least not its most ambitious ones. In the worst cases, Japanese firms lost their most ambitious employees to U.S. and western European firms and were left with poor-performing local staff who sought job stability with lower wage rates rather than less security but opportunity for job advancement. Lower-skill production workers in Japanese (and U.S.) firms tend to stay in their positions due to limited job opportunities, but ambitious (and capable) white-collar staff leave for other firms. In one extreme case, a Japanese chemical company lost its entire research team to U.S. and European subsidiaries.[67]

Bonuses

Japanese firms offer bonuses to both managerial and non-managerial staff alike, usually twice a year, a pattern that resembles Chinese practice, albeit with a stronger linkage to group performance. Firms determine bonuses according to company performance and individual appraisal. Over time, such bonuses have varied in size, diminishing in recent years, but each bonus tallies one or more months' worth of base wages. Within a company, bonuses differed little as a share of monthly base wages, an egalitarian aspect of Japanese remuneration. If a worker opts to leave in the middle of a work year, the worker would lose a substantial portion of his or her salary in the form of a foregone bonus.

In Shanghai, most Japanese firms gave out bonuses that varied based on workers' job grades and pay levels, a replication of parent company practice.[68] For example, a Japanese general manager in a Sino-Japanese JV described how the JV adopted the Japanese parent company's bonus system: "We give bonuses out according to a worker's grade (5 grades). This is completely according to the Japanese company model. The bonus differences are determined by the grade and worker's pay level. People at the same level and pay get the same bonus."[69] Both Chinese and Japanese managers in Japanese-invested enterprises came to recognize that the Japanese bonus model inadequately motivated Chinese workers.[70] A Chinese human resources manager analyzed Japanese firms' approach to pay and the resulting flat pay scale:

> Japanese people have a guiding principle, that the company's success is a collective enterprise rather than an individual's enterprise. They emphasize collectivism rather than individualism. They really emphasize this point, and it shapes their compensation structure. Fixed

wages are relatively large, but bonuses are very, very small. Such a small bonus really has no use. At the same time, their wage structure is very flat. I get a bonus that is just a couple hundred *yuan* more than an average worker.[71]

Japanese labor institutions focus on collective work and appraisal, which has limited their capacity to use individual performance as a basis of constructing wage and even bonus reforms.

Wage and Bonus Reform

By 2000, Japanese firms had begun to introduce wage and bonus reforms because Japanese firms in Shanghai encountered two problems: higher-than-expected labor turnover (to be discussed in chapter 6) and poor worker motivation. Rather than inducing greater firm loyalty and motivation to make the firm succeed, flat, seniority-plus-merit pay schemes induced the opposite. In Shanghai, Japanese firms encountered labor market conditions quite different from those in Japan, namely workers with short time horizons and keen competition for hiring mid-career workers. Japanese firms' reforms had two main thrusts: to allow greater salary differentiation and to enhance compensation for individual performance. To do so, Japanese managers had to depart from company norms. Using bonuses as an incentive for individual work was, according to one Japanese manager, "alien to the Japanese way of thinking."[72]

A Japanese general manager explained some of the radical steps taken to alter the wage structure and culture of work in the Shanghai subsidiary that he managed:

We have started a new wage system, in which fixed wages will be determined by workers' performances. Previously, fixed wages were determined by seniority...Mainly, we want to use a clear method to indicate workers' performances. We have nothing like this in Japan: on a wall in the factory, we have a chart showing each worker's productivity so that all can see how they are doing. This helps motivate workers to perform.[73]

Such a reform is especially significant because their previous model was a combination of Japanese and Chinese institutions implemented by Chinese human resources managers. Ultimately, the JV rejected the Japanese parent company's approach in pursuit of a U.S.-inspired pay-for-performance model.

Another Japanese firm posted workers' daily output on a board, but added an element, foul cards ("red" and "yellow," as in soccer) to show workers who had failed to meet a quota or quality standards.[74] The factory adopted a bonus system that gave out widely varying bonuses, which appealed to the Chinese assistant manager.[75] Clearly, the above methods rewarded high-performing workers but also disciplined poor performers. A third Japanese factory also instituted the soccer foul approach to discipline workers:

> We have to add pressure (*yali*) to make them work hard. We use yellow and red cards to assign penalties to workers. For example, workers are supposed to be back from lunch at a certain time. If they come in late, it is a penalty. We do not use fines, but total the points during the year. Each penalty is assigned a number of points. If during the year a person receives 100 or more penalty points, he or she can have their contract terminated. We also have averages for productivity in each position. You do not have to be above average to receive incentives, but you cannot fall below a minimum standard. These methods may be related to a Japanese style of management. If this was a factory that started hiring workers from scratch, we would not have to do this. We have a lot of former SOE employees.[76]

According to the Chinese assistant manager, the Japanese company's labor incentives failed to mesh well with Chinese workers' interests, especially those who were accustomed to the "iron rice bowl" model, which forced the firm to use the threat of coercion to increase labor productivity. The comments underscore a problem of institutional change: it is more difficult to alter the informal, taken-for-granted labor practices (or "cognitive scripts") of old workers in an existing factory than it is to introduce new scripts to recently hired workers in new factories.[77]

In some JVs, Japanese managers were reluctant to depart from their parent company compensation practices. A Japanese manager of a trading company in Shanghai explained how company practices and norms discouraged reforms in overseas subsidiaries, "The local staff has worked here for many years, but the Japanese staff changes every three years. If we do not have trouble with our tenure here, we will have no trouble transferring back to Japan after our three years are over. If we try to change things much here, we might have trouble transferring back to Japan. Some Japanese managers avoid scolding staff because they fear that it might cause trouble."[78] Rather than risk undertaking unsuccessful reforms or disrupting harmony within their subsidiary's operation, many seasoned Japanese managers stuck to company rules and norms.

Young local managers who had weak attachment to Japanese and Chinese SOE labor institutions, however, readily identified poor-performing parent company institutions and pressed for compensation reforms in some Japanese-invested firms. Within Japanese JVs, Japanese managers sometimes reined in attempts by Chinese managers to devise pay-for-performance schemes. Chinese managers' support for compensation reforms helped to convince the Japanese manager that introducing such reforms would not create divisions within the firm. As outsiders in Japanese-invested enterprises, Chinese managers were less committed to the Japanese bonus system than expatriate managers. Hence, Chinese managers were more open to revising Japanese institutions in Shanghai, while many Japanese managers cleaved to parent company practices.

Parent Company and Subsidiary Wage Reforms

Analyzing Japanese subsidiaries' wage reforms is complicated by shifting compensation practices in Japanese parent firms. When the Japanese recession of the mid- and late 1990s deepened, parent companies in Japan undertook their own human resource reforms, which sought to model some aspects of U.S. practice. In particular, many Japanese parent firms adopted "management by objective" (MBO) programs, which linked wages and promotion to evaluations of performance on meeting objectives or targets.[79] Japanese firms introduced MBO to attack the collectivist orientation in Japanese companies and to spur individual labor productivity, which were partly blamed for Japan's prolonged economic slump of the 1990s.

In Tokyo human resources managers complained about the difficulty of implementing MBO methods in Japanese companies. The introduction of MBO hinged on two aspects of individuals' definition in Japanese firms—clarification of job descriptions and differentiated pay—both of which conflicted with firm-level norms. Parent companies shaped some of the wage reforms in their subsidiaries in China. Initially, Japanese parent firms were reluctant to allow their subsidiaries in Shanghai to have free rein to revise the wage and bonus system. Despite the gradual shift toward an American model of quicker promotion and greater pay differentiation in Japan, parent companies slowed what they considered to be too aggressive institutional reforms in subsidiaries. For example, one company was shocked by a request from its expatriate manager in Shanghai to raise a particular worker's salary 100 percent in a single year.[80] Ultimately, many parent companies determined that foreign subsidiaries should enjoy a fair amount of autonomy in devising their human resource systems.[81]

In 2000, a Sino-Japanese JV in the machinery industry revised its pay system to enhance the role of bonuses in workers' pay. The JV made bonuses approximately 50 percent of workers' total pay. By making one-half of the total pay variable, the company sought to raise labor productivity.[82] Similar to the MBO model, the Sino-Japanese JV used standardized performance criteria to determine the size of workers' bonuses.[83] In 2000, a Japanese high-tech company introduced a bonus system that allowed individuals' bonuses to vary between 50–250 percent of the average bonus. Bonuses were linked to semi-annual appraisals by managers who were uncomfortable in their new role of assigning differentiated grades for workers. The company headquarters' human resources division had to conduct extensive training for managers to learn how to conduct such evaluations. Interestingly, according to a human resources manager at the parent company headquarters, the company introduced the same reforms in its Shanghai JV three years earlier.

> All along, we were eager to change. But in Japanese society, it was
> difficult to apply the changes. Reforms were easier to apply abroad—
> people there were eager to adopt a western system. Local workers easily
> adapted to such a system. Especially in the case of China, where there
> is a law forcing employers to have labor contracts, we had to have very
> clear policies on salaries and evaluations. It was easier to propose and
> to implement wage reforms under such conditions. We are only on our
> way to such a change in Japan.[84]

The case study is significant not just because of the different responses of
workers in Japan and China to the company's labor reforms, but also because
the Japanese company made greater headway in its wage and bonus reforms
in China than in Japan. The company did not learn from China how to organize its pay system, but it used its Chinese JV as a laboratory for experimenting with reforms.[85] Among Chinese managers and workers, Japanese labor
institutions were less routinized than in Japan and, therefore, the cognitive
scripts were easier to rewrite.

Despite efforts to reform wage and bonus systems in Japanese subsidiaries, interviewees in 2003 and 2005 complained that Japanese firms still faced
problems within their firms because of flat pay scales. Japanese firms' progress in developing pay-for-performance schemes fell short of their U.S. and
European competitors, and Japanese firms remained disappointed with the
meshing of their labor institutions with the Chinese labor force. In particular,
Chinese managerial staff were frustrated by the modest reforms introduced
by their Japanese employers. Some of the Chinese staff became proponents
of pay-for-performance schemes in Japanese enterprises.

Case Study of a Japanese Electronics JV

In Japan, major corporations typically face very low labor turnover, yet a
well-known Japanese electronics manufacturer in Shanghai encountered
10–15 percent labor turnover on an annual basis. The Shanghai affiliate
had no record of firing workers, so labor turnover was a function of voluntary quits. The firm in question had a well-developed company culture and
human resources management system, which it diligently transferred to its
Shanghai facility. Indeed, the parent company spent a large amount of time
and money inculcating their company culture among employees and training workers. Such a labor turnover rate indicates that the Japanese company's
human resource program had failed to achieve its desired outcome: a loyal,
well-trained labor force. A brief account of the company's labor turnover
woes highlights three points: (i) the difficulty of meshing Japanese business
culture with Shanghai staff; (ii) the interconnectedness of various components of the firm's human resources program; and (iii) Japanese companies'
need to adapt parent-company institutions to China's environment.

The Japanese parent company transferred its wage and bonus tables, which linked wages to a worker's position and skills to the Shanghai subsidiary. Differences among workers' wages and, particularly, bonuses were quite compressed. Parent company wage tables kept employees' starting salaries quite low. Recent college graduates in China often have the highest skill levels in factories, yet they were asked to accept pay below the local standard for the industry and position, which caused dissatisfaction and turnover. In addition, workers underwent annual evaluations and received letter grades, from "A" to "D," to determine bonus amounts. A worker who received an "A" grade was awarded the equivalent of 1.6 months' pay for their semi-annual bonus; a "B" received 1.4 months' pay, a "C" earned 1.2 months' pay, and a "D" earned 0.9 months' pay, a quite flat allocation. According to the Chinese assistant general manager, the bonus compression created a troubling response: "Good workers view such bonuses as too low, but mediocre workers think the bonuses are very satisfying."[86] The polarized opinions caused able workers to seek employment at other firms, while average and poor-performing workers stayed with the company.

In Japan, wage and bonus compression is acceptable because of long-term employment and a clear, if slow, promotional pattern. Company rules stipulated that workers spend at least five years with the company prior to consideration for promotion and that the subsidiary could only promote workers from within the company. The seniority-based promotion system caused young Chinese workers' dissatisfaction with employment at the company. The Chinese assistant manager lamented, "College graduates are not happy with our company's system; they think that our promotion system is too slow....If the young hires keep leaving the firm, we will face a future problem of having no young managers to promote. So, we are reconsidering our promotion system."[87] The poor meshing of company rules with local labor market conditions and local workers' values contributed to the company's labor turnover problems.

Japanese workers have observed the operation of their companies' human resource system and have grown accustomed to working within such a framework. Shanghai workers who are drawn to foreign-invested enterprises seek an alternative to the SOE culture. In particular, local workers seek fast promotion, high pay, and clear rewards for hard work. Those workers who cleave to "iron rice bowl" principles may be satisfied with Japanese slow promotion, but they may not be the best performing staff. Ultimately, the Japanese-invested company slowly began to insert more incentives and earlier consideration for promotion into their human resource system to suit the Chinese workforce. In the year 1999, the Shanghai subsidiary began to offer new recruits and managers special compensation for educational achievement. Such a program may help to stem the outflow of talented young local managers, but it clearly violates parent company norms, if not rules, on compensation. Importantly, Chinese managers and staff, and not Japanese managers, raised the above concerns and pushed for reforms in the Sino-Japanese JV.

U.S. Firms and Shanghai Workers

In many respects, U.S. and Japanese labor institutions bear little resemblance to one another: pay, promotion, and training methods are all distinct, especially for white-collar staff.[88] In U.S. firms, market principles shape most human resources practices. White-collar employees' pay is differentiated at the point of hiring and through subsequent evaluations, while blue-collar employees' pay tends to be relatively uniform.[89] Kazuo Koike has observed that large U.S. firms segment their labor forces into white-collar and blue-collar workers, and firms apply distinct human resources practices to each segment. For example, U.S. firms typically offer to white-collar workers clear and quick promotion opportunities,[90] incentive-laden pay, and evaluations to determine pay and promotion; while blue-collar workers have fewer opportunities for career advancement and, where unions operate, receive pay based on position and seniority. In U.S. firms, production workers are paid base wages with few incentives for performance and infrequent evaluations.[91] White-collar workers are frequently evaluated, which affects their pay and promotion. Within a U.S. firm, one can find yawning income gaps, particularly between levels of staff. Blue-collar employees tend to receive base wages and limited benefits, and their income does not increase very much in the same position. White-collar staff receive performance-based pay (including bonuses), which gives them a steeper rise in income. Consequently, the income gap between managers and workers is greater in U.S. than in Japanese firms, and the income differential has rapidly expanded since 1980.

Human resources managers in Shanghai-based U.S. firms confirmed that they applied the same market-based approach to setting pay levels as found in the United States.[92] Rather than rely on pay determination for a position based on strict company policy, managers in U.S. MNCs research the appropriate wage rate for a position and the person whom they wish to hire for the position.[93] Following such a method requires paying top market rates for strategic appointments in the firm and allows paying low rates to production workers, resulting in a differentiated pay scheme.

American corporations in China offer faster promotion and pay raises to white-collar workers than do Japanese and Chinese firms. In the first three years of employees' careers, firms identify skilled employees and speed their promotion through the managerial hierarchy. Unlike the Japanese system of promotion, which is based on evaluations by supervisors and a slow but clear promotion track, U.S. firms typically use a "post-and-bid" system for non-managerial staff.[94] Under the latter model, open jobs are posted and employees within and outside the firm may apply. Post-and-bid fosters movement between firms, while the Japanese internal market model of promotion discourages such transfers to new firms. The post-and-bid approach limits the weight given to seniority in promotion and pay.

The post-and-bid model of hiring and advancement suits China's current labor market. A Chinese human resources manager in a U.S.-funded enterprise thought that the U.S. approach matched Chinese workers' interests:

> Top personnel in China like the American way of thinking, quick results and advancement. I want money, and I want to see my life change quickly. I want to change my generation; I cannot wait until the next generation for change to happen. I think that this change in mindset is a good match with the US model. This is one of the reasons why U.S. companies have succeeded in China.[95]

Chinese workers' short time horizons for advancement lead them to prefer working for U.S. over Japanese firms. In Japanese firms, promotion and slow pay raises discouraged loyalty from ambitious workers, while U.S. firms were willing to make determinations on individuals based on their performance and the manager's perception of what the market could bear.

In Shanghai-based subsidiaries, U.S. firms replicated their home country practices of segmentation of production and managerial staff along with performance-based, inegalitarian income distribution.[96] Indeed, a manager of an international human resources firm reported that U.S. subsidiaries had an even more unequal distribution of income in Shanghai than in home-country operations. The manager explained the difference according to market principles: in Shanghai, production workers are abundant and good managerial candidates are scarce.[97] To attract talented workers, U.S. firms paid market rates for new hires. Unlike Japanese and Chinese firms that had rigid wage schemes, U.S. firms had flexible hiring practices built on competitive market principles, which allowed them to adapt easily to local market conditions.[98]

As did Japanese firms, U.S. firms sought to design labor regimes with an eye to improving the performance of their local employees. In some cases, this entailed revising compensation systems, but in others it was a matter of negotiating with and disciplining local workers. A U.S. assistant general manager described how he worked with the local general manager to improve worker productivity:

> The Chinese labor system is based on the time necessary to complete a product. So, if the standard is to make three valves in an hour, if a worker makes three, he gets all of his pay; if he makes more than three, he earns more. The per unit production times that workers had were padded. If I ask our GM to raise productivity, he says, "No problem." He just renegotiates and readjusts the norms for productivity, just squeezing a few minutes off the per unit production time.[99]

In more extreme cases, corporations introduced piece rates as a means to encourage labor productivity gains.[100]

General managers of U.S. corporations had to tailor their compensation practices to suit China's labor market. A manager in a U.S. WFOE and a former manager in a Sino-U.S. JV explained how he adjusted his pay system:

> I am starting to hire new employees at low pay rates and then raise them very quickly, as much as 20% per year. My approach is to hire at low salaries and work people very hard. If they perform well, then I raise their pay very quickly. That way, they feel good about their improvement and feel challenged in their work. The situation here is very different from the U.S. in terms of pay raises. In the U.S., the highest pay raise in a firm may be 10% in a year, but people expect big raises here.[101]

In China's labor market for white-collar employees, managers must offer higher percentage pay raises to top performers than they do in the United States. Conversely, low or no pay raises signal to workers that they are not valued by the company and may wish to leave. U.S. firms were applying similar market principles to compensation as they do at home but were scaled to Chinese market conditions.

Bonuses

American corporations are known for giving hefty bonuses to their executive staff, but few corporations give regular bonuses to production workers and other non-managerial staff.[102] Certainly, U.S. firms do not offer one or two months' pay as bonuses as a matter of course in the same way that Japanese and Chinese firms do. In Shanghai, U.S. subsidiaries adopted the norm of offering bonuses to managerial staff and production workers. In fact, many general managers from the United States and Japan operated under the false impression that they must give out at least the equivalent of one month's salary to workers as a bonus.[103] Unlike many Japanese and western European companies that have parent company rules to follow on giving one or two months' wages as bonuses to all employees, U.S. firms had to devise new practices for the Shanghai compensation norm.

A look at the aggregate figures reveals that there were no meaningful differences between the size of workers' bonuses in Japanese and U.S. firms. As a percentage of yearly salary, Japanese trading offices and factories, on average, gave their employees 11.7 percent and 19.5 percent, respectively, of their pay as bonus, while U.S. trading offices gave employees bonuses of 24 percent of their total pay as bonus and U.S. manufacturers gave 17.7 percent. U.S. trading offices usually offered their sales staff commissions, whereas many Japanese firms did not, which helps to explain the higher average bonus for U.S. trading firms than Japanese trading firms. The aggregate averages, however, mask important differences in how Japanese and U.S. companies distributed bonuses.

American firms tended to use one of two methods to distribute their bonuses. Many U.S. firms perfunctorily offered small, roughly equivalent bonuses to all workers, which followed the logic of home-country operations in which unionized production workers receive few incentives to increase productivity. A few firms' U.S. managers who gave out bonuses in an egalitarian manner opposed the idea that bonuses and floating pay improved worker productivity. One U.S. manager claimed that productivity-based bonuses and floating pay caused workers to focus on quantitative output and to neglect quality controls, a serious concern in Shanghai.[104] Yet, some U.S. firms created a new approach of giving out widely varying bonuses to induce higher labor productivity in Chinese subsidiaries. They adopted a Chinese (and Japanese) practice of giving bonuses to all workers, but they adapted it to suit U.S. firms' values of using variable pay to encourage strong performance. One manager for a U.S. firm with several operations in China criticized the obligatory 13th-month of pay as bonus:

> If everyone gets 13 months pay in that analysis, what is the effectiveness of a bonus? We give a large proportion of a worker's salary in the form of a bonus. Even if a person receives no bonus, his/her base wages would be sufficient to support a family. Still, they would be around the tenth percentile in terms of JV salaries for our industry. However, bonuses can double or more than double one's salary. If workers receive their total bonus, then they end up around the 75th percentile for pay in our industry. Our pay system combines risk and fixed components. This was difficult at the beginning; people had some trouble adjusting.[105]

The regional manager's comment that "people had some trouble adjusting" suggests that the firm's approach to using bonuses was new to many workers. According to a management consultant at one of Watson Wyatt's China offices, U.S. firms are learning how to use bonuses effectively in China, mainly by strengthening their "pay-for-performance" element along the lines of the above example.[106]

Distinct parent-company institutions account for the differences between the Japanese and U.S. firms' approaches to bonuses in Shanghai. In Japan, firms have instituted bonuses as a means to supplement the working wage and to create group performance incentives by tying bonuses to firm or factory profits and production. Within a Japanese firm, bonuses as a percentage of salary do not vary a great deal from one worker to another. In the United States, bonuses are used less frequently but when adopted are linked to individual and/or company performance. The crucial difference is the emphasis on individual performance in U.S. corporations, in contrast to the group performance in Japanese firms. Hence, U.S. subsidiaries tended to give very small bonuses or to offer widely divergent bonuses linked to individual performance.

Some U.S. corporations in Shanghai offered few incentives in the form of bonuses or floating wages, but they contributed to the reform of pay systems in other ways. For example, some companies introduced stock options to their workers. In China, stock options were not offered prior to their introduction by U.S. and European corporations, and Chinese authorities initially balked at stock options for Chinese workers in FIEs. Indeed, China was a latecomer to publicly held companies, and China's state has tried to limit foreign ownership of Chinese equity shares. In this case, a U.S. high-tech WFOE offered all workers stock options, but the number of shares offered in the global corporation varied according to one's rank in the company.[107] Thus, advancement in the company was rewarded with greater investment opportunities.[108]

Another way in which (primarily U.S.) companies altered the pay system was a decrease in the number of subsidies and allowances. SOEs had a dizzying number of allowances such as those for day care, housing, bus passes, and, even, haircuts. Foreign enterprises, especially U.S. WFOEs, sought to move to a single form of base pay rather than the numerous allowances. A human relations consultant explains the rationale, "By segregating pay into base pay and allowances, it does not add to workers' pay, but it does add to the company's administrative burden. Companies are trying to move toward a concept of total pay. Foreign companies are involved in an education process."[109] Another human resources consultant explained how Chinese firms are replicating this shift:

> There is now a clear trend towards an American model. Companies are adopting higher base pay, variable bonuses, and fewer allowances. Chinese firms are raising the base wage, getting rid of allowances, and letting the people spend the money as they like. This is a big change for the Chinese. Suddenly, they are given the opportunity to make their own decisions and to be more individualistic. Basically, this is adoption of an American model.[110]

Rather than adopting a Japanese model of human resources practices, as some authors have predicted,[111] Chinese SOEs, at least in recent years, have shifted in the direction of an American model.

Case Study of a U.S. High-tech JV

In contrast to the case study of a Japanese subsidiary described above, the American manufacturing JV under consideration was not set up with the same level of attention to transferring parent company culture and norms but was burdened by a number of SOE managers who became assistant managers. The JV's former SOE managers initially transferred an egalitarian pay structure with few incentives, drawn from the SOE partner. The Chinese partner in the venture transferred several older members of its managerial staff to the JV, and those assistant general managers carried a set of values and expectations that were steeped in SOE culture. The U.S. company dispatched a Singaporean Chinese to become the general manager, and he quickly tried to change the pay structure and culture of the JV. The case study reveals the dynamics of changing informal institutions and cognitive scripts in JVs, especially regarding human resource issues.

Upon arrival in Shanghai, the JV's general manager encountered a wage system that was established by the human resources department, under the control of the Chinese partner. The general manager, representing the U.S. partner, took issue with the pay scheme and introduced an incentive-laden plan, which extensively used evaluations. "We are trying to change our pay system. Everyone started at about the same pay scale. Nobody complained about this, but I looked at it and thought it was wrong. Now, everyone gets graded on their work… [T]heir grades determine their salary and bonus."[112] Evaluations have been used by state-owned enterprises, but their significance was minimized by the egalitarian distribution of wages and bonuses and by the practice of lifelong employment. In addition, the new pay scheme increased the size of the bonus to over one-half of total pay and instituted a wide gap between staff bonuses, thus linking pay to performance.

Changes to the pay scheme and the culture generated conflict among the JV's staff. The general manager analyzed staff reaction to the new system:

> Some of the workers come back and say, "That's great, but it cannot be done in China." Our facility has developed into two camps: those who believe miracles can happen in China and those who do not. The workers who are trained and believe that the workplace can be transformed are the believers and are under the other expatriate staff. The other side is composed of the human resources people and most of the Chinese deputy managers who do not believe that we can bring such an approach to China.[113]

In many JVs, older managers who came from the SOE partner resisted the pay-for-performance model. As older managers were replaced by younger Chinese human resources managers who were trained by foreign investors, Chinese managers shifted to supporting the pay-for-performance models.

In 2000, the outcome of the new approach was unclear, but there were some indications from this case study and others that suggest the viability of such an approach.[114] In 1999, labor turnover at the JV was just a few percent, significantly below the average for foreign invested manufacturers in Shanghai.[115] Additionally, the JV profitably operated from its inception and had a growing market for its products. The general manager believed that workers positively responded to the JV's changes. At a Sino-Hong Kong JV that had undertaken similar reforms and that encountered similar resistance from local managers and some workers, it took just a couple of years to transform the workplace and the workforce's attitudes.

The Direction of Chinese Compensation since 1994

In the mid- and late 1990s, two forces brought increasing pressure to bear on Chinese SOEs to reform their human resources policies: (i) a surge of foreign direct investment in China; and (ii) anticipation of China's accession to the WTO. With so many foreign firms entering China or expanding their operations, China could not meet demand for capable workers and managerial staff. Foreign investors paid high wages and bonuses to white-collar staff in order to attract them to their operations. Many ambitious white-collar workers abandoned their jobs in SOEs to seek their fortunes in foreign invested enterprises, leaving SOEs with the double burden of rising debt and poor managerial talent to right their sinking ship. Concomitantly, the 1994 Labor Law and a more permissive political climate increased FIEs' leeway to innovate pay schemes, and these provided models for SOEs to emulate.

WTO accession further opened up China's market, exposing Chinese firms to heightened competition with producers from advanced capitalist countries. Related, China's anticipation of and actual WTO accession brought a new wave of foreign direct investment. State reformers determined that China must fundamentally reform its wage and labor systems in SOEs to make the remaining enterprises under their control competitive. To remedy this situation, SOEs had to increase their managerial wages, but many of them also faced tremendous financial stress, which placed them in a double bind. Pressure to offer higher managerial wages, forced SOEs to lower production workers' wages by: (i) relying more heavily on contract migrant workers who had fewer benefits, lower wages, and high levels of productivity;[116] (ii) reducing redundant staff through mass layoffs; and (iii) revising their internal wage policies to stimulate productivity. Chinese SOEs began to drop their egalitarian pay structures to reflect market demand in a segmented workforce. Managerial talent was in short supply due to the constant demand for it, generated by foreign direct investment flows, while China possesses a seemingly endless supply of unskilled and semi-skilled production workers due to the underemployment of rural workers.[117]

International consulting firms and foreign firms have diffused international hiring and compensation practice to Chinese firms (both SOEs and non-SOEs), especially reliance on external markets, variable pay components, and differentiated pay schemes. Chinese private companies have moved particularly fast in the direction of variable pay components. According to an international consultant, in private enterprises over one-half of workers' pay is "at risk," or variable.[118] China's state has produced internal documents to compel SOEs to reform their compensation systems, often along U.S. lines.[119] Another consultant noted that SOEs have moved to emulate U.S. firms by raising the base wages in their factories, reducing subsidies, and increasing the variable components of pay.[120] To compete with foreign enterprises, some SOEs offer higher compensation to managers than FIEs do, an indirect indication of the growing wage stratification in SOEs.[121] To set their new pay scales, SOEs are purchasing salary surveys compiled by international consulting companies, clearly indicating their interest in adjusting their pay to market rates.[122]

At least as early as 1986, Chinese economists and reformers sought such a conversion of subsidies to regular wages. Wang Ju, an economist at

Zhongshan University, called for higher wages and the elimination of sub-sidies.[123] Essentially, Wang's prescription mirrored compensation reforms that foreign companies carried out in recent years but that got bogged down in SOEs in the 1980s and 1990s. Foreign firms and international consulting firms provided examples of how to implement such wage systems, and a combination of competition and state guidance compelled Chinese SOEs to adopt such compensation models.

Indeed, labor reforms in the SOE and FIE sectors played off one another. Officials developed reforms to address problems in SOEs and FIEs, but politically FIEs were better positioned to undertake such reforms. Therefore, FIEs appear to be leading the way in labor reforms, with SOEs following in their wake. The assertion that FIEs helped to propel Chinese labor reforms by providing a model of reform and by instituting competitive pressure for reform begs two questions: Toward which model(s) are Chinese labor institutions shifting? And, why are they moving in such a direction(s)? Even though competition among firms for able staff played a role in propelling wage and labor reforms in SOEs, the state still played some role in guiding the process of reform.

In the mid-1990s, China appeared destined to adopt a Japanese model for the following reasons: (i) it more closely approximated Chinese practices and, therefore, would make for an easier transition; (ii) it had led to high levels of labor productivity and low levels of unemployment in Japan; and (iii) it routinized labor bargaining with few instances of strikes and industrial conflict. Authors argued for the Japanese model because it would raise labor productivity while adhering to egalitarianism, unlike the U.S. model. In fact, many Chinese workers and officials did like the way that Japan's labor model combined security, productivity, and relative equality in factories. Yet, transplanting Japan's labor relations to China resulted in poor performance, according to managers—both Chinese and Japanese—who work in Japanese-invested enterprises. Chinese workers voted with their feet by leaving Japanese firms for employment in U.S., western European, and recently, Chinese firms. By the year 2000, Japanese firms in China, too, had begun to move toward a U.S. model of wage determination, and Chinese firms followed quickly on their heels. Foreign firms created models for SOEs to follow and lobbied for looser labor restrictions, but, as a Chinese human resources consultant reported, "A more profound reason for the reforms is the general intention of Chinese government to make China a true place of market economy, whereby many of the practices have to be re-engineered to meet the international standards and practices of which labor management is a part."[124]

Policy Networks and Information Flows

Over the course of the reform period, a policy network took shape that bridged foreign investors, SOEs, and state officials. Consultants—both foreign and Chinese—played important roles in providing information to the people in a position to reform compensation practices. Initially, consultants disseminated information about local labor regulations and about local pay scales, which allowed foreign investors to construct wage systems with less dependence on Chinese human resources managers, some of who were resistant to labor reforms. Such information was crucial, especially through the mid-1990s, when China's regulatory environment was more opaque and information more scarce than it is today and when many new investors entered China. Consultants first helped foreign investors to loosen their dependence on Chinese human resources managers from their SOE partners, and later taught Chinese firms about foreign labor institutions and their implementation. Latterly, human resources consultants have been instrumental in introducing new cognitive scripts in the form of industrial relations institutions to Chinese firms.

Chinese actors have become consultants on human resources matters, too. Foreign consulting firms hire and train local human resources consultants to work with companies that need guidance on how to devise successful human resource practices. Some of these trained local consultants move into human resources managerial positions in local firms or start up their own consulting firms. An interviewee described a Chinese management consultant whom she met in an MBA program in the United States. The consultant worked for Cisco Systems for three years, which took him to Singapore for training. After completing the MBA program, the Chinese manager returned to Shanghai to start up a very lucrative private managerial consulting firm. Chinese firms hire such consultants because they "are anxious to use international companies as a benchmark for themselves."[125]

Once foreign firms began to establish compensation practices that reflected their parent-country practices, they trained local human resources managers on how to apply such labor institutions. Many Chinese human resources managers were sent abroad to learn how the parent company operated and applied its business model. China's labor market has encouraged well-trained local managers to hop from job to job, and they carry their past training to their new setting. In recent years, local private and state-owned enterprises have begun to hire away Chinese human resources managers from FIEs.[126] Foreign firms are transferring their soft technology—or business institutions—to Chinese employees who, in turn, take that soft technology and diffuse it to Chinese state-owned and private enterprises. A Chinese human resources manager explained how foreign enterprises, especially U.S. firms, were contributing to the invigoration of local firms:

> I think that if China can develop in the next ten years or so to a certain
> level, it too will need to hire some of the many Chinese people who
> have been trained by foreign companies. The Chinese people who will
> become managers will be trained by American companies. I think
> that Chinese persons' way of thinking is actually quite a good fit with
> American culture, especially the emphasis on getting results.[127]

In fact, one of the early reasons that Chinese leaders established the foreign investment policy was to facilitate the transfer of foreign managerial techniques to China. The effect of such consulting work is to diffuse institutional practices from the sub-regime established by U.S. corporations to other organizations in the Chinese economy. Hence, such adoption of foreign business institutions is, at least partly, the realization of a Chinese state goal rather than the triumph of foreign investors over Chinese interests.

Path Dependence and Remaking Business Institutions Abroad

This chapter has contended that foreign investors at the micro level and business consultants at the meso level have influenced changes in China's human resources practices, thus contributing to a growing literature on the interaction of foreign investors and Chinese labor and managerial reforms.[128] Yet, it builds upon and challenges previous arguments in three ways. First, it distinguishes the influence of foreign investors from different countries on Chinese labor institutions, whereas most previous studies have approached foreign invested enterprises as a unified bloc.[129] Second, it specifies policy networks, acting at the meso level, that bring together foreign firms, state officials including SOE managers, and foreign firms, as mechanisms for transmitting wage models from foreign enterprises to SOEs. Finally, it claims that both Chinese SOEs and Japanese investments in China have begun to move toward a U.S. model of wages and against much of the prevailing wisdom that Chinese reforms are taking shape around Japanese labor institutions.

Evolving compensation practices in FIEs and SOEs provide rich material to examine path dependence and institutional change. Path dependency theory posits that institutional change should occur incrementally because inherited institutions and related ideological predispositions shape actors' attitudes toward institutions and institutional change.[130] Policy makers look for positive feedback on the operation of their institutions, but incrementally change existing institutions rather than undertaking fundamental change. Even when policy makers change formal institutions, at the ground level, people often continue to follow their unconscious norms and practices, or cognitive scripts. In the case of human resource practices in China, the state initially tried to control FIEs' labor practices through their organizational ties in JVs, but as foreign firms increasingly used the WFOE investment structure, a sub-regime of labor practices emerged to contend with the dominant labor practices in SOEs. Business consultants played a crucial role in aggregating information on hiring methods, compensation patterns, and Chinese regulations to formulate models to disseminate to SOEs and FIEs. The number of firms that adopted such models and recommendations grew, thus expanding the sub-regime until it eclipsed the SOEs' "iron rice bowl" model.

The case of Japanese and U.S. investors in China also provides an opportunity to reflect on the adjustment process of MNCs in new host environments. After the period of heavy regulation of FIEs' human resource practices waned, the main area in which U.S. firms adjusted to the local market was the proliferation of bonuses. In that case, U.S. firms initially followed the local practice of doling out an undifferentiated thirteenth month of pay as bonus, but more recently, U.S. firms have shifted to pay-for-performance bonuses, another indication of market principles at work. The actions of U.S.-invested enterprises in China follow the logic of path dependency because they apply home-country principles to the Chinese labor market conditions, but the reforms of SOEs and of Japanese-invested enterprises require a more detailed explanation.

Pay-for-performance institutions contributed to the formation of a new model or sub-regime of institutions that was attractive to many employees in China and which became a model to emulate by Japanese and Chinese firms. Japanese firms in China and at home shifted toward an American-inspired model of compensation. While such an institutional shift marks a break from their institutional heritage, Japanese wage reforms reflect many aspects of path dependent institutional change. First, in Japanese firms, formal compensation institutions were more easily revised than actual practice. Ideas of egalitarianism and seniority colored Japanese managers' way of thinking, even after formal rules had been altered. Second and related, young Chinese human resources managers played an important role in identifying problems in the way that Japanese compensation practices meshed with Chinese workers. Chinese managers were less influenced by Japanese managerial culture and, thus, were in a better position to reflect critically on Japanese institutions. Third, institutional reforms that Japanese managers believed were radical departures from their egalitarian wage system still fell short of many U.S. investors' market-based practice. Just as path dependency theorists would predict, institutional inheritance (in this case, cognitive scripts of egalitarian labor practices) acts as an anchor that limits firms' capacity to reform institutions. Against the predictions of organizational learning theory on firms' ability to adapt to new environments, subsidiaries are weighted down by parent-company institutions, thereby limiting adaptation.

Chinese labor reforms also bear the imprint of path dependent reform in at least two ways. First, as with Japanese reforms, Chinese policy makers found it easier to revise formal rules of the game than to change actors within the Chinese economy. Even after the state gave authority and encouragement to SOE managers to experiment with compensation reforms, the latter were reluctant to do so. Managers and employees continued to follow egalitarian norms, and dissatisfied ambitious employees left the firms for greener pastures in foreign and private firms. Second, many of the Chinese managers who pressed for compensation reforms were young human resources managers who had been trained by foreign enterprises. Thus, they were less committed to Chinese SOE institutions and more open to foreign compensation institutions than older Chinese managers. In order to alter the scripts followed in SOEs and Sino-foreign JVs, a new cast had to be assembled with fresh institutional models.

The ultimate direction of Chinese compensation reforms, toward a U.S.-inspired compensation model rather than a Japanese model, is somewhat perplexing. Japanese compensation institutions more closely resembled China's wage and bonus model, so one might expect Chinese reformers to move in that direction. Yet, China opted for a deeper institutional reform based on an American compensation model. Path dependency suggests that policy makers cleave to their experience with past institutions, causing them to undertake limited, incremental reforms. In China's case, reformers, as early as 1976, rejected the "iron rice bowl" model and encouraged the adoption of pay schemes that were similar to U.S. compensation systems. Under such conditions, Chinese reformers sought new institutions that helped meet the goals of their reform efforts. American compensation practices helped to break up the "iron rice bowl" without the same degree of punitive and exploitative methods employed by mainly Hong Kong and Taiwanese investors in SEZs such as Shenzhen. State officials guided the process of globalization and institutional change, encouraging SOEs to adopt particular patterns of labor institutions and not others.

Finally, through their movement on the labor market at the micro level, Chinese employees indirectly affected compensation reforms. American and European companies introduced new labor models that formed a subregime, which appealed to an ambitious minority of workers who previously labored under an egalitarian labor regime. The attraction of many high-flying managers to the new regime created pressure for other firms to adapt to these new principles. To compete, Chinese firms had to mimic and even outdo U.S. firms for compensation given to top employees. In this fashion, Chinese firms shifted from their egalitarian commitments to polarized incomes within firms.

6

Dismissal and Labor Turnover

The previous chapter analyzed Chinese efforts to reform compensation practices and the lessons drawn from the operation of Japanese and U.S. models in China. Chinese state interests established guideposts to shift away from the "iron rice bowl" model, and feedback from workers in the labor market and the lessons learned by human resources managers and diffused by the policy community helped to construct the path toward a U.S. model of compensation. The present chapter looks at two other crucial aspects of employment: hiring and retention/dismissal practices. As in the previous chapter, state officials identified loosening lifetime employment in SOEs as a target of reform efforts, but, frustrated by the intransigence of SOE staff and managers, officials turned to FIEs as models of how to handle hiring, retention, and dismissal of employees. In these regards, Japanese and U.S. investors presented very distinct institutional models, and ambitious Chinese workers in the market came to prefer U.S. (and European) human resources management practices. Chinese human resources managers and some Japanese general managers drew lessons from the pattern of Chinese workers' reactions to Japanese labor practices, although many general managers persisted with their parent-company practices or only introduced moderate reforms. The pattern of FIEs' influence on Chinese hiring and dismissal practices illuminates micro-level dynamics in the process of state-guided globalization, especially the role that FIEs and business consultants played in diffusing market-based labor practices to China.

China began its economic reforms and open-door policy without a free market to allocate labor, and they initially sought to control how foreign investors hired and managed their labor force. Bureaucrats assigned workers to employers often for life (or longer),[1] and manifold regulations prevented the free movement of workers between work units.[2] Under China's socialist model, the state also heavily regulated employers to manage the allocation, training, evaluation, and retention/dismissal of employees. Beginning in 1978, the state sought to develop market-based labor institutions that would improve incentives, rationalize labor allocation and, destroy the "iron rice bowl," a term that encapsulated the high level of security enjoyed by state owned enterprise workers.[3] China endeavored to alter the state owned enterprises' (and large collective enterprises') pattern of employment relations and work culture by introducing a variety of measures that fostered freer movement of labor and that enhanced managerial control over workers. To introduce market principles in the allocation of labor, China had to create new institutions or revise existing ones. Since 1978, China gradually has reformed the entire process of recruiting and contracting labor, including dismantling the state's unified labor allocation system, but no measure was more significant or politically charged than empowering firms to dismiss workers. Worker dismissals and layoffs challenged the ideological tenets and the political commitments of the Communist Party to protect the interests of workers, yet reformers considered it an important step in increasing the authority of industrial managers. Along with corruption, the shift of core commitments by the Communist Party has driven much of the urban protest by Chinese workers during the reform era.[4]

As China has searched for appropriate labor market models, Japanese and U.S. firms have supplied starkly different approaches to recruitment, training, and dismissal of employees. In the process of constructing China's emerging labor market, how did foreign firms contribute to the development and implementation of new labor institutions? If we think of institutional reform in terms of a "menu of plausible broad arrangements,"[5] U.S. and Japanese firms offered two new choices to Chinese reformers and firms to consider. Institutional reformers build on an existing institutional foundation and in light of their reform goals, which makes some options on the menu more palatable than others. In this regard, Japanese labor institutions, which share some common features with the legacy of China's "iron rice bowl" model, appeared a logical choice of least resistance.[6] Yet, Chinese reformers after a period of favoring Japanese practices in the early and mid-1990s have veered toward a pattern that is more premised on U.S. principles than those of Japan. Foreign investors, especially those from the United States and Europe, implemented market-based hiring and firing practices that became a sub-regime and catalyzed institutional reform and diffusion. To understand how labor market reforms unfolded and the roles played by FIEs in that process, the chapter compares how Japanese and U.S. approaches to labor markets have contributed to the course of Chinese labor institutional reform.

The rest of the chapter details the dynamic process of institutional change—both reform of Chinese labor market institutions and adjustment of U.S. and Japanese institutions that operate in China-based subsidiaries. As with other reforms, labor market development evinces a familiar pattern: an initial period of domestic opposition to institutional changes[7] and state attempts to isolate and control foreign investors, followed by a period during which foreign investors were given more leeway to introduce a variety of home-country institutions to China, concluding with a shift toward a U.S.-inspired sub-regime of labor market institutions. The sub-regime led to the gradual diffusion of radical labor reform measures, many of which had antecedents in the early discussion of SOE labor reforms. The chapter begins with a discussion of attempts to reform labor market practices during the period 1978–1992, including the introduction of labor contracts and state attempts to manage FIEs' labor market practices through organizations such as the Foreign Employment Services Company (FESCO). Next, I analyze labor reform efforts since 1992, especially focusing on the Labor Law of 1994, the Japanese and U.S. labor market institutions that firms brought to China, and the demonstration effects of U.S. and Japanese labor models in China. I conclude with a discussion of micro-level dynamics in the process of state-guided globalization and reform of labor market institutions.

FIEs made three contributions to the development of China's labor contract system and the formation of a labor market. First, FIEs were much quicker to implement the labor contract system than were SOEs. Second, FIEs pressed for signing Chinese workers to labor contracts that were shorter in duration than Chinese reformers initially sought, thus creating more flexibility for their managers to adjust their work rolls. SOEs followed the FIEs' examples and adopted similar practices. Third, FIEs provided models on how to operate in a labor market such as the creation of job advertisements, evaluation and promotion systems, and termination procedures. Chinese firms could observe and mimic these practices, and Chinese workers within FIEs, especially human resource managers, acquired a detailed knowledge of such institutions, which they could transfer to new employers. Since 1992, foreign firms have developed a sub-regime of labor institutions related to hiring, training, and dismissal that has been emulated by Chinese firms and diffused to the rest of the Chinese economy.

Building the Institutions of a Labor Market, 1978–1992

During the initial period of labor market development, state attempts to break down the "iron rice bowl" model of lifetime employment met with resistance from SOE managers and workers because of their socialization to the "iron rice bowl" model and due to a lack of incentives to undertake such changes. The state granted FIEs in SEZs more leeway in constructing labor practices along the lines of free market principles, but they, too, faced obstacles from local officials and Chinese JV partners to free hiring and dismissal of employees. Hence, China's labor market reforms made modest and uneven progress during this period, even though many reformers and FIEs pressed for instituting such practices.

To facilitate the free(r) movement of workers, China had to change its regulatory environment and informal norms on employment. Prior to full application of the labor contract system, China's state controlled the allocation of approximately one-half of China's urban labor force through the unified allocation system (*tongyi fenpei*).[8] No job advertisements existed, and workers did not freely pursue employment in a transparent system. Any dismissal or transfer of an employee required the enterprise to report the matter to the local labor department,[9] which was reluctant to approve such requests. Once assigned to a unit, it was difficult for a worker to leave it because the worker depended on the firm for many welfare provisions.[10]

Labor departments pressed SOEs to take on extra workers and were reluctant to approve dismissals because of the mounting unemployment and underemployment in China's cities.[11] Both management and workers found themselves locked into an employment model in which management hoarded high-quality workers, poor-performing laborers cleaved to the security of state owned enterprises, and local party and state agents sought to inflate employment rolls even at the expense of labor productivity. The predictable result was overstaffing and poor productivity in SOEs.[12] A survey in Xiamen found that 33–50 percent of SOE staff was made redundant after merging with a foreign company to form a JV, an indication of the depth of overstaffing in SOEs.[13] Hong Yung Lee cites a number of studies from inside and outside China that estimated 8.7–40.0 percent of state-owned enterprises' staff was redundant.[14]

To induce greater labor productivity and to improve the matching of workers' skills to employers' needs, the state had to give managers more control over the hiring process and the power to terminate employees in order to eliminate poor performing or redundant workers. In 1979, reformers began the process of altering the rules on hiring and dismissal with the introduction of a labor contract system. Nevertheless, SOE managers and their employees resisted many state attempts to introduce new norms and rules on labor in factories because of their deeply ingrained cognitive scripts.

Development of the Labor Contract System

Against opposition, in 1980, the State Council introduced labor contracts as a means to attack the SOEs' "iron rice bowl." Contracts included length of employment as one of their terms, implicitly creating a terminal date for the employment relationship, unless a contract was renewed or extended.[15] Additionally, Chinese commentary on labor contracts advanced the policy as crucial to developing a labor market in which workers and employees would have greater flexibility in voluntarily finding appropriate matches.[16] Due to staunch resistance from a conservative faction of party leaders and some bureaucratic agencies,[17] the state proceeded cautiously, allowing nine cities and provinces to experiment with labor contracts during the period 1980–1983 before expanding their scope.[18] Beginning in 1981, Shanghai experimented with the labor contract model, and by 1986, had 150,000 workers operating under labor contracts.[19] According to Hillary Josephs, officials in Beijing and Shanghai—two pilot cities for the labor contract system— resisted or reversed aspects of the labor contract system.[20] Workers in SOEs opposed the labor contract model because they suspected that it imperiled lifelong employment, a suspicion that was proved correct. Authorities praised the results of the labor contracts, claiming that labor productivity improved and, dubiously, that workers liked the new system.[21]

Foreign firms in special economic zones helped to lead the implementation and development of the labor contract system, such as Shenzhen's 1980 experiment with introducing labor contracts rather than lifelong employment.[22] The 1980 *Regulations on Labor Management in Joint Ventures Using Chinese and Foreign Investment* called for JVs to sign workers to contracts, which gave legal endorsement to Shenzhen's reforms.[23] Implementing procedures issued in 1983 clarified that all JV personnel should be under contract, negotiated between management and trade unions.[24] FIEs had to register labor contracts at the local Labor Bureaus, which gave the state agencies power to monitor and to approve labor practices in FIEs. In 1983, Chinese authorities expanded experimentation with the contract labor system, allowing provinces to select municipalities to establish labor contract systems in SOEs, based on Shenzhen's and other experiments' success.[25] In designated cities, SOEs introduced labor contracts but only for new employees or, in a few cases, to convert permanent employees to contract workers. The two-track model of industrial relations was meant gradually to move all employees into contracted employment.[26] Regulations mandating that all workers in SOEs sign labor contracts, however, did not appear until 1994. The labor contract system improved enterprise financial performance, in part, by reducing the firm's (especially FIEs') obligations to pay workers benefits, which pared payroll expenses.[27] Legally, enterprises were required to offer the same benefits to contract workers as to permanent employees, but anecdotal information suggests that the enterprises did otherwise.[28]

Most Chinese articles cited Shenzhen FIEs as models for its labor contract system reforms, and certainly, the introduction of labor contracts went more smoothly in FIEs located in the SEZs than in SOEs in other cities that experimented with labor contracts. In contrast to Shanghai and Beijing, which had strong and entrenched state-owned enterprise interests represented among local officials and ministries, Shenzhen was basically an unindustrialized rural area in 1980 and lacked many SOEs or officials with interests to oppose the labor reforms.[29] Typically, workers in Shenzhen were new entrants to the industrial workforce who came from the countryside with minimal employment demands, unlike the long-standing SOE employees with their expectations of an "iron rice bowl" with minimal employment demands. Initially,

Chinese authors heaped praise on the Shenzhen model of labor contracts for its role in "improving enterprise management and labor efficiency,"[30] for increasing labor productivity,[31] and for helping to match appropriate workers with jobs.[32]

In 1986, China's State Council determined that the labor contract system gradually would become universal for all new employees in state-owned enterprises, though existing permanent workers would retain their status. The contract regulations suggested that long-term workers sign five-year contracts, short-term workers sign three- to five-year contracts, and temporary workers sign contracts up to one year in duration.[33] SOE managers, however, continued to treat new hires as permanent workers, which assuaged workers' fears of becoming mere temporary workers but undermined the creation of a flexible workforce.[34]

The 1989 protest movement and its violent repression temporarily stalled further labor reforms in SOEs. In addition to the ascendance of a conservative leadership group and policy retrenchment, officials were concerned about alienating urban workers who—along with students, entrepreneurs, and unemployed people—actively participated in the June 4 1989, protest movement. Until they were disbanded, workers formed autonomous unions that threatened Communist Party hegemony. After 1989, China faced lingering protests from workers angered by their crumbling job security.[35] In the three years following the event, central and local leaders sought to avoid harsh policies that would cause further worker consternation.[36]

Progress on bringing SOE workers under the contract system moved very slowly until the mid-1990s. Figure 6.1 details the expansion of the contract labor system in terms of number of employees. By 1991, less than 14 percent of employees in all ownership types of enterprises and just 14.6 percent of SOE employees worked under contract. Moreover, many work units persisted in internal hiring, especially employing children of current workers, a practice that violated hiring rules.[37] From the inception of the labor contract system, a higher percentage of employees in foreign and private enterprises (included in the "others" column of Figure 6.1) worked under contracts than did state-owned or urban collective enterprises. Up through the early 1990s, FIEs employed only a small share of China's workforce, but almost all of the FIEs involving Western or Japanese investors had labor contracts. The pattern indirectly supports the claim that greater opposition to the spreading labor contract system arose in SOEs than in FIEs.[38] It is more difficult to change the institutions (and behavior of people) in long-standing enterprises with deeply embedded norms of behavior and expectations of lifelong employment such as SOEs than it is to transplant institutions into newly created enterprises.[39] Additionally, the higher percentage of workers under labor contracts in FIEs than in SOEs put the foreign investors in a better position to dismiss unwanted or poor-performing workers when restrictions and norms on doing so loosened.

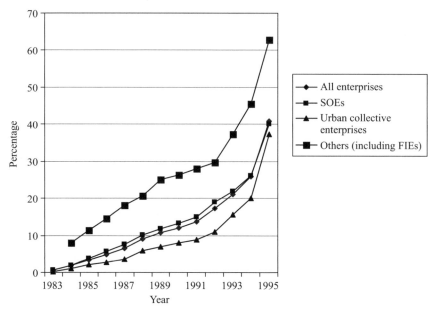

Figure 6.1   Percentage of Employees under Labor Contracts by Enterprise Type.
Source: Chinese Economic Statistical Yearbook Editorial Committee, *Chinese Economic Yearbook* (Beijing: Chinese Economic Yearbook Publishers, various years).

Controlling the Labor Market: Labor Service Centers and FESCO

China's early shift toward the labor contract system loosened the strictures on employment, but the state sought to regulate the flow of workers in and out of enterprises—both SOEs and FIEs. First, the labor contract system addressed the terms of employment rather than enterprises' hiring practices. Throughout this period, China persisted with a unified employment system for urban workers. Consequently, job descriptions and advertisements were largely absent.[40] By law, SOEs were required to hire workers according to their qualifications rather than through internal recruitment (*dingti* or *neizhao*),[41] but until the mid-1990s, they were still learning to utilize free labor market institutions.[42] The *Labor Law* (1994) would dispense with the state unified allocation of urban workers in enterprises, but until that time, labor market hiring practices such as job fairs, advertisements, and headhunters remained a small sub-regime of labor practices in the FIE sector.

Fearful of political repercussions from unemployment, the state managed and surveilled the growing number of unemployed and laid-off workers and people "waiting for work" (*daiye*)[43] through local labor departments and their ancillary organizations, labor service companies, and foreign-related labor service companies such as the FESCO. Around 1980, the state introduced labor service companies to act as intermediaries between workers and domestic enterprises in the operation of the nascent labor market and to monitor workers who were not employed or who sought temporary employment in urban areas.[44] Labor service companies were encouraged to offer worker-training programs and to operate labor employment service enterprises, which were collective enterprises designed to provide limited employment opportunities for dismissed or laid-off staff.[45] The labor service companies were established to hold "reservoirs" of workers who were ready to fill new openings in China's enterprises. As jobs opened in enterprises, the labor service companies recommended applicants to fill those posts, whether they were permanent or temporary positions.

FIEs and private firms enjoyed a bit more freedom to hire from society, but the state regulated them, too. Foreign invested enterprises could hire workers "from society," which, under most circumstances, would facilitate the emergence of free labor market institutions, but in China such institutions and practices only slowly emerged.[46] The state did not allocate workers to foreign enterprises as it did to SOEs, but the state retained three means to limit the operation of a free labor market for FIEs. First, in JVs, the Chinese (SOE) partner exercised control over human resource management.[47] Most employees in JVs transferred in from SOE partners rather than being hired on an open market. In fact, foreign enterprises were not given the right to publicly announce job openings until 1988.[48] In the absence of transparent formal mechanisms, workers relied on informal mechanisms such as *guanxi* (social ties) to learn about job openings and to seek employment, and SOEs looked to labor service companies and illegal internal hiring for recruitment.[49] FIEs could hire college graduates straight out of school, but the firms had to pay the educational institution a fixed sum of money.[50] Second, regulations required trade representative offices and WFOEs to hire personnel through designated labor service companies for foreign businesses such as the FESCO.[51] The Chinese state owned the foreign-related labor service companies,[52] which enabled local labor departments to monitor labor relations in two types of foreign enterprises (representative offices and WFOEs) that typically lacked trade unions or party branch organizations. Foreign enterprises could select their workers, but the FESCO shaped the pool of candidates that foreign enterprises saw. FESCO was responsible for making sure that all employees hired through it had proper labor contracts with their employers[53] and that foreign companies paid payroll taxes, high wages, and covered all benefits for its workers. Third, the local labor bureaus exercised rights to approve job openings (and dismissals) in foreign operations.

Dismissals and Layoffs

Severe overstaffing in SOEs and, to a lesser degree, in JVs acted as a drag on labor productivity and allowed poor work norms to persist. In order to rectify the situation, managers needed to trim their work rolls, not just to eliminate surplus laborers but also to inculcate a norm of hard work. According to the

1980 *Regulations on Labor Management in Joint Ventures Using Chinese and Foreign Investment,* rules on the dismissal of employees in foreign invested enterprises were to be included in laborers' contracts.[54] Article 4 allowed JVs to dismiss "superfluous" workers due to "changes in production," or to discharge employees who severely broke the JV's rules and regulations. The prevalence of JVs, however, limited the capacity of FIEs to reduce the number of employees via dismissals because Chinese human resources managers who transferred into JVs from SOEs and who typically were Communist Party members also were reluctant to abandon their cognitive scripts and to use dismissal as a means of promoting efficiency.

If an employer—SOE or FIE—dismissed an employee, responsibility for monitoring the former worker fell into the hands of the local labor department and its labor service companies. Before an enterprise could dismiss a worker, the enterprise had to discuss the matter with the trade union branch and inform the local labor bureau.[55] The procedures for handling dismissed workers from foreign invested enterprises varied, depending on the type of foreign business involved. The onus of placing a worker fired from a JV fell on the Chinese JV partner, on the local labor department, or on the department in charge of the JV.[56] In the case of employees dismissed from WFOEs or foreign representative offices, responsibility fell into the laps of the local labor department or the foreign labor service company.[57] Local officials and labor service companies had little incentive to encourage employers to dismiss workers. Assuming that employers dismissed their least effective or most troublesome employees, labor service companies faced an uphill struggle to find suitable new matches for dismissed workers. In the 1980s and early 1990s, tight budgets and local pressure to inflate employment combined to cause local labor departments to resist efforts to dismiss and lay off workers.[58] In addition, a faction of conservative national leaders continued to thwart attempts to move toward a free labor market and dismissal of redundant employees.[59] Up to the early 1990s and more definitively the passage of the 1994 Labor Law, the state was reluctant to devolve a great deal of control over unemployment, layoffs, and labor markets to all types of enterprises. The combined power of local labor bureaus and Chinese human resources managers impeded JVs from exercising their power to dismiss employees through the 1980s.

Despite acknowledgement of overstaffing problems and the discussion of dismissal, such reforms made little headway in providing relief from overstaffing because of practical restrictions on managers' ability to dismiss workers.[60] Overstaffing was ideologically supported by the egalitarian principle that it was better to employ many workers at low wages than it was to employ few workers at high wages in the pursuit of efficiency.[61] Addressing the rules on dismissal proved controversial, but altering the norms in SOEs was even more difficult.[62] SOE managers, despite other reforms designed to increase their powers and profit motives, still had much of their profitability determined by state pricing of inputs and goods sold to end producers rather than wage bills, so state-owned enterprise managers had little incentive to dismiss redundant workers.[63] Even FIEs, headed by foreign managers interested in using dismissal procedures, made little headway in carrying out dismissals due to the intransigence of Chinese bureaucrats and human resources managers.[64] China's reformers attempted to use FIEs' practices and use of contracts to spread such institutions to SOEs. Through 1991, labor reforms in SOEs, however, stalled; the core institutions—unified placement, restrictions on dismissals, and norms of lifelong employment—persisted in SOEs. The breakthrough in the construction of free labor markets required a new "script" on how to manage labor, which came with the promulgation of the 1994 *Labor Law*.

Employment Institutions since 1992

Deng Xiaoping's "southern tour" of 1992, on which he affirmed the path of opening to the outside world, reinvigorated Chinese economic reforms and marked a turning point in labor relations, when the state took a harsher, more juridical stance on industrial relations in all enterprises and allowed FIEs greater freedom to manage their own industrial relations. During the period 1992–1995, China's State Council and other central government organs produced a series of laws, regulations, and circulars related to labor relations in China, mostly designed to deal with labor redundancies and the anticipated ensuing conflict. The impressive slate of legislation passed includes *The Trade Union Law* (1992), *Regulations on the Placement of Surplus Staff and Workers of State Owned Enterprises* (1993), *Regulations Governing the Settlement of Labor Disputes in Enterprises in the People's Republic of China* (1993), *Regulations Concerning Minimum Wages in Enterprises* (1993), *Regulations Governing Labor Management of Foreign-Invested Enterprises* (1994), *Regulations on Retrenchment of Workforce by Enterprises for Economic Reasons* (1994), *The Labor Law of the People's Republic of China* (1995), *State Council Regulations on Working Hours of Employees* (1995), and *Regulations Governing Collective Contracts* (1995). Very rapidly, the state altered the legal framework for managing labor in all enterprises located in China and began to establish a new approach for state and trade union action on labor relations. Since 1992, China has made great progress in constructing market-based labor institutions, including: (i) unifying labor regulations for all enterprises; (ii) significantly loosening restrictions on market-based hiring; (iii) eliminating unified labor allocation for urban workers; and (iv) promoting a new set of norms for all enterprises by giving freer rein to market principles and adding pressure to follow such principles. FIEs have modeled many of the institutions in their sub-regime, which Chinese firms have emulated.

Since 1992, four factors have shaped the direction of shifting labor relations. First, a group of reformers who pursued economic and legal reforms in tandem and who saw the interconnection of these two domains took the reins in 1992. In the 1990s, President Jiang Zemin and Premier Zhu Rongji propelled a number of reforms related to industrial relations in SOEs and loosened reins on FIEs to institute their labor practices. Concomitantly, they put through legislation on labor arbitration and other measures that gave rise to formal means of addressing labor issues and concerns. Second, the shift away from the JV investment structure and toward the WFOE model weakened government and Chinese partners' influence on the daily operations of FIEs. Third, the growing financial crisis of SOEs caused the Chinese state to take extreme measures and to force SOEs finally to adopt earlier reform measures such as the labor contract system. In addition to allowing some SOEs to go bankrupt and to be bought out by private and foreign investors, Chinese leaders also compelled SOEs to undertake massive layoffs in order to improve efficiency and labor productivity.

Finally, the takeoff of foreign investment and private business combined with the difficulties faced by SOEs to cause a significant shift of the relative shares of industrial production and employment held by SOEs and FIEs. When China opened to foreign investors in 1978, SOEs employed the lion's share of China's urban workers, and all but a fraction of the remainder were in collective enterprises. Beginning in 1979, foreign investment trickled into China and, although employment in FIEs was much discussed in the Chinese and foreign press, the share of urban workers employed in FIEs (including those from Hong Kong, Macao, and Taiwan) did not top one percent until 1991, and in 1985, workers employed by SOEs outnumbered those employed by FIEs by a ratio of approximately 1500:1. The relatively small role that foreign enterprises played in China limited the effect of foreign investors over Chinese labor institutions and workers as well as the relative bargaining power of FIEs. In 1993, China's state announced impending layoffs from SOEs (and from the bureaucracy), just as a period of frenetic foreign investment into China began. By the time the investment frenzy cooled slightly in 1999, the ratio of SOE employees to FIE employees dropped dramatically to 14:1. Layoffs persisted in the SOE sector, while foreign investment continued at a very high rate, so that in 2005, the ratio of SOE employees to FIE employees had narrowed to 5.2:1. Over the period 1978–2005, SOEs' share of total urban employees tumbled from 78 to approximately 24 percent, so the scope of the dominant labor regime shrank. The sub-regime of FIEs' labor institutions simultaneously enjoyed fewer restrictions and expanded its zone of operation. The shift in SOEs' and non-state enterprises' (especially FIEs and private enterprises) relative positions in the economy directly altered competition among firms and created greater pressure (to which the state added its directives) on SOEs to reform their approaches to the labor market in order to recruit and retain talented staff.[65] The structural and policy shifts had a ripple effect out from Beijing and from the FIEs' emerging sub-regime, altering hiring and dismissal practices throughout China.

Hiring

By 1993, the state effectively had dismantled its worker allocation system (although remnants of the system lingered in some cities for a few more years), allowing job fairs, advertisements, labor employment centers, and headhunters to emerge to fill the gap.[66] Foreign firms, especially those from the United States and Europe, were well prepared for this shift to a free labor market, while Japanese firms were somewhat less adept at operating in China's market.

Instituting China's labor market required the state, in addition to clearing the way for new mechanisms for allocating labor to emerge, to compel SOEs to adjust their human resource practices. Until recently, SOEs lacked autonomy to make decisions about their human resources. The state has now devolved control over personnel decisions—how many staff and what types of position are needed—to SOE managers. SOEs are given fixed human resources budgets and are allowed more freedom to decide on wage allocation and the number of staff necessary.[67] Given the power and responsibility to develop human resources strategies, SOE managers have developed job descriptions and have conducted job searches. In this manner, SOEs followed U.S. and European firms' practices, but less so Japanese firms, which lack detailed job descriptions. The introduction of free labor markets and the unification of labor regulations for all firms caused SOEs to revise existing institutions and create new ones, though SOEs were slow to do so. If their institutions fell short of some of the foreign models that they used as guides, it is more due to the logic of incremental reform, slow shifts in personnel, and the persistence of cognitive scripts than formal impediments to institutional change.

Dismissal

In 1993, the State Council issued regulations on handling laid-off SOE workers.[68] The regulations presaged massive layoffs in the state sector, which began in 1993 and established a severance policy, a lump sum payment equivalent to one month's pay for each year of employment with the enterprise. More important, the long-awaited 1994 *Labor Law* altered the landscape for workers and managers. Among other provisions, the 1994 *Labor Law* mandated all workers be employed under labor contracts.[69] The *Labor Law* (and the mandating of labor contracts) was a Faustian bargain for workers: the law enhanced protection of employees by stipulating limitations on work hours, mandating vacations, guaranteeing the rights of women to maternity leave, extending workers' right to form trade unions, and providing legal recourse for workers who felt that their rights were violated, among other provisions, but it also provided a legal framework to dismiss workers.[70]

The *Labor Law* still requires all enterprises seeking to dismiss workers to consult the enterprises' trade union branches or the labor representative committees.[71] If the trade union or the labor representative committee raises no objections to the dismissal, the enterprise may proceed. The firm also must notify the local labor bureau of any dismissal, but it is not clear if the local labor department can or under what circumstances would block such dismissals. To contest a dismissal, within 30 days workers have to raise objections with their trade union or file a complaint with the labor department. A trade union may reexamine a case, and the labor department may refer a case to labor arbitration. If the dismissal is not overturned, the dismissal is registered and, thus, approved. Sheila Oakley cites numerous examples of dismissed workers challenging their SOE employers through labor arbitration committees in the 1990s when these procedures took hold.[72] In many of those cases, workers clearly violated labor discipline or other aspects of their labor contract but challenged the dismissal based on their expectations of lifelong employment, which suggests the persistence of workers' "iron rice bowl" cognitive scripts. Unlike the heyday of the "iron rice bowl" model, however, many such dismissals were registered.

After 1994, the central government and bureaucratic agents felt compelled to harden their position on dismissals and layoffs, in part, due to the growing fiscal crisis in SOEs. Facing mounting deficits in SOEs in 1993, the state began to lay off millions of SOE workers to bring the enterprises closer to solvency. The severity of the state-owned enterprises' crisis compelled the state to allow SOE managers to institute harsher rules and practice on dismissal and to impose layoffs. The degree of overstaffing and financial crisis faced by SOEs is demonstrated by a report from the State Council that stated 25.5 million people were laid off during the period 1998–2001, of whom 16.8 million were reemployed.[73]

Against the financial and market pressure to restructure SOEs and to push through layoffs and dismissals, the state has to weigh its concerns with social stability and its (weakening) commitments to protecting workers' interests. Within the restructuring efforts, SOEs and state agencies were encouraged to help laid-off workers find new assignments. Large SOEs dispatched redundant workers to ancillary organizations that offered less lucrative employment,[74] but even these related firms faced pressures to restructure.[75] Through the 1990s, the desire to maintain stability through nearly full employment weakened the state's commitment to restructuring and opened the door to some large SOEs to resist pressure to lay off workers.[76] Restructuring efforts and mass layoffs were more easily implemented in SOEs that were privatized as part of the state's policy of letting go of the small and medium-sized enterprises and keeping hold of large SOEs.[77]

Nevertheless, the state, until recent years, found it difficult to force through restructuring measures due to the norms of workers and managers who operated under the state. In Shanghai, despite years of encouragement to do so, major SOEs were putting through labor restructuring measures, such as early retirement offerings, as late as 2007. Faced with an aging workforce that earns relatively high salaries but lacks requisite skills for the contemporary economy, SOEs may offer to buy out the remaining years of workers' contracts and pay the normal pension when such workers' reach the mandatory retirement age. Such a golden parachute method entails a huge financial burden for SOEs, but managers believe it is necessary to compete with FIEs on products and for personnel in the marketplace. Even SOEs that enjoy monopoly status have adopted such measures due to stepped up pressure from the state, which has issued special bulletins to SOEs to push through restructuring plans. Without such pressure from the state and FIEs, SOE personnel might persist with their pattern of lifelong employment and overstaffing.[78]

Once regulations were in place and the state's attitude more permissive,[79] foreign enterprises were poised to take quick advantage of the rules. Indeed, they were more willing and eager to reduce overstaffing through dismissals and non-renewal of contracts than SOEs. By law, a firm that fires an employee for any one of the disciplinary reasons that do not require 30 days' notice, such as conviction of a crime, owes the fired worker no compensation. Firms have to compensate employees who are terminated in the middle of a contract or for reasons that require 30 days notice with one month's pay for each year of employment with the company.[80] State rules on severance pay, which mimicked Western business practices, clarified and endorsed the procedures for dismissal. As long as FIEs dismiss employees with cause and pay an appropriate severance package, workers and trade unions have little legal ground on which to block dismissals.

Since 1994, China's attitude toward protecting workers' interests, especially those in FIEs, has undergone a significant change. For example, the FESCO, which previously blocked dismissals and toed the party line on high levels of employment, has changed to not only allow but to facilitate dismissal of unwanted Chinese workers. In the late 1990s, some trade representative offices simply informed the FESCO that there was a problem with a worker, presented the evidence, and asked to have the worker dismissed. The FESCO then handled the termination of the labor contract.[81] In the words of an office manager, "the FESCO provided a healthy legal structure" for dismissing workers.[82] Such comments evince the depth of change at the FESCO. In another case, the local labor bureau, where all dismissals must be registered, never intervened in a Japanese company's efforts to dismiss employees, so the manager continued to discharge employees.[83] Over the course of the 1990s, direct state control over labor service companies for domestic enterprises and foreign enterprises weakened as free labor market practices proliferated and the impediments to labor mobility were eroded and removed.

Hiring Practices and Managing Labor Turnover in Japanese and U.S. Firms

The above account lays out the changing legal framework and structural factors that conditioned China's shift toward a free labor market. It leaves unanswered why China moved in a direction of a U.S. style of employment relations rather than a Japanese one. Sharing a common pattern of life-long employment and egalitarian wage distribution with China's "iron rice bowl," Japanese institutions were rather easily transferred to China. Initially, Chinese officials were interested in Japanese advanced training techniques and the prospect of upgrading workers' skills without destabilizing the Chinese workforce,[84] but they ultimately rejected Japanese labor institutions because the latter replicated many problems found in SOEs.[85] In the late 1990s, managers in Japanese-invested enterprises in China went through a period of adjustment, weakening their commitment to lifelong employment and increasing their interest in dismissing employees. American institutions on dismissal and labor turnover, which were quite distinct from the "iron rice bowl," at first met resistance from officials and Chinese managers but later were more widely accepted, if not emulated by Chinese and Japanese firms in Shanghai.

Japanese and U.S. Firms' Approaches to Hiring

Typically, in Japan, firms recruit new employees from high schools or universities as a cohort for their general skills and without particular job assignments during the hiring seasons. After a period of initial general training, a firm assigns new employees to a division for work and further training. An employee within a Japanese firm may shift between divisions or receive training in many components of the firm's operations. Such an approach is premised on a conception of "job" that is not neatly defined.[86] Instead, the company is conceived of as a community, and its work is a shared endeavor, so employees are trained in many aspects of the company's operation and jobs remain fuzzily defined.[87] Advancement within a Japanese firm is slow, involving completion of a series of training exercises and job-related tasks. Japanese firms rely on internal labor markets, meaning that when a job comes open, human resources managers promote an existing employee within the firm to fill the post. Hence, Japan has a very limited market for mid-career appointments, and company rules create incentives to stay with a company.

In contrast, U.S. firms' home country practices are structured around a flexible labor force and expectations of moderate labor turnover. The U.S. system of hiring is called post-and-bid, in which a well-defined job is posted, and people inside and, often, outside the firm may apply.[88] The model facilitates workers' job mobility and relies on mid-career hiring, so they are not exclusively dependent on promotion from the ranks of their staff, as is the case in Japan.[89] In China, U.S. firms drew on their labor institutions to poach talented staff from other firms and to fill vacated positions. Chinese regulations have wavered on protecting the right of foreign invested enterprises to recruit employees away from state-owned enterprises.[90] SOEs were reluctant to give up their most talented employees but were also too strapped financially to offer competitive wages. Regulations thwarted the free movement of mid-career employees, but cash-starved SOEs came to settle for monetary compensation from FIEs who hired away their workers.[91] Headhunters, a Western human resources institution, are now a common feature of China's labor market. In China and Japan, seniority played an important role in promotions, thus creating disincentives to mid-career job-hopping, while U.S. reliance on post-and-bid recruitment fostered job mobility. Since 1992, the new wave of labor market institutional reforms and flood of foreign investment have given rise to a labor market that has been characterized by rapid turnover among well-educated and trained white-collar staff. In China, the shift from unified labor allocation with little job movement after the initial employment relationship to a robust mid-career labor market with attendant job advertisements and headhunters evinces the effect of U.S. and European labor institutions. SOEs were reluctant to undertake meaningful hiring reforms, but Chinese staff favorably responded to new opportunities presented by foreign investors' sub-regime of labor institutions.

Japanese and U.S. Firms' Approaches to Training and Retention

In Japan, large corporations achieved remarkably low rates of labor turnover and employee dismissal by constructing a set of institutions that rewarded loyalty and facilitated employee development.[92] Japanese firms' "late promotion" and "promotion from within" patterns of advancement developed loyal workers with a high level of enterprise-specific skills and allowed for careful observation and evaluation before promoting staff.[93] To Shanghai, Japanese firms brought their (somewhat watered-down) commitment to life-long employment and slow promotion, but those institutions did not produce very desirable results among Chinese white-collar employees. For most of Japan's postwar period, internal promotion evoked workers' loyalty to the firm because hiring norms and firm-specific training programs limited opportunities to leave the firm for jobs in other companies.[94] In Shanghai, those same conditions did not apply, and Japanese institutions produced quite different results. Beginning in the early 1990s, the tidal wave of foreign direct investment opened up numerous job opportunities for ambitious Chinese managers and white-collar staff. Consequently, white-collar staff in foreign-invested enterprises quickly turned over in their positions, and workers displayed short time horizons, a pattern at odds with Japanese norms.[95] Shanghai's high level of foreign direct investment flows caused human resource woes for all foreign investors, especially for Japanese investors who lacked institutions to replace staff who departed in the middle of their careers.

In Shanghai, Japanese companies complained that the long-term employment and internal promotion systems did not evoke worker identity with and loyalty to the firm. A Japanese manager in a Sino-Japanese electronics JV noted, "[I]n a Japanese factory the workers have a type of collective consciousness. They understand that they work for the firm and that if they work well, the factory will succeed. In China, there is a weak collective consciousness. Each worker is concerned with him/herself."[96] In his explanation for high levels of Chinese staff turnover in Japanese firms, a Chinese staff member conceded that Chinese workers "don't have any moral principles; they just think about themselves."[97] A Japanese office manager found that workers lacked commitment to the firm: "We expect loyalty from workers in terms of their basic work in exchange for high base salaries. This method does not work in China."[98] Many Japanese managers complained of Chinese workers' desire to hop to jobs in other firms.[99] Chinese white-collar workers' short time horizons compelled Japanese firms to reconsider and to revise their labor institutions in China, for example their decision to enhance individual performance-based pay, described in chapter 4.

In fact, Japanese companies have faced problems gaining white-collar workers' loyalty in their subsidiaries throughout Asia. Experts on Japanese labor practices noted,

> Japanese management style is willingly accepted by blue-collar workers in Asia. The Japanese companies train workers a lot and provide high levels of job security. The Japanese management style is not very well accepted by white-collar workers. Managers often complain about late promotion, relatively low salaries, and a reluctance to entrust duties and to extend authority to local managers.[100]

The guarantees provided by Japanese employment suited many Chinese blue-collar workers who watched mass layoffs from SOEs, but security combined with slow promotion had little appeal to the young entrepreneurial managers in China, who had greater prospects for advancement due to the high demand for talented managers.[101]

Rochelle Kopp contends that Japanese subsidiaries are loath to promote local managers to higher positions, a pattern she describes as a "rice paper ceiling,"[102] which drives many aspiring managers to depart Japanese firms. An impediment to advancement in Japanese-invested enterprises is the large numbers of expatriates that many Japanese companies send to China and other countries. With Japanese staff occupying the top layer(s) of operations in many facilities, Chinese employees cannot climb very high up the managerial ladder. A Chinese human resources manager in a Japanese corporation explained how this affects Chinese workers' attitudes towards their companies:

> Japanese companies determine how many expatriates to send to their subsidiaries prior to hiring local workers, and all of the Japanese hold the leadership positions for the departments. The problem for Chinese staff is that there is no clear promotional track. This is something that U.S. and European companies have done very well. They plan for a person's development to become a manager. In a Japanese company, they don't give you increasing responsibility and difficult tasks to help

you train to be a manager. You just get your pay raise, and that's that. Many people leave the company after a couple of years because they feel that they have limited growth opportunities.[103]

The Chinese human resources manager's criticism indicates a new cognitive script—one that emphasizes job advancement and individual reward over long-term security—among an emerging wave of foreign-trained, young white-collar staff.

Japanese parent firms offer extensive training programs to their home-country workers and managerial staff in order to develop multi-skilled workers,[104] but some Japanese firms limited training of local staff in their overseas subsidiaries.[105] In Tokyo, a personnel manager's comments reflected his company's latent bias against local staff in their foreign subsidiaries: "We don't bring foreign workers to Japan for training; *that is only for company members.* We set up training programs for them in their local countries."[106] In this case, the distinction between a company member and a non-company member was not determined by working for the company in question but being Japanese or foreign. Another personnel manager in a large Japanese manufacturing company who previously worked in China noted a systemic company bias toward foreign staff, "The training programs are mainly for Japanese staff. There are many very talented workers in China, but no one is interested in them in our Japanese operations. No one wants to bring them to Tokyo for training."[107] Chinese staff view overseas training programs both as job rewards and as opportunities for career development. Chinese interpret denial of such opportunities, then, as a double slight.

Without a training program equal to the one afforded to Japanese employees, Chinese managers were at a disadvantage when being considered for promotions in Japanese-invested operations. In turn, Japanese managers were frustrated by Chinese workers' lack of loyalty and poor performance, and they were unwilling to invest significant training in employees who might quickly leave the company. Slow promotions and poor training put off Chinese workers, so they were anxious to look for better job opportunities with other firms. The mutual dissatisfaction of local employees and Japanese managers reinforced Japanese fears of disloyal Chinese workers and Chinese beliefs that they could not be promoted, which pushed up labor turnover and dismissal rates.

American firms tend to use a mixture of market-based compensation, training, and upward mobility to retain white-collar staff.[108] Chinese interviewees lauded U.S. firms for their approaches to training and promotion. U.S. firms use advertisements and headhunters to hire Chinese for specific managerial positions, and they construct training around achieving specific goals for the person hired for the position. Some Chinese employees in U.S.-invested enterprises claimed that U.S. firms were better at training workers for long-term professional growth than Japanese firms. A Chinese human resources manager offered this explanation for the discrepancy:

> U.S. firms' training programs are able to completely train a person to become a mature businessperson. After 3–5 years, a person is able to understand the firm's business model and to make good decisions on his/her own to solve similar problems. American companies are good at spotting people with fast learning curves, and they give such workers higher salary bumps than other workers. U.S. companies want to spend money on training and are willing to take the risk that once the person is trained that s/he may join another company. Thus, I think this training issue is a major reason why Chinese people prefer to work under the American model.[109]

To retain top employees, U.S. firms give additional compensation, training, and other rewards to signal to the employees that the firm values their work. Such training also helps to diffuse U.S. institutions to other firms through managers who depart U.S. firms to establish their own or to work for other companies.

Although several U.S. firms tried to train their employees to solve problems on their own, this required a change in the cognitive script of Chinese workers, who grew up in a school system that did not emphasize creative problem solving. A research director in a U.S. high-tech firm explains the problems that he encountered training some of his Chinese staff:

> We believe in delegating responsibility, trust, performance evaluation. We are finding a good reception to these principles among Chinese; education and training are other matters. We have to adapt them to a working model. In China, we expect workers to ask questions in a training class. In the west we are taught to ask questions and challenge opinions. We respect autonomy and creativity. Here, classes are very repetitive in math, and not very conceptual. It is not surprising that the repetition and lack of conceptualization lead to weak autonomy and creativity among Chinese students.[110]

Not all Chinese were able to develop problem-solving skills, but U.S. investors attempted to train Chinese staff to have critical analytical skills, which they could use to advance their careers and could take with them to other foreign and Chinese firms. Several of the U.S. firms send their Chinese employees who hold key positions in their Shanghai operations to the United States for training. Such training trips are a reward in themselves, but, in addition to technical matters, the trips also expose Chinese employees to the culture and values of their companies. The opportunity to receive such training and to employ them in research and other responsibilities were more important than pay for some Chinese staff. A researcher at a U.S. high-tech company explained his motivation for staying with the U.S. company, "If I were making my work decision strictly on salary, I would probably leave. I would go work in a disco. Here, I can do advanced work, which is a great opportunity."[111]

Clarifying requirements for promotion, providing appropriate training, and following through with promotions and financial rewards encouraged strong performers to stay with U.S. firms. In fact, a general manager of a U.S.-invested firm argued that opportunities for advancement were more important than salary when it comes to retention. A salary survey conducted on behalf of Japanese firms found that their pay by type of position was higher than average, which led a Chinese human resources manager to conclude that promotion opportunities rather than pay increases caused white-collar turnover in Japanese firms.[112]

The clearest evidence of the promotional paths available to Chinese employees in U.S. operations is the high degree of "localization" of the general manager's position. Of the U.S. firms interviewed in 2000, 38 percent of their general managers were local (Chinese), 44 percent were from the United States, and the remainder came from third countries such as Singapore and Taiwan. Of the Japanese companies interviewed, 94 percent of the general managers were from Japan, 4 percent from third countries, and only 2 percent from China. Clearly, U.S. firms held out greater hope of promotion to the very top reaches of management in their China-based operations. Only a few select Chinese employees ever climb very far up the corporate ladder in U.S. firms, but Chinese workers do not perceive the same "rice paper ceiling"[113] as they do in Japanese-invested firms.

Japanese Firms' Approaches to Dismissal and Retention

Japanese firms have experienced low levels of labor turnover in their home-country operations, in part, because Japanese firms are reluctant to dismiss employees in their home-country operations. Japanese firms applied similar principles to their Shanghai operation. A Chinese assistant general manager in a Sino-Japanese JV described how his company dealt with lax workers: "The workers from the SOE came from a situation that was too comfortable. It was difficult to change them. Many U.S. firms offer a severance package (*anzi fei*) to get rid of unwanted SOE workers who are transferred to a JV. Japanese firms do not believe that this pays off (*bu hesuan*). We believe that you should train workers to try to change them."[114] Such an approach led Japanese firms in China to focus on retraining poor-performing staff, while top employees left for better opportunities in other companies. Through the mid-1990s, Japanese managers generally tried to retrain rather than fire poor performing staff, but in the late 1990s Japanese firms began to change their approach.[115]

In Japan, firms emphasize training and retraining of employees to find an appropriate position in the firm rather than dismissing poor performers. A Chinese deputy general manager in a Sino-Japanese JV explained how his company applied such an approach to Shanghai staff:

> When we have a person who performs badly, we try to switch that person to a new position. If, after further training and switching

positions the person still is not working out, we tell them such. If they don't work out after switching posts, they usually leave on their own. Japanese firms usually do not fire workers. The Chinese management team thinks that it is a little strange.[116]

Rather than lauding the Japanese firm's commitment to Chinese workers, the Chinese manager expressed dismay over retraining efforts. The comments reflect the views of the new wave of Chinese managerial staff who worked in FIEs during the late 1990s.

By the late 1990s, Japanese managers (and Chinese assistant general managers) became dissatisfied with the way that the Japanese human resource system meshed with local workers' cognitive scripts on employment and the performance that Japanese institutions induced from Chinese workers. Some Japanese managers cleaved to their firms' retraining principle and took personal responsibility for their failure to overcome their Chinese employees' poor performance, but, beginning in the late 1990s, others came to China and adopted a more confrontational approach to workers in their new appointments. For example, after he was appointed to a Shanghai office in 1999, one Japanese trading office manager effectively "cleaned house." In 1999, the trading office had run in the red, and the newly appointed office manager determined to institute new employment practices, including a willingness to get rid of unwanted employees. In one year, the office manager pushed out (without formally firing anyone) 7 of 24 employees, a remarkable 29 percent of the staff.[117] In a rural production facility where labor turnover tends to be low, a Japanese manager fired 30 of the 50 original production workers who held non-technical jobs. In addition, after beginning operations with three-year labor contracts, the company quickly moved to one-year contracts for new hires because non-renewal of a contract is much easier than firing workers in the middle of contracts.[118] Still, some Japanese managers were quick to shift toward a modified version of lifelong employment. For example, a Japanese general manager of a Sino-Japanese JV offered all Chinese employees two-year contracts, but employees who stayed on for five years were offered unlimited contracts, essentially lifelong employment.[119] Japanese firms' revised labor contracting practices reflect a compromise of parent-company institutions to cope with China's labor market.

For the year 1999, the average labor turnover in Shanghai-based foreign invested enterprises was approximately 15 percent.[120] For the same year, on average, surveyed Japanese manufacturers experienced 5.5 percent labor turnover, and Japanese offices 6.2 percent in Shanghai. These figures fall far below the oft-quoted 15 percent labor turnover rate for Shanghai-based foreign invested enterprises for 2000. Objectively, the Japanese firms were doing well with regard to labor turnover, but the turnover figures unsettled most Japanese managers who had experienced minimal labor turnover in Japan.[121] Japanese managers complained that they lost employees to U.S. and western European firms, a troubling pattern that one might be tempted to explain by Chinese workers' lingering bias against their Japanese employers left over from World War II. Yet, many of the white-collar employees studied Japanese to improve their employment prospects in such firms, which suggests that they did not harbor such a bias.[122]

Growing competition for top managerial and technical staff also has forced Japanese firms to reconsider their parent-company institutions. A general manager of a high-tech company explains how anticipated competition forced his Sino-Japanese JV to changes personnel policies, including use of dismissal procedures:

> I am afraid that many other companies will grab our employees. We must keep our excellent people. I am looking to shift wages and personnel around, so that our better people get higher pay and our average workers receive lower pay or are eliminated. People with no ability sometimes cause mistakes, and we do not need such people. Some of these workers we must dismiss; others we may keep but at a lower salary. We must focus on the best workers.[123]

As foreign investors flooded China, Japanese-invested firms had to reform their institutions to cope with the competition, which entailed abandoning egalitarian distribution of income and trimming unnecessary staff rather than retraining poor performers.

Japanese firms partially abandoned their home-country commitment to retraining employees and the model of firm as family. In the late 1990s, Japanese managers found local actors willing to help carry out dismissals. On the matter of firing workers, one Japanese manager in Shanghai said, "In Japan, it is very difficult to fire workers, but here in Shanghai it is very easy."[124] Such an attitude helps to explain why, in 2000, the manager lost (mostly fired) approximately 12 percent of his staff. In the same year, the subsidiary's parent company in Japan only lost about 20 employees, excluding retirements, a sharp contrast to the recent dismissals in the China facility.[125] The changing local institutional environment provided a framework for instituting dismissal measures in firms that sought to get rid of unwanted employees, whereas the Japanese home environment did not.

Japanese firms were not at the forefront of efforts to push China to reform its policies or, even, norms regarding labor dismissals. To the contrary, Japanese firms were late to try to institute aggressive dismissal practices in their Chinese subsidiaries, and only then in reaction to their frustration with poor results of their home-country institutions in China's labor environment and with some prodding from Chinese managerial staff. Japanese firms' reliance on recruitment of recent high school or college graduates for training and long-term employment with the firm made it difficult for Japanese firms to resolve the problem of mid-career labor turnover in China. Despite relatively low turnover rates, the number of staff, especially managers who quit firms, unsettled Japanese managers in Shanghai. Due to their internal labor market institutions, they were unaccustomed to hiring low- and middle-level managers from outside the firm. To address their human resource problems in Shanghai, some Japanese firms altered their approach to promotion and retention, although many firms were slow to respond to feedback from labor market signals on their institutions. Japanese firms in Shanghai that did undertake significant reforms increasingly resembled U.S.-invested companies.

U.S. Approaches to Dismissal and Retention

In the 1980s and early 1990s, some U.S. managers found dismissing Chinese employees quite difficult or "nearly impossible."[126] For example, at Beijing Jeep, one of the early major U.S. investments in China, U.S. managers had trouble getting the Chinese managers to discipline workers, even more so to dismiss them.[127] A foreign manager of a Sino-U.S. JV could not dismiss several deputy general managers who were incompetent but who enjoyed the backing of Chinese partners.[128] During the late 1990s many U.S. manufacturers established WFOEs rather than JVs or converted existing JVs to WFOEs (see chapter 3), in which foreign managers were unlikely to face entrenched party and trade union representatives and Chinese partners who could thwart dismissals.[129] The WFOE model facilitated greater foreign control over labor management and, indirectly, worker dismissal.

By the late 1990s, U.S. managers found it easier to release or fire unwanted workers. In part, this resulted from a lesson learned to reduce the length of workers' contracts. When state officials introduced labor contracts, they suggested that contracts would be three to ten years in duration.[130] Such long contracts would introduce an element of mid- and long-term flexibility to firms' workforces, but managers would not be able to react very quickly to short-term changes in production needs or poor performance by workers. Initially, managers of FIEs sought more flexibility to manage their workforces, but their JV partners prevented them from offering short contracts. Over the course of the 1990s, managers of FIEs learned from earlier "mistakes" in offering three- and five-year contracts to all employees, and Chinese human resource managers softened their insistence on such long contracts. One-year contracts allowed firms to dispense with unwanted employees at the end of their contract with little or no opposition from the workers' trade union or the local labor bureau. U.S. investors moved to shorten the contracts in their firms, a pattern that Japanese investors mimicked. U.S. firms tended to offer one- and two-year contracts to their Chinese workforce, until the firms are "confident in the employee's ability."[131] Unlike Japanese subsidiaries, U.S. firms were not tied to a firm-wide policy but offered contracts of different lengths, depending on the position and the person holding it. A Sino-U.S. JV offered two-year contracts to most employees, one-year contracts to employees who were not performing very well, and five-year contracts to staff in crucial positions.[132] Another U.S. subsidiary began operations with three-year contracts, but switched to one-year initial contracts because "three years leaves no latitude in firing."[133] With one-year contracts, a firm has a short period to wait until releasing unwanted employees at the expiration of the contract. Japanese firms moved to shorten the duration of their contracts from five years to three, two, or even one year because of rapidly changing market conditions[134] and the inability to dismiss poor-performing employees in the midst of long-term contracts.[135]

Some aspects of Chinese labor regulations, especially the 1994 *Labor Law*, better suited U.S. firms' approach to hiring and firing than they did Japanese firms. The dismissal process built into the 1994 *Labor Law* also quickly evolved into a practice of offering workers a severance package in exchange for dismissal, a model that mimicked U.S. institutions and marked a departure from Chinese (and Japanese) approaches to dismissal. American firms are accustomed to rapidly evaluating new hires and judging their potential.[136] China's *Labor Law* established a three-month probationary period during which a firm can dismiss poor-performing employees without financial repercussions[137] that suited U.S. evaluation practices. Typically, new hires in U.S. subsidiaries underwent a brief period of intense training and observation, in some cases just three months, after which, the firm evaluated the employee and determined whether to retain or let the worker go. A manager in a rapidly expanding U.S. manufacturer callously referred to his firm's strategy as "mining gold and getting rid of dirt...If a person does not work out, we just get rid of them before a year has passed."[138] In 1999, 10 of 54 employees (18.5%) in that manager's trading office "left" the company, albeit none of them voluntarily.

Some local workers could not adjust to the fast pace of U.S. operations and the rapid determination of an employee's quality. In Sino-U.S. JVs, workers who transferred in from SOEs often faced difficulties in meshing with the new rigorous work requirements. A Chinese human resources manager in a Sino-U.S. JV reported that workers were surprised by the strictness of labor management, which led many to flee the company after just a few months' work.[139] Unlike Japanese corporations, which trained and retrained hires who have difficulty adjusting to their new company, U.S. corporations were much more likely to dismiss or not renew contracts of workers who slowly adapted to their new work environment. The different models are also related to distinct approaches to defining jobs. Japanese firms recruit generalists and can (re)define a person's role in the course of a career, whereas U.S. firms hire employees for specific functions, and failure to fulfill those functions can lead to dismissal.

In their home country operations, U.S. and Japanese firms have significantly different labor turnover rates.[140] Yet, sampled Japanese and U.S. operations in Shanghai had remarkably similar turnover rates in 1999. On average, U.S. trading and representative offices had a slightly higher labor turnover (7.6 percent) rate than Japanese (6.2 percent), but U.S. manufacturing subsidiaries had a slightly lower rate (4.8 percent) than Japanese (5.5 percent).

In light of the U.S. post-and-bid system and Japanese internal promotion principles, it is somewhat surprising that the labor turnover rates were so similar and suggests that Japanese procedures induced worse-than-anticipated results, and U.S. firms enjoyed better results than expected.[141] The causes of labor turnover appear distinct in the two countries' facilities. Japanese-invested enterprises faced higher levels of employee dissatisfaction than U.S. firms, which caused labor turnover, an opinion corroborated by Chinese interviewees' complaints about Japanese firms in Shanghai.[142] In Japanese firms, voluntary quits were equally or more important than dismissals as the cause of Japanese firms' labor turnover. Generally, managers of U.S. firms controlled their labor turnover by forcing out unwanted employees and using high salaries to retain prized employees. American firms, too, lost employees to competitors who offered better compensation or promotions, but U.S. managers were able to address staff turnover with their post-and-bid hiring model, whereas Japanese firms' internal promotion schemes could not overcome their labor turnover.

A New Script for Chinese Human Resources Managers

In JVs and especially in WFOEs, foreign managers were able to ingrain their parent companies' values and approaches to labor relations in Chinese managerial staff. In the early years of JVs, such efforts met resistance from recalcitrant Chinese managers who earned their managerial stripes during the late Mao era and who took control over human resources positions and limited transplantation of foreign labor institutions. State controls over FIEs' labor practices diminished as trade unions and Communist Party cells became more pliant than in the 1980s and scarcely existed in foreign invested enterprises, especially in WFOEs.[143] Additionally, the state allowed freer flow of personnel throughout the country, which simultaneously undermined the household registration (*hukou*) and dossier (*dang'an*) systems of worker dependency.[144] Managers of foreign firms eroded China's institutional legacies that created opposition to dismissal, replacing them with new norms and new personnel. By the late 1990s, many Chinese managers who were imbued with socialist principles had retired from JVs, and a new cadre of younger, more market-driven managers had emerged. Many of the younger Chinese managers identified more with their foreign partners than with local workers and socialism.[145] Such colleagues contributed to firing employees, pressured workers to raise productivity, and did not necessarily protect workers' interests or state goals. A Chinese general manager of a Sino-U.S. JV electrical appliance firm described how the Chinese partners' approach to labor changed:

> We rarely used to fire workers. Personnel matters were handled by the trade union. Many of our workers came in from the old (SOE) factory, and it was difficult to fire them unless they broke the law. Recently,

our JV partner introduced us to the western style of personnel management. We have already fired many workers. The Chinese side was very soft on this, so it is a big change for us to fire workers.[146]

In the same company, management worked with its trade union representatives to restructure the company's five JVs, forcing 440 employees to accept layoffs and to institute a more stratified compensation system.[147]

Chinese human resources managers in Japanese-invested enterprises evinced some of the same values, but Japanese managers tended to temper such enthusiasm for firing employees. Indeed, Chinese managers in Japanese-invested enterprises sometimes were dismayed by Japanese managers' willingness to retain poor performers. Foreign investors introduced Chinese managers to new labor institutions and trained them in the logic of such institutions' practice. With these new cognitive scripts, Chinese managers began to take on the values of their foreign managers, which they used in FIEs or could take with them to new firms. They also received training from chambers of commerce and management consultants that operate at the meso level, forming a policy community with a shared set of values and analytical tools.

Both Japanese and Chinese firms moved toward the U.S. model of labor turnover and dismissal. In China, Japanese firms have begun to revise their promotion and retention practices, including dismissal, due to frustrations with the meshing of their home-country practices with local workers. Chinese firms, too, have shifted toward mass layoffs, downsizing, and a willingness to fire workers because of the combination of financial difficulties, learning from foreign investors' institutions, and human resources reorganization born of competition for talented staff. In addition, the Chinese government has pressed SOEs to allow workers to accept severance packages to depart the firm in much the same way that is standard practice in foreign-invested enterprises.[148] Labor turnover spilled over into the SOE sector, especially when foreign enterprises poached top young managers who may have had their promotional track blocked by a top-heavy older set of managers in SOEs. In recent years, SOEs responded in kind; they now poach from foreign firms in Shanghai, which indicates greater mobility in China's labor market and SOEs' adoption of more aggressive hiring practices.[149]

The 2007 *Labor Contract Law:* Slowing the Influence of FIEs' Labor Practices?

Critics have contended that China's reform of labor institutions and the adoption of contentious labor relations have shifted too far in eroding the safety net for workers.[150] Under Hu Jintao's leadership (2002–present), China has sought to buttress the power of trade unions and to protect the interests of workers. The *Labor Contract Law* signals such an effort to shore up the rights of workers. The new law strengthens rules on extending lifelong contracts to employees with more than ten years' experience or who have completed more than two consecutive labor contracts with a corporation as well as shortened the term of some workers' probationary periods during which they could be dismissed without grounds for challenging the decision.[151]

The use of dismissal by Chinese and foreign-invested enterprises has, at times, violated principles of appropriate conduct, even measured by Chinese labor standards, an indication of Chinese firms' shift in the direction of conflictual labor practices. For example, at the end of 2007, a number of high-profile incidents occurred involving Chinese and foreign firms dismissing long-term Chinese employees prior to the new *Labor Contract Law* going into effect on January 1, 2008. Allegedly, Huawei, one of China's leading corporations and exporters, compelled 7000 employees to resign before the new law went into effect to avoid extending such workers open-ended contracts. Some of the resigning employees were allowed to sign new labor contracts with the firm.[152] Officially, Huawei is a private company, but it is referred to as a "national champion" and has historical linkages to government-sponsored research labs.[153] In a similar case, workers at Transpo Electronics, a U.S.-invested enterprise in Shanghai staged a demonstration on the roof of their enterprise to protest their forced layoffs before the new Labor Contract Law took effect.[154] The All-China Federation of Trade Unions stepped up pressure in these and other cases in Shenzhen and Shanghai to thwart inappropriate dismissals of staff by foreign and domestic investors,[155] and the companies backed away from these labor violations. These cases demonstrate the degree to which foreign and local firms have adopted similar logic with regard to labor contracts and flexibility.

At first blush, the *Labor Contract Law* appears a challenge to foreign investors' use of dismissals, and, indeed, many foreign investors balked at the law's tightened restrictions when it was in its draft stage. The *Labor Contract Law* does strengthen the hand of workers and trade unions in their relations with employers, but two aspects of the law's gestation are suggestive of the continued importance of foreign investors' influence. First, the new law equally targets domestic firms, not just FIEs. Second, the process of writing the legislation marked something of a breakthrough in terms of political transparency. When a draft version of the *Labor Contract Law* was introduced, state officials called for two rounds of commentary—one open and the other by invitation—to solicit the views of civil society organizations. Both domestic and international organizations in China were allowed to participate in this process. For example, business organizations such as the American Chamber of Commerce and the US-China Business Council offered responses to the draft legislation.[156] In redrafting the legislation, the National People's Congress took into account some of the concerns raised by organizations. In a letter posted on its website, the American Chamber of Commerce-Shanghai praised the legislative process involved in enacting the *Labor Contract Law* calling it, "an almost unprecedented call by the government for public comments on drafts of the law," and concluded, "The *Labor Contract Law* is an excellent example of government and business groups working together to craft legislation."[157] Although the *Labor Contract Law* does contain provisions that encroach on FIEs' human resources practices, the process of enacting legislation was a welcome advance in the development of transparency and the inclusion of FIEs' interests.

Foreign Firms, Local Interests, and Flexible Labor

Returning to the pair of questions posed at the start of this chapter, we can now summarize the role that foreign investors played in reforming the "iron rice bowl" and how Japanese and U.S. firms' approaches to dismissal and labor turnover meshed with China's "iron rice bowl" culture. In general, foreign firms—more so U.S. firms than Japanese firms—contributed to labor reform in four ways.

First, foreign firms shortened the term of labor contracts from the three- to ten-year contracts, which the authorities initially recommended, to one- to three-year contracts. Such a shift greatly increased the FIEs' control over staffing and helped to break the security of the "iron rice bowl." Second, foreign firms helped to bridge the gap between formal changes in Chinese labor law and regulations, on the one hand, and labor practices, on the other. The Ministry of Labor and Social Services faced difficulty instituting a new pattern of behavior in firms that had developed an "iron rice bowl" culture. Reformers found a more receptive audience in foreign enterprise managers and a sub-set of workers who also responded favorably to institutional sub-regimes. Third, foreign, especially U.S., firms imparted values to their staff that changed the ethos of labor relations in foreign invested enterprises. Many Chinese managers accepted the market-driven values of foreign firms and private Chinese enterprises. Judging by Chinese managers' critical comments about their Japanese counterparts' practices in JVs, Chinese staff more quickly adopted a flexible labor perspective than Japanese managers did. Fourth, foreign firms introduced a number of practices and institutions such as headhunters, training programs, mid-career hiring, and evaluation procedures that propelled labor market reforms. Foreign investors helped to sketch in the details for constructing the labor market based on the rough blueprints generated by early reformers.

The development of China's labor contract system and labor market practices sheds light on state-guided globalization and institutional change. As was the case with compensation reform, Chinese officials determined in the early stages of the reform period that they needed to introduce labor contracts as a means to insert a degree of labor flexibility for managers and to break the "iron rice bowl." The Chinese state changed the formal institutions related to contracts and labor markets, but it was difficult to change behavior under the reformed institutions because actors had internalized "iron rice

bowl" norms. Foreign firms that were eager to adopt labor market principles led the way in implementing labor contracts. They also introduced new
methods of hiring, training, and managing staff retention, which constituted
a sub-regime of labor institutions. Foreign investors succeeded in doing so
because, in the 1990s, a new cohort of Chinese human resources managers were trained by their employers, and foreign firms gained control over
human resources functions as they shifted investment to WFOEs. As the
sub-regime expanded and grew in popularity, other firms operating under
the dominant regime opted to mimic the sub-regime's practices.

Japanese and U.S. firms supplied distinct models for China to consider and to emulate. Earlier works on reforms to Chinese labor institutions
have suggested that China was likely to move toward human resource practices imbued with Japanese characteristics.[158] The above analysis gives little support to those claims; indeed, I assert that China is moving toward a
U.S. model of managing labor turnover and dismissal practices.[159] Existing
Chinese institutions and the desires of many reformers to maintain social
stability may be more in line with Japanese institutions, but several Japanese
managers and Chinese managers grew disillusioned with Japanese recruitment, training, promotion, and dismissal policies. Crucial to this change of
course was feedback supplied by workers on the labor market who left firms,
thus, informing judgments on firm-level labor institutions. Chinese human
resources managers typically recognized the varying responses to Japanese
and U.S. labor institutions, but Japanese firms did not always affect reforms
in response. The lessons were not lost on Chinese human resources managers
and meso-level actors, however, who could diffuse such knowledge to other
companies. In addition, there was a conflict between the fundamental goal
of the labor contract system, to break down state-owned enterprises' lifelong employment system, and the Japanese model of long-term training and
employment. In fact, many Japanese firms and managers partially abandoned
their home-country institutions in China. Firms did not offer training programs to the same degree as in Japan, revised their pay systems, and weakened their commitment to lifelong employment. The Japanese model held the
promise of social stability and extensive worker training, but in practice, the
model gradually induced stunted training, white-collar labor turnover, and
a higher degree of industrial conflict than in U.S.- and European-invested
enterprises. Japanese firms' slow and partial response to negative feedback
suggests that organizational learning models do not very well predict firms'
responses to new information in a host environment. Rather, path dependent
approaches better explain their cleaving to parent-era institutions.

While foreign enterprises contributed to Chinese reforms, Chinese
authorities adopted many of the policies, at least as pilot projects that foreign firms wanted to institute as practice. Foreign firms did not bully China
into adopting policies, but the two sides arrived at common interests in labor
practices that would attract foreign capital and help to make China's firms

more efficient. One long-time U.S. management consultant in China put it this way,

> Multinational corporations wanted greater flexibility on some issues such as flexible scheduling of work hours and greater freedom in the hiring and firing process. I would describe the changes as evolutionary in nature and as meeting the needs both of the government and of foreign businesses, not as the result of pressure or complaints from the foreign side.[160]

Other human resource consultants in China noted that China "would not have changed its rules if it was not interested in doing so,"[161] and "lobbying only explains part of the labor reforms; a more profound reason is the general intention of the Chinese government to make China a true market economy."[162] Still, China's officials have become more transparent about their writing of laws and are more welcoming of actors' input on draft legislation, as the *Labor Contract Law* shows.

Such comments lend support to the claim that foreign investors helped Chinese reformers to institute practices that they wished to adopt. In the cases of some labor reforms, new policies initially proved politically difficult to implement in state-owned enterprises, but foreign invested enterprise managers were receptive to the changes. FIEs created a sub-regime of labor practices based on their home-country practices, and Chinese workers indicated their institutional preferences through their movement on the labor market. As FIEs' structural position in China's economy expanded, SOEs began to mimic FIEs' models. SOEs did so because of the perceived success of foreign firms, to improve their standing among firms competing for top staff in China, and in response to state pressure to reform. Moreover, Chinese human resources managers moved between foreign and domestic enterprises, diffusing foreign institutional models. Thus, Chinese reformers gave wind to foreign corporations to advance new labor practices where they found resistance among state-owned enterprises. As labor markets formed, competition between the dominant regime and sub-regime of institutions forced SOEs, with encouragement from state officials, to adopt more aggressive human resource practices to retain their top employees and to continue to improve.

7

"Remade in China": Foreign Investors and Chinese Actors Negotiate Institutional Change

China's opening to foreign investment, trade, and culture generated consternation among foreign leaders and citizens. To some critics, China is a gross violator of human rights, a country that lacks commitment to legal principles, and a rising military power, all of which cause them to approach China as a country bent on changing the norms, standards, and rules of international society.[1] For others, China is growing into the role of a reliable international actor that is slowly adopting the norms and practices of international society. This book has detailed how China gradually has shifted from tightly restricting the movement of foreign ideas, capital, and goods into China to embracing foreign investment, trade, and many international and foreign business institutions. Since 1978, China has become deeply engaged in the world economy, measured in terms of investment flows, trade, and membership in multilateral organizations. Additionally, China has reformed many of its domestic institutions to move closer to the norms and expectations of members of international society. China has reaped economic rewards from its greater openness, boasting an extraordinary growth rate of over 9 percent per year since it commenced its reforms in 1978. China's gradual approach to reform has resulted in startling cumulative changes, but certainly, China is far from a liberal democratic country. Despite its economic, political, and societal transformations, China has come under intense scrutiny for its persistent shortcomings with regards to international norms of behavior. Some 30 years after the introduction of its open-door policy, it is appropriate to take stock of China's progress toward adhering to international norms and the success of international organizations and foreign countries in diffusing new institutions to China.

The study of China's state-guided globalization directs our attention to a key point of contention in this debate: institutional change. Specifically, is China adjusting its macro-level institutions to comply with international norms and standards of conduct? Equally important, our focus on the operation of organizations and the diffusion of institutions to the micro and meso levels indicates: (i) new points of pressure on Chinese reformers; and (ii) China's compliance with international norms beyond formal rule changes at the macro level. This line of analysis leads to two sets of questions. First, is the flow of foreign investment into China serving China's interests and undermining the goals that foreign powers and international society hold for China? Have 30 years of engagement with China remolded China's interests, fostered interdependence, and made China less of a threat to international society? What kind of state and society are emerging from China's 30 years of opening to the outside world? Is China emerging as a member of international society that complies with international norms and, therefore, is less dangerous now than in 1978? Second, in comparison to other developing countries, why was China able to guide its globalization with such success, rather than have institutional change forced upon it by international organizations? What lessons about how to manage integration with the global economy might other countries learn from China's successful record? What does China's experience with globalization tell us about interdependence, international institutions, and state autonomy? The answers to the latter questions help us to understand and measure the cumulative effect of three decades of incremental reform.

An Overview of the Politics of China's Deepening Engagement with the Global Economy

Initially, China endeavored to control global integration to maximize its benefits from foreign investment and trade flows, but the dynamics of globalization were not fully controllable, and the Chinese state was left trying to guide foreign investors and other agents of globalization. In the early part of the reform period, the state elaborated control mechanisms over foreign investors by quarantining FIEs in SEZs, pressuring foreign firms to form JVs with SOE partners, constructing a mercantilist trade regime, and even issuing a special currency for trading with foreign currencies to regulate the outflow of Chinese money. Although these mechanisms did enhance state control, they also thwarted China's ability to accrue benefits to its economy and to achieve development goals. To fulfill long-term strategic economic goals, China's state had to compromise its immediate concerns with controlling the process of globalization, allowing foreign investors, in particular, the ability to operate in a wider set of geographic locations, in more industries, and under looser restrictions. Since that early period, China has gradually but significantly departed from its efforts to micromanage foreign investors, instead attempting to use foreign investors to advance institutional reforms that the state found difficult to impose on Chinese organizations.

For their part, foreign countries have sought to shape and to manage China's position in the world order. Since 1978, the United States, most of the other advanced capitalist economies, and China's neighbors primarily have approached China with a policy of engagement hedged by realist balancing measures.[2] Randall L. Schweller defines engagement as "the use of non-coercive means to ameliorate the non-status quo elements of a rising major power's behavior. The goal is to ensure that this growing power is used in ways that are consistent with peaceful change in regional and global order."[3] In addition to bilateral discussions between countries, two of the primary means to pursue engagement are economic interdependence and inclusion of a rising power in multilateral organizations. Economic interdependence helps to socialize countries to peaceful exchanges and to increase the economic opportunity costs of pursuing warfare, thereby lessening the appetite for belligerence. Multilateral organizations embed rising powers in rules-based means of resolving conflict and establish a cooperative framework for international relations. China's open-door policy has fostered a high level of interdependence with other nations and has allowed China to enter many multilateral organizations. The work of foreign investors, lawyers, and consultants in China directly touches upon both means of pursuing engagement: interdependence and adherence to international institutions. Foreign investment is a primary method of creating interdependence, and the fact that foreign investors in China actively trade increases their contribution to China's economic engagement. Foreign investors, lawyers, and business consultants, as demonstrated in the chapters above, carry detailed models of international institutions to host countries and help to transmit them to local actors. By adopting institutional designs that follow international norms and participating in multilateral organizations, China signals to others that it is committed to charting its development within a framework acceptable to international society.[4]

In the aftermath of the dramatic events of 1989 that played out in China and in eastern and central Europe, countries have intensified their efforts to guide China's entry into international society, especially as China has enjoyed robust economic growth and has upgraded its military capabilities. Depending on their theoretical and ideological vantage points, international relations analysts advocate distinct approaches to China. For realist theorists of international relations, Chinese economic success is a point of grave concern because, based on historical analogies, rising powers convert economic strength into military might.[5] Hawkish politicians and structural realists believe that, in the anarchy of international relations, states must guard their interests against rising powers, a form of zero-sum politics. Consequently, they argue on behalf of a modified form of containment in approaching relations with China, just as the former Soviet Union was contained during the Cold War, because a rising power such as China imperils the international leadership of the United States and its allies in Asia and beyond.[6]

For nearly two decades, economic engagement with China has sparked political controversy in the United States and in other advanced capitalist countries, despite China's deepening commitment to economic engagement and involvement in multilateral institutions, regional organizations, and bilateral relations. Many press accounts and much political debate on contemporary China emanating from the United States and, to a lesser degree, from Europe is highly critical of China and calls for a reassessment of engagement policy. Critics of China charge that by investing in, trading with, and cooperating with China, the United States and other countries are contributing to the ascendance of a new great power that remains uncommitted to liberal political, social, and economic institutions. Specifically, they argue that engaging China has rewarded a country that violates human rights, suppresses labor, soaks up employment opportunities from advanced capitalist economies, engages in mercantilist trade and currency policies, lacks democracy, undermines U.S. leadership, abets dictatorial regimes, and seeks military power to challenge the United States.[7] In other words, engagement may be helping China to gain on and surpass the United States, Europe, and Japan in terms of power, thereby posing a danger to global human rights, liberal economies, and international security. Such accounts contrast sharply to claims advanced by supporters of engagement with China within scholarly and business communities who contend that economic exchanges with China are contributing to the gradual reform and pacification of China[8] as well as the continued dynamic growth of the U.S. economy, which keeps the United States ahead of China's technological capacity.[9] Both sides of the debate agree that global integration has promoted Chinese economic growth and has enhanced its position in international affairs. The crux of the disagreement in the debate concerns how China is using and plans to use its enhanced power.

What I have hinted at throughout the earlier chapters, I assert here: China is emerging as a country increasingly concerned with international norms and rules-based conduct due to a mixture of domestic actors' interests and foreign actors' influence. Such a development has clear ramifications for domestic political economy and legal development, but it also applies to the way in which China conducts its international relations. The difficulty for China and for others that are engaged with China is how the rules of the game will be defined. I argue that foreign investors are affecting China's interests in compliance with international institutions by: (i) fostering economic interdependence that increases the opportunity costs of warfare; (ii) diffusing international and foreign norms down to the micro level of Chinese society; and (iii) influencing the values of Chinese citizens and organizations, thereby decreasing their interest in belligerent international relations and increasing their interests in further institutional reform. Many analyses of engagement focus on the first point,[10] a few touch upon the second,[11] while the third point marks a new way of approaching the topic. Unlike international organizations and states acting through bilateral relations, MNCs, business organizations, and legal and business consultants come into contact with local state agents and micro-level actors whom they help socialize to international and foreign institutions. Chinese actors—from state officials to workers on the job market—are interested in access to foreign organizational models and their accompanying institutions. The process of socialization to international norms and new values is slow and hard to measure, but it holds the greatest hope for sustaining and deepening China's compliance with the rules of international society. Such an approach enhances our understanding of the role of MNCs in China's global integration, including compliance with international institutions.

Foreign Investment, Engagement, and China

Despite a growing literature on the study of foreign investment in China,[12] surprisingly few studies have discussed foreign investment and engagement in depth.[13] The lacuna is significant because a core argument of engagement theory claims that economic exchanges and integration of a country into international society socialize a potentially hostile country to international norms and rules and lessen the likelihood of conflict by fostering interdependence and by reducing the conflict of interests among states. Foreign investment is one of the main mechanisms for fostering interdependence and, unlike trade, it has the capacity to transfer institutions to host economies. Thus, foreign investment allows for a deep form of global engagement.

As Rosemary Foot asserts, China has been interested in joining the members of international society and becoming a great power, both of which require meeting standards of the international community.[14] Over the last 30 years, China has joined many treaty organizations and signed many international conventions in the realms of security, human rights, rule of law, and international economy—signs that China is following the form of a good member of international society. More controversial is whether China has accepted the norms of international society and accordingly has adjusted its behavior,[15] has selectively adapted to international norms,[16] or has entered international society and organizations in order to alter the status quo.[17] Some analysts contend that Chinese leaders seek to revise international norms and institutions rather than subordinate their interests to international society,[18] while others claim that China's commitment to abide by international norms is uneven or unclear.[19] Judging China's actions against international norms is complicated by the evolving norms of elite membership in the international community. In particular, since the collapse of the Cold War, the norms of membership in international society have been raised to include greater protection of human rights and democratic forms of rule.[20]

While China has been accused of wishing to revise the rules of international society, their rhetoric and actions, such as their voting record on the United Nations Security Council, have been less disruptive to the efforts of powerful members of that organization than analysts feared,[21] and China's voting pattern suggests that China adheres to an earlier conception of international obligations, especially guarding sovereignty as the core principle of international society, rather than revising rules of international society.[22] China rarely exercises its veto power on UN Security Council measures in order to avoid appearing obstructive of such efforts and to follow a recent norm on abstaining rather than vetoing Security Council sanctions.[23] Although they made principled arguments in the UN Security Council, China did not veto legislation that would have hampered the two missions in Iraq and the mission in Afghanistan. Yong Deng and Thomas Moore argue that China has moved from a reluctant participant in engagement and interdependence to embracing globalization and interdependence.[24] The below account examines how international engagement is affecting China's compliance with three crucial areas of analysis: security norms, human rights, and rule of law.

Engagement and Security Norms

Engagement theory is of significant concern to those studying international (especially, Sino-U.S.) relations, and understandably, security analysts have dominated the discussion because the greatest immediate threat of an emerging power is in the security realm. American critics of engagement with China tend to advance one or both of the following lines of argument: (i) that engagement has contributed to China's economic takeoff and subsequent growth in military spending, which makes China a strategic threat to Asia and the United States; and (ii) that China has failed to abide by the rules of international society and is intent on expanding its power and, perhaps, territory as it ascends to great power status. According to these critics, foreign investors have fueled China's economic rise, transferred technology with military applications, and facilitated China's conversion of economic might into military power.[25] Moreover, they claim that China's growing ties to regional economies and multilateral organizations, which liberals assert help to dampen conflict, are inducing regional actors' dependence on China.[26] For example, heavy investment and trade with China by South Korea, Japan, and Australia, among other regional states, potentially reduces those states' will to oppose China in times of conflict. Rather than interdependence constraining Chinese behavior, it could have the effect of weakening liberal states' will to balance Chinese power. By these accounts, multilateralism in Asia, built on economic cooperation and more recently, on security cooperation, has created a "bandwagon effect" in which states go along with China as a new regional leader.[27] They point to China's deepening economic ties to regional states and China's emerging leadership in the Shanghai Cooperation

Organization (SCO) and in "ASEAN Plus Three"—both of which exclude the United States as a member, as evidence that China is pursuing multilateral relations in Asia to foster China's power at the expense of the United States.[28] Robert G. Sutter, who harbors doubts about the capacity of engagement to cause China to pursue peace and development, found, however, that Asian government leaders were concerned about China's emerging role and sought to hedge against China's regional leadership with measures such as retaining the United States in an important regional security role, which undermines the argument of regional bandwagoning.[29] Zhang Yunling and Tang Shiping capture well this dilemma from the Chinese leadership's perspective, "If China actively participates in regional affairs and norms, some in the United States will take it as a sign that China is aiming to challenge U.S. dominance. At the same time, international politics is becoming more regional...."[30] Liberals tend to view such binding multilateral ties in a positive light, noting that the SCO and ASEAN Plus Three address non-traditional security matters such as fighting terrorism,[31] while critics of engagement argue that China is using such ties to emerge as a new leader, displacing U.S. influence in Asia.[32]

Using security norms and treaties to constrain China are also bound to fail, according to critics of engagement.[33] As part of its effort to join international society, China has signed many arms and technology control regimes—some of which it may have violated. The alleged violations were most common through the mid-1990s[34] when China's military was highly decentralized and was allowed to operate independent economic organizations in order to raise funds for its own budget.[35] For example, China directly or indirectly aided Pakistan, Libya, and Iran in their nuclear weapons programs.[36] The decentralized control over the military branches and their freedom to engage in economic transactions made it very difficult for the central government to control its own military and to abide by weapons regimes. Since the forced military divestment in 1998, China's government has sought to clean up the corruption in its military,[37] and compliance with weapons regimes has improved,[38] although Chinese firms still face financial incentives to transfer weapons technology.[39] Allegations of weapons proliferation prompted the Chinese government, in 2002, to establish new controls on the export of military technology, although concerns remain about technical exchanges between China and Pakistani scientists in the area of nuclear technology.[40] According to a member of the Bush administration, China has reduced its arms trade, although it still violates the Missile Technology Control Regime (MTCR).[41] Still, shipments of conventional arms to gross violators of human rights such as Zimbabwe have provoked international condemnation of China for a lack of commitment to human rights and to security norms.[42]

A long-standing charge against China is that its decision-making process and military budget are opaque, making it difficult to determine China's strategic intentions and commitment to international norms. Against assertions that China's military budgets have become more transparent since China recentralized control over military spending, security analysts and the U.S. Department of Defense continue to complain about lack of transparency.[43] China has begun to issue reports on its military spending to try to assuage concerns about its military development and interests. The United States has begun military exchanges with China to help foster better understanding of each side's intentions, thereby reducing the security dilemma between the two countries.[44] Nevertheless, security analysts worry that China is acquiring weapons (mainly from Russia) and developing the military capacity necessary to retake Taiwan (an entity that China has claimed is an integral part of its nation-state) and to keep the United States at bay if conflict with Taiwan broke out.[45] Indeed, China's rhetoric on Taiwan and its opposition to U.S. hegemony in Asia feed such security concerns, but Chinese leaders view their military development as defensive in nature (preventing the loss of claimed national territory and in response to U.S. weapons sales in the region, especially to Taiwan) rather than expansionist (securing Taiwan as a new territory). The closest China has come to warfare with Taiwan was during the dramatic 1996 Taiwanese presidential campaign, but since that year and especially as the Nationalist Party gradually returned to power on Taiwan, there has been some easing of tensions across the Taiwan Straits. The easing of tensions is demonstrated by the visit of Nationalist Party leader Lien Chan to Beijing in 2005 to meet with President Hu Jintao.[46] Most security analysts acknowledge that China's effort to reform its military to acquire weaponry is focused on limited goals and is mostly a defensive posture. In particular, China lacks the ability to project its force by sea or air beyond limited regional conflicts.[47] Chinese military development, however, does appear aimed at either retaking Taiwan or, more benignly, preventing Taiwan's potential attempts to assert formal independence.

In recent years, the U.S. and Chinese militaries have engaged in a series of exchanges and cooperative endeavors in order to enhance transparency and understanding of each sides' military capabilities, thereby reducing the security dilemma, which many believe is likely to arise around the status of Taiwan.[48] Robert Gates, U.S. secretary of defense, has suggested that military exchanges can help overcome the non-transparency issues of China's military development and ease the security dilemma.[49] With an eye to developing closer relations with its neighbors—some of whom have had territorial disputes with China—China's military has carried out peacekeeping and counterterrorist practice exercises with SCO members and India, reducing potential antagonism with members of the multilateral organizations.[50] Some realists criticize China for creating bandwagon effects by deepening relations with members of Asian multilateral organizations,[51] but others note that China's multilateral partners harbor concerns about China's rise and hedge against China's potential regional leadership.[52] It would appear that Asian regional partners in multilateral organizations that include China harbor no illusions about China's potential for belligerence in the future.

Economic actors can do little directly to affect monitoring of or compliance with security norms other than promote greater political transparency. In addition to the military exchanges to develop mutual understanding and to reduce the security dilemma, there is some evidence of greater transparency in Chinese legislating and in the circulation of new laws and regulations—both of which were requirements of China's WTO accession. For example, China's Standing Committee and National People's Congress have recently adopted a practice of inviting one or more rounds of commentary from civil society organizations, including foreign business organizations, on draft legislation such as the Labor Contract Law (2008).[53] As Chinese political institutions become less opaque, even if not completely transparent, the difficulty of interpreting China's actions and goals should abate.

The research reported here cannot offer a direct counterargument to realist assumptions on China's security interests and actions. Much of the debate between liberal institutionalists and realists with regard to China stems from how to interpret China's actions and context rather than from concrete differences in their data. Drawing on realist theories that rising powers use economic growth as a basis for military development, critics of engagement often use China's annual GDP growth rate, which has hovered near 10 percent for the last three decades,[54] as evidence that China has the capacity to develop a significant military threat, a point partially supported by double-digit annual percentage increases in defense spending since the mid-1990s. Still, as Avery Goldstein points out, China began its period of economic growth and military spending increases from a very low baseline, making China's takeoff steeper but less worrisome than realists' claims.[55] According to the Pentagon, China's military spending for the year 2003 was as much as three times the stated budget, and they project China's military budget to rise to as high as $320 billion (in 2005 U.S. dollars) by the year 2025, more than a threefold increase on 2005 spending figures.[56] Some security analysts even claim that Chinese defense spending is 10 times greater than its stated budget, when off-budget items are included and calculated according to purchasing power parity recalculations.[57] Such claims exaggerate China's spending for two reasons: they calculate spending based on old purchasing power parity measures that predate Chinese price reforms, and they disregard inefficiencies in Chinese defense industry that inflate the cost of producing weaponry.[58] The Rand Corporation and other think tanks have challenged the Pentagon's figures for China's current military spending and projections into the future. According to Rand, China's 2003 military spending was 40–70 percent greater than China's reported spending (not 200 percent greater, as the Pentagon suggested), and based on economic modeling, China's 2025 military expenditure will be approximately 60 percent of the U.S. military budget for 2003.[59]

The strongest argument that economic engagement theorists can make against realist security claims, however, is that interdependence indirectly diminishes security threats from a rising power by creating a context in which rivals would potentially lose economic benefits if they chose conflict over peace. China increasingly depends on the U.S. economy and other (mainly, regional) economies—through trade and foreign investment—for its continued growth, which likely moderates potential conflict between China and its Asian neighbors and the United States. Phillip C. Saunders claims that "China's growing economic dependence on the United States and on the world economy act as a passive restraint on Chinese behavior."[60] Since 1978, economic growth has increasingly become the key tool for Chinese leaders to legitimate themselves in the eyes of citizens (sometimes referred to as "GNPism"[61]), so an economic slowdown would entail not just an economic but also a political crisis. Such considerations simultaneously increase China's ability to defend itself but also dampen Chinese leaders' enthusiasm for foreign confrontation.

China's reliance upon foreign investors is greater than appears at first glance. While foreign investment has provided important technology, managerial models, and funds for capital construction, the percentage of Chinese urban workers employed by FIEs, in recent years, has hovered around 5 percent—not a very high percentage when considered alone, but the number of workers employed in firms that supply FIEs likely is much greater. Thus, a large segment of the urban (and rural industrial) workforce is directly or indirectly dependent on FIEs for all or part of their income. Chinese industry also has become heavily dependent on foreign enterprises for its total output. In 1999, when foreign investors had already flooded China, FIEs contributed 15 percent of China's gross value of industrial output, but in 2006, the contribution of FIEs to China's gross value of industrial output soared to 31 percent.[62] Figures on foreign trade, which has become a great source of political debate, especially in the United States, demonstrate an emerging domination by foreign investors. In 1993, FIEs in China were responsible for approximately 34 percent of China's trade, according to Chinese statistics. By 2000, FIEs' contribution to Chinese overall trade had risen to 50 percent, and in 2005 and 2006, the figures had climbed to over 58 percent. The figures for FIEs' contribution to exports leaving China show an even steeper climb, growing from 27 percent of China's total exports in 1993 to 58 percent by 2006 (see Figure 7.1).

Strategic analysts are concerned about China's trajectory of economic growth based on recent growth rates, combined with steeply climbing military spending. Strategists use these figures to argue that China has greatly closed the economic gap on the United States, and even that it will surpass the United States in the coming decades. While realists appropriately argue that China's macroeconomy is rapidly expanding and creating the capacity for military development, engagement theorists are correct to indicate that China's growth relies significantly on foreign investment. Moreover, as Yasheng Huang points out, control over the profits from such exporting activities remain in the hands of foreign enterprise owners, relegating China's share mainly to wages and income generated by inputs from local suppliers.[63]

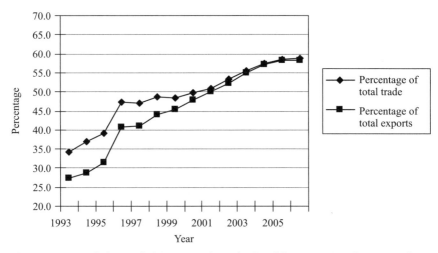

Figure 7.1   FIEs' Share of Chinese Trade. Calculated from: National Bureau of Statistics of China, *China Statistical Yearbook* (Beijing: China Statistics Press, various years) (http://www.stats.gov.cn/english/statisticaldata/yearlydata/).

China's population has grown increasingly dependent on employment in foreign-invested enterprises, which puts a brake on interest in conflict and rivalry. If strategic entanglements rock relations with countries that invest in China, foreign investors could lose substantial stakes in their investment, but China would lose out on managerial skills and export markets. Nothing guarantees that Chinese leaders will follow economic interests in their strategic decisions, but their economic interests in keeping international peace are significant and growing.

A cursory examination of macroeconomic data can lead one to overlook two important matters. First, beneath many of China's macroeconomic trends, there are troubling signs for Chinese leaders who stake their legitimacy on providing stable economic growth.[64] Although China's GDP, investment flows, and foreign trade have all expanded very quickly for three decades, China still faces an extremely high rate of unemployment, which creates a domestic powder keg for China's leaders.[65] The prospect of deepening unemployment in a country that already has an unofficial unemployment rate of, likely, 14 percent (or more)[66] and that faces significant and growing labor unrest must be a frightening scenario for Chinese leaders. Moreover, in 2008 the IMF recalibrated its calculations of purchasing power parity (or PPP, its methodology for comparing GDP across currencies and time), which sharply lowered the PPP value of China's 2005 GDP by 40 percent.[67] Consequently, China, which was believed to have a GDP that reached the point of two-thirds the size of the U.S. economy and double the Japanese GDP,[68] had its GDP reduced to just 43 percent of the U.S. economy.[69] Hence, China is catching up with the rest of the world less quickly than previously believed, based on the new comparative measurement,[70] undermining arguments by proponents of containment that China is rapidly closing the gap in terms of economic and military capacity on the United States and its allies.

Using economic growth to avoid domestic instability has deeply colored China's grand strategy, which Zhang Yunling and Tang Shiping summarize as being, "to secure and to shape a security, economic, and political environment that is conducive to China concentrating on its economic, social, and political development."[71] Chinese diplomatic efforts can be understood as attempting to create a context that will allow for China's continued economic rise. Second, glancing at China's macroeconomic statistics does not capture the institutional and value changes taking place in China, which alters the context in which security decisions are made. As China has moved from a planned economy to a market economy with swelling private ownership, the number of firms and people directly supported by the state has declined. Concomitantly, citizens—especially the emerging white-collar class of professionals—display a growing affinity with international practices and institutions, which makes them less prone to approach international relations from a belligerent posture. Their interest in amassing a growing fortune aligns their interest with deep economic engagement—either through employment with an FIE or through a domestic firm that is likely to engage in trade—and interdependence rather than belligerence and isolation.

Engagement and Human Rights Norms

China's record on human rights (including labor rights) has divided scholars, the business community, and human rights groups (including labor organizations). Many human rights and labor organizations have claimed that China has a very poor record of protecting human rights, even asserting that foreign investors have worsened the situation in the following ways: (i) rewarding China with investment despite abuses and perhaps because of weak labor protections; (ii) lowering Chinese standards by hiring migrant workers rather than permanent employees at higher compensation; and (iii) transmitting low labor standards to other countries by pitting workers in different countries against the standards of China.[72] According to this argument, China's economic rise threatens international standards on labor and human rights. Such assertions about the direction of Chinese human and labor rights as well as the effect of foreign investors on labor standards have provoked intense debate from proponents of engagement both inside and outside China. Members of the business and academic communities tend to look more favorably upon China's human rights record, noting the long-term progress that China has made in developing its human rights.[73] Alastair I. Johnston points out that international human rights norms contain both individual and collective principles, which make China's compliance with international norms difficult to determine.[74] Part of the difficulty of articulating a clear set of universal human rights is that the 13 core legal instruments designated by the UN Office of the High Commissioner on Human Rights overlap a great deal and have some important distinctions in their approach. For example, the UN Universal Declaration on Human Rights[75] and the International Covenant on Civil and Political Rights[76] emphasize individual political rights, including the right to elect one's government, while the International Covenant on Economic, Social, and Cultural Rights[77] places greater emphasis on the rights to subsistence, education, and social security. The Vienna Declaration and Programme of Action highlights that cultures and peoples have differing approaches to human rights and that countries have the right to develop, a form of collective right.[78] The document, however, goes on to state that the "lack of development may not be invoked to justify the abridgement of internationally recognized human rights."[79] In general, China emphasizes collective human rights principles over individual rights and meeting developmental needs of citizens over extending political rights.[80] The prioritization of economic and social rights over political rights is quite pronounced in the Bangkok Declaration, originally adopted by ASEAN states in 1967 and later adopted by the Asian regional meeting in preparation of the World Conference on Human Rights.[81]

Without denying that China violates human rights as defined by the UN Declaration of Human Rights and that Chinese labor standards are lower than those in advanced capitalist countries, there are several problems with the assertions raised by the above criticisms of China' human rights. First, many analysts agree that the general movement of China's human rights practices and protections is in a positive direction, although the protections are uneven over time and among segments of the population, so the argument that Chinese human rights are worsening (as opposed to remaining below international standards) is controversial.[82] For example, China uses the death penalty more extensively than any country in the world, but since October 2006 the Supreme People's Court must approve any exercise of the death penalty by lower courts, resulting in a significant drop in the use of the punishment.[83] Second, Chinese firms—mostly private and collective enterprises—rather than FIEs, are responsible for the worst forms of labor abuse in China.[84] Extreme cases of laborers held against their will to perform labor at low wages require local government involvement or complicity, which is more likely in collective enterprises, in private firms with strong connections to local officials, or in firms in which the local government has an investment share.[85] Thus, the introduction of foreign capital typically is not the cause of labor abuses; corrupt local officials who fail to monitor or who actively participate in such business activities and the managers of such businesses are to blame for breaking China's *Labor Law*. Third, many FIEs bring labor standards that are superior to those required by Chinese regulations, even though some FIEs or subcontractors for FIEs do not meet Chinese labor standards. Monitoring labor practices in supply chains is an extremely nettlesome issue.[86] Many (though not all) FIEs are providing their employees critical thinking skills, a workplace independent of state control, and significant relief from poverty.[87] The fact that FIEs pay, on average, higher wages to contracted employees than domestic enterprises also suggests that foreign firms are lifting the wage standards of Chinese workers rather than lowering them.[88] FIEs from different countries have brought varying approaches to Chinese labor. Studies have shown that FIEs from China's neighbors such as South Korea, Taiwan, and Hong Kong have harsher practices than Japanese, European, and U.S. firms;[89] interviewees tended to prefer U.S. and European firms to those from Japan, with South Korean, Taiwanese, and Hong Kong firms near the bottom of their preferences.[90] Additionally, labor-intensive firms, mostly from China's neighboring economies, which seek to extend the lifetime of their textile and electronics manufacturers, are more likely to employ harsh labor practices to ensure profits than capital-intensive firms that seek knowledgeable, long-term employees.[91]

Even though many FIEs follow Chinese labor rules and improve workplace conditions, their introduction of polarized labor compensation through market-based pay schemes may have a mixed effect on labor rights and on conditions of employment in China. While average pay rates in FIEs have gone up, not all have benefited equally, and those workers at the bottom of the employment ladder, particularly migrant laborers, face job uncertainty and (maybe) less pay. Still, many workers in lower job classifications in FIEs hail from villages, where their employment prospects and earning potential are much worse, so employment in FIEs marks an improvement in their living standards, too. The case of migrant workers and overtime, which is limited by China's *Labor Law,* for instance, is extremely complicated. Migrant workers, who wish to maximize their income in a short period of time in order to return home with as much money as possible, seek out employment with the prospect of long overtime hours and may leave a position without such overtime in excess of labor regulations.[92] Labor abuse and incarceration are serious matters, but migrant workers' interest in working long hours puts managers who wish to follow China's labor regulations in a conundrum. More fruitfully, as foreign investors have expanded employment opportunities in places like Shanghai and Shenzhen, labor supplies have tightened and forced up wages for even the lowest-paid workers.[93]

In addition to foreign investors' contribution to the improvement of labor standards discussed in chapters 5 and 6 above, China's current (in 2007–2008) campaign to introduce corporate social responsibility (CSR) illustrates the interplay between international human rights norms, China's state, and international actors. CSR is a relatively recent development in the business world, and, according to Chinese interviewees, China has no indigenous concept equivalent to CSR.[94] Pressure from international NGOs and negative media reports on the labor practices of FIEs and domestic firms in China has compelled China's government and foreign firms to improve the labor standards in FIEs and throughout FIEs' supply chains.[95] The Chinese government and media have called on foreign and local firms to practice CSR by improving their internal labor standards and by helping their communities through charitable donations of labor, money, and in-kind gifts and through collaborative projects with NGOs.[96] Due to the novelty of these practices in China, the Chinese Ministry of Commerce has pressed foreign investors to take the lead in CSR, thereby demonstrating to local firms how to improve labor standards, to work with civil society, and to act benevolently.[97] Business organizations such as the Shanghai American Chamber of Commerce have established special committees to help members develop and implement CSR policies and activities. A few Chinese companies have established their own CSR programs, and others are likely to follow. According to Chinese citizens working with local and foreign companies on their CSR practices, the greater a Chinese company's contact with and reliance upon foreign markets and with foreign investors, the more likely the same company is to take seriously CSR.[98] At each stage of the development of CSR in China, international actors and ideas were crucial in raising the human rights practices of FIEs and domestic enterprises in China: NGOs transmitted norms such as SA8000 and ISO 14000 and created pressure on China's government to comply with labor and environmental standards, respectively; FIEs and foreign business organizations took the lead in developing new practices; and the FIEs modeled practices for domestic enterprises to emulate. Finally, China's state officials helped to guide this process and to diffuse practices from FIEs to local firms. The rise of CSR in China illustrates the positive effect that economic engagement can have in the human rights realm and on Chinese business practices.

Although many interviewees were skeptical about how deeply the CSR campaign has taken root in China, the public response to the devastating Sichuan earthquake on May 12, 2008, indicates that the concept has begun to gain traction among Chinese citizens and companies. In the weeks following the Sichuan earthquake, which killed nearly 70,000 and wounded more than 370,000 citizens, private relief donations surpassed government relief expenditures.[99] Many individual citizens donated time, money, and blood through NGOs, and many Chinese corporations joined foreign companies to speed funding to victims of the earthquake. Internet discussion groups praised companies that donated large amounts of money and derided companies that gave meager sums or no money.[100] The flurry of discussion suggests growing societal consciousness of corporate social responsibility, and the large donations indicate acceptance of such responsibility. More broadly, the emerging CSR practices point to a nascent fusing of business and ethics that is supportive of international labor and human rights norms. Protests indicate societal will to organize and engage in collective protest to demand political change.

Engagement and Legal Norms

As argued in chapter 4, China has improved its legal system through the interplay of domestic leaders' interests, international norms, and foreign actors' pressure and information. Without reprising those arguments, it is worthwhile to consider three new items in assessing China's seriousness with regard to developing rule of law: improving standards of China's legal system in terms of quality of judges; efforts to protect the disadvantaged; and growing interest in rules-based management of international relations, such as compliance with its treaty obligations and other international commitments. These three points, while general, help to assess China's macro-level commitment to rule of law. The third matter directly touches upon the liberal approach to international security, which calls on using engagement and international institutions to develop a rules-based means of resolving conflict rather than reversion to warfare. According to G. John Ikenberry, "The United States cannot thwart China's rise, but it can help ensure that China's power is exercised within the rules and institutions that the United States and its partners have crafted over the last century, rules and institutions that can protect the interests of all states in the more crowded world of the future."[101]

Foreign lawyers, politicians, activists, and MNCs have pointed out the shortcomings of China's legal system, but many also indicate that China's legal system has made strides to improve the quality of its justice. For example, in 2001, China revised its rules on the appointment of judges and, for the first time, established an examination system to qualify judicial appointees.[102] Application of the examination system was initially limited to new appointees to the bench and unevenly applied to different levels of the court system and areas of the country, but it nevertheless marked an improvement in the legal system.[103] Xiao Yang, former head of China's Supreme People's Court, ushered in that procedure, which was an important step toward raising the standards of the courts' judgments. Additionally, China has allowed more engagement with foreigners in the legal realm through numerous rule-of-law programs operated by international NGOs and foreign universities—many of them run out of the United States. Such programs improve the qualifications of attorneys, judges, and other legal staff, and, more importantly, create advocates within China's legal community for systemic reform along the lines of international models.

More generally, average Chinese citizens and the Chinese government use the language of rights, embedded in laws and rules, to assert claims of justice. In the countryside, citizens petition higher officials to report abuses of their rights as well as other forms of rights-based contentious action.[104] Disadvantaged citizens are turning to legal aid stations, most of them established by the government and many partially underwritten by foreign foundations, for help in protecting their rights.[105] Most legal aid stations offer free legal advice and representation to qualifying citizens, usually determined by a person's income level. As Mary Gallagher has shown, labor arbitration cases are on the rise,[106] and the passage of the New Labor Contract Law is likely to increase demand for rules-based settlement of grievances, as well as better protection of laborers' rights.[107] Over the reform period, citizens increasingly have used legal means to hold fellow citizens, firms, and state agents accountable to the laws and regulations that the government has established. While the development of rule of law, especially in holding state officials accountable to legal statutes, is far from perfect, the legal activity gives a strong indication of the emerging legal consciousness among average citizens. The growing interest in legal methods also suggests rising popular confidence in the efficacy of such means to protect rights.

Micro-level legal activity positively interacts with macro-level commitments to legal principles, albeit limited by conflicting state interests in legal reform. China's government, too, uses the rules and dispute settlement mechanisms of international organizations to protect its interests. For example, China has been party to several dispute settlement cases that have come before the WTO, including the successful case against U.S. steel import tariffs in 2003.[108] China both is being forced to follow rules and has pledged to use WTO rules to protect its interests through dispute settlement procedures in international organizations.[109] The U.S. Trade Representative reports to Congress each year on China's compliance with its WTO commitments, and the reports, while noting China's shortcomings, especially in the area of protection of intellectual property rights, enforcement of laws, and transparency of rules, praise China's efforts to comply with WTO commitments.[110] Pitman B. Potter notes that through 2005, China was subject to 338 antidumping measures by fellow WTO member states, which, he argues, is part of a pattern of "selective adaptation" to WTO rules on free trade.[111] Free trade norms, though, have begun to shape the ideas and rhetoric of state officials. When explaining its reforms, Chinese officials often refer to the imperative of international norms and globalization. Indeed, Xiao Yang called for China "to learn from the experience of various countries and keep pace with the global legal development."[112] Chinese leaders, thus, are paying attention to international rules and norms in dealing with foreign countries and as a rationale to push through domestic reforms. Once rules and laws are created, Chinese officials face pressure from average citizens and organizations to follow domestic laws.[113] A similar logic applies to international relations. Yong Deng and Thomas G. Moore assert that China is using multilateralism to limit the U.S. exercise of arbitrary power,[114] but, in playing to multilateral rules, surrenders part of its own autonomy.

Even in the area of security affairs, China shows a growing commitment to rules-based conflict resolution. China's increased participation and, in a few cases, leadership in multilateral regional organizations that have security dimensions, point to China's determination to manage international relations through multilateral, peaceful means. In its bilateral relations, over the last decade China has worked hard to settle many of its territorial disputes with Russia and former Soviet Republics,[115] although outstanding claims remain over the Spratley (also known as the Diaoyutai or Senkaku) Islands and, of course, over Taiwan.[116] Advocates of containing China argue that China's growing military might poses a danger because of China's many outstanding security issues with its neighbors. As China settles those matters in a peaceful way, it both demonstrates a non-belligerent stance and reduces the potency of realists' concerns about China's expansionism. According to M. Taylor Fravel's study of China's handling of territorial disputes, China "has compromised more frequently than it has used force" and "has been less belligerent than leading theories of international relations might have predicted for a state with its characteristics."[117] Chinese military officials discuss security reforms in the context of international norms and rules, with an eye to improving China's standing in the international community.[118] These examples illustrate China's slow internalization of rules-based norms and how to use rules to augment their power. By adopting and applying such rules, China makes its own behavior more open to evaluation based on the same rules.

China does not meet its full obligations under treaty organizations and international conventions that it has joined. China has, though, displayed steady improvement in its compliance with international norms. In the case of the WTO, China faced more strenuous reform obligations to accede than most other countries.[119] According to the US-China Business Council and the U.S. Trade Representative's Office, China receives high marks for meeting the "letter of its requirements" as dictated in its accession agreement, but it does not necessarily abide by the spirit of the agreement or follow the logic of the WTO rules.[120] Improvement in China's level of compliance with international norms is, in part, a function of foreign businesses and lawyers who work in China, observing China's practice, pointing out the shortcomings of China's compliance, and helping to train Chinese practitioners to observe international norms. Chapter 4 demonstrated how foreign actors worked with Chinese actors to bring China closer to full compliance with international norms on international commercial arbitration and enforcement as defined by the UNCITRAL Model and the New York Convention. To move toward compliance with international norms on enforcing arbitration decisions, China's Supreme Court intervened to assert its power over lower courts, a move that fit into a broad, gradual reorganization of the courts that is bringing China closer into alignment with the hierarchical nature of justice systems in the United States and elsewhere.[121] In other words, efforts to comply with international norms have entailed institutional and organizational reforms with repercussions for the distribution of power between political and economic actors. Such reforms and progress inherently are more difficult to measure than GNP growth and military budgets, but they are significant nonetheless.

In a similar vein, foreign investors, business associations, and lawyers have brought pressure to bear on Chinese authorities to improve its protection of intellectual property rights, as mandated by China's WTO accession agreement, and to improve environmental standards and to apply them equally to all businesses—foreign and domestic—operating in China. While still not meeting the standards of intellectual property protection sought by foreign businesses, foreign actors in China have increased the vigilance with which China addresses this admittedly nettlesome issue.[122] For example, the U.S. Trade Representative has mixed technical exchanges, bilateral discussions, and dispute settlement procedures to compel China to improve its compliance with the TRIPS Agreement on intellectual property rights protection.[123]

China may fall short of Western standards of rule of law, but it is making strides to improve its legal system. The current situation of legal reform demonstrates a linkage of international institutions and agents to domestic actors, norms, and interests, in the development of rule of law, a familiar pattern from earlier chapters. It is worth recalling that China's initial push to develop rule of law was very limited, a means to avoid gross abuses of arbitrary power by leaders. After 1978, the rise of capitalism, especially the opening to foreign direct investment, ushered in a set of actors who sought legal protection and stimulated people moving into the legal profession. Many of China's best-trained attorneys have participated in educational programs abroad, especially in the United States, and now are leading advocates of further legal reform or are engaged in public interest legal work that expands notions of citizens' rights. Bilateral technical exchanges such as that between Australia and China have diffused important legal practices and norms to Chinese attorneys and legal officials.[124] China, working with foreign foundations, NGOs, and law schools, has also expanded its legal aid centers throughout the country to better protect disadvantaged citizens' rights in the legal system, including the civil, administrative, and criminal realms.[125] Such an endogenous dynamic that draws on international legal norms and principles bodes well for the long-term development of legal consciousness, rights-based initiatives, and commitment to rules-based resolution of conflict.

Engagement and Micro-level Institutional Dynamics

Unlike many studies of engagement, which focus on macroeconomy and macro-level institutional development, this chapter contends that micro-level dynamics, too, have affected Chinese institutional development and commitment to institutional change. The level of economic interdependence between China and its trading and investment partners is the starting point for analyzing engagement, but foreign investors are contributing to a deeper set of societal and ideational changes in China. While state-level interests and actions are important in any study of the consequences of engagement, here I have taken a more expansive view of engagement, examining whether economic interaction and interdependence transform the institutions and popular values in a country such as China rather than a narrower examination of the interaction of interdependence with commitments to international institutions and security threats.[126]

Along with multilateral organizations and foreign states, a set of micro- and meso-level foreign actors, including MNCs, lawyers, business associations, and business consultants, are helping to diffuse new models and norms to China and to reshape China's employment structure. At the micro level, average citizens voted with their feet, opting to join foreign-funded enterprises over the declining job security offered by SOEs. Through the early 1990s, when the state still allocated most labor to factories through the unified labor allocation system and when SOEs transferred employees into JVs, the dominant investment vehicle at that time, it was difficult to get a clear sense of Chinese workers' preferences for employment in FIEs. With the rise of WFOEs to dominance and loosening of state controls over labor allocation, workers' preferences for employment in FIEs, especially in U.S.- and European-invested firms, became clearer. Certainly, Chinese staff enjoyed higher-than-average compensation in FIEs, but several interviewed Chinese staff asserted that U.S. institutions and their logic appealed to Chinese workers, and they contrasted such company cultures to those of Chinese and Japanese enterprises. More specifically, white-collar workers in U.S.-invested firms in China praised the autonomy, responsibility, creativity, and opportunity for advancement that they enjoyed in the workplace.[127] In Chinese and Japanese firms, interviewees noted a more circumscribed autonomy and set of responsibilities, as well as limited advancement opportunities.[128]

As citizens' values and interests shift, they bring pressure to bear on leaders to revise institutions. Underlying much of the analysis in earlier chapters is the emergence of new cognitive scripts among Chinese citizens, particularly among those working in FIEs. FIEs are altering the values of China's workforce, thereby reducing the potential for international conflict and improving the prospects of endogenous institutional change. Through employment in many FIEs, white-collar Chinese workers are exposed to foreign values, Western definitions of human rights, critical analytical skills, and responsibility, which impart new standards of evaluating their environment.[129] Although Chinese workers and managers in JVs initially resisted efforts by U.S. investors to transplant work standards and norms, as FIEs recruited a new generation of Chinese staff and established green-field investments in the form of WFOEs, Chinese workers took to U.S. (and European) labor institutions, including values such as responsibility, evaluation, and initiative. Obviously, not all workers found such work norms to their liking, nor did all workers perform well under all labor institutions from the variety of foreign investors. Nevertheless, given a choice on positions in the growing array of firms, Chinese citizens tend to prefer to work for U.S. and European firms. This outcome is a function of both high pay and the values embedded in the workplace constructed by such firms. FIEs helped to provide an institutional sub-regime in which such ideas and values, previously inchoate or submerged in pockets of China's population, could flourish.

If cognitive scripts were so deeply rooted among Chinese workers, why did foreign firms, and especially U.S. and European human resources institutions, attract such interest? While social norms may be widespread, they are far from universally accepted within a population, and new institutions and cognitive scripts can appeal to those dissenters who feel stymied by dominant social norms. The rewards in the form of increased compensation and enhanced promotion opportunities gave positive reinforcement to those staff willing to shift to the U.S. model of business operations. In contrast, Japanese firms could offer improved pay with limited chances for promotions, thus making them less attractive to entrepreneurial white-collar workers. American institutions tapped previously latent interest in performance-based compensation among Chinese workers, especially underpaid skilled workers whose talents were widely sought but in short supply, and adventurous workers gravitated toward U.S. and other foreign firms who offered fewer employment guarantees but higher pay rates. Over the course of the reform period, interest in the U.S. model and institutional sub-regime grew, and the sub-regime expanded to the point of challenging the dominant regime. Consequently, China's society and economy evince growing pluralism, both in terms of values and institutional forms.

The timing of white-collar workers' growing interest in this sub-regime roughly coincided with shifting bases of power within the Chinese Communist Party, away from blue-collar workers to the emerging middle class. President Jiang Zemin's "three represents" policy, which called for inclusion of "advanced elements of society" in the party, elaborated and punctuated this shift in party doctrine. Since 1992, a small minority of the Chinese workforce, young professionals and managers, have enjoyed disproportionate power in Chinese politics, leading the government to pay attention to their needs and preferences. To attract and retain young engineers, managers, and professionals, firms had to compete with U.S. and other foreign firms on compensation, promotion, and work environment. Such changes were not easy for SOEs and other Chinese firms, so they hired consultants to help train them in institutional forms and accompanying practices. Thus, the sub-regime incorporated more firms and broadened its attractiveness.

The appeal of U.S. and foreign institutions in China relates to the issue of changes in U.S. and Chinese "soft power," which recently has become a focal point of discussion.[130] While the U.S. government may have lost some of its influence and esteem abroad, people in China and elsewhere still hold U.S. institutions in high regard, mainly due to the work of U.S. businesses and educational institutions.[131] Additionally, Asian leaders and populations remain leery of China's rise and some of its institutions and values. Amitav Acharya asserts, "China has neither the regional social capital nor the ideological appeal to dominate the region's ideational landscape."[132] In China, U.S. institutions began with three groups that have served as strong spokespersons and, over time, have added a fourth. Many managerial consulting firms peddle their advice on U.S. human resources and management practices in China. Chinese firms are anxious to acquire documentation on compensation markets, various pay models, and evaluation procedures, so that they can compete with foreign enterprises for hiring and training personnel. In some cases, the Chinese firms may end up with an incomplete understanding of how the models function in practice, but the basic institutions are diffused and localized. Business groups such as the American Chamber of Commerce hold numerous sessions each year on U.S. human resources and legal practices, primarily targeting Chinese young professionals. American law firms and law schools also diffuse international and foreign legal forms and norms by training domestic lawyers and offering special training to judges and others in the legal field. Finally, the cumulative efforts of MNCs, law firms, and consultants have given rise to a policy community that is informed by their knowledge of international and U.S. institutions and practices.[133] While analysts lament the rise of China's "soft power" and the decline of the U.S. government's "soft power,"[134] business and legal communities continue to spread and attract a following for U.S. institutions.[135]

Structural Underpinnings of China's State-guided Globalization

In this chapter, I have asserted that foreign investors, lawyers, business consultants, and organizations have helped Chinese officials and average citizens to improve their institutional compliance with foreign and international institutions. Concomitantly, China has sought to maintain a degree of autonomy in order to guide its globalization process. The issue of financial autonomy is crucial to understanding the process of state-guided globalization. Despite growing reliance on foreign direct investment flows, China has been able to guide foreign investors to help meet many of China's evolving state economic interests. How did they do it? Arguably, China's enormous size and market potential contributed to its ability to structure the terms on which global actors engaged China, but the enormity of China's economy cuts two ways. On one hand, it enhanced China's bargaining with MNCs. On the other, international economic organizations such as the WTO and foreign countries have been concerned about the effect of such a large economy on the global political economy, so they have raised the entry requirements for China to join the WTO and more assiduously have monitored China's strategic and human rights policies, for example.[136] China's relative success has been due to its ability to manage foreign capital, especially to attract the kind of foreign capital it sought.

A salient factor in gauging state autonomy is the degree of dependence on foreign capital and the type of foreign capital that flows into a country. Countries have three main options for attracting foreign capital: foreign direct investment, foreign loans, and financial instruments such as the sale of stocks and bonds. China began the open-door era lacking any foreign financial capital in its borders and, therefore, any influence of foreign capitalists, so it was able to build its approach to foreign capital with no direct external influence. After an initial period of relative reliance on foreign loans, China shifted to greater use of FDI and curtailed its foreign borrowing (see chapter 2); it did not sell stock shares to foreign investors until 2001. China avoided being saddled with the same foreign debt burdens faced by many Latin American economies, central and eastern European economies, and the Asian economies most deeply affected by the Asian financial crisis. Compared to a group of countries that have faced financial crises in recent decades—Argentina, Brazil, Indonesia, Mexico, and Thailand—in 1990, China's debt in real terms was the lowest. Although China has increased its debt in real terms since 1990, its ability to repay its mounting debt has improved. Using two standard measures of a country's capacity to repay a debt—total debt as a percentage of exports and total debt as a percentage of gross national income—China has improved its debt position since 1990 and, especially, since drawing lessons from its neighbors' financial crises in 1997–1998. In contrast, Argentina's and Brazil's debt positions have worsened since 1990, Indonesia's and Thailand's debt positions approximate their 1990 circumstances (both have improved since the 1997–1998 Asian financial crisis), while only Mexico joins China as having improved its debt position since 1990. Still, Mexico's debt position is worse than China's in terms of ratios of debt to gross national income and debt to exports (see Figures 7.2 and 7.3).

Reliance on foreign debt and stocks and bonds, especially destabilizing short-term debt and financial instruments, restricts a state's capacity to chart its own course through the globalization process. Although developing countries may borrow from a variety of sources—private international banks, foreign governments, or international financial organizations such as the IMF or World Bank—heavily indebted countries are exposed to the

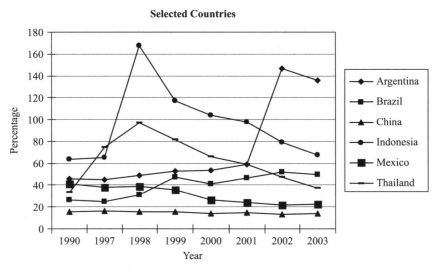

Figure 7.2   Total Standing Debt as a Percentage of GNI, Selected Countries. Source: World Bank, *Global Development Finance* (Washington, DC: World Bank, 2005).

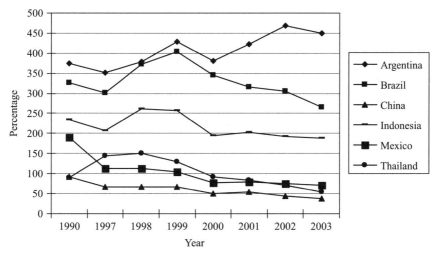

Figure 7.3   Total Standing Debt as a Percentage of Total Exports. Source: World Bank, *Global Development Finance* (Washington, DC: World Bank, 2005).

ebb and flow of investors' confidence. Heavily indebted countries that mismanage resources can face financial crises, which, in turn, can lead to economic bailouts and the imposition of institutional changes engineered by multilateral organizations and foreign banks. Such has been the case in the financial crises in Mexico (1982 and 1994), Argentina (2001–2002), Thailand (1997–1998), Indonesia (1997–1998), and Brazil (1998–1999). Concerned with borrowers' long-term capacity to repay loans, in the last two decades the IMF has increased its demands for structural adjustments of economic and political institutions. The IMF's prescriptions have varied over time, but it tends to dole out a version of political economic orthodoxy that is current at the time of the crisis.[137] Heavy debtors are prone to crises, which strip them of the capacity to select among institutional models and to moderate the pace of institutional change. When combined with large foreign reserves and a burgeoning trade surplus, China's low debt burden makes it less susceptible to financial crises and to unwanted interventions by international economic organizations.

In recent years, China has become the world's leading recipient of foreign direct investment, which most dependency theorists argue undermines local control over economic development. Unlike foreign lenders, foreign investors bring a variety of institutional models to developing countries, as well as a set of interests and institutions. Foreign investors' physical presence in a host economy adds to their clout and their capacity to displace local firms and induce dependency. Hence, foreign direct investment brings a set of risks to state autonomy that is distinct from foreign loans. States that manage foreign loans well can maximize state autonomy because they can channel resources into sectors and industries according to the state's development goals. South Korea pursued such a strategy of restricting foreign direct investment but borrowing heavily,[138] and its state did enjoy a great deal of autonomy until the Asian financial crisis hit in 1997–1998, after which it had to make significant structural adjustments to receive funds from the IMF to bailout its economy. Foreign investors have lobbied for changes to China's legal and business environments, introduced new institutional models, and diffused new norms to many young managerial staff. Those processes, though, took decades, during which the Chinese state was able to manage the pace of change and to work with foreign investors to find common goals and interests. Foreign investment flows in over a period of time into fixed assets, which cannot be easily liquidated at a moment's notice, a sharp contrast to the "hot money" of the Southeast Asian and Latin American financial crises. Thus, foreign direct investment provides greater financial stability and fewer risks than foreign borrowing.

Importantly, China has succeeded in attracting foreign investors from a wide variety of economies, reflecting distinct institutional models, business practices, and levels of technological development. Most countries with recent colonial histories face legacies of ties to firms from the former colonizing country, which perpetuates dependency on a single economy.[139] China's 30-year break from colonialism and any form of foreign investment undid any such lingering ties. Moreover, the perceived potential of the "China market" attracted foreign investors from most advanced capitalist economies, and China's cheap labor induced foreign investment from regional economies such as Taiwan, Hong Kong, and South Korea. The flood of investment from so many economies enhanced China's ability to authorize investment projects and selectively to adopt institutional models from foreign investors that helped to meet Chinese economic goals.

Through the decades of its gradual opening, China's state succeeded in defining parameters for foreign investors that guided some of the investment into sectors and industries according to state targets. The approval process for foreign investment projects grew decentralized after the mid-1980s; yet, the central government alone could approve large projects, those involving investment over $30 million. The investment projects that required the most capital also involved higher-end technology and machinery, which met state goals of industrial upgrading. Even under a relatively decentralized investment approval regime, the Chinese central government could exercise control over the types of investment that matter the most to it. Moreover, the state was able to restrict investment into a number of industries or at least postpone opening weak areas of its economy, such as the financial sector, until state-owned firms had an opportunity to prepare for competition from investors.[140]

China's globalization path points to the importance of controlling the borrowing of capital at the macro level (defaulted foreign loans taken out by firms often fall on states to repay) and devising institutions to attract foreign investment projects that facilitate meeting state economic goals such as technological upgrading and managerial and labor reforms at the micro level. China's path may be difficult to replicate, however, because it began its globalization process in the unusual position of being without significant foreign influence on its economy. Today, few other countries enjoy such an advantage. Nevertheless, China's management of globalization also evinces lessons that relate to dependency theory. First, foreign direct investment, when managed well, can facilitate economic development and help states to meet their strategic goals. Second, developing economies should try to attract investment flows from a number of countries, thus enabling host states to extract different lessons from the varieties of foreign investors' experiences. While foreign direct investment does not prevent institutional diffusion to the host economy, it grants the host state more discretion over the pace and direction of institutional reform and, indirectly, limits the capacity of international actors to force the host economy to comply with international norms.

Engagement, Interdependence, and State-guided Globalization

Studies of the Chinese pattern of economic reform through the mid-1990s used the Chinese idiom, "crossing the river by feeling for stones" to describe the unplanned way in which China's reformers plunged into a reform process without a clear blueprint.[141] A more accurate and updated metaphor for the current period might be driving a car with a GPS system. The GPS system, developed abroad, can be used to program a specific destination and it recommends a best path to follow. While the driver may veer from the preferred path, the system advises the driver, sometimes in an annoying tone, to return to the scheduled path. Finally, the system may irritate the driver to the point of wishing to turn it off or to unplug it, but the system is so useful that the driver persists in using it and comes to rely on its guidance.

China has opted to join the elite members of international society, which calls for multilateralism, engagement, and a policy of globalization—all of which structure its path of institutional reform. China can try to drive off the preferred path, but a chorus of multilateral organizations, foreign countries, MNCs, and increasingly domestic actors such as local attorneys and people in the business community complain about such actions. Chinese officials' desire to become a great power compels them to heed such feedback. Through the complex interplay of foreign efforts to diffuse international institutions to China and China's attempts to protect its interests and guide globalization to achieve strategic ends, China is emerging as a powerful state that is increasingly embedded in international norms and values. Most impressive is the cumulative effect of a series of modest institutional reforms. Multilateral organizations and foreign states have framed a course of international legitimacy for China, which China has been following, although progress on the path has been uneven, episodic, and painstakingly slow. Multinational corporations have helped supply feedback on shortcomings of China's reform efforts, modeled institutional change at the micro level, and affected values and norms of policy communities who diffuse institutional forms to state officials and firms. None of these changes would have been possible or sustainable without the willing participation of local actors, including state officials, Chinese policy communities, and workers in the job market. Chinese officials established a grand course for reforms that became clear with its efforts at WTO accession. It also set parameters for foreign investors at the micro level in order to guide development to meet strategic ends. Policy communities, which emerged out of the growing market for legal and business consultation that foreign and local businesses have demanded, have dispensed advice to organizations at the micro level and to state officials at various levels of the bureaucracy on how to improve its legal and regulatory environment. Workers on the job market gave important signals to consultants and, indirectly, to state officials on what they value in employers and how they respond to distinct incentive models.

Initially, China's state undertook open-door policies for the purpose of economic development, but it increasingly has come to embrace globalization and institutional change as a necessity to achieving a broader goal: emerging as a great power. Providing a definitive synopsis of China's attitude toward international norms and rules is complicated by the "hedging" strategy that China, like the United States, has adopted.[142] Much like the approach that the United States, Japan, and other major powers have taken to China, China has opted for a mixed strategy that emphasizes engagement and interdependence but also builds a strong military to enhance its clout in international affairs by making its security threat credible.

Although some have asserted that China is attempting to revise international rules, China is better characterized as making uneven progress toward adherence to the norms of international society, which vary in their clarity and codification. China has played a positive role as interlocutor between advanced capitalist states and other developing countries to help work on free trade principles by pushing forward the agenda set out at the Doha round of WTO discussions, on human rights by contributing to the Bangkok Conference on human rights, and security issues most notably by sponsoring talks on halting North Korea's nuclear weapons program. China's institutional reforms have not yet fully met the standards of international society, but it is moving in the direction of greater compliance with international norms and practices and it is proving itself a useful partner in international society. In its globalization, adoption of macro-level institutions is a rather straightforward process, but adherence to institutional reforms throughout China, which is large and has an institutional inheritance that veers widely from international norms, is difficult to achieve. The central argument offered here is that foreign investors, lawyers, and business organizations have contributed to a deepening of international norm diffusion to

China's micro level. By helping to develop a cohort of citizens, especially white-collar professionals who have knowledge of international institutions and a vested interest in their adoption, foreign actors have helped to catalyze an internal dynamic that calls for further institutional reform. The localization of international norms and institutions has created a sustainable pattern of globalization that will propel China further along the path of following the norms and strictures of international society. The presence of foreign investors with varying institutions will continue to provide Chinese officials and organizations with alternative models to consider as they seek to guide China's globalization path.

Appendix: List of Interviewees

President and general manager of Sino-U.S. JV (C-2000–001), interview by author, Shanghai, China (2000).

Officer at U.S. Consulate in Shanghai (C-2000–002), interview by author, Shanghai, China (2000).

Officer at foreign business association (C-2000–003), interview by author, Shanghai, China (2000).

Officer at foreign business association (C-2000–004), interview by author, Shanghai, China (2000).

General manager at U.S. WFOE (C-2000–005), interview by author, Shanghai, China (2000).

Managing director of U.S. firm's operations in China (C-2000–006), interview by author, Shanghai, China (2000).

Lawyer at Chinese law firm (C-2000–007), interview by author, Shanghai, China (2000).

President of U.S. firm's operation in Greater China (C-2000–008), interview by author, Shanghai, China (2000).

President of U.S. investment firm (C-2000–009), interview by author, Shanghai, China (2000).

Engineer for Sino-U.S. JV (C-2000–010), interview by author, Shanghai, China (2000).

Human resources manager in Sino-U.S. JV (C-2000–011), interview by author, Shanghai, China (2000).

Researcher in U.S. WFOE (C-2000–012), interview by author, Shanghai, China (2000).

Attorney in U.S. law firm (C-2000–013), interview by author, Shanghai, China (2000).

Legal consultant in U.S. law firm (C-2000–014), interview by author, Shanghai, China (2000).

Assistant general manager in Sino-Japanese JV (C-2000–015), interview by author, Shanghai, China (2000).

Attorney in Japanese law firm (C-2000–016), interview by author, Shanghai, China (2000).

Chief representative of U.S. firm's operations in Greater China (C-2000–017), interview by author, Shanghai, China (2000).

General manager of U.S. WFOE (C-2000–018), interview by author, Shanghai, China (2000).

Attorney in Japanese law firm (C-2000–019), interview by author, Shanghai, China (2000).

Attorney in Chinese law firm (C-2000–020), interview by author, Shanghai, China (2000).

Assistant general manager in Sino-Japanese JV (C-2000–021), interview by author, Shanghai, China (2000).

Human resources manager in U.S. WFOE (C-2000–022), interview by author, Shanghai, China (2000).

Chief representative in U.S. representative office (C-2000–023), interview by author, Shanghai, China (2000).

Regional manager in French representative office (C-2000–024), interview by author, Shanghai, China (2000).

Trade union representative in Sino-Japanese JV (C-2000–025), interview by author, Shanghai, China (2000).

Trade union representative in Sino-Hong Kong JV (C-2000–026), interview by author, Shanghai, China (2000).

Assistant head Shanghai trade union branch (C-2000–027), interview by author, Shanghai, China (2000).

President of Japanese representative office (C-2000–028), interview by author, Shanghai, China (2000).

General manager of Japanese representative office (C-2000–029), interview by author, Shanghai, China (2000).

General manager of U.S. representative office (C-2000–030), interview by author, Shanghai, China (2000).

Account manager of Chinese human resources company (C-2000–031), interview by author, Shanghai, China (2000).

General manager of Sino-Japanese JV (C-2000–032), interview by author, Shanghai, China (2000).

President of Japanese WFOE (C-2000–033), interview by author, Shanghai, China (2000).

General manager of Sino-Japanese JV(C-2000–034), interview by author, Shanghai, China (2000).

Managing director of U.S. WFOE (C-2000–035), interview by author, Shanghai, China (2000).

General manager of Sino-Japanese JV (C-2000–036), interview by author, Shanghai, China (2000).

General manager of Sino-Hong Kong JV (C-2000–037), interview by author, Shanghai, China (2000).

Chief representative of Japanese representative office (C-2000–038), interview by author, Shanghai, China (2000).

Chief representative of Japanese representative office (C-2000–039), interview by author, Shanghai, China (2000).

CEO and president of Sino-U.S. JV (C-2000–040), interview by author, Shanghai, China (2000).

General manager of Sino-U.S. JV (C-2000–041), interview by author, Shanghai, China (2000).

Research and development manager of U.S. WFOE (C-2000–042), interview by author, Shanghai, China (2000).

Human resources manager in Sino-Japanese JV (C-2000–043), interview by author, Shanghai, China (2000).

Human resources manager in Sino-U.S. JV (C-2000–044), interview by author, Shanghai, China (2000).

Chief representative of Japanese representative office (C-2000–045), interview by author, Shanghai, China (2000).

General manager of Japanese WFOE (C-2000–046), interview by author, Shanghai, China (2000).

General manager of Sino-U.S. JV (C-2000–047), interview by author, Shanghai, China (2000).

General manager of Sino-Japanese JV (C-2000–048), interview by author, Shanghai, China (2000).

General manager of U.S. WFOE (C-2000–049), interview by author, Shanghai, China (2000).

President of Japanese representative office (C-2000–050), interview by author, Shanghai, China (2000).

General manager of Sino-Japanese JV (C-2000–051), interview by author, Shanghai, China (2000).

General manager of Sino-Hong Kong JV (C-2000–052), interview by author, Shanghai, China (2000).

Office manager of Japanese representative office (C-2000–053), interview by author, Shanghai, China (2000).

Vice president of Sino-U.S. JV (C-2000–054), interview by author, Shanghai, China (2000).

Human resources manager of Sino-Japanese JV (C-2000–055), interview by author, Shanghai, China (2000).

Human resources manager of Sino-Japanese JV (C-2000–056), interview by author, Shanghai, China (2000).

Office manager of Japanese representative office (C-2000–057), interview by author, Shanghai, China (2000).

Director and general manager of Sino-Japanese JV (C-2000–058), interview by author, Shanghai, China (2000).

Deputy general manager of Sino-Japanese JV (C-2000–059), interview by author, Shanghai, China (2000).

General manager of Sino-U.S. JV (C-2000–060), interview by author, Shanghai, China (2000).

General manager of U.S. firm's China operations (C-2000–061), interview by author, Shanghai, China (2000).

President of Japanese WFOE (C-2000–062), interview by author, Shanghai, China (2000).

Human resources manager in U.S. WFOE (C-2000–063), interview by author, Shanghai, China (2000).

General manager of Sino-U.S. JV (C-2000–064), interview by author, Shanghai, China (2000).

General manager of Japanese representative office (C-2000–065), interview by author, Shanghai, China (2000).

General manager of Sino-U.S. JV (C-2000–066), interview by author, Shanghai, China (2000).

Deputy general manager of Sino-Japanese JV (C-2000–067), interview by author, Shanghai, China (2000).

General manager of Japanese representative office (C-2000–068), interview by author, Shanghai, China (2000).

Lawyer in Chinese law office (C-2000–069), interview by author, Shanghai, China (2000).

General manager of Sino-Japanese JV (C-2000–070), interview by author, Shanghai, China (2000).

General manager of Sino-U.S. JV (C-2000–071), interview by author, Shanghai, China (2000).

Program manager of Japanese company (J-2001–001), interview by author, Tokyo, Japan (2001).

Officer of Japanese business association (J-2001–002), interview by author, Tokyo, Japan (2001).

Personnel manager of Japanese company (J-2001–003), interview by author, Tokyo, Japan (2001).

Senior director of personnel of Japanese company (J-2001–004), interview by author, Tokyo, Japan (2001).

Personnel manager of Japanese company (J-2001–005), interview by author, Tokyo, Japan (2001).

Chairman of Japanese labor organization (J-2001–006), interview by author, Tokyo, Japan (2001).

Personnel manager of Japanese company (J-2001–007), interview by author, Tokyo, Japan (2001).

International human resources manager of Japanese company (J-2001–008), interview by author, Tokyo, Japan (2001).

Human resources manager of Japanese company (J-2001–009), interview by author, Tokyo, Japan (2001).

Human resources manager of Japanese company (J-2001–010), interview by author, Tokyo, Japan (2001).

Human resources manager of Japanese company (J-2001–011), interview by author, Tokyo, Japan (2001).

Public relations director of Japanese business organization (J-2001–012), interview by author, Tokyo, Japan (2001).

Professors of Japanese labor relations (J-2001–013), interview by author, Tokyo, Japan (2001).

Manager of international division of Japanese company (J-2001–014), interview by author, Tokyo, Japan (2001).

Human resources manager of Japanese company (J-2001–015), interview by author, Tokyo, Japan (2001).

Human resources manager of Japanese company (J-2001–016), interview by author, Tokyo, Japan (2001).

Managing consultant of international human resources company (C-2003–001), interview by author, Shanghai, China (2003).

Consultant of international human resources company (C-2003–002), interview by author, Shanghai, China (2003).

President of international human resources company (C-2003–003), interview by author, Shanghai, China (2003).

Human resources manager in U.S. WFOE (C-2005–001), interview by author, Shanghai, China (2005).

Human resources manager in Sino-Japanese JV (C-2005–002), interview by author, Shanghai, China (2005).

Director of international business organization (C-2005–003), interview by author, Shanghai, China (2005).

Lawyer in Chinese law firm (C-2005–004), interview by author, Shanghai, China (2005).

Officer in international business organization (C-2008–001), interview by author, Shanghai, China (2008).

Chinese management professor (C-2008–002), interview by author, Shanghai, China (2008).

Notes

Introduction

1. Qian Qiao, "Lin Zexu, a Patriot Who Opened His Eyes to the World," *Renmin Ribao*, 22 June 1981, translated in Joint Publication Research Service, *China Report: Political, Sociological, and Military Affairs* (hereafter, *JPRS*), no. 78640 (30 July 1981), pp. 8–10.

2. Margaret Pearson, *Joint Ventures in the People's Republic of China* (Princeton: Princeton University Press, 1991), pp. 37–51, lays out the positions taken by reformers and conservatives on the issue of learning from the west in the early days of the Deng era reforms.

3. Peter Gries, *China's New Nationalism* (Berkeley: University of California Press, 2005), pp. 46–52, analyzes the continuing effect of the "century of humiliation" on China's foreign policy.

4. David Held and Anthony McGrew, David Goldblatt, and Jonathan Perraton, *Global Transformations: Politics, Economics, and Culture* (Stanford: Stanford University Press, 1999), p. 276; and Kenichi Ohmae, *The End of the Nation State: The Rise of Regional Economies* (New York: The Free Press, 1995).

5. Stephan Haggard, *Developing Nations and the Politics of Global Integration* (Washington, DC: Brookings Institution Press, 1995), pp. 19–20; James R. Markusen, "The Theory of the Multinational Enterprise: A Common Analytical Framework," in *Direct Foreign Investment in Developing Economies and Structural Change in the Asia-Pacific Region*, ed. Eric D. Ramstetter (Boulder: Westview, 1992), pp. 26–27.

6. Doug Guthrie, *Dragon in a Three-Piece Suit: The Emergence of Capitalism in China* (Princeton: Princeton University Press, 1999), p. 39.

7. Douglass C. North, *Institutions, Institutional Change and Economic Performance* (Cambridge: Cambridge University Press, 1999), p. 83; Paul Pierson,

219

Politics in Time: History, Institutions, and Social Analysis (Princeton: Princeton University Press, 2004), pp. 108–122; John L. Campbell, *Institutional Change and Globalization* (Princeton: Princeton University Press, 2004), p. 77; and Kathleen Thelen and Sven Steinmo, "Historical Institutionalism in Comparative Politics," in *Structuring Politics: Historical Institutionalism in Comparative Analysis*, eds. Sven Steinmo, Kathleen Thelen, and Frank Longstreth (Cambridge: Cambridge University Press, 1992), p. 17.

8. North, *Institutions, Institutional Change*, pp. 73, 83, 89, 101; Pierson, *Politics in Time*, pp. 137–139; Margaret Weir, "Ideas and the Politics of Bounded Innovation," in *Structuring Politics*, pp. 194–195; Campbell, *Institutional Change*, pp. 65, 69–73.

9. Robert Boyer, "The Convergence Hypothesis Revisited: Globalization but Still the Century of Nations?" In *National Diversity and Global Capitalism*, eds. Suzanne Berger and Ronald Dore (Ithaca, NY: Cornell University Press, 1996), pp. 29–59; Mauro F. Guillen, *The Limits of Convergence: Globalization and Organizational Change in Argentina, South Korea, and Spain* (Princeton: Princeton University Press, 2001); Peter Hall and David Soskice, eds., *Varieties of Capitalism: The Institutional Foundation of Comparative Advantage* (Oxford: Oxford University Press, 2001); North, *Institutions, Institutional Change;* Louis W. Pauly and Simon Reich, "National Structures and Multinational Corporate Behavior: Enduring Differences in the Age of Globalization," *International Organization* 51, no. 1 (Winter 1997), pp. 1–30; Pierson, *Politics in Time;* and Robert Wade, "Globalization and Its Limits: Reports of the Death of the National Economy Are Greatly Exaggerated," in *National Diversity and Global Capitalism*, eds. Suzanne Berger and Ronald Dore (Ithaca, NY: Cornell University Press, 1996), pp. 60–88.

10. Shah M. Tarzi, "Third World Governments and Multinational Corporations: Dynamics of Host's Bargaining Power," in *International Political Economy* (3rd ed.), eds. Jeffry A. Frieden and David Lake (New York: St. Martin's Press, 1995), pp. 154–164.

11. Anita Chan, "Labor Relations in Foreign-funded Ventures, Chinese Trade Unions, and the Prospects for Collective Bargaining," in *Adjusting to Capitalism: Chinese Workers and the State*, ed. Greg O'Leary (Armonk, NY: M. E. Sharpe, 1998), pp. 122–149.

12. John Child, *Management in China during the Age of Reform* (Cambridge: Cambridge University Press, 1994); John Ravenhill, "Japanese and U.S. Subsidiaries in East Asia: Host Economy Effects," in *Japanese Multinationals in Asia: Regional Operations in Comparative Perspective*, ed. Dennis J. Encarnation (New York and Oxford: Oxford University Press, 1999), pp. 261–284.

13. Scott Wilson, "Law Guanxi: Multinational Corporations, State Actors, and Rule of Law in China," *Journal of Contemporary China* 17, no. 54 (February 2008), pp. 25–51.

14. Guthrie, *Dragon in a Three-Piece Suit*, pp. 62–63; Mary Gallagher, *Contagious Capitalism: Globalization and the Politics of Labor in China* (Princeton: Princeton University Press, 2005), pp. 14–18; David Zweig, *Internationalizing China: Domestic Interests and Global Linkages* (Ithaca, NY: Cornell University Press, 2002), p. 29.

15. Pearson, *Joint Ventures;* Margaret M. Pearson, "Erosion of Controls over Foreign Capital in China, 1979–1988," *Modern China* 17, no. 1 (January 1991), pp. 112–150.

16. Pearson, *Joint Ventures*, pp. 3–4.

17. Guthrie, *Dragon in a Three-Piece Suit;* and Gallagher, *Contagious Capitalism.*

18. Guthrie, *Dragon in a Three-Piece Suit,* p. 53.

19. Gallagher, *Contagious Capitalism,* pp. 14–18.

20. Zweig, *Internationalizing China,* p. 29.

21. *Ibid,* pp. 268–269.

22. Anita Chan, "Labor Relations in Foreign-funded Ventures," p. 124; Malcolm Warner and Zhu Ying, "The Origins of Chinese Industrial Relations," in Malcolm Warner, ed. *Changing Workplace Relations in the Chinese Economy* (New York: St. Martin's Press, 2000), pp. 28 and 30.

23. Agent of international human resources company (C-2003–01), interview by author, Shanghai (2003).

24. Gallagher, *Contagious Capitalism,* p. 3.

25. Guthrie, *Dragon in a Three-Piece Suit,* p. 5.

26. This argument follows the "constructivist" school's line of reasoning that international society affects the actions of states by shaping the normative fabric and identities in which states operate. Christian Reus-Smith, "Constructivism," in *Theories of International Relations,* eds. Scott Burchill et al. (Houndsmill, Basingstoke, Hampshire, UK: Palgrave MacMillan, 2005), pp. 188–212; Audie Klotz, "Norms Reconstituting Interests: Global Racial Equality and U.S. Sanctions Against South Africa," *International Organization* 49, no. 3 (Summer 1995), pp. 451–478; Richard Price, "A Geneology of the Chemical Weapons Taboo," *International Organization* 49, no. 1 (Winter 1995), pp. 73–103; Alexander Wendt, "Anarchy Is What States Make of It," *International Organization* 46, no. 2 (Spring 1992), pp. 391–425; and Alexander Wendt, "Constructing International Politics," *International Security* 20, no. 1 (Summer 1995), pp. 71–81.

27. James V. Feinerman calls China's record on compliance with the international legal order "mixed." According to Feinerman, "[Chinese] practice shows both admirable compliance with, and complete disregard of, international law…" James V. Feinerman, "Chinese Participation in the International Legal Order: Rogue Elephant or Team Player?" *The China Quarterly,* no. 141 (March 1995), p. 210.

28. China's strategy of preferring foreign borrowing to foreign direct investment appears to have mimicked South Korea's take-off strategy. On South Korea's development experience, see: Alice Amsden, *Asia's Next Giant: South Korea and Late Industrialization* (Oxford: Oxford University Press, 1992); and Robert Wade, *Governing the Market: Economic Theory and the Role of Government in East Asian Industrialization* (Princeton: Princeton University Press, 1990).

29. Sherman Cochran, *Encountering Chinese Networks: Western, Japanese, and Chinese Corporations in China, 1880–1937* (Berkeley: University of California Press, 2000), takes a similar approach to the one followed here, albeit during a different time period.

30. Margaret Pearson, *Joint Ventures,* for example, focuses almost exclusively on joint ventures because, at the time of her writing, few WFOEs were established in China.

31. In Shanghai, I drew a random sample of Hong Kong, Japanese, and U.S. companies in the electronics, industrial machinery, and chemical industries from a list of representative offices in Shanghai from 上海市对外经济贸易委员会和新闻报社编 (Shanghai Foreign Trade Committee and News Press, ed.), 台港澳、外国企业驻沪机构年鉴 1999 (*1999 Yearbook of Taiwan, Hong Kong, Macao and Foreign*

Enterprises in Shanghai), (中国纺织大学出版社 , 1999) (Chinese Textile University Press, 1999).

Chapter One

1. Some authors have contended that industrialization, international regimes, and globalization cause institutions in different countries to converge. Clark Kerr, *The Future of Industrial Societies: Convergence or Continuing Diversity?* (Cambridge, MA: Harvard University Press, 1983); Dennis J. Encarnation and Louis T. Wells, Jr., "Sovereignty en Garde: Negotiating with Foreign Investors," *International Organization* 39, no 1 (1985), p. 48; and Colin J. Bennett, "What Is Policy Convergence and What Causes It?" *British Journal of Political Science* 21, no. 2 (April 1991), pp. 225–227.

2. Mauro F. Guillen, *The Limits of Convergence: Globalization and Organizational Change in Argentina, South Korea, and Spain* (Princeton and Oxford: Princeton University Press, 2001); Peter A. Hall and David Soskice, eds., *Varieties of Capitalism: The Institutional Foundations of Comparative Advantage* (Oxford: Oxford University Press, 2001); Paul Pierson, *Politics in Time: History, Institutions, and Social Analysis* (Princeton: Princeton University Press, 2004); Paul Pierson, "Increasing Returns, Path Dependence, and the Study of Politics," *American Political Science Review* 94, no. 2 (June 2000), pp. 251–267; and Douglass C. North, *Institutions, Institutional Change and Economic Performance* (Cambridge: Cambridge University Press, 1999). Steven D. Krasner, "Review: Approaches to the State: Alternative Conceptions and Historical Dynamics," *Comparative Politics* 16, no. 2 (Jan. 1984), pp. 240–241, articulates a path dependent theory of institutional resilience. Avner Greif and David D. Laitin, "A Theory of Endogenous Institutional Change," *American Political Science Review* 98, no. 4 (November 2004), pp. 633–652, criticizes Paul Pierson's definition of increasing returns in terms of positive feedback, which sidesteps the issue of negative feedback—poor performance or "noise" from institutions.

3. Wolfgang Streeck and Kathleen Thelen, "Introduction: Institutional Change in Advanced Political Economies," in *Beyond Continuity: Institutional Change in Advanced Political Economies,* eds. Wolfgang Streeck and Kathleen Thelen (Oxford: Oxford University Press, 2005); Paul Pierson, *Politics in Time;* David Stark, "Path Dependence and Privatization Strategies in East Central Europe," *East European Politics and Societies* 6, no. 1 (Winter 1992), pp. 17–54; John L. Campbell, *Institutional Change and Globalization* (Princeton: Princeton University Press, 2004); Douglass C. North, *Institutions, Institutional Change;* and Wolfgang Streeck and Kozo Yamamura, eds., *The Origins of Nonliberal Capitalism: German and Japan in Comparison* (Ithaca, NY: Cornell University Press, 2001).

4. Pierson, "Increasing Returns," p. 251; and Pierson, *Politics in Time,* p. 18.

5. Krasner, "Review: Approaches to the State," pp. 234–235.

6. Streeck and Thelen, "Introduction," p. 16; Pierson, *Politics in Time;* Campbell, *Institutional Change;* G. John Ikenberry, "Institutions, Strategic Restraint, and Persistence of American Postwar Order," *International Security* 23, no. 3 (Winter 1998–1999), pp. 43–78; North, *Institutions, Institutional Change.*

7. Magnus Henrekson, "Sweden's Relative Economic Performance: Lagging Behind or Staying on Top?" *The Economic Journal* 106 (November 1996),

pp. 1747–1759; Wolfgang Streeck and Kozo Yamamura, "Introduction," in *The End of Diversity? Prospects for German and Japanese Capitalism*, eds. Kozo Yamamura and Wolfgang Streeck (Ithaca, NY, and London: Cornell University Press, 2003), pp. 1–50; Steven K. Vogel, "The Re-Organization of Organized Capitalism: How the German and Japanese Models are Shaping Their Own Transformations," in *The End of Diversity? Prospects for German and Japanese Capitalism*, eds. Kozo Yamamura and Wolfgang Streeck (Ithaca and London: Cornell University Press, 2003), pp. 306–333; Marie Anchordoguy, "Japan at a Technological Crossroads: Does Change Support Convergence Theory?" *Journal of Japanese Studies* 23, no. 2 (Summer 1997), pp. 395–396.

8. Doug Guthrie, *Dragon in a Three-Piece Suit: The Emergence of Capitalism in China* (Princeton: Princeton University Press, 1999).

9. Ken-ichi Ohmae, *The Borderless World* (London: Harper Collins, 1995). Paul Hirst, "The Global Economy—Myths and Realities," *International Affairs* 73, no. 3 (July 1997), pp. 409–425, argues that MNCs remain rooted in domestic economies and are governable.

10. Peter J. Katzenstein and Nobuo Okawara, "Japan's National Security: Structures, Norms, and Policies," *International Organization* 17, no. 4 (Spring 1993), pp. 117.

11. Andrew G. Walder, "Wage Reform and the Web of Factory Interests," *The China Quarterly*, no. 109 (March 1987), pp. 22–41; and John L. Campbell, *Institutional Change*, p. 43. Several studies of MNCs moving to new contexts have documented worker resistance to foreign institutions, including: Diane Rosemary Sharpe, "Globalization and Change: Organizational Continuity and Change within a Japanese Multinational in the UK," *in The Multinational Firm: Organizing across Institutional and National Divides*, eds. Glenn Morgan, Peer Hull Kristensen, and Richard Whitley (Oxford and New York: Oxford University Press, 2001), pp. 196–221; Laurie Graham, *On the Line at Isuzu-Subaru: The Japanese Model and the American Worker* (Ithaca, NY: Cornell University ILR Press, 1995).

12. Wolfgang Streeck and Kozo Yamamura, "Introduction," pp. 5 and 11; Steven K. Vogel, "The Re-Organization," pp. 329–332.

13. US-China Business Council, "China's Implementation of Its World Trade Organization Commitments," Written Testimony by the US-China Business Council, submitted to the Office of the U.S. Trade Representatives, (28 September 2006), p. 5, discusses the issue of Chinese compliance with "national treatment," an example of potential non-compliance with treaty obligations.

14. Judith Teichman, *Freeing the Markets of Latin America: Chile, Argentina, and Mexico* (Chapel Hill: University of North Carolina Press, 2001); Thomas Risse-Kappen, "Ideas Do not Float Freely: Transnational Coalitions, Domestic Structures, and the End of the Cold War," *International Organization* 48, no. 2 (Spring 1994), pp. 186 and 196–204; Amitav Acharya, "How Ideas Spread: Whose Norms Matter? Norm Localization and Institutional Change in Asian Regionalism," *International Organization* 58, (Spring 2004), pp. 239–275.

15. Richard Whitley, *Divergent Capitalisms: The Social Structuring and Change of Business Systems* (Oxford and New York: Oxford University Press, 1999), p. 22.

16. Peter A. Hall and David Soskice, "An Introduction to Varieties of Capitalism," in *Varieties of Capitalism: The Institutional Foundations of Comparative Advantage*, eds. Peter A. Hall and David Soskice (New York and Oxford: Oxford University Press, 2001), p. 9.

17. Thorstein Veblen, *The Theory of the Leisure Class* (Penguin Classics, 1994); Karl Polanyi, *The Great Transformation: The Political and Economic Origins of Our Time* (Boston: Beacon Press, 1944); and Mark Granovetter, "Economic Action and Social Structure: The Problem of Embeddedness," *American Journal of Sociology* 91 (November 1985), pp. 481–510.

18. Ronald Dore, *Taking Japan Seriously: A Confucian Perspective on Leading Economic Issues* (Stanford: Stanford University Press, 1987), pp. 169–192; Scott Wilson, "Face, Norms, and Instrumentality," in *Social Connections in China: Institutions, Culture, and the Changing Nature of Guanxi,* eds. Thomas Gold, Doug Guthrie, and David Wank (Cambridge: Cambridge University Press, 2002), pp. 163–178; Gary Hamilton and Nicole Woolsey Biggart, "Market, Culture, and Authority: A Comparative Analysis of Management and Organization in the Far East," *American Journal of Sociology* 94, Supplement, pp. S52-S94; Gary G. Hamilton, "Patterns of Asian Network Capitalism: The Cases of Taiwan and South Korea," in *Networks, Markets, and the Pacific Rim: Studies in Strategy,* ed. W. Mark Fruin (New York: Oxford University Press, 1998), pp. 195–196; Marc Orru, "Practical and Theoretical Aspects of Japanese Business Networks," in *Business Networks and Economic Development in East and Southeast Asia,* ed. Gary G. Hamilton (Hong Kong: Center of Asian Studies, University of Hong Kong, 1991), pp. 244–271.

19. Whitley, *Divergent Capitalisms,* pp. 18–19.

20. Colin Hay, "Contemporary Capitalism, Globalization, Regionalization and the Persistence of National Variation," *Review of International Studies* 26 (2000), pp. 509–531, contends that regional institutions shape economies' propensity for convergence and that Asia's institutions limit convergence with the "Washington Concensus." Louis W. Pauly and Simon Reich, "National Structures and Multinational Corporate Behavior: Enduring Differences in the Age of Globalization," *International Organization* 51, no. 1 (Winter 1997), pp. 1–30; Paul Doremus et al., *The Myth of the Global Corporation* (Princeton: Princeton University Press, 1999); Ronald Dore, "The Distinctiveness of Japan," in *Political Economy of Modern Capitalism: Mapping Convergence and Divergence,* eds. Colin Crouch and Wolfgang Streeck (London: Sage Publications, 1997), pp. 19–33; and Marc Orru, "Practical and Theoretical Aspects," pp. 244–271; Colin Crouch and Wolfgang Streeck, "Introduction" in *Political Economy of Modern Capitalism,* eds. Colin Crouch and Wolfgang Streeck (Thousand Oaks, CA: Sage Publications, 1997), pp. 1–18; Robert Boyer, "The Convergence Hypothesis Revisited: Globalization but Still the Century of Nations?" in *National Diversity and Global Capitalism,* eds. Suzanne Berger and Ronald Dore (Ithaca: Cornell University Press, 1996), pp. 46–47; Sven-Erik Sjostrand, "The Many Faces of Capitalism," in *Institutional Change: Theory and Empirical Findings,* ed. Sven-Erik Sjostrand (Armonk, NY: M. E. Sharpe, 1993), pp. 399–404.

21. Cal Clark and K. C. Roy, *Comparing Development Patterns in Asia* (Boulder: Lynne Rienner, 1997), pp. 68–93; Dore, *Taking Japan Seriously,* pp. 169–192; Gary Hamilton and Nicole Woolsey Biggart, "Market, Culture, and Authority," pp. S52-S94; Gary G. Hamilton, "Patterns of Asian Network Capitalism," pp. 195–196; Robert Wade, *Governing the Market: Economic Theory and the Role of Government in East Asian Industrialization* (Princeton: Princeton University Press, 1990); Alice Amsden, *Asia's Next Giant: South Korea and Late Industrialization* (Oxford: Oxford University Press, 1989); S. Gordon Redding, "Weak Organizations and Strong Linkages: Managerial Ideology and Chinese Family Business Networks," in *Business*

Networks and Economic Development in East and Southeast Asia, ed. Gary Hamilton (Hong Kong: Center of Asian Studies, University of Hong Kong), pp. 42–46; Alice Amsden, *The Rise of "the Rest": Challenges to the West from Late-Industrializing Economies* (Oxford: Oxford University Press, 2001); Ezra F. Vogel, *The Four Little Dragons: The Spread of Industrialization in East Asia* (Cambridge, MA: Harvard University Press, 1991); Chalmers Johnson, "Political Institutions and Economic Performance: The Government-Business Relationship in Japan, South Korea, and Taiwan," in *The Political Economy of the New Asian Industrialism,* ed. Frederic C. Deyo (Ithaca, NY: Cornell University Press, 1987); Chalmers Johnson, *MITI and the Japanese Miracle: The Growth of Industrial Policy, 1925–1975* (Stanford: Stanford University Press, 1982).

22. Dore, *Taking Japan Seriously,* pp. 169–192; Jeffrey H. Dyer, "To Sue or Keiretsu: A Comparison of Partnering in the United States and Japan," in *Networks, Markets, and the Pacific Rim: Studies in Strategy,* ed. W. Mark Fruin (New York and Oxford: Oxford University Press, 1998), pp. 233–254.

23. W. Brian Arthur, *Increasing Returns and Path Dependence in the Economy* (Ann Arbor: University of Michigan Press, 1994), cited in Pierson, "Increasing Returns," p. 254.

24. It might be equally or more accurate to think of institutional commitments in terms of "sunk costs" rather than "increasing returns." Establishing and organizing institutions require significant resources, and increasing the number of people affected by the institutions raises the expense of coordinating behavior and implementing policies that flow from institutions such as social security. Changing institutions and reorganizing coordination would cause people to lose significant resources (sunk costs) in the transition. Krasner, "Review: Approaches to the State," p. 235.

25. Ronald Dore, *Flexible Rigidities: Structural Adjustment in Japan: 1970–1982* (Stanford: Stanford University Press, 1986); Ken-ichi Imai, "Japan's Corporate Networks," in *The Political Economy of Japan, Vol. 3: Cultural and Social Dynamics,* eds. S. Kumon and H. Rosovsky (Stanford: Stanford University Press, 1992), pp. 198–230; Ichiro Numazaki, "Networks of Taiwanese Big Business," *Modern China* 12, no. 4 (October 1986), pp. 487–534; Tong Chee Kiong and Yong Pit Kee, "Guanxi Bases, Xinyong and Chinese Business Networks," *British Journal of Sociology* 49, no. 1 (March 1998), pp. 75–96; Hamilton and Woolsey Biggart, "Market, Culture, and Authority," pp. S52–S94.

26. Krasner, "Review: Approaches to the State," p. 236.

27. Elizabeth S. Clemens and James M. Cook, "Politics and Institutionalism: Explaining Durability and Change," *Annual Review of Sociology* 25 (1999), pp. 445–446; Paul J. Dimaggio and Walter W. Powell, "The Iron Cage Revisited: Institutional Isomorphism and Collective Rationality in Organizational Fields," in *The New Institutionalism in Organizational Analysis,* eds. *idem,* pp. 63–82; and Peter L. Berger and Thomas Luckman, *The Social Construction of Reality: A Treatise of Sociology of Knowledge* (Garden City, NY: Anchor Books, 1966).

28. Clemens and Cook, "Politics and Institutionalism," p. 449.

29. Human resources manager of Japanese corporation (J-2001–10), interview by author, Tokyo (2001); human resources manager of Japanese corporation (J-2001–08), interview by author, Tokyo (2001); and staff member of Japanese Institute of Labor (J-2001–06), interview by author, Tokyo (2001). Andrew G. Walder, *Communist Neo-Traditionalism: Work and Authority in Chinese Industry*

(Berkeley: University of California Press, 1986), pp. 239–240; and Walder, "Wage Reform and the Web of Factory Interests," pp. 22–42.

30. North, *Institutions, Institutional Change*, pp. 95–96; and Pierson, Politics *in Time*, p. 126.

31. North, *Institutions, Institutional Change*, pp. 8, 23, 25, and 107; Pierson, *Politics in Time*, pp. 38–40.

32. North, *Institutions, Institutional Change*, pp. 8, 23, and 44.

33. Barbara Levitt and James G. March, "Organizational Learning," *Annual Review of Sociology* 14 (1988), pp. 319–340.

34. North, *Institutions, Institutional Change*, p. 23.

35. I remain skeptical about organizational learning theory's approach to firm's handling of new information. While I accept their claim that firms organize knowledge and may expand to new environments that lack their knowledge, I am more pessimistic on how organizations—both states and firms—handle new and negative information. On the latter point, institutionalists raise significant arguments with regard to the limits of cognition.North, *Institutions, Institutional Change*, pp. 95–96; and Pierson, *Politics in Time*, p. 126.

36. Krasner, "Review: Approaches to the State," p. 235.

37. Krasner, "Review: Approaches to the State," p. 235.

38. Hall and Soskice, "An Introduction," pp. 58 and 63.

39. Clemens and Cook, "Politics and Institutionalism," p. 452; Richard Deeg, "Change from Within: German and Italian Finance in the 1990s," in *Beyond Continuity: Institutional Change in Advanced Political Economies*, eds. Wolfgang Streeck and Kathleen Thelen (Oxford: Oxford University Press, 2005), pp. 169–202.

40. Deeg, "Change from Within," pp. 182, 195–196.

41. Krasner, "Review: Approaches to the State," p. 234.

42. Stark, "Path Dependence," pp. 17–54. Marie Anchordoguy, "Japan at a Technological Crossroads," makes a similar claim about Japanese economic reform.

43. North, *Institutions, Institutional Change*, p. 89.

44. Peter Gourevitch, *Politics in Hard Times: Comparative Responses to International Economic Crises* (Ithaca, NY: Cornell University Press, 1986), p. 33; Hay, "Contemporary Capitalism," pp. 511–515.

45. Charles Tilly, "War Making and State Making as Organized Crime," in *Bringing the State Back In*, eds. Peter B. Evans, Dietrich Rueschmeyer, and Theda Skocpol (Cambridge: Cambridge University Press, 1985), pp. 169–191; Margaret Levi, *Of Rule and Revenue* (Berkeley: University of California Press, 1988); Krasner, "Review: Approaches to the State," pp. 238–240.

46. Krasner, "Review: Approaches to the State," pp. 242–243; Streeck and Thelen, "Introduction," p. 20; Kathleen Thelen, "Historical Institutionalism in Comparative Politics," *Annual Review of Political Science* 2 (1999), pp. 369–404; and Pierson, *Politics in Time*, pp. 55–58.

47. Krasner, "Review: Approaches to the State."

48. Vogel, "The Reorganization," pp. 306–333.

49. Jose Alvarez, "The WTO as Linkage Machine," *American Journal of International Law* 96, no. 1 (January 2002), p. 149; and Steven Bernstein and Benjamin Cashore, "Globalization, Four Paths of Internationalization and Domestic Policy Change: The Case of EcoForestry in British Columbia, Canada," *Canadian Journal of Political Science* 33, no. 1 (March 2000), pp. 81–83.

50. Martha Finnemore and Kathryn Sikkink, "International Norm Dynamics and Political Change," *International Organization* 52, no. 4 (Autumn 1998), pp. 887–917; and Kathryn Sikkink, "Transnational Politics, International Relations Theory, and Human Rights," *PS: Political Science and Politics* 31, no. 3 (September 1998), pp. 516–523.

51. Dimaggio and Powell, "The Iron Cage Revisited," p. 67.

52. Martin Feldstein, "Refocusing the IMF," *Foreign Affairs* 77, no. 2 (March/April 1998), pp. 20–33; Judith A. Teichman, *The Politics of Freeing Markets in Latin America: Chile, Argentina, and Mexico* (Chapel Hill: University of North Carolina Press, 2000); Judith A. Teichman, *Privatization and Political Change in Mexico* (Pittsburgh: University of Pittsburgh Press, 1996); Nora Lustig, *Mexico: The Remaking of an Economy,* 2nd ed. (Washington, DC: Brookings Institution Press, 1998); Stephan Haggard, *Developing Nations and the Politics of Global Integration* (Washington, DC: The Brookings Institution, 1995). Miles Kahler, "International Financial Institutions and the Politics of Adjustment," in *Fragile Coalitions: The Politics of Economic Adjustment,* ed. Joan M. Nelson (New Brunswick: Transaction Books, 1989), pp. 144–149, contends that the IMF and World Bank have tried to use conditionality and structural adjustment loans as levers for changing developing countries' policies, but these approaches have had limited success.

53. Acharya, "How Ideas Spread," pp. 239–275; and Hay, "Contemporary Capitalism," pp. 509–531.

54. Clyde Prestowitz, "Beyond Laisse Faire," *Foreign Policy* 87, (Summer 1992), pp. 67–87.

55. Geoffrey Garrett and Peter Lange, "Internationalization, Institutions and Political Change," in *Internationalization and Domestic Politics,* eds. Robert O. Keohane and Helen V. Milner (Cambridge: Cambridge University Press, 1996), p. 54; John L. Campbell, *Institutional Change,* pp. 18–22.

56. Audie Klotz, "Norms Reconstituting Interests: Global Racial Equality and U.S. Sanctions Against South Africa," *International Organization* 49, no. 3 (Summer, 1995), pp. 451–478; Hans-Peter Schmitz, "Mobilizing Identities: Transnational Social Movements and the Promotion of Human Rights Norms," in *Global Institutions and Local Empowerment,* ed. Kendall Stiles (New York: St. Martin's Press, 2000), pp. 85–113; and Christian Reus-Smith, "Constructivism," in *Theories of International Relations* (2nd ed.), eds. Scott Burchill, et al. (Basingstroke, Hampshire, and New York: Palgrave Macmillan, 2001), pp. 209–231, contend that states are concerned with their identities in international affairs and act according to how international society perceives them.

57. Robert Rohrschneider, "The Democracy Deficit and Mass Support for an EU-Wide Government," *American Journal of Political Science* 46, no. 2 (April 2002), pp. 463–475; and Amy Verdun, "The Institutional Design of EMU: A Democratic Deficit?" *Journal of Public Policy* 18, no. 2 (May–August 1998), pp. 107–132.

58. Guthrie, *Dragon in a Three-Piece Suit,* pp. 151–153.

59. Pierson, *Politics in Time,* p. 43; and David Zweig, *Internationalizing China: Domestic Interests and Global Linkages* (Ithaca, NY: Cornell University Press, 2002), p. 29.

60. Deeg, "Change from Within," pp. 182, 195–196.

61. Pierson, *Politics in Time,* p. 137.

62. Clemens and Cook, "Politics and Institutionalism," pp. 445, discusses cognitive scripts.

63. Pauly and Reich, "National Structures," pp. 1–30; and Doremus et al., *The Myth of the Global Corporation.*

64. Sharpe, "Globalization and Change;" and Graham, *On the Line.*

65. Sharpe, "Globalization and Change," pp. 200 and 211; Peer Hull Kristensen and Jonathan Zeitlin, "The Making of a Global Firm: Local Pathways to Multinational Enterprise," in *The Multinational Firm: Organizing Across Institutional and National Divides,* eds. Glenn Morgan, Peer Hull Kristensen, and Richard Whitley (Oxford: Oxford University Press, 2001), p. 192.

66. Guthrie, *Dragon in a Three-Piece Suit,* pp. 61–63.

67. Mary Gallagher, *Contagious Capitalism: Globalization and the Politics of Labor in China* (Princeton: Princeton University Press, 2005), pp. 6 and 10–14.

68. Barbara Levitt and James G. March, "Organizational Learning," *Annual Review of Sociology* 14 (1988), p. 319, assert that organizational learning is distinct from bargaining power explanations of firms.

69. Bruce Kogut, "Joint Ventures: Theoretical and Empirical Perspectives," *Strategic Management Journal* 9, no. 4 (1988), p. 323; and Yadong Luo, "Toward a Cooperative View of MNC-Host Government Relations: Building Blocks and Performance Implications," *Journal of International Business Studies* 32, no. 3 (2001), pp. 401–419.

70. Mary M. Crossan, Henry W. Lane, and Roderick E. White, "An Organizational Learning Framework: From Intuition to Institution," *Academy of Management Review* 24, no. 3 (1999), p. 525; and Levitt and March, "Organizational Learning," pp. 319–340.

71. Kogut, "Joint Ventures," p. 323; and Bruce Kogut and Udo Zander, "Knowledge of the Firm and the Evolutionary Theory of the Multinational Corporation," *Journal of International Business Studies* 24, no. 4 (1993), pp. 625–645.

72. However, Levitt and March, "Organizational Learning," p. 335, argue, "Learning does not always lead to intelligent behavior."

73. Richard Whitley, *Divergent Capitalisms,* p. 128.

74. Guthrie, *Dragon in a Three-Piece Suit.*

75. Klotz, "Norms Reconstituting Interests," pp. 451–478; Schmitz, "Mobilizing Identities," pp. 85–113; and Christian Reus-Smith, "Constructivism," in *Theories of International Relations* (2nd ed.), eds. Scott Burchill, et al (Basingstoke, Hampshire; New York: Palgrave Macmillan, 2001), pp. 209–231.

76. Pierson, *Politics in Time,* pp. 160–162.

77. Krasner, "Review: Approaches to the State," p. 235.

78. Kogut, "International Joint Ventures"; Yadong Luo, "Joint Venture Success in China: How Should We Select a Good Partner?" *Journal of World Business* 33, no. 2 (Summer 1998), pp. 145–166; and James P. Walsh, ErPing Wang, and Katherine R. Xin, "Same Bed, Different Dreams: Working Relationships in Sino-American Joint Ventures," *Journal of World Business* 34, no. 1 (1999), pp. 69–92.

79. Deeg, "Change from Within," p. 183.

80. Risse-Kappen, "Ideas Do not Float Freely," pp. 185–214.

81. Finnemore and Sikkink, "International Norm Dynamics," pp. 887–917; and Sikkink, "Transnational Politics," pp. 516–523.

82. Teichman, *The Politics of Freeing Markets,* pp. 59–60.

83. Wolfgang H. Reinicke, "The Other World Wide Web: Global Public Policy Networks," *Foreign Policy,* No. 117 (Winter 1999–2000), pp. 44–57; Finnemore and

Sikkink, "International Norm Dynamics," pp. 887–917; and Sikkink, "Transnational Politics," pp. 516–523.

84. Walter Hatch and Kozo Yamamura, *Asia in Japan's Embrace: Building a Regional Production Alliance* (Cambridge: Cambridge University Press, 1996), p. 25.

85. Paul Pierson, "Coping with Permanent Austerity: Welfare State Structuring in Affluent Democracies," *Revue Francaise de Sociologie* 43, no. 2 (April–June 2002), p. 372, discusses veto points.

86. Matthew Evangelista, "The Paradox of State Strength: Transnational Relations, Domestic Structures and Security Policy in Russia and the Soviet Union," *International Organization* 49, no. 1 (Winter 1995), pp. 1–38.

87. Rosemary Foot, "Chinese Power and the Idea of a Responsible State," *The China Journal,* no. 45 (January 2001), pp. 1–19.

88. Joshua Kurlantzick, *Charm Offensive: How China's Soft Power Is Transforming the World* (New Haven and London: Yale University Press, 2007), discusses China's attempts to spread its influence and appeal in international society.

89. Alastair Iain Johnston, "Is China a Status Quo Power?" *International Security* 27, no. 4 (2003), pp. 5–56, addresses China's commitments to international institutions in the context of its international ambitions.

90. Feng Chen, "Industrial Restructuring and Workers' Resistance in China," *Modern China* 29, no. 2 (April 2003), pp. 237–262; and Andrew G. Walder, "Wage Reform."

91. Feng Chen, "Industrial Restructuring," pp. 237–262; William Hurst and Kevin J. O'Brien, "China's Contentious Pensioners," *The China Quarterly,* no. 170 (June 2002), pp. 345–360; Scott Kennedy, *The Business of Lobbying in China* (Cambridge: Harvard University Press, 2005); Kevin J. O'Brien and Lianjiang Li, *Rightful Resistance in Rural China* (Cambridge: Cambridge University Press, 2006); He Baogang, "The Making of a Nascent Civil Society in China," in *Civil Society in Asia,* eds. David C. Schak and Wayne Hudson (Hampshire: Ashgate, 2003), pp. 114–139; Jude Howell, "Seizing Spaces, Challenging Marginalization, and Claiming Voice: New Trends in Civil Society in China," in *Civil Society,* eds. Marlies Glasius, David Lewis, and Hakan Seckinelgin (Abingdon: Routledge, 2004), pp. 121–129; and Tony Saich, "Negotiating the State: The Development of Social Organizations in China," *China Quarterly,* no. 161 (March 2000), pp. 124–141.

Chapter Two

1. In the *People's Daily,* (14 December 1981), pp. 1–4, Deng Xiaoping was quoted as saying that China had to open to foreign investment in order to meet its Four Modernizations program. Cited in Fuh-Wen Tzeng, "The Political Economy of China's Coastal Development Strategy," *Asian Survey* XXXI, no. 3 (March 1991), pp. 270.

2. Liu Xiao and Zheng Youjing, "About Operating Enterprises Jointly with Foreign Capital," *Jingji Guanli* (Hong Kong), No. 4 (25 April 1979), pp. 20–23, translated in *JPRS,* no. 73870 (19 July 1979), pp. 82–88; Xu Dixin, "Views on Special Economic Zones," *Shijie Jingji Daobao* (in Chinese), No. 37 (15 June 1981), p. 3, translated in *JPRS,* No. 78684 (5 August 1981), pp. 31–32; and Fang Zhoufen, "On the Nature of China's Special Economic Zones," *Jingji Yanjiu,* no. 8 (20 August

1981), pp. 54–58, translated in *JPRS, China Report,* No. 79100 (30 September 1981), pp. 41–42.

3. Mary Gallagher, *Contagious Capitalism: Globalization and the Politics of Labor in China* (Princeton: Princeton University Press, 2005), pp. 14–15; and David Zweig, *Internationalizing China: Domestic Interests and Global Linkages* (Ithaca, NY: Cornell University Press, 2002), p. 29.

4. Sarah Tong, "The US-China Trade Imbalance: How Big Is It Really?" *China: An International Journal* 3, no. 1 (March 2005), pp. 149–150.

5. Calculated from Chinese Economic Statistical Yearbook Editorial Committee, *Chinese Economic Yearbook* (Beijing: Chinese Economic Yearbook Publishers, various years).

6. Margaret Pearson, *Joint Ventures in the People's Republic of China* (Princeton: Princeton University Press, 1991), pp. 21–25, argues than in the early years of China's opening, leftists, conservatives, and reformers formed a consensus that foreign investors and their influence had to be limited.

7. Pearson, *Joint Ventures,* pp. 59–62 and 64. "Economic Zones in Guangdong Promote Four Modernizations," *Nanfang Ribao* (in Chinese) (4 September 1980), p. 1, translated in *JPRS-CEA,* 76913 (2 December 1980), p. 10; Zhongshan University Shenzhen Investigation Team, "A Useful Insight: An Investigation into Wage System Reform in the Shekou Industrial Zone," translated in *Chinese Economic Studies* XIX, no. 2 (Winter 1985–1986), p. 67; and Xu Dixin, "Views on Special Economic Zones," p. 31, argue that China should protect its sovereignty while opening SEZs.

8. Fang Lin, "Indiscriminate Copying Foreign Experiences Criticized," *Jingji Guanli,* no. 1 (January 1985), pp. 41–42, translated in *JPRS-CEA,* 75643 (7 May 1980), pp. 31–32, criticizes the idea of "takeoverism" by foreign or Western powers.

9. Xia Gu, "Promote the Virtue of Patriotism," *Shaanxi Ribao,* 11 March 1981, p. 3, translated in *JPRS,* 78312 (17 June 1981), p. 23.

10. David Bachman, "Differing Visions of China's Post-Mao Economy: The Ideas of Chen Yun, Deng Xiaoping, and Zhao Ziyang," *Asian Survey* 26, no. 3, pp. 292–321.

11. Liu Xiao and Zheng Yongjing, "About Operating Enterprises Jointly," pp. 82–88.

12. "Economic Zones in Guangdong," p. 10; and Zhao Yuanhao, "Talk about Ways To Demonstrate Guangdong's 'Superiority,'" *Yangcheng Wanbao* (5 August 1981), p. 2, translated in *JPRS,* 79518 (24 November 1981), p. 57.

13. Xu Dixin, "Views on Special Economic Zones," p. 30.

14. Joseph Fewsmith, "Special Economic Zones in the PRC," *Problems of Communism* (November–December 1986), pp. 78–85; David Zweig, "China's Stalled 'Fifth Wave': Zhu Rongji's Reform Package of 1998–2000," *Asian Survey* 41, no. 2 (April 2001), pp. 231–247; and Bachman, "Differing Visions," pp. 292–321.

15. Pearson, *Joint Ventures,* pp. 37–51, lays out the positions taken by reformers and conservatives on the issue of learning from the West in the early days of the Deng era reforms.

16. Hsiao Cheng, "'Cheng Ming' Optimistic on Joint Ventures Plan," *Cheng Ming* (Hong Kong), in Chinese (1 July 1979), pp. 11–12, translated in *JPRS-CEA,* 74003 (14 August 1979), p. 42; Liu Xiao and Zheng Yongjing, "About Operating Enterprises Jointly," pp. 20–23, translated in *JPRS,* 73870 (19 July 1979), p. 87.

17. Fang Zhoufen, "On the Nature of China's Special Economic Zones," p. 41; Xu Dixin, "Views on Economic Zones," p. 3; and Ji Honggeng and Li Zhaofen, "Make

the Best of Their 'Special Points'—Commenting on the Work Done in China's Four Special Economic Zones over the Past Year and Future Prospects," *Renmin Ribao*, 15 July 1981, p. 2, both translated in *JPRS-CEA*, 78684 (5 August 1981), pp. 29–37.

18. Zhao Yuanhao, "Talk about Ways To Demonstrate Guangdong's 'Superiority,'" *Yangcheng Wanbao* (5 August 1981), p. 2, translated in *JPRS*, 79518 (24 November 1981), pp. 57–59; and "Speech by Sun Ru," *Wen Wei Po* (Hong Kong, in Chinese), (9 March 1980), p. 8, translated in *JPRS*, 75423 (2 April 1980), pp. 58–59, discusses taking advantage of compatriots in Hong Kong and Macao who want to invest in China.

19. Xia Gu, "Promote the Virtue of Patriotism," pp. 23–24.

20. Zhao Yuanhao, "Talk about Ways,'" p. 57.

21. The Chinese government first issued the FEC in 1980. "Provisional Regulations on the Bank of China Foreign Exchange Certificate," issued by Bank of China (19 March 1980). http://novexcn.com/fec_forex.html.

22. *Law of the People's Republic of China on Joint Ventures Using Chinese and Foreign Investment*, adopted by the National People's Congress (1 July 1979), Article 9, "encourage[d]" JVs to export their products. By 1986, the rules limited joint venture domestic sales to products "that China urgently needs or imports," essentially an import substitution policy. *Regulations for the Implementation of the Law of the People's Republic of China on Joint Ventures Using Chinese and Foreign Investment*, revised by the State Council (15 January 1986), Article 61.

23. Bachman, "Differing Visions," pp. 300–302.

24. Pearson, *Joint Ventures*, pp. 80 and 82.

25. *Law of the People's Republic of China on Enterprises Operated Exclusively with Foreign Capital*, adopted by National People's Congress (12 April 1986), legalized WFOEs, but the flood of investment in the WFOE structure did not occur until much later. He Xinhao, "Use of Foreign Capital to Speed Up Development Urged," *Guoji Maoyi Wenti* (International Trade Journal, in Chinese), no. 2 (June 1980), pp. 16–21, translated in *JPRS-CEA*, 76614 (14 October 1980), p. 7, notes that China should limit WFOEs to instances where Chinese enterprises are incapable of producing items through JVs. Moreover, the author contends that loans would be preferable to WFOEs where shortage of capital is the main concern.

26. Xu Dixin, "Views on Special Economic Zones," pp. 31–32.

27. Calculated from State Statistical Bureau, *Statistical Yearbook of China, 1986* (Oxford: Oxford University Press, 1986), p. 500.

28. Jonathan Kaufman, "Suspicions of Western, Japanese Business Surface," *South China Morning Post*, (29 May 1979), in *JPRS*, 73781 (28 June 1979), pp. 49–50.

29. Peng Zhen, "Several Questions on the Socialist Legal System," *Hongqi* (2 November 1979), pp. 3–7, translated in *FBIS-CHI*, 779–229 (27 November 1979), pp. L2-L8; and Li Biyun, "The Scientific Nature of the Concept of Rule by Law," *Faxue Yanjiu* (Legal Studies), no. 1 (1982), pp. 6–11, translated in *JPRS*, 80911 (26 May 1982), pp. 29–38.

30. Wang Shouchun, "Role of Special Economic Zones Discussed," *Guoji Maoyi Wenti* (International Trade Journal), no. 1 (1981), pp. 40–44, translated in *JPRS-CEA*, 78309 (16 June 1981), p. 68.

31. Carol A. G. Jones, "Capitalism, Globalization and Rule of Law: An Alternative Trajectory of Legal Change in China," *Social and Legal Studies* 3 (1994), pp. 195–221; and Pitman B. Potter, "Guanxi and the PRC Legal System: From Contradiction to Complementarity," in *Social Connections in China*, eds. Thomas

Gold, Doug Guthrie, and David Wank (Berkeley: University of California Press, 2002), pp. 179–196.

32. Thomas B. Gold, "'Just in Time!' China Battles Spiritual Pollution on the Eve of 1984," *Asian Survey* 24, no. 9 (September 1984), pp. 947–974.

33. Susan Shirk, *How China Opened Its Door* (Washington, DC: The Brookings Institution, 1994), pp. 39–44.

34. Li Honglin, "*Shehui zhuyi he dui wai kaifang,*" *Renmin Ribao,* October 15, 1984, p. 5, translated as "Socialism and Opening Up to the Outside World," *Chinese Economic Studies* XIX, no. 1 (Fall 1985), p. 35; and Zou Erkang, "Special Economic Zone Typifies Open Policy," *Beijing Review* 27, no. 48 (26 November 1984), pp. 19–22, reprinted in *Chinese Economic Studies* XIX, no. 1 (Fall 1985), p. 82.

35. Ye Xiangping, "Theoretical Basis for Evaluating Open Door Results," *Fujian Luntan* (Fujian Forum), no. 10 (5 October 1985), pp. 19–21, translated in *JPRS-CEA*, 86–004 (9 January 1986), pp. 91–95; "Ideological Problems in Shenzhen SEZ Discussed," *Shenzhen Tequ Bao* (Shenzhen SEZ Report), (8 September 1985), p. 1, translated in *JPRS-CEA,* 86–038 (9 April 1986), pp. 87–88. Suzanne Pepper, "China's Special Economic Zones: The Current Rescue Bid for a Faltering Experiment," *Bulletin of Concerned Asian Scholars* 20, no. 3 (1988), pp. 10–15.

36. *Provisions of the State Council on the Encouragement of Foreign Investment,* issued by State Council (11 October 1986), Article 14. http://www.novexcn.com/encour_foregn_invest.html

37. Wei Ge, *Special Economic Zones and the Economic Transition in China* (Singapore: World Scientific, 1999), pp. 50–52; and Robert Kleinberg, *China's "Opening" to the Outside World: The Experiment with Foreign Capitalism* (Boulder: Westview Press, 1990), pp. 214–215.

38. *Decisions on Personnel Management of Foreign Invested Enterprises,* issued on 12 October 1988 by the Ministry of Labor and Personnel, approved by the State Council (15 December 1988). http://www.novexcn.com/personal_management_for_jv.html

39. *Ibid.,* Article 5.

40. *Regulations for the Autonomous Right of the Enterprise with Foreign Investment to Employ Personnel, the Wages and Salaries, and the Expenses for Insurance and Welfare Benefits for Staff Members and Workers,* promulgated by the Ministry of Labor and Personnel (10 November 1986), Article 2a. http://www.novexcn.com/wages_salaries_jv_employ.html

41. Jim Mann, *Beijing Jeep: A Case Study of Western Business in China* (Boulder, CO: Westview Press, 1997), p. 174, discusses the difficulty of exporting from Beijing Jeep.

42. *State Council's Regulations on the Balance of Foreign Exchange in Joint Ventures Using Chinese and Foreign Investments,* promulgated by the State Council (15 January 1986), articles 4 and 5, translated in *JPRS-CEA,* 86–020 (27 February 1986), pp. 41–44.

43. Pearson, *Joint Ventures,* p. 138.

44. Gallagher, *Contagious Capitalism,* p. 56–57; Yu Jianxun, "A Brief Discussion of China's Absorption of Direct Foreign Investment," *Guoji Maoyi Wenti,* no. 5 (30 May 1991), pp. 58–60, 57, translated in *JPRS-CAR,* 91–051 (13 September 1991), pp. 59–61; Shirk, *How China Opened Its Door,* pp. 39–44.

45. Shirk, *How China Opened Its Door,* pp. 41–42.

46. Gallagher, *Contagious Capitalism,* pp. 41–42.

47. Chinese Economic Statistical Yearbook Editorial Committee, *Chinese Economic Yearbook* (Beijing: Chinese Economic Yearbook Publishers, various years).

48. Hong Kong and Taiwan were important investors during this time, but their importance is somewhat overstated for two reasons: (i) many Western and Japanese companies funneled foreign investment in China through Hong Kong subsidiaries; and (ii) many Chinese firms deposited cash in Hong Kong and brought it back into China to be invested as a "foreign party," thus reaping the tax incentives granted to foreign investors.

49. Calculated from Chinese Economic Statistical Yearbook Editorial Committee, *Chinese Economic Yearbook* (Beijing: Chinese Economic Yearbook Publishers, various years). In 1985, China did not include separate statistics on investment from Taiwan.

50. Wang Hongying, *Weak States, Strong Networks: The Institutional Dynamics of Foreign Direct Investment in China* (Oxford: Oxford University Press, 2001); Youtien Hsing, *Making Capitalism in China: The Taiwan Connection* (Oxford: Oxford University Press, 1998); and Qunjian Tian, "'Like Fish in Water': Taiwanese Investors in a Rent-Seeking Society," *Issues and Studies* 35, no. 5 (September/October 1999), pp. 61–94.

51. Anita Chan, "Labor Relations in Foreign-funded Ventures," in *Adjusting to Capitalism: Chinese Workers and the State*, ed. Greg O'Leary (Armonk, NY: M. E. Sharpe, Inc., 1997), pp. 129–133; and Ching Kwan Lee, "From Organized Dependence to Disorganized Despotism: Changing Labour Regimes in Chinese Factories," *China Quarterly*, no. 157 (March 1999), pp. 44–70.

52. Many of the most egregious cases of abusive labor practices in China were instituted by Hong Kong, Taiwanese, and domestic Chinese (private) firms in the light industrial sector, which relies heavily on labor inputs. Michael A. Santoro, *Profits and Principles: Global Capitalism and Human Rights in China* (Ithaca, NY: Cornell University Press, 2000), pp. 18–20; and Anita Chan, *China's Workers under Assault* (Armonk, NY: M. E. Sharpe, 2001), pp. 11–13.

53. United Nations, *Convention on the Recognition and Enforcement of Foreign Arbitral Awards*, adopted by diplomatic conference (10 June 1958) (hereafter, New York Convention), http:www.uncitral.org/english/texts/arbitration/NY-conv.htm.

54. "Officials Try to Woo Foreign Investors," *Hong Kong Standard* (17 June 1989), reprinted in *FBIS-CHI*, 89–117 (20 June 1989), pp. 36–37; "Gansu Adopts Measures to Lure Foreign Investors," Lanzhou Gansu Provincial Service (9 August 1989), translated in *FBIS-CHI*, 89–154 (11 August 1989), p. 41; "Special Treatment Continues for Foreign Investors," *Wen Wei Po* (Hong Kong) (12 February 1990), translated in *FBIS-CHI*, 90–030 (13 February 1990), p. 19; Chou Wen-chiang, "Shantou: The SEZ Develops According to Its Own Ability," *Wen Wei Po* (in Chinese, Hong Kong), (17 December 1989), p. 2, translated in *JPRS-CAR*, 90–016 (28 February 1990), p. 55; and Lin Yu-tung, "Whither the Special Economic Zones?" *Wen Wei Po* (in Chinese, Hong Kong), (9 December 1989), p. 1, translated in *JPRS-CAR*, 90–016 (28 February 1990), p. 46.

55. Lucille A. Barale, "The New WFOE Implementing Regulations," *The China Business Review*, no. 7–8 (July–August 1991), pp. 8–11.

56. "Twenty High-Tech Zones Will Upgrade Industry," *Hong Kong Standard* (3 July 1990), p. 1, reprinted in *JPRS-CAR*, 90–049 (11 July 1990), pp. 72–73.

57. Walter Arnold, "Japanese Investment in China after Tiananmen: The Case of Pudong Special Economic Zone in Shanghai," In *China in Transition: Economic, Political and Social Development,* ed. George T. Yu (Lanham: University Press of America, 1993), pp. 165–179; and Lin Xiaoli, "Development and Opening Up of Pudong New Zone Attracts Worldwide Attention, Evokes Widespread Interest and Serious Attention in Japanese Economic and Entrepreneurial Circles," *Wen Hui Bao* (in Chinese, Shanghai), (17 July 1990), p. 1, translated in *JPRS-CAR,* 90–066 (29 August 1990), pp. 74–75.

58. Shirk, *How China Opened Its Door,* p. 67, describes these measures as a response to the U.S. passage of the 1988 Omnibus Trade Act, which contained section 301 (often called, "Super 301"), authorizing the U.S. Trade Representative to take countermeasures against countries that violate free trade.

59. Shirk, *How China Opened Its Door,* pp. 39–41.

60. Shirk, *How China Opened Its Door,* p. 47; and Zweig, *Internationalizing China,* pp. 92–97.

61. Daniel H. Rosen, *Behind the Open Door: Foreign Enterprises in the Chinese Marketplace* (Washington, DC: Institute for International Economics, 1999), pp. 47–48; and Gallagher, *Contagious Capitalism,* pp. 43–44.

62. General manager of Japanese WFOE (C-2000–046), interview by author, Shanghai (2000); general manager of Sino-Hong Kong JV (C-2000–052), interview by author, Shanghai (2000); Gallagher, *Contagious Capitalism,* p. 44. In fact, Chinese regulations do not require WFOEs to allow party organizations to form, but all firms with more than 25 employees are required to allow trade union branches to form.

63. Gallagher, *Contagious Capitalism,* pp. 16–18, notes the gradual convergence of labor regulations for SOEs and FIEs in China around the rules established for FIEs.

64. "Chinese International Economic and Trade Arbitration Commission: Introduction," CIETAC website at http://www.cietac.org.cn/english/introduction/intro_1.htm, notes the connection between the new Arbitration Law and CIETAC's reforms in 1995 and 1998.

65. A notable example of such an effort to develop rule of law is the US-China Legal Cooperation Fund, established by the US-China Business Council.

66. Nicholas R. Lardy, *Integrating China into the Global Economy* (Washington, DC: Brookings Institution Press, 2002), pp. 63–64.

67. Zweig, *Internationalizing China,* pp. 29. Pierson, *Politics in Time,* pp. 43, notes that institutional designers have a similar motivation to lock future leaders on an institutional path of development.

68. Lardy, *Integrating China,* pp. 65–80.

69. Margaret M. Pearson, "China's Integration into the International Trade and Investment Regime," in *China Joins the World: Progress and Prospects,* eds. Elizabeth Economy and Michel Oksenberg (New York: Council on Foreign Relations, 1999), pp. 161–206.

70. Lardy, *Integrating China,* pp. 32–48, 150, 151, and 153.

71. Mary E. Gallagher, "'Use the Law as Your Weapon!': Institutional Change and Legal Mobilization in China," in *Engaging the Law in China: State, Society, and Possibilities for Justice,* eds. Neil J. Diamant, Stanley B. Lubman, and Kevin J. O'Brien (Stanford: Stanford University Press, 2005), pp. 54–83; and Kevin J. O'Brien

and Lianjiang Li, "Suing the State: Administrative Litigation in Rural China," in *Engaging the Law in China: State, Society, and Possibilities for Justice,* eds. Neil J. Diamant, Stanley B. Lubman, and Kevin J. O'Brien (Stanford: Stanford University Press, 2005), pp. 31–53.

72. Representative from Shanghai office of global consulting company (C-2003–02), interview by author, Shanghai (2003).

Chapter Three

1. Exceptions include the following works: Helen Chen and Janet Shanberge, "The Future of the Joint Venture," *EuroBiz Magazine* (April 2004), http://www.sinomedia.net/eurobiz/v200404/story0404.html; Ping Deng, "WFOEs: The Most Popular Entry Mode into China," *Business Horizons* 44, no. 4 (2001), pp. 63–72; and Yaodong Luo and Min Chen, "Financial Performance Comparison between International Joint Ventures and Wholly Foreign-Owned Enterprises in China," *The International Executive* 37, no. 6 (1995), pp. 599–614.

2. Jim Mann, *Beijing Jeep: A Case Study of Western Business in China* (Armonk, NY: M. E. Sharpe, Inc., 1997); John Child and Yanni Yan, "Investment and Control in International Joint Ventures: The Case of China," *Journal of World Business* 34, no. 1 (1999), pp. 3–15; Haochun Dong, Peter J. Buckley, and Hafiz Mirza, "International Joint Ventures in China from a Managerial Perspective: A Comparison between Different Sources of Investment," in *Internationalization Strategies,* eds. George Chryssochoidis, Carla Millar, and Jeremy Clegg (Basingstoke, UK: Macmillan Press, 1997), pp. 171–191; Elizabeth Li, "Marital Discord: A Clash of Values and Assumptions for Transforming Organizations: Implications for Sino-Foreign Joint Ventures," *Advances in Chinese Industrial Studies,* vol. 5 (JAI Press, 1997), pp. 69–92; and James P. Walsh, ErPing Wang, and Katherine R. Xin, "Same Bed, Different Dreams: Working Relationships in Sino-American Joint Ventures," *Journal of World Business* 34, no. 1 (1999), pp. 69–93.

3. Li, "Marital Discord," pp. 69–92, andWalsh, Wang, and Xin, "Same Bed, Different Dreams," pp. 69–93.

4. Michel Delapierre and Christian Milelli, "Japanese Direct Investment in China," in *China and India: Economic Performance and Business Strategies of Firms in the Mid-1990s,* eds. Sam Dzever and Jacques Jaussaud (New York: St. Martin's Press, 1999), pp. 62–63.

5. Mary Gallagher, *Contagious Capitalism: Globalization and the Politics of Labor in China* (Princeton: Princeton University Press, 2005), pp. 40–41.

6. Barry Naughton, *Growing out of the Plan: Chinese Economic Reform, 1978–1993* (Cambridge: Cambridge University Press, 1996), p. 288, notes that reforms recommended at the end of 1990.

7. Dali L. Yang, "China Adjusts to the World Economy: The Political Economy of China's Coastal Development Strategy," *Pacific Affairs* 64, no. 1 (Spring 1991), pp. 42–64; and Gallagher, *Contagious Capitalism,* p. 44, contend that the rise of WFOEs was due to fundamental changes in foreign investors' bargaining power resulting from the coastal development strategy in 1988. While the coastal development strategy was important, the causes of the shift to WFOEs are more numerous and complicated than Yang and Gallagher note.

8. "There Are Methods That Can Be Depended On, There Are Rules That Can Be Followed and There are Clear Objectives for Doing a Good Job on the Special Economic Zones for Further Serving the Four Modernizations," *Nanfang Ribao*, (4 September 1980), p. 1, translated in *JPRS-CEA*, no. 76913 (2 December 1980), p. 10; "High-level CCP Meeting Has Not Yet Made Plans for a Complete Breakthrough Regarding Shenzhen Special Zone Issue," *Cheng Ming Jih Pao* (in Chinese, Hong Kong), (18 June 1981), p. 1, translated in *JPRS-CEA*, no. 78487 (10 July 1981), pp. 32–33; Li Honglin, "Shehui Zhuyi he Dui Wai Kaifang," *Renmin Ribao*, (15 October 1984), p. 5, translated in *Chinese Economic Studies* XIX, no. 1 (Fall 1985), p. 33.

9. Daniel H. Rosen, *Behind the Open Door: Foreign Enterprises in the Chinese Marketplace* (Washington, DC: Institute for International Economics, 1999), pp. 215–218, discusses FIEs' woes guarding intellectual property.

10. Margaret Pearson, "The Erosion of Controls over Foreign Capital in China, 1979–1988: Having Their Cake and Eating It Too?" *Modern China* 17, no. 1 (January 1991), pp. 112–150.

11. President of U.S.-based investment company in Shanghai (C-2000–009), interview by author, Shanghai, China (2000).

12. Mann, *Beijing Jeep*, p. 68.

13. *Provisional Regulations on the Political and Ideological Activities for Chinese Employees of Sino-Foreign Equity and Contractual Joint Ventures*, jointly promulgated by the State Economic Commission, the Propaganda Department of the Central Committee, the Organization Department of the Central Committee, the All-China Federation of Trade Unions, and the Communist Youth League (11 August 1987), Article 7. Margaret M. Pearson, "Erosion of Controls," p. 133 and 134, notes that internal (*neibu*) party documents called for party cells to be established in JVs, but party cells were "inactive" even prior to 1989.

14. *EJV Law*, Article 6.

15. *Regulations on Joint Ventures' Balance of Foreign Exchange Revenue and Expenditure*, promulgated by the State Council (15 January 1986), Article 9, allows foreign investors with multiple investments to shift funds among firms to balance the firms' overall balance of foreign exchange. See also Margaret M. Pearson, *Joint Ventures in the People's Republic of China* (Princeton: Princeton University Press, 1991), p. 138.

16. *Regulations on Joint Ventures' Balance of Foreign Exchange Revenue and Expenditure*, Article 5; *Measures Relating to the Import Substitution by Products Manufactured by Chinese-Foreign Equity Joint Ventures and Chinese-Foreign Cooperative Ventures*, promulgated by the State Planning Commission (1 October 1987).

17. *Law of the People's Republic of China on Chinese-Foreign Equity Joint Ventures*, revised and adopted by National People's Congress (4 April 1990), Art. 6. http://www.lehmanlaw.com/resource-centre/laws-and-regulations/foreign-investment/sino-foreign-equity-joint-venture-law-1990.html

18. "Situation, Problems Absorbing Direct Foreign Investment," *Guoji Maoyi Wenti*, no. 6 (30 June 1988), pp. 45–47, translated in *JPRS-CAR*, 88–052 (2 September 1988), p. 43; and "Shanghai's Foreign Entrepreneurs Face Problems," *Wen Hui Bao* (Shanghai, in Chinese), (12 December 1989), pp. 1 and 3, translated in *JPRS-CAR*, 90–021 (20 March 1990), p. 51.

19. "Shanghai's Foreign Entrepreneurs Face Problems," p. 53.

20. See the interviews cited in Hongying Wang, *Weak State, Strong Networks: The Institutional Dynamics of Foreign Direct Investment in China* (Oxford and New

York: Oxford University Press, 2001), pp. 92–105. See also Wilfried R. Vanhonacker, "*Guanxi* Networks in China," *The China Business Review* (May–June 2004), pp. 48–53.

21. President of China operations of U.S. manufacturer (C-2000–008), interview by author, Shanghai, China (2000).

22. General manager of U.S. WFOE (C-2000–005), interview by author, Shanghai, China (2000).

23. Dong, Buckley, and Mirza, "International Joint Ventures in China," pp. 180–182, found that both Japanese and U.S. investors were interested in developing *guanxi* to build distribution networks, and that Japanese particularly were interested in developing government relations.

24. For example, Susan Shirk documents local officials' creation of "special economic zones" in violation of central government policy. Susan Shirk, *How China Opened Its Door* (Washington, DC: Brookings Institution Press, 1994), pp. 41–44.

25. Walsh, Wang, and Xin, "Same Bed, Different Dreams," pp. 69–93; Li, "Marital Discord," pp. 69–92; and Delapierre and Milelli, "Japanese Direct Investment in China."

26. General manager of Sino-U.S. JV (C-2000–054), interview with author, Shanghai, China (2000); and deputy general manager of Sino-Japanese JV (C-2000–067), interview with author, Shanghai, China (2000).

27. Xiong Qingchuan, "A Simple Analysis of the Nine Major Problems in the Management of Chinese-Foreign Joint Ventures," *Jingji Yu Guanli Yanjiu*, no. 4 (8 August 1989), pp. 45–49, translated in *JPRS*, 90–011 (12 February 1990), p. 43; "Improving Conditions for Joint Ventures," p. 43; Wang Yihe, "Rethinking Traditional Joint Ventures," *Guoji Maoyi*, no. 12 (27 December 1987), pp. 33–36, translated in *JPRS-CAR*, 88–013 (14 March 1988), p. 52; Jiang Qingyun, "A Look at the Foreign-Invested Enterprises' Problem with Autonomy," *Guoji Shangbao*, (22 April 1989), p. 3, translated in *JPRS-CAR*, 89–062 (14 June 1989), pp. 28–30; and Li Xiangyang, "On the Selection of Sectors to Receive Direct Foreign Investment," *Guoji Maoyi Wenti*, no. 1 (31 January 1990), pp. 14–20, translated in *JPRS-CAR*, 90–046 (26 June 1990), p. 43.

28. Managing director of U.S. FIEs in China (C-2000–06), interview by author, Shanghai, China (2000).

29. Walsh, Wang, and Xin, "Same Bed, Different Dreams," pp. 69–93.

30. State Statistical Bureau, *Statistical Yearbook of China* (Hong Kong: Economic Information Agency, 2002), p. 266. Even after nearly two decades of reforms in state-owned enterprises, in 2002 Chinese central and local governments subsidized loss-making enterprises 25.9 billion Chinese yuan. State Statistical Bureau, *Statistical Yearbook of China*, (2006), p. 281.

31. Delapierre and Milelli, "Japanese Direct Investment in China," pp. 62–63.

32. President of U.S. investment firm in Shanghai (C-2000–009), interview by author, Shanghai, China (2000).

33. General manager of a Sino-U.S. JV (C-2000–064), interview by author, Shanghai, China (2000).

34. "Shanghai Foreign Entrepreneurs Face Problems," *Wen Hui Bao* (12 December 1989), pp. 1 and 3, translated in *JPRS*, 90–021 (20 March 1990), p. 51.

35. General manager of a Sino-U.S. JV (C-2000–066), interview by author, Shanghai, China (2000). Jiang Qingyun, "A Look at the Foreign-Invested Enterprises' Problem with Autonomy," p. 29, notes that foreign investors in Shanghai were not

allowed to pay wages to their workers that were 20–50 percent higher than the average in similar SOEs, even though it was permitted by state regulations.

36. "'Improving' Conditions for Joint Ventures," *Xinhua* (15 June 1988), translated in *JPRS-CAR,* 88–042 (1 August 1988), p. 43. At Beijing Jeep, an early Sino-U.S. JV, a vehicle took 86 labor hours to assemble, whereas the same vehicle only required 20–26 labor hours to assemble in the United States. Mann, *Beijing Jeep,* pp. 256–257.

37. "Situation, Problems Absorbing Direct Foreign Investment," p. 43.

38. President of investment management firm (C-2000–009), interview by author, Shanghai, China (2000).

39. Xu Xinli, "Efficiency Analysis of Enterprises of 'Three Capital Sources' in Shanghai," *Caijing Yanjiu,* no. 1 (3 January 1991), pp. 20–23, translated in *JPRS-CAR,* 91–028 (22 May 1991), p. 65.

40. He Xiaoying, "Foreign Businesses Investing in Shanghai Report Greater Confidence and Are More Complimentary of the Municipality and Their Investment Is Growing Rapidly and Is Becoming More Rational," *Shijie Jingji Daobao* (27 February 1989), p. 10, translated in *JPRS-CAR,* no. 89–032 (10 April 1989), p. 37; "'Improving' Conditions for Joint Ventures," p. 45, similarly calls for handing over control of JVs to foreign partners.

41. President of U.S. investment company in Shanghai (C-2000–008), interview by author, Shanghai, China (2000).

42. Director of U.S. business organization in Shanghai (C-2000–003), interview by author, Shanghai, China (2000); manager of U.S. WFOE (C-2000–018), interview by author, Shanghai, China (2000); general manager of Sino-Japanese JV (C-2000–034), interview by author, Shanghai, China (2000); general manager of Sino-Japanese JV (C-2000–036), interview by author, Shanghai, China (2000); general manager of Sino-U.S. JV (C-2000–040), interview by author, Shanghai, China (2000); and general manager of Sino-Japanese JV (C-2000–048), interview by author, Shanghai, China (2000). In contrast, Hong Kong, Taiwanese, and Korean investors tended to use China as an export platform, relying on low-wage Chinese labor to keep costs down.

43. Xiong Qingchuan, "A Simple Analysis," p.44.

44. *Regulations for the Implementation of the Law of the People's Republic of China on Chinese-Foreign Equity Joint Ventures,* promulgated by the State Council (20 September 1983), Article 60 and 61.

45. Local officials were sometimes able to carve out domestic, or at least local, access for JV products. For example, Zhu Rongji, former mayor of Shanghai, worked out a deal for Shanghai Volkswagon to sell its Santanas to a Shanghai taxi company to help the JV become profitable. Eric Harwit, "Foreign Passenger Car Ventures and Chinese Decision-Making," *The Australian Journal of Chinese Affairs,* no. 28 (July 1992), p. 155.

46. *Provisions of the State Council on the Encouragement of Foreign Investment,* promulgated by the State Council (11 October 1986), Articles 2, 5, and 7–11. http://www.novexcn.com/encour_foregn_invest.html.

47. *Regulations of Joint Ventures' Balance of Foreign Exchange Revenue and Expenditure,* promulgated by the State Council (15 January 1986), Article 1. http://www.novexcn.com/jv_balance_forex_expend.html.

48. *Regulations for the Implementation of the Law of the People's Republic of China on Joint Ventures Using Chinese and Foreign Investment,* promulgated by

the State Council (20 September 1983), Article 57; and *Law of the People's Republic of China on Enterprises Operated Exclusively with Foreign Capital,* adopted by the National People's Congress (12 April 1986), Article 15. The local content requirement for WFOEs was changed in 2001, to come into compliance with the "national treatment" principle of the WTO.

49. Mann, *Beijing Jeep,* p. 157; and Eric Harwit, "Foreign Passenger Car Ventures," p. 154.

50. Director of U.S. business organization in Shanghai (C-2000–003), interview by author, Shanghai, China (2000); manager of U.S. WFOE (C-2000–018), interview by author, Shanghai, China (2000); general manager of Sino-Japanese JV (C-2000–034), interview by author, Shanghai, China (2000); general manager of Sino-Japanese JV (C-2000–036), interview by author, Shanghai, China (2000); general manager of Sino-U.S. JV (C-2000–040), interview by author, Shanghai, China (2000); and general manager of Sino-Japanese JV (C-2000–048), interview by author, Shanghai, China (2000).

51. Andrew H. Wedeman, *From Mao to Market: Rent Seeking, Local Protectionism, and Marketization in China* (Cambridge: Cambridge University Press, 2003), pp. 157–192.

52. Hongying Wang, *Weak State, Strong Networks,* p. 97.

53. "Shanghai Foreign Entrepreneurs," pp. 51–52.

54. U.S. lawyer in Shanghai office (C-2000–013), interview by author, Shanghai, China (2000).

55. President of Sino-U.S. JV (C-2000–040), interview by author, Shanghai, China (2000).

56. Chief representative of Greater China office for U.S. company (C-2000–017), interview by author, Shanghai, China (2000).

57. Manager of U.S. company's representative office (C-2000–023), interview by author, Shanghai, China (2000).

58. Manager of U.S. WFOE (C-2000–018), interview by author, Shanghai, China (2000).

59. He Xinhao, "Actively Use Foreign Capital to Speed Up Economic Development," *Guoji Maoyi Wenti,* no. 2 (June 1980), pp. 16–21, translated in *JPRS-CEA,* no. 76614 (14 October 1980), p. 2; "There Are Methods that Can Be Depended on," p. 10; Xu Dixin, "Views on Special Economic Zones," *Shijie Jingji Daobao,* no. 37 (15 June 1981), p. 3, translated in *JPRS-CEA,* no. 78684 (5 August 1981), p. 31.

60. "There Are Methods that Can Be Depended on," p. 10; Wang Shouchun and Li Kanghua, "A Brief Discussion of the Role of Special Economic Zones in Our Country," *Guoji Maoyi Wenti,* no. 1 (1981), pp. 40–44, translated in *JPRS-CEA* (16 June 1981), p.66; Xu Dixin, "Views on Special Economic Zones," p. 31.

61. Wang Shouchun and Li Kanghua, "A Brief Discussion," p. 65.

62. Wang Shouchun and Li Kanghua, "A Brief Discussion," p. 65; Xu Dixin, "Views on Special Economic Zones," p. 32.

63. "There Are Methods That Can Be Depended on," p. 10; Wang Shouchun and Li Kanghua, "A Brief Discussion," p. 66; Xu Dixin, "Views on Special Economic Zones," p. 31; Fang Zhoufen, "On the Nature of China's Special Economic Zones," *Jingji Yanjiu,* no. 8 (20 August 1981), pp. 54–58, translated in *JPRS-CEA,* no. 79100 (30 September 1981), p 41.

64. Nie Haiying, "Thoughts Related to the Use of Direct Foreign Investment," *Renmin Ribao* (8 May 1989), p. 6, translated in *JPRS*, no. 89–065 (26 June 1989), p. 35.

65. Li Xiangyang, "On the Selection of Sectors to Receive Direct Foreign Investment," p. 42.

66. Liu Guoguang, "Several Problems Concerning the Development Strategy of China's Special Economic Zones," *Caimao Jingji*, no. 2 (1987), translated in *Chinese Economic Studies* 25, no. 3 (Spring 1992), p. 9; and Zhao Yuanhao, "Talk about Ways To Demonstrate Guangdong's 'Superiority,'" *Yangcheng Wanbao* (5 August 1981), p. 2, translated in *JPRS*, 79518 (24 November 1981), pp. 57–59; and "Speech by Sun Ru," *Wen Wei Po* (Hong Kong,), (9 March 1980), p. 8, translated in *JPRS*, 75423 (2 April 1980), pp. 48–49.

67. Wang Shouchun and Li Kanghua, "A Brief Discussion," pp. 64 and 66.

68. Many analysts and politicians were concerned, too, that China faced persistent trade deficits in the mid-1980s. According to Dali Yang and Mary Gallagher, the trade deficit led Zhao Ziyang to emphasize light industrial exports as part of the coastal development strategy. Yang, "China Adjusts to the World Economy," pp. 56–57; and Gallagher, *Contagious Capitalism*, p. 40.

69. Anita Chan, "Labor Relations in Foreign-Funded Ventures," pp. 129–133; and Ching Kwan Lee, "From Organizational Dependence to Disorganized Despotism: Changing Labour Regimes in Chinese Factories," *The China Quarterly*, no. 157 (March 1999), pp. 44–71.

70. Reported in Deng Jianqin, "Foreign Capital Infusion Should Emphasize Direct Foreign Investment—On the Strategic Readjustment of China's Foreign Capital Structure," *Guoji Maoyi Wenti*, no. 2 (28 February 1991), pp. 2–7, translated in *JPRS-CAR*, 91–032 (13 June 1991), p. 64.

71. "Official Explains Draft Amendment to Joint Ventures Law," *Xinhua* (in English), (31 March 1990), reprinted in *JPRS-CAR*, 9–030 (24 April 199), p. 44.

72. Zhang Lin, "GNP Boost Anticipated," *China Daily* (5 March 1991), p. 1, reprinted in *JPRS*, 91–025 (8 May 1991), p. 42. According to Barry Naughton, *The Chinese Economy: Transition and Growth* (Cambridge: MIT Press, 2007), p. 410, by 2003 there were over 100 special investment zones backed by the central government and many more established by local authorities without central government backing.

73. "Update on Three Shanghai Economic Development Zones," *Jiefang Ribao*, (3 June 1990), pp. 1, 3, translated in *JPRS-CAR*, 90–064 (17 August 1990), pp. 40–42.

74. Deng Jianqin, "Foreign Capital Infusion," p. 66.

75. Walter Arnold, "Japanese Investment in China after Tiananmen: The Case of Pudong Special Economic Zone in Shanghai," in *China in Transition: Economic, Political, and Social Developments*, ed. George T. Yu (Lanham: University Press of America, 1993); Wu Weicheng, "Shanghai's Foreign-Invested Enterprises Present Five Characteristics," *Shijie Jingji Daobao* (4 January 1988), p. 11, translated in *JPRS-CAR*, 88–013 (14 March 1988), p. 57; and Di Jiangrong, "Zhu Rongji Addresses U.S. Joint Trade Session," *Jiefang Ribao* (21 June 1988), p. 1, translated in *JPRS-CAR*, 88–050 (25 August 1988), p. 39.

76. Li Xiangyang, "On the Selection of Sectors to Receive Direct Foreign Investment," p. 42.

77. Lo Keng, "Many and Few—Problems in Sino-Foreign Joint Ventures Examined," *Ching Chi Tao Pao*, no. 25 (26 June 1989), p. 8, translated in *JPRS-CAR*, 89–101 (5 October 1989), p. 45.

78. Deng Jianqin, "Foreign Capital Infusion," p. 65.

79. He Ying, "Ramblings on Chinese Use of Foreign Investment," *Guoji Maoyi Wenti*, (31 March 1990), pp. 2–8, 41, translated in *JPRS-CAR*, 90–054 (20 July 1990), p. 54.

80. Xu Xinli, "Efficiency Analysis of Enterprises," p. 65.

81. Yue Haitao, "Trade Union and Party Organizations," *Beijing Review* 30 (7 September 1987), p. 27.

82. Xiong Qingchuan, "A Simple Analysis," p. 43.

83. Nie Haiying, "Thoughts Related to the Use of Direct Foreign Investment," p. 36.

84. President of U.S. investment company in Shanghai (C-2000–09), interview by author, Shanghai, China (2000).

85. *WFOE Law* (1986).

86. *WFOE Law* (1986), Article 3.

87. *WFOE Law* (1986), Article 3; general manager of Sino-Japanese JV (C-2000–034), interview by author, Shanghai, China (2000); and general manager of Sino-U.S. JV (C-2000–047), interview by author, Shanghai, China (2000).

88. *Detailed Rules for Implementing the Law of the People's Republic of China on Enterprises Operated Exclusively with Foreign Capital,* approved by the State Council on 28 October 1990 and promulgated by MOFCOM (12 December 1990).

89. *Detailed Rules* (1990), Article 3.

90. Gallagher, *Contagious Capitalism*, p. 41.

91. He Ying, "Ramblings on Chinese Use of Foreign Investment," p. 53; Yu Jianxun, "A Brief Discussion of China's Absorption of Direct Foreign Investment," *Guoji Maoyi Wenti*, no. 5 (30 May 1991), pp. 58–60, 57, translated in *JPRS-CAR*, 91–051 (13 September 1991), p. 59.

92. Lin Yu-Dong, "A Program for Further Opening Up Shenzhen," *Wen Wei Po*, (10, 11, 12, 13 December 1989), translated in *JPRS-CAR*, 90–016 (28 February 1990), pp. 47–56.

93. *Ibid.*, p. 52.

94. *Ibid.*, p. 54.

95. *Detailed Implementing Rules for the Law of the People's Republic of China on Wholly Foreign-Owned Enterprises,* amended by the State Council (12 April 2001). http://www.lehmanlaw.com/resource-centre/laws-and-regulations/foreign-investment/detailed-implementing-rules-for-the-law-of-the-peoples-republic-of-china-on-wholly-foreign-owned-enterprises-2001.html

96. *Ibid.*, Article 43.

97. *Ibid.*, Article 44.

98. *Ibid.*, Article 42.

99. U.S. Consulate officer in Shanghai (C-2000–002), interview by author, Shanghai, China (2000).

100. Chen and Shanberge, "The Future of the Joint Venture."

101. National Bureau of Statistics, *China Statistical Yearbook, 1995* (Beijing: 1995).

102. Deng Jianqin, "Foreign Capital Infusion," pp. 2–7, 64.

103. Lo Keng, "Many and Few—Problems in Sino-Foreign Joint Ventures Examined," p. 45, notes that Chinese managers have difficulty assimilating foreign technology, even in JVs.

104. Wang Songji, "Macroeconomic Policies—Reflections on the Past Ten Years," *Jinrong Shibao* (18 January 1989), p. 3, translated in *JPRS-CAR*, 89–020 (8 March 1989), p. 9; and Naughton, *Growing out of the Plan*, pp. 276 and 283.

105. Director U.S. business organization's Shanghai office (C-2000–03), interview by author, Shanghai, China (2000).

106. Wang Yihe, "Rethinking Traditional Joint Ventures," p. 51, laments the declining rate of foreign capital contribution to JVs.

107. Xiong Qingchuan, "A Simple Analysis," p. 42.

108. Wang Yihe, "Rethinking Traditional Joint Ventures," p. 51.

109. "Thumbs up for WFOEs," *China Business Review* (July–August 1991), p. 10.

110. Lucille A. Barale, "Wholly Foreign Owned Enterprises," *The Chinese Business Review* (January–February 1990), p. 30.

111. *Ibid.*, p. 30; He Ying, "Ramblings on Chinese Use of Foreign Investment," p. 54.

112. Nie Haiying, "Thoughts Related to the Use of Direct Foreign Investment," p. 36; He Ying, "Ramblings on Chinese Use of Foreign Investment," pp. 54.

113. Official in U.S. consulate in Shanghai (C-2000–002), interview by author, Shanghai, China (2000); director of U.S. business organization's Shanghai office (C-2000–003), interview by author, Shanghai, China (2000); Head of U.S. company's representative office (C-2000–037), interview by author, Shanghai, China (2000).

114. Deputy general manager in Sino-Japanese JV (C-2000–059), interview by author, Shanghai, China (2000).

115. Yang, "China Adjusts to the World Economy," p. 47, notes, for example, the 1984 Hainan SEZ car import scandal.

116. Dali Yang, "China Adjusts to the World Economy," p. 58.

117. Barale, "Wholly Foreign Owned Enterprises," pp. 30–35.

118. Nie Haiying, "Thoughts Related to the Use of Direct Foreign Investment," p. 36.

119. Quoted in Lu Yu-dong, "A Program for Further Opening up Shenzhen," *Wen Wei Po* (Hong Kong, in Chinese), 10, 11, 12, and 13 December 1989, translated in *JPRS-CAR*, 90–016 (28 February 1990), p. 51.

120. Li Yu-tung, "Whither the Special Economic Zones?" *Wen Wei Po* (Hong Kong, in Chinese), (9 December 1989), p. 1, translated in *JPRS-CAR*, 90–016 (28 February 1990), p. 46.

121. Deng Jianqin, "Foreign Capital Infusion," p. 67; and Nie Haiying, "Measures Proposed to Stimulate Direct Foreign Investment," p. 36. Walter Arnold, "Japanese Investment in China after Tiananmen," p. 165, notes that Chinese efforts to compromise with Japan to attract upper-end investors began in 1988 with the signing of the Sino-Japanese Investment Protection Act. The Tiananmen Square demonstrations postponed Japanese investment, which surged in mid-1990 (p. 170). Zhang Dong, "New Characteristics of Japan's Overseas Investment and Several Issues Deserving China's Attention in Absorbing Japanese Investment," *Guoji Maoyi Wenti*, no. 7–8 (30 August 1989), pp. 12–14, translated in *JPRS-CAR*, 89–119 (19 December 1989),

pp. 23–24, advocates softening investment restrictions to encourage technology transfer by Japanese firms.

122. Gallagher, *Contagious Capitalism,* p. 41, persuasively argues that Zhao Ziyang's 1988 coastal development strategy, by decentralizing approval for foreign investment projects, also enhanced foreign investors' bargaining power.

123. A good deal of the increased investment flow in 1990 was from projects scheduled to come on line in 1989 but that investors postponed during the period following June 4, 1989. FDI in 1991 is a better indication of renewed confidence in China's investment environment.

124. William P. Alford, *To Steal a Book Is an Elegant Offense: Intellectual Property Law in Chinese Civilization* (Stanford: Stanford University Press, 1995).

125. Former manager in Sino-U.S. JV (C-2000–037), interview by author, Shanghai, China (2000).

126. Ping Deng, "WFOEs."

127. U.S. attorney in Shanghai (C-2000–013), interview by author, Shanghai, China (2000); and general manager of Sino-Japanese JV (C-2000–032), interview by author, Shanghai, China (2000).

128. Manager of Japanese WFOE (C-2000–033), interview by author, Shanghai, China (2000). Manager of Sino-U.S. JV (C-2000–047), interview by author, Shanghai, China (2000), also claimed that Chinese lacked sophisticated enough machinery to copy his company's products well.

129. Research and development director for a U.S. WFOE (C-2000–042), interview by author, Shanghai, China (2000).

130. General manager of U.S. WFOE (C-2000–005), interview by author, Shanghai, China (2000).

131. General manager of U.S. WFOE (C-2000–049), interview by author, Shanghai, China (2000).

132. Chinese deputy general manager of Sino-Japanese JV (C-2000–059), interview by author, Shanghai, China (2000).

133. Office director of U.S. business organization (C-2000–003), interview by author, Shanghai, China (2000); Chinese human resources manager in Sino-Japanese JV (C-2000–055), interview by author, Shanghai, China (2000).

134. Chen and Shanberge, "The Future of the Joint Venture."

135. U.S. manager of a Sino-U.S. JV (C-2000–064), interview by author, Shanghai, China, (2000).

136. Jiang Qingyun, "A Look at the Foreign-Invested Enterprises' Problem with Autonomy," p. 29.

137. President of Sino-U.S. JV (C-2000–040), interview by author, Shanghai, China (2000).

138. General manager of a U.S. WFOE (C-2000–018), interview by author, Shanghai, China (2000).

139. *Regulations for the Autonomous Right of the Enterprises with Foreign Investment to Employ Personnel, the Wages and Salaries, and the Expenses for Insurance and Welfare Benefits for Staff Members and Workers,* promulgated by the Ministry of Labor and Personnel (10 November 1986), Art. 1 (a).

140. General manager of a U.S. WFOE (C-2000–005), interview by author, Shanghai, China (2000).

141. *Ibid.*

142. Human resources manager in U.S. WFOE (C-2000–063), interview by author, Shanghai, China (2000).

143. General manager of Sino-U.S. JV (C-2000–066), interview by author, Shanghai, China (2000).

144. Manager of U.S. WFOE (C-2000–05), interview by author, Shanghai, China (2000).

145. Engineer in Sino-U.S. JV (C-2000–010), interview by author, Shanghai, China (2000); and general manager of U.S. WOFE (C-2000–049), interview by author, Shanghai, China (2000).

146. *Regulations for the Implementation of the Law of the People's Republic of China on Joint Ventures Using Chinese and Foreign Investment,* promulgated by the State Council (20 September 1983), Article 95, http://www.novexcn.com/jv_use_chin_for_invest.html; *Provisional Regulations on the Provision of Political Ideological Activities for Chinese Employees of Sino-Foreign Equity and Contractual Joint Ventures,* Article 7; *Labor Law of the People's Republic of China,* promulgated by the President (5 July 1994), Article 7.

147. Citing a CCP journal, The Economist reported that, in 1999, only 17% of all foreign invested enterprises had established party cells. "The Withering Away of the Party," *The Economist* (May 30, 2002). http://www.economist.com/world/asia/displayStory.cfm?story_id=1159535.

148. "Shan Wei: A Joint Venture Party Branch Head," *China Daily* (11 November 2002). http://www.china.org.cn/english/features/48441.htm.

149. *Provisional Regulations on the Political and Ideological Activities for Chinese Employees of Sino-Foreign and Contractual Joint Ventures,* jointly promulgated by the State Economic Commission, the Propaganda Department of the Central Committee, the Organization Department of the Central Committee, the All-China Federation of Trade Unions, and the Communist Youth League (11 August 1987), Article 7.

150. "Strengthening Party in Foreign-Owned Enterprises," *Dangxiao Luntan* (Party School Tribune), no. 12 (5 December 1993), pp. 49–51, translated in *JPRS-CAR,* 94–018 (18 March 1994), pp. 4–6.

151. Manager of Japanese WFOE (C-2000–046), interview by author, Shanghai, China (2000).

152. "Unions Urge 'Tougher Action' Against Foreign Firms," p. 47, notes that local officials fail to force FIEs to comply with safety regulations that prevent industrial accidents, an example of officials siding with investors over the interests of workers and in violation of the law.

153. Doug Guthrie, *Dragon in a Three-Piece Suit: The Emergence of Capitalism in China* (Princeton: Princeton University Press, 1999), p. 62.

154. Jiang Qingyun, "A Look at the Foreign-Invested Enterprises' Problem with Autonomy," p. 30. See also Xiong Qingchuan, "A Simple Analysis," p. 43.

155. Human resources manager for U.S. WFOE (C-2005–01), interview by author, Shanghai, China (2005).

Chapter Four

1. *La guanxi* is a Chinese expression, meaning "to pull strings (to get things done)." An earlier, abbreviated version of this chapter was published by the *Journal of*

Contemporary China 17, no. 54 (February 2008), pp. 25–51, and this chapter reprints large excerpts from that article with the journal's permission.

2. James V. Feinerman, "Chinese Participation in the International Legal Order: Rogue Elephant or Team Player?" *The China Quarterly* 141 (March 1995), pp. 189–190; and Pitman Potter, "China and the International Legal System: Challenges of Participation," *The China Quarterly*, no. 191 (September 2007), pp. 699–715.

3. "Government Drafts First Commercial Arbitration Law," *China Daily*, translated in *FBIS-CHI*, 94–123 (27 June 1994), p. 51; "Arbitration Commission to Resolve Disputes," *Xinhua* in *FBIS-CHI*, 95–204 (23 October 1995), p. 57; and Song Lianbin, "*Zhongguo Zhongcai de Guojihua, Bentuhua yu Minjianhua*," [Chinese Arbitration's Internationalization, Localization, and Popularization], (9 January 2006), http:www.china-arbitration.com/3a1.asp?id=1763&name=仲裁研究.

4. Although I use the term "diffusion" to analyze the transmission of norms from the international realm to China, "layering" more accurately describes the process of institutional change in China. According to Paul Pierson, diffusion refers to "wholesale replacement of institutions," while layering involves partial institutional change and adoption of institutions parallel to existing institutions. Paul Pierson, *Politics in Time: History, Institutions, and Social Analysis* (Princeton: Princeton University Press, 2004), pp. 137–138.

5. "'Rule by Law' Versus 'Rule by Man,'" *Faxue Yanjiu* [Legal Research], no. 1 (1982), pp. 6–11, trans. in *JPRS*, no. 80911 (26 May 1982), pp. 29–38.

6. "Peng Zhen Speech at Law Society Meeting," *Xinhua*, (29 September 1982), in *FBIS-CHI* (5 October 1982), p. K8.

7. "Qiao Shi Interviewed on Role of NPC," *Xinhua* (14 December 1996), trans. in *FBIS-CHI*, 96–242, cited in Stanley B. Lubman, *Bird in a Cage: Legal Reform in China after Mao* (Stanford: Stanford University Press, 1999), p. 148.

8. "Vice Premier Qiao Shi Speaks on Law Research," *Xinhua* (21 May 1986), trans. in *FBIS-CHI* (27 May 27 1986), p. K 28.

9. Quoted in "Qiao Shi 5 July Speech at Lawyers' Congress," *Renmin Ribao* (8 July 1986), trans. in *FBIS-CHI*, (14 July 1986), K 26–27.

10. "Zhao Ziyang-Proposed Group Works on Economic Law," *FBIS-CHI* (23 May 1985), p. K11.

11. Xiao Yang, "Law is the Basic Language with Which We Communicate with the World," from speech at the inaugural meeting of the China Organizing Committee for the Congress on the Law of the World (24 March 2005). http://www.chinacourt.org/zhuanti1/22clw/e_detail.php?id=155574

12. James V. Feinerman, "Chinese Participation in the International Legal Order," p. 188, notes that China feels a "perceived need to pay lip-service to international legal standards," although he is skeptical about Chinese commitment to such standards.

13. Randall Peerenboom, "Globalization, Path Dependency and the Limits of Law: Administrative Law Reform and the Rule of Law in the People's Republic of China," *Berkeley Journal of International Law* 19 (2001), p. 190.

14. National Bureau of Statistics of China, *China Statistical Yearbook* (Beijing: China Statistics Press, various years).

15. Chinese Economic Statistical Yearbook Editorial Committee, *Chinese Economic Yearbook* (Beijing: Chinese Economic Yearbook Publishers, 2003).

16. For a list of attributes of rule of aw, see Thomas Carothers, The Rule of Law Revival," *Foreign Affairs* 77, no. 2 (March–April 1998), p. 96.

17. A burgeoning literature on *guanxi* exists. See Fei Xiaotong, *From the Soil*, trans. and intro. by Gary G. Hamilton and Wang Zhen (Berkeley: University of California Press, 1992); Ambrose Yeo-chi King, "Kuan-hsi and Network Building: A Sociological Interpretation," *Daedalus* 120, no. 2 (Spring 1991), pp. 63–84; Kwang-kuo Hwang, "Face and Favor: The Chinese Power Game," *American Journal of Sociology* 92, no. 4 (January 1987), pp. 944–74; Yunxiang Yan, *The Flow of Gifts* (Stanford: Stanford University Press, 1996); J. Bruce Jacobs, "A Preliminary Model of Particularistic Ties in Chinese Political Alliances," *China Quarterly* 78 (June 1979), pp. 237–273; Thomas Gold, "After Comradeship," *China Quarterly* 104 (1985), pp. 657–75; Thomas Gold, Doug Guthrie, and David Wank, eds. *Social Connections in China: Institutions, Culture, and the Changing Nature of Guanxi* (Cambridge: Cambridge University Press, 2002); and David Wank, *Commodifying Capitalism* (New York: Cambridge University Press, 1999).

18. Edmund C. Duffy, "Business Law in China: Evolutionary Revolution," *Journal of International Affairs* 49, no. 2 (Winter 1996), p. 557; and Randall Peerenboom, "Globalization," p. 177.

19. Doug Guthrie, *Dragon in a Three-Piece Suit: The Emergence of Capitalism in China* (Princeton: Princeton University Press, 1999), pp. 20 and 196–197.

20. Hsing You-tien, *Making Capitalism in China: The Taiwan Connection* (New York: Oxford University Press, 1998), p. 133; and Hongying Wang, *Weak State, Strong Networks: The Institutional Dynamics of Foreign Direct Investment in China* (Oxford and New York: Oxford University Press 2001), p. 87.

21. Wank, *Commodifying Communism.*

22. Carol A. G. Jones, "Capitalism, Globalization and Rule of Law: An Alternative Trajectory of Legal Change in China," *Social and Legal Studies* 3 (1994), pp. 200 and 216.

23. Pitman Potter, "*Guanxi* and the PRC Legal System: From Contradiction to Complementarity," in *Social Connections in China: Institutions, Culture, and the Changing Nature of Guanxi,* eds. Thomas Gold, Doug Guthrie, and David Wank (Cambridge: Cambridge University Press, 2002), p. 183. Robb M. Lakritz, "Comment: Taming a 5000 Year-Old Dragon: Toward a Theory of Legal Development in Post-Mao China," *Emory International Law Review* 11 (Spring 1997), pp. 264–265.

24. Jerome A. Cohen, "Opening Statement Before the First Public Hearing of the U.S.-China Commission," Washington, DC (June 14, 2001), http:www.uscc. gov/textonly/transcriptstx/txtescoh.htm, contends that *guanxi* affects CIETAC and court decisions. Julius Melnitzer, "Reforms Make Arbitration in China a Safer Bet; Regs Still Not up to U.S. Standards," *Corporate Legal Times* (July 2005), p. 19, http://0-web.lexis-nexis.com.library.acaweb.org/universe, quotes Jerome Cohen on a case he argued in front of CIETAC in which the opposing counsel was a recently named vice chairman of CIETAC and, hence, a supervisor of the arbitrators. See also Pitman Potter, *The Chinese Legal System: Globalization and Local Legal Culture* (New York: Routledge, 2001), p. 32.

25. Pierson, *Politics in Time,* p. 137; and Gunther Teubner, "Legal Irritants: How Unifying Law Ends up in New Divergences," in *Varieties of Capitalism: The Institutional Foundations of Comparative Advantage,* eds. Peter A. Hall and David Soskice (Oxford University Press, 2001), p. 435, uses the term "coupling" to refer to a similar process.

26. *Model Law on International Commercial Arbitration,* adopted by United Nations Commission on International Trade Law (21 June 1985) (hereafter,

UNCITRALModel),http:www.uncitral.org/uncitral/en/uncitral_texts/1985Model_ arbitration_status.html.

27. *New York Convention* (1958).

28. Judith Teichman, *The Politics of Freeing Markets in Latin America* (Chapel Hill: University of North Carolina Press, 2001), pp. 20–21; and Douglass C. North, "Privatization, Incentives, and Economic Performance," in *The Privatization Process: A Worldwide Perspective,* eds. Terry L. Anderson and Peter J. Hill (Boston: Rowman and Littlefield, 1996), p. 33.

29. Shyam J. Kamath, "Foreign Direct Investment in a Centrally Planned Developing Economy: The Chinese Case," *Economic Development and Cultural Change* 39, no. 1 (October 1990), p. 123.

30. Michael A. Santoro, *Profits and Principles: Global Capitalism and Human Rights in China* (Ithaca, NY: Cornell University Press, 2000), pp. 33–43 and 151.

31. Teichman, *The Politics of Freeing Markets,* pp. 16–22; and Martha Finnemore and Kathryn Sikkink, "International Norm Dynamics and Political Change," *International Organization* 52, no. 4 (Autumn 1998), p. 902.

32. Amitav Acharya, "How Ideas Spread: Whose Norms Matter? Norm Localization and Institutional Change in Asian Regionalism," *International Organization* 58, (Spring 2004), pp. 250–254; Potter, "China and the International Legal System," pp. 699–715.

33. This point is supportive of sociological institutionalists' and constructivists' arguments that expectations of appropriateness affect behavior. Finnemore and Sikkink, "International Norm Dynamics," pp. 898 and 912; and James G. March and Johan P. Olsen, "The Institutional Dynamics of International Political Orders," *International Organization* 52, no. 4 (Autumn 1998), p. 958.

34. Fei, *From the Soil,* pp. 94–107; Lakritz, "Comment," pp. 242–246.

35. Potter, *The Chinese Legal System,* pp. 10–12.

36. Stanley Lubman, *Bird in a Cage: Legal Reform in China after Mao* (Stanford: Stanford University Press, 1999), pp. 100–101.

37. UNCITRAL, Status 1985-UNCITRAL Model Law on International Commercial Arbitration, http:www.uncitral.org/uncitral/en/uncitral_texts/arbitration/ 1985Model_arbitration_status.html

38. John Haley Owen, *The Spirit of Japanese Law* (Athens: The University of Georgia Press, 1998), pp. 9–12.

39. Frank K. Upham, *Law and Social Change in Postwar Japan* (Cambridge and London: Harvard University Press, 1989), pp. 17–18; John Owen Haley, *Authority without Power: Law and the Japanese Paradox* (New York: Oxford University Press, 1991), p. 169.

40. Hoken S. Seki, "Perspectives: Effective Dispute Resolution in United States-Japan Commercial Transactions," *Northwestern Journal of International Law and Business* 6 (Winter 1984–1985), pp. 985–986.

41. Michelle L. D. Hanlon, "The Japan Commercial Arbitration Association: Arbitration with the Flavor of Conciliation," *Law and Policy in International Business* 22, no. 3 (1991), p. 615.

42. R. Daniel Kelemen and Eric C. Sibbitt, "The Globalization of American Law," *International Organization* 58, no. 1 (Winter 2004), p. 106; and Robert A. Kagan and Lee Axelrad, "Adversarial Legalism: An International Perspective," in *Comparative Disadvantages? Social Regulations and the Global Economy,* ed. Peter S. Nivola (Washington, DC: Brookings Institution Press, 1997), p. 152. Jeffrey H. Dyer,

"To Sue or *Keiretsu,*" in *Networks, Markets, and the Pacific Rim: Studies in Strategy,* ed. W. Mark Fruin (New York and Oxford: Oxford University Press, 1998), pp. 233–254, compares U.S. and Japanese legal cultures.

43. *United States Federal Arbitration Act,* United States Code, Title 9, enacted 12 February 1925, and amended 3 September 1954, 31 July 1970, 19 November 1988, 15 August 1990, 15 November 1990, 1 December 1990, and 7 May 2002.

44. Symposium: In Support of International Commercial Arbitration and the Need for Federal Legislation, "It's Time to Adopt the UNCITRAL Model Law on International Commercial Arbitration," *Transnational Law and Contemporary Problems* 8, no. 3 (Spring 1998), p. 3. The UK's 1996 Arbitration Law is largely based on the UNCITRAL Model, as are the rules of the American Arbitration Association in the United States. James H. Carter, "Best Practices: Litigation Management; Trends in International Commercial Dispute Resolution," *The Metropolitan Corporate Counsel,* Greater New York Metro Edition (May 1998), p. 45, http://0-web. lexis-nexis.com.library.acaweb.org/universe.

45. The model offered here is similar to Amitav Acharya's model of norm diffusion in which "transnational norm entrepreneurs" mobilize information about international norms, and "local agents" work to "localize" those norms. Acharya, "How Ideas Spread," p. 254.

46. The interests of some of the NPC leaders, especially Qiao Shi, may have been to use legislation as a means of establishing credentials to rise to the position of party chairman rather than interest in lawmaking as an end.

47. Hsing You-tien, *Making Capitalism in China,* p. 133; and Qunjian Tian, "'Like Fish in Water': Taiwanese Investors in a Rent-Seeking Society," *Issues and Studies* 35, no. 5 (September–October 1999), pp. 61–94.

48. Daniel H. Rosen, *Behind the Open Door: Foreign Enterprises in the Chinese Marketplace* (Washington, D.C.: Institute for International Economics, 1999), pp. 31–32.

49. Keidanren, "Japan-China Relations in the 21st Century," (20 February 2001), http://www.keidanren.or.jp/english/policy/2001/006.html, http:www.keidanren. or.jp/english/policy/2001/006.html; and American Chamber of Commerce in Shanghai, *White Paper, 2000,* http:www.amcham-shanghai.org/AmChamPortal/ MCMS/Presentation/Publication/WhitePaper/ChairmanMessage.aspx?Year=2001.

50. http:www.uschinalegalcoop.org/prior/html.

51. Kelemen and Sibbitt, "The Globalization of American Law," p. 111.

52. "Foreign Law Firms Set up 103 Offices in China," *People's Daily* (12 April 2001), http:fpeng.peoplesdaily.com.cn/200104/12/eng20010412_67578.html.

53. *Regulations on Administration of Foreign Law Firms' Representative Offices in China,* adopted by State Council (19 December 2001), Article 15A.

54. "China Brings Legal System into Line with International Practice," *Xinhua* (11 December 1995), http://0-web.lexis-nexis.com.library.acaweb.org/ universe.

55. Shanghai lawyer (C-2005–04), interview by author, Shanghai, China (2005), worked for nineteen years in the Japanese legal system.

56. Foreign environmental attorney in Shanghai (C-2007–064), interview by author, Shanghai, China (2008).

57. *Regulations on Administration of Foreign Law Firms' Representative Offices in China,* promulgated by the State Council (19 December 2001), article 16. http:// www.gov.cn/english/laws/2005–08/24/content_25816.htm

58. Representative of foreign business group (C-2007–01), interview by author, Shanghai, China (2007).

59. Anthony Lin, "Shanghai Bar Association Goes after Foreign Law Firms," *New York Law Journal* (May 18, 2006). http://www.law.com/jsp/llf/PubArticleLLF.jsp?id=1147856732635

60. Susan Beck, "McDermott Entering into Alliance with Chinese Law Firm," *The American Lawyer* (30 January 2007). http://www.mwe.com/info/pubs/amlaw-mwechina.pdf

61. Feinerman, "Chinese Participation in the International Legal Order," p. 189.

62. Peter Hays Gries, *China's New Nationalism* (Berkeley: University of California Press, 2005), p. 21.

63. Susan Shirk, *How China Opened Its Door* (Washington, DC: The Brookings Institution, 1994), pp. 39–42.

64. "Chinese Arbitration Organization Attracts Attention," *Xinhua* (26 September 1989), http://0-web.lexis-nexis.com.library.acaweb.org/universe.

65. "First Arbitration Law Expected by End of 1994," *China Daily,* trans. in *FBIS-CHI,* 94–126 (30 June 1994), p. 36.

66. Song Lianbin, Zhao Jian, and Li Hong, "Approaches to Several Issues Related to the Amendment to Arbitration Act 1994 of PR China," *Explore and Research Forum in Arbitration,* 2002, no. 2, pp. 4, 8, 13, and 14, http:www.arbitration.org.cn/en/viewcontent.asp?id=50; and Song Lianbin, "Zhongguo Zhongcai" [Chinese Arbitration].

67. *China International Economic and Trade Arbitration Commission Arbitration Rules, 1998* (hereafter, *CIETAC Rules*) (1998), revised and adopted by China Chamber of International Commerce (6 May 1998), Article 2. http:web.singnet.com.sg/~arbiter/cietac.html

68. Charles Kenworthey Harer, "Arbitration Fails to Reduce Foreign Investors' Risk in China," *Pacific Rim Law and Policy Journal* 8, no. 2 (1999), p. 400.

69. Li Hu, "Enforcement of the International Commercial Arbitration Awards and Court Intervention in the People's Republic of China," *Journal of International Arbitration* 20, no. 2 (2004), p. 6.

70. CIETAC, "Stipulations for the Appointment of Arbitrators." http:www.cietac.org.cn/english/arbitrators/arbitrators.htm.

71. Zhang Kewen, "Commercial Arbitration Rules of Procedure Amended," *China Daily,* (20 September 1988), p. 4, trans. in *FBIS-CHI,* 88–183 (21 September 1988), p. 43.

72. U.S. lawyer in Shanghai (C-2000–13), interview by author, Shanghai, China (2000).

73. http:www.cietac.org.cn/english/news/news_3.htm.

74. *CIETAC Arbitration Rules, 2000,* adopted by the Chinese Council for the Promotion of International Trade/China Chamber of International Commerce (1 October 2000), Article 24.

75. *UNCITRAL Model,* Article 11(5). The International Chamber of Commerce, *Rules of Arbitration* (Paris: 1998), Article 9(5), also call for the Court to appoint a third, presiding panelist from a country that is not party to the case.

76. U.S. attorney (C-2000–013), interview by author, Shanghai, China (2000); Matthew Miller, "Disputes Tribunal Powers Widened," *South China Morning Post* (9 April 1998), *China Business Review,* p. 2, http://0-web.lexis-nexis.com.library.acaweb.org/universe.

77. "Government Drafts First Commercial Arbitration Law," *China Daily,* trans. in *FBIS-CHI*, 94–123 (27 June 27 1994), p. 51.

78. "Overhaul of Court System Overdue," *The Standard* (8 August 2005), http://0-web.lexis-nexis.com.library.acaweb.org/universe.

79. *CIETAC Rules,* (2005), Article 21(2). If the parties agree to such a selection process, CIETAC must approve of the selected arbitrators for them to become panelists.

80. In addition, CIETAC tightened its rules on panelists' ethics and the right to remove panelists. *CIETAC Rules,* (2005), Articles 25–27.

81. *CIETAC Rules,* (2005), Article 22(3).

82. Chinese attorney (C-2000–069), interview by author, Shanghai, China (2000).

83. The relevant IBA regulation is Article 4, cited in Huang Yanming, "The Ethics of Arbitrators in CIETAC Arbitration," *Journal of International Arbitration* 12 (June 1995), p. 10. For the relevant Chinese regulation, see *CIETAC Rules, 2000,* Article 28.

84. *CIETAC Rules, 2000,* Article 29.

85. Symposium: In Support of International Commercial Arbitration and Litigation: The Need for Federal Legislation, "It's Time to Adopt," pp. 6–7.

86. *CIETAC Rules, 2000,* Article 22.

87. U.S. JV manager (C-2000–047), interview by author, Shanghai, China (2000).

88. Japanese attorney (C-2000–019), interview by author, Shanghai, China (2000).

89. Japanese attorney (C-2000–016), interview by author, Shanghai China (2000).

90. President of U.S. management consulting company (C-2000–009), interview by author, Shanghai, China (2000).

91. Jerome Cohen, "Opening Statement," p. 4; Jerome Cohen, "Time to Fix China's Arbitration," *Far Eastern Economic Review,* (January/February 2005), http:www.feer.com/articles1/2005/0501/free/p031.html; and Harpole, "Following Through on Arbitration," *China Business Review* 25, no. 5 (Sept./Oct. 1998), pp. 36–38.

92. *UNCITRAL Model,* Article 26(1).

93. Russell Thirgood, "A Critique of Foreign Arbitration in China," *Journal of International Arbitration* 17, no. 3 (2000), p. 99, discusses the case.

94. *CIETAC Arbitration Rules,* adopted by Standing Committee of the Second National Congress of the China Council for the Promotion of International Trade (1 June 1994), Article 40; and Thirgood, "A Critique of Foreign Arbitration in China," p. 99.

95. *Civil Procedure Law,* adopted by the National People's Congress and promulgated by the President of the People's Republic of China (9 April 1991), Article 259. http://www.cietac-sz.org.cn/English/Convention/Cp101.htm.

96. David Howell, "An Overview of Arbitration Law and Practice in the PRC," *Arbitration Developments in China* (December 2000), Baker & McKenzie, p. 4, http:www.bakerinfo.com/Publications/Documents/1539_tx.htm. During the period 1990–1996, the most common reason for non-enforcement was the non-existence of assets available for distribution. See Harpole, "Following Through," p. 37. Liu Zuoxiang, *"Zhongguo Sifa Difang Baohu Zhuyi zhi Pipan"* [Criticism of Chinese

Legal Protectionism], *Faxue Yanjiu* [Legal Research], no. 1 (2003), p. 92 , cites a study by Zou Zongshan that claims some Chinese local courts fail to enforce up to 50 percent of financial awards. Randall Peerenboom, "Seek Truth from Facts: An Empirical Study of Enforcement of Arbitral Awards in the PRC," *American Journal of Comparative Law* 49 (2001), p. 254.

97. U.S. attorney (C-2000–013), interviewed by author, Shanghai, China (2000).

98. Matthew D. Bersani, "Enforcement of Arbitration Awards," *The China Business Review,* nos. 5–6 (1992), pp. 51–52.

99. *Civil Procedure Law,* (1991), Article 260, details five grounds for not enforcing an arbitral award: (i) the parties' failure to reach an arbitration agreement; (ii) an invalid arbitration agreement; (iii) improper notification of the arbitration proceedings; (iv) defects in the arbitration proceedings; and (v) the arbitration organ did not have jurisdiction in the case. See Pitman Potter, *Foreign Business Law in China: Past Progress and Future Challenges* (Burlingame, CA: 1990 Institute, 1995), p. 74. Shanghai attorney (C-2000–014), interview by author, Shanghai, China (2000).

100. U.S. attorney (C-2000–014), interview by author, Shanghai, China (2000); "Overhaul of Court System Overdue."

101. Cited in Li Hu, "Enforcement of the International Commercial Arbitration Award," p. 13.

102. *UNCITRAL Model* (1985), Article 36 (1) (b) (ii).

103. *CIETAC Rules* (2000), Article 23.

104. Liu, "Criticism," p. 91.

105. Peerenboom, "Seek Truth," pp. 254–255.

106. Peerenboom, "Seek Truth," pp. 292–293.

107. *New York Convention* (1958), Article II(3).

108. The Court's ruling violated Chinese law as well. *Regulations for the Implementation of the Law on Joint Ventures* (1983), Article 110, http:www.novexcn. com/jv_use_chin_for_invest.html

109. Robert R. Aronson, "Prepared Statement Before the House Committee on Ways and Means, Trade Subcommittee," *Federal News Service* (23 May 1995); and Robert R. Aronson, "Testimony Before the Subcommittee on Trade of the House Committee on Ways and Means, Hearing on the Future of United States-China Trade Relations and the Possible Accession of the World Trade Organization" (4 November 1997), http://0-web.lexis-nexis.com.library.acaweb.org/universe/document?_m=86 7cbfd850aeef8b875edcad6161394e&_docnum=14&wchp=dGLbVtz-zSkVA&_md5= 7ac671cf5cf37338faf327844c423830.

110. Until new rules were issued in 1998 requiring enforcement within two months of a court's acceptance of an application of enforcement, the courts could indefinitely delay any order to enforce a CIETAC award. Li Hu, "Enforcement of the International Commercial Arbitration Award," pp. 9 and 33. The 2005 Rules further sped the process of rendering arbitral decisions from nine months to six months. *CIETAC Rules* (2005), Article 42(1).

111. This, too, violated international arbitration rules. As a clear parent company of SFAIC, the Ministry of Aeronautics and Astronauts is legally liable for paying compensation owed by SFAIC. Information on the case comes from Nigel Holloway, "Arbitrary Justice: Breach of Contract in China Becomes Test Case," *Far Eastern Economic Review* (20 July 1995), p. 78; Li Hu, "Enforcement of the International Commercial Arbitration Award," pp. 28–29; Robert Aronson, "Prepared Statement";

Robert Aronson, "Testimony"; U.S. attorney in Shanghai (C-2000–013), interview by author, Shanghai, China (2000); and Chinese attorney in international law firm (C-2000–014), interview by author, Shanghai, China (2000).

112. Peerenboom, "Seek Truth," p. 297; and Li Hu, "Enforcement of the International Commercial Arbitration Award," p. 23.

113. Li Hu, "Foreign Arbitral Awards," p. 178.

114. http:www.uschinalegalcoop.org/prior.html.

115. Harpole, "Following Through," p. 35. The Supreme Court announced this position on August 28, 1995, in *The Supreme People's Court Notice on Several Questions Concerning the People's Court's Handling with the Issues in Relation to Foreign-related Arbitration and Foreign Arbitration* (1995), Paragrap. 2.

116. *Regulation of the Supreme People's Court on Several Issues Concerning the Jurisdiction over Foreign-related Civil and Commercial Actions,* (2002), cited in Li Hu, "Enforcement of Foreign Arbitral Awards and Court Intervention in the People's Republic of China," *Journal of International Arbitration* 20, no. 2 (2004), p. 170.

117. "TriNorth's Application for Enforcement Order Referred to Supreme Court of China," *Canadian Corporate Newswire* (23 September 2003), http://0-web.lexis-nexis.com.library.acaweb.org/universe. Information about the Supreme Court verdict and collection of the award was found at the TriNorth corporate website. http:www.trinorthcapital.com/pr2.html.

118. "Overhaul of Court System Overdue"; and Stanley Lubman, "Law of the Jungle," *China Economic Review* (September 2004), pp. 24–25, analyze the Zidell cases.

119. Howard Davies et al., "The Benefits of 'Guanxi,'" *Industrial Marketing Management* 24, (1995), p. 211; K. R. Xin and J. Pearce, "*Guanxi:* Good Connections as Substitutes for Institutional Support," *Academy of Management Journal* 39, no. 6 (1996), pp. 1641–1658; and Wilfried R. Vanhonacker, "*Guanxi* Networks in China," *The China Business Review* (May–June 2004), pp. 48–53.

120. Shirk, *How China Opened*, pp. 41–42.

121. Japanese attorney (C-2000–16), interview by author, Shanghai, China (2000).

122. Sino-Japanese JV manager (C-2000–062), interview by author, Shanghai, China (2000) (emphasis added).

123. U.S. commercial officer (C-2000–002), interviewed by author, Shanghai, China (2000).

124. U.S. WFOE manager (C-2000–018), interview by author, Shanghai, China (2000).

125. U.S. WFOE manager (C-2000–005), interview by author, Shanghai, China (2000).

126. Sino-U.S. JV manager (C-2000–047), interview by author, Shanghai, China (2000).

127. U.S. regional manager for China (C-2000–008), interview by author, Shanghai, China (2000).

128. General manager of U.S. WOFE in Shanghai (2000–06), interview by author, Shanghai, China (2000).

129. Regional manager of U.S. corporation (C-2000–008), interview by author, Shanghai, China (2000).

130. In the areas of civil, administrative, and even, criminal law, international NGOs are having a positive effect on Chinese legal reforms, according to

interviews that I conducted with attorneys and representatives of NGOs conducted in 2007–2008.

131. Potter, "China and the International Legal System," pp. 707–708, refers to this process as "selective adaptation" to international legal norms.

132. Symposium: In Support of International Commercial Arbitration and Litigation: The Need for Federal Legislation, "It's Time to Adopt," pp. 6–12, notes several of the U.S. FAA's shortcomings, some of which have analogs to complaints raised by MNCs and attorneys about the rules and practice of CIETAC.

Chapter Five

1. Minquan Liu, Luodan Xu, and Liu Liu, "Wage-Related Labor Standards and FDI in China: Some Survey Findings from Guangdong Province," *Pacific Economic Review* 9, no. 3 (2004), pp. 225–243. While wage data do not lend much support to a deleterious overall effect on wages among Chinese workers, there are strong indications that foreign direct investment is contributing to growing wage inequality.

2. Sek Hong Ng and Malcolm Warner, "Industrial Relations versus Human Resource Management in the PRC: Collective Bargaining 'with Chinese Characteristics'" in *Changing Workplace Relations in the Chinese Economy,* ed. Malcolm Warner (New York: St. Martin's Press, 2000), p. 102; Andrew G. Walder, *Communist Neo-Traditionalism: Work and Authority in Chinese Industry* (Berkeley: University of California Press, 1988), pp. 76–81; and Zhongshan University Shenzhen Investigation Team, "A Useful Insight: An Investigation into Wage System Reform in the Shekou Industrial Zone," *Chinese Economic Studies* XIX, no. 2 (Winter 1985–1986), p. 63.

3. "Is the 'Iron Rice Bowl' Really Something We Cannot Bear to Part With?" *Renmin Ribao* (18 November 1986), p. 2. Translated in *FBIS-CHI* (21 November 1986), p. K15. In 1988, another journalist, Zhou Qiren estimated that 15–20 million workers in state-owned enterprises were redundant. "Smashing 'Iron Rice Bowl' Necessary for Reform," *Shijie Jingji Daobao* (19 September 1988), translated in *FBIS-CHI*, 88–196 (11 October 1988), p. 29.

4. John Child, *Management in China during the Age of Reform* (Cambridge: Cambridge University Press, 1994), p. 176.

5. Jim Mann, *Beijing Jeep: A Case Study of Western Business in China* (Boulder: Westview Press, 1988), pp. 256–258. Japanese investors also complained about the poor productivity of Chinese workers. Japanese manager in Sino-Japanese JV (C-2000–036), interview by author, Shanghai, China (2000); Japanese manager in Sino-Japanese JV (C-2000–034), interview by author, Shanghai, China (2000).

6. Child, *Management in China;* Mary Gallagher, *Contagious Capitalism: Globalization and the Politics of Labor in China* (Princeton: Princeton University Press, 2005); Doug Guthrie, *Dragon in a Three-Piece Suit: The Emergence of Capitalism in China* (Princeton: Princeton University Press, 1999); and Sally Sargeson, "Assembling Class in a Chinese Joint Venture Factory," in *Organizing Labour in Globalising Asia,* eds. Jane Hutchinson and Andrew Brown (London and New York: Routledge, 2001), pp. 48–70.

7. Joseph Fewsmith, "Special Economic Zones in the PRC," *Problems of Communism* 35, no. 6 (November–December, 1986), p. 78; Guthrie, *Dragon in a Three-Piece Suit,* p. 5; and Gallagher, *Contagious Capitalism,* pp. 11–18.

8. Nailin Bu and Ji-Liang Xu, "Work-Related Attitudes among Chinese Employees *vis-à-vis* 'American' and 'Japanese' Management Models," in *Changing Workplace Relations in the Chinese Economy*, ed. Malcolm Warner (New York: St. Martin's Press, 2000), pp. 185–203; Anita Chan, "Labor Relations in Foreign-funded Ventures, Chinese Trade Unions, and the Prospects for Collective Bargaining, in *Adjusting to Capitalism: Chinese Workers and the State*, ed. Greg O'Leary (Armonk, NY: M. E. Sharpe, 1998), pp. 122–149; Child, *Management in China;* and John Ravenill, "Japanese and U.S. Subsidiaries in East Asia: Host-Economy Effects, in *Japanese Multinationals in Asia: Regional Operations in Comparative Perspective*, ed. Dennis J. Encarnation (New York and Oxford: Oxford University Press, 1999), pp. 261–284, are exceptions.

9. Anita Chan, "Chinese *Danwei* Reforms: Convergence with the Japanese Model?" in *Danwei: The Changing Chinese Workplace in Historical and Comparative Perspective*, eds. Xiaobo Lu and Elizabeth J. Perry (Armonk, NY: M.E. Sharpe, 1997), pp. 91–113.

10. Mark W. Frazier, *The Making of the Chinese Industrial Workplace: State, Revolution, and Labor Management* (Cambridge: Cambridge University Press, 2002), pp. 153–154 and 213; "Piece Work Wage System Discussed," *Jingji Yanjiu*, translated in *JPRS* (16 July 1979), pp. 27–28; and Andrew G. Walder, *Communist Neo-Traditionalism*, pp. 118–120 and 137–139.

11. For an overview of the pre-reform pay system, see Walder, *Communist Neo-Traditionalism*, pp. 76–81.

12. *Ibid.*, pp. 68–71.

13. Deng Xiaoping, "Jianchi Anlao Fenpei Yuanze," *Deng Xiaoping Wenxuan (1975–1982)* (Beijing: Renmin Daban She, 1983) (author's translation).

14. Michel Korzec and Martin King Whyte, "Reading Notes: The Chinese Wage System," *China Quarterly*, no. 86 (June 1981), p. 259.

15. "It Is Fine Not To Hold the 'Iron Rice Bowl'—Sixth Discussion on Stopping the Practice of 'Eating from the Same Big Pot,'" *Renmin Ribao* (4 February 1983), p. 1, translated in *FBIS-CHI* (16 February 1983), p. K11.

16. Zhou Jing, "A Piece Rate Wage System Should Be Put into Practice," *Zhejiang Ribao* (6 September 1980), p. 3, translated in *JPRS*, no. 76913, pp. 4–7; "Piece Work Wage System Discussed," *Jingji Yanjiu*, no. 2 (February, 1979), translated in *JPRS, No. 73845 (16 July 1979), pp. 27–36.

17. On the introduction of floating wages see, Kang Yonghe, "*Tichang he Tuiguang Xiaoyi Gongzi*" (Encourage and Spread Profit-linked Wages), *Renmin Ribao* (22 May 1983). Reprinted in Zhongguo, *Fuyin Baokan Ziliao*, 1983, no. 6 (*Laodong Jingji yu Renkou*) (Beijing: Renmin Daxue Shubao Ziliao She, 1983), pp. 55–56; Xiao Mei, "Xiantan Fudong Gongzi," (A Discussion of Floating Wages), *Jingjixue Zhoubao* (5 May 1983). Reprinted in Zhongguo, *Fuyin Baokan Ziliao* (1983), no. 6 (*Laodong Jingji yu Renkou*) (Beijing: Renmin Daxue Shubao Ziliao She, 1983), p. 48; and Gong Yu, "Fudong Gongzizhi," (Floating Wage System), *Jingji Ribao* (18 April 1983). Reprinted in Zhongguo, *Fuyin Baokan Ziliao* (1983), no. 6 (*Laodong Jingji yu Renkou*) (Beijing: Renmin Daxue Shubao Ziliao She, 1983), p. 52.

18. Child, *Management in China*, p. 187.

19. "*Jingji Yanjiu* on Wage, Profit Reform," *FBIS-CHI*, 88–149 (3 August 1988), p. 39.

20. Chen Xiao, "Good and Bad in Contract System," *China Daily* (10 March 1992), p. 4, in *FBIS-CHI* (11 March 1992), p. 37; and Zhao Ziwen, "Investigation in

20 Cities Shows Fast Development of Contract System," *Renmin Ribao* (29 December 1987), p. 1, translated in *FBIS-CHI,* 88–007 (12 January 1988), p. 27.

21. Huang Jian, "Wage System of Enterprises Should Not Be Reformed All at Once," *Shijie Jingji Daobao* (27 May 1985), p. 5, translated in *JPRS-CEA,* 85–070 (6 August 1985), p. 79, called for linking wage funds to enterprise profit taxes.

22. Zhu Ying, "Major Changes Under Way in China's Industrial Relations," *International Labor Review* 134, no. 1 (1995), pp. 37–49. "Positional wages" refer to a portion of compensation linked to a worker's post and its grade.

23. "A Piece Rate System Should Be Put into Practice," p. 4; and "Piece Rate Wage System Discussed," p. 75.

24. Andrew G. Walder, "Wage Reform in the Web of Factory Interests," *The China Quarterly,* no. 109 (1987), pp. 22–41; and Child, *Management in China,* p. 176.

25. Jeanne Wilson, "Labor Policy in China," *Problems of Communism* (September-October 1990), pp. 63–65, notes the chilling effect that the suppression of the June 4, 1989, protests had on the ACFTU and worker activism.

26. Malcolm Warner, "Introduction: Whither the Iron Rice Bowl," in *Changing Workplace Relations in the Chinese Economy,* ed. Malcolm Warner (New York: St. Martin's Press, 2000), p. 4. Kazuo (John) Fukuda, "Japanese Companies in China: Problems of Human Resource Management," *Journal of Far Eastern Business* 1, no. 4 (1995), p. 53; and Andrew G. Walder, "Wage Reform," pp. 25–27.

27. Child, *Management in China,* pp. 190–191.

28. *Ibid.,* p. 206, found little variation in bonus amounts within enterprises in surveys conducted in 1985 and 1990.

29. Wilson, Labor Policy in China," pp. 58–59; and Andrew G. Walder, "China Transitional Economy: Interpreting Its Significance," *The China Quarterly,* no. 144 (December, 1995), pp. 973–974.

30. Wilson, "Labor Policy in China," pp. 58–59.

31. Minghua Zhao and Theo Nichols cite interviews with workers who noted with irony that the bonus system was used to reduce their pay by fining workers for slow performance. Minghua Zhao and Theo Nichols, "Management Control of Laborers in State-Owned Enterprises," in *Adjusting to Capitalism: Chinese Workers and the State,* ed. Greg O'Leary (Armonk, NY: M. E. Sharpe, 1998), pp. 92–94.

32. Many of the workers—and the ones with the harshest labor conditions—in the textile firms analyzed by Zhao and Nichols were peasant contract workers. Zhao and Nichols, "Management Control of Labor." Anita Chan notes, "For many formerly privileged workers in state-owned industrial sector...working conditions, benefits, and job security have declined precipitously over the past fifteen years." Anita Chan, *China's Workers under Assault* (Armonk, NY: M.E. Sharpe, 2001), p. 13. Chan goes on to lament the harsh conditions endured by migrant workers.

33. Zhou Qiren, "It Is Necessary to Curb Inflation and Promote Reform: Smashing the Big Pot Is More Pressing Than Ever Before," *Shijie Jingji Daobao* (Shanghai), (19 September 1988), p. 6, translated in *FBIS-CHI,* 88–196 (11 October 1988), p. 29.

34. Gallagher, *Contagious Capitalism;* Zhongshan University Shenzhen Investigation Team, "A Useful Insight: An Investigation into Wage System Reform in the Shekou Industrial Zone," *Chinese Economic Studies* XIX, no. 2 (Winter 1985–1986), pp. 59–70; "Wage System in Shenzhen Special Economic Zone," *Renmin Ribao* (11 January 1983), translated in *JPRS,* no. 82822 (8 February 1983), p. 117; and

Guangming Ribao, "Shenzhen and Shekou Industrial Areas Reform Wage System," *Chinese Economic Studies* XIX, no. 2 (Winter 1985–1986), pp. 71–78.

35. "Guangdong Enterprises Study Experiences of Shenzhen," *Yangcheng Wanbao* (11 April 1984), p. 1, translated in *JPRS*, CEA-84–073 (29 August 1984), pp. 127–128.

36. "Wage System in Shenzhen Special Zone," p. 118; and "Shenzhen and Shekou Industrial Areas Reform Wage System," *Guangming Ribao*, translated in *Chinese Economic Studies* XIX, no. 2 (Winter 1985–1986), pp. 71–72.

37. "Wage System in Shenzhen Special Zone," p. 117; and "'Renmin Ribao' on Efficiency in Shenzhen," *Renmin Ribao* (15 January 1983), translated in *JPRS*, no. 82822 (8 February 1983), p. 114.

38. "'Renmin Ribao' on Efficiency in Shenzhen," *Renmin Ribao*, 15 January 1983, translated in *JPRS*, no. 82822 (8 February 1983), p. 115.

39. *Regulations of the People's Republic of China on Labor Management in Joint Ventures Using Chinese and Foreign Investment*, promulgated by the State Council (26 July 1980), Article 9.

40. *Regulations for the Implementation of the Law of the People's Republic of China on Joint Ventures Using Chinese and Foreign Investment*, promulgated by the State Council (20 September 1983), Article 34.

41. *Regulations on Labor Management in Joint Ventures* (1980), Article 2.

42. Ibid., Article 8. *Procedures for the Implementation of the Provisions for Labor Management in Joint Ventures Using Chinese and Foreign Investment*, promulgated by the Ministry of Labor and Personnel (19 January 1984), Article 12, clarified the average wage in SOEs used to determine the appropriate wages in JVs.

43. For example, see Mann, *Beijing Jeep*.

44. Gallagher, *Contagious Capitalism*, p. 15.

45. "Shenzhen Zone Cracks Down on Child Labor," *Xinhua*, translated in *FBIS-CHI*, 88–153 (9 August 1988), pp. 41–42; "Shenzhen Businesses Exploit Children, Workers," Beijing Domestic Service, translated in *FBIS-CHI*, 88–163 (23 August 1988), pp. 40–41.

46. "Shenzhen Businesses Exploit Children, Workers," pp. 40–41.

47. Ibid., pp. 40–41.

48. Katherine Forestier, "Capitalist Impact on Shenzhen Discussed," *South China Morning Post* (Business Post), 16 May 1988, p. 4, reprinted in *FBIS-CHI*, 88–095 (17 May 1988), p. 55.

49. "Frequent Strikes Reported in Shenzhen," *Ming Pao* (Hong Kong), translated in *FBIS-CHI*, 91–020 (30 January 1991), p. 67.

50. "Shenzhen to Unionize 40 Percent of Foreign Enterprises," *South China Morning Post*, reprinted in *FBIS-CHI*, 94–058 (25 March 1994), p. 68.

51. Anita Chan, "Chinese Trade Unions and Workplace Relations in the State-Owned and Joint Venture Enterprises," in *Changing Workplace Relations in the Chinese Economy*, ed. Malcolm Warner (London: Macmillan, 2000), pp. 46–47.

52. Keith Goodall and Malcolm Warner, "Enterprise Reform, Labor-Management Relations, and Human Resource Management in a Multinational Context: Empirical Evidence from Sino-Foreign Joint Ventures," *International Studies of Management and Organization* 29, no. 3 (Fall 1999), pp. 21–36.

53. Child, *Management in China*, p. 158; and Kazuo (John) Fukuda, "Japanese Companies in China: Problems of Human Resource Management," *Journal of Far Eastern Business* 1, no. 4 (1995), p. 53; and Keith Goodall and Malcolm

Warner, "Enterprise Reform, Labor-Management Relations, and Human Resource Management in a Multinational Context," *International Studies of Management and Organization* 29, no. 3 (Fall 1999), pp. 22–23. Diana Rosemary Sharpe, "Globalization and Change: Organizational Continuity and Change within a Japanese Multinational in the UK," in *The Multinational Firm: Organizing across Institutional and National Divides,* eds. Glenn Morgan, Peer Hull Kristensen, and Richard Whitley (Oxford: Oxford University Press, 2001), pp. 211–215, makes a similar point regarding brown-field and green-field Japanese investments in the United Kingdom.

54. See also Child, *Management in China,* p. 281.

55. Makoto Kumazawa, "Ability-Oriented Management in Japanese Firms," translated in *The Japanese Economy* 25, no. 6 (November-December 1997), pp. 4–5.

56. According to the Nikkeiren, the job performance qualification system "often operated based on a de facto seniority basis." See Nikkeiren, *The Current Labor Economy in Japan.* (Tokyo: Nikkeiren, 2000), p. 40.

57. Kazuo Koike, "White Collar Workers in Japan and the United States." In *The Transformation of the Japanese Economy,* ed. Kazuo Sato (Armonk, NY: M.E. Sharpe, 1999)," p. 194.

58. Clair Brown et al., *Work and Pay in the United States and Japan* (Oxford: Oxford University Press, 1997), pp. 120–121.

59. Kazuo Koike, "White Collar Workers," pp. 176–177.

60. Japanese manager in a Japanese trading company (C-2000–050), interview by author, Shanghai, China (2000).

61. Japanese general manager of Sino-Japanese JV (C-2000–036), interview by author, Shanghai, China (2000).

62. Chinese consultant in an international management consultant firm (C-2003–02), interview by author, Shanghai, China (2003), made essentially the same point.

63. Chinese human resources manager in Japanese firm (C-2005–02), interview by author, Shanghai, China (2005).

64. Chinese consultant in an international management consultant firm (C-2003–02), interview by author, Shanghai, China (2003); and Chinese human resources manager in a U.S. WFOE (C-2000–063), interview by author, Shanghai, China (2000).

65. Japanese manager of Japanese trading company (C-2000–028), interview by author, Shanghai, China (2000).

66. Chinese human resources manager in Japanese subsidiary in Shanghai (C-2005–02), interview by author, Shanghai, China (2005).

67. Japanese manager of Sino-Japanese JV (C-2000–062), interview by author, Shanghai, China (2000).

68. *Ibid.*

69. Japanese manager in a Sino-Japanese JV (C-2000–48), interview by author, Shanghai, China (2000).

70. Japanese manager in a Sino-Japanese JV (C-2000–036), interview by author, Shanghai, China (2000); and Chinese human resources manager in a Sino-Japanese JV (C-2005–02), interview by author, Shanghai, China (2005).

71. Chinese human resources manager in a Japanese subsidiary in Shanghai (C-2005–02), interview by author, Shanghai, China (2005).

72. Chinese human resources manager in a Sino-Japanese JV (C-2000–043), interview by author, Shanghai, China (2000).

73. Japanese manager of a Sino-Japanese JV (C-2000–051), interview by author, Shanghai, China (2000).

74. Chinese deputy general manager of a Sino-Japanese JV (C-2000–067), interview by author, Shanghai, China (2000).

75. *Ibid.*

76. Chinese assistant general manager in a Sino-Japanese JV (C-2000–015), interview by author, Shanghai, China (2000).

77. Sharpe, "Globalization and Change," pp. 211–215 and 217.

78. Japanese manager of Japanese trading company in Shanghai (C-2000–029), interview by author, Shanghai, China (2000).

79. Nikkeiren, *Creating a Society Rich in Choices: Nikkeiren Position Paper 2001* (Tokyo: Japan Federation of Employers' Association, 2001), pp. 19–22. Japanese human resources managers in Tokyo admitted that it was difficult to change the managers' pattern of grading workers; managers still tended to grade workers very close to the mean. Human resources manager in Japanese manufacturing firm (J-2001–010), interview by author, Tokyo, Japan, 2001.

80. Human resources manager in Japanese trading company (J-2001–009), interview by author, Tokyo, Japan (2001).

81. Project manager in Japanese manufacturing firm (J-2001–001), interview by author, Tokyo, Japan (2001); human resources manager in Japanese manufacturing firm (J-2001–005), interview by author, Tokyo, Japan (2001); international human resources manager in Japanese manufacturing firm (J-2001–008), interview by author, Tokyo, Japan (2001); human resources manager in Japanese trading company (J-2001–009), interview by author, Tokyo, Japan (2001); human resources manager in Japanese manufacturing firm (J-2001–010), interview by author, Tokyo, Japan (2001); and human resources manager in Japanese trading company (J-2001–011), interview by author, Tokyo, Japan (2001).

82. Japanese general manager of a Sino-Japanese JV (C-2000–034), interview by author, Shanghai, China (2000).

83. *Ibid.* At the time of the interview, the system had not been in place long enough to determine its effect on workers' performance.

84. Senior human resources director in Japanese manufacturing firm (J-2001–04), interview by author, Tokyo, Japan (2001).

85. *Ibid.*

86. Chinese deputy general manager in Sino-Japanese JV (C-2000–059), interview by author, Shanghai, China (2000).

87. *Ibid.*

88. Brown et al., *Work and Pay*, p. 18.

89. Brown et al., *Work and Pay*, p. 100, analyzes the distinction between U.S. white-collar and blue-collar pay in terms of distinct norms of fairness. White-collar workers perceive fairness to be a function of equal opportunities, and blue-collar workers understand fairness in terms of equal pay.

90. Kazuo Koike, "White Collar Workers," p. 174.

91. Brown et al., *Work and Pay*, p. 101.

92. U.S. representative in Watson-Wyatt (consulting firm) in Shanghai (C-2003–01), interview by author, Shanghai, China (2003); Chinese representative in U.S. consulting firm in Shanghai (C-2003–02), interview by author, Shanghai, China (2003); and Chinese human resources manager in U.S. WFOE (C-2005–01), interview by author, Shanghai, China (2005).

93. Chinese human resources manager for U.S.-invested company (C-2005–01), interview by author, Shanghai, China (2005).

94. Brown et al., *Work and Pay*, p. 12.

95. Chinese human resources manager for U.S.-invested company (C-2005–01), interview by author, Shanghai, China (2005).

96. Child, *Management in China*, p. 270, notes that U.S. firms linked wages to performance more so than Japanese and western European investors in China.

97. Chinese management consultant in international consulting firm (C-2003–002), interview by author, Shanghai, China (2003).

98. Chinese management consultant for an international consulting firm (C-2003–02), interview by author, Shanghai, China (2003); and Chinese human resources manager in U.S. corporation (C-2005–01), interview by author, Shanghai, China (2005).

99. U.S. vice president of Sino-U.S. JV (C-2000–054), interview by author, Shanghai, China (2000).

100. Chinese human resources manager in Sino-U.S. JV (C-2000–022), interview by author, Shanghai, China (2000).

101. Manager of U.S. WFOE (C-2000–018), interview by author, Shanghai, China (2000).

102. Exceptions to that rule are found in the high-tech industries of Silicon Valley, where firms offer bonuses, stock options, and profit-sharing schemes to retain highly talented employees in a rapidly expanding field. U.S. management consultant for an international consulting firm (C-2003–001), interview by author, Shanghai, China (2003).

103. U.S. general manager of Sino-U.S. JV (C-2000–064), interview by author, Shanghai, China (2000).

104. General manager of a Sino-U.S. JV (C-2000–047), interview by author, Shanghai, China (2000).

105. Regional manager of U.S. firm in China (C-2000–061), interview by author, Shanghai, China (2000).

106. Chinese management consultant for an international consulting firm (C-2003–002), interview by author, Shanghai, China (2003).

107. Human resource officer in U.S. WFOE (C-2000–063), interview by author, Shanghai, China (2000).

108. Chinese management consultant in an international consulting firm (C-2003–002), interview by author, Shanghai, China (2003). Zhuang Li and Lu Xiongwen, "*Yuangong Chigu he Guanliceng Chigu: Cong Meiguo Dao Zhongguo*" (Employee Stock Options and Management-level Stock Options: From the U.S. to China), *Jingji Lilun yu Jingji Guanli* (Economic Theory and Economic Management), no. 3 (2000), pp. 11–15, discusses the transfer of stock options to China.

109. *Ibid.*

110. U.S. management consultant for an international consulting firm (C-2003–001), interview by author, Shanghai, China (2003).

111. Anita Chan, "Chinese *Danwei* Reforms: Convergence with the Japanese Model?" in *Danwei: The Changing Chinese Workplace in Historical and Comparative Perspective*, eds. Xiaobo Lu and Elizabeth J. Perry (Armonk, NY: M.E. Sharpe, 1997), pp. 91–113, Ma Zaixin, "What To Learn from the Japanese: The Process of Japanese-Style Management Transfer to China," in *Management in China: The Experience of Foreign Businesses*, ed. Roger Strange (London and Portland: Frank Cass, 1998),

pp. 118–131; and Malcolm Warner and Zhu Ying, "The Origins of Chinese 'Industrial Relations,' " pp. 28 and 30. Chan premises her argument more on the introduction of collective bargaining practices to China rather than the structure of compensation. As I show in the next chapter, even China's collective bargaining practices are not very similar to Japanese practice.

112. Singaporean president of a Sino-U.S. JV (C-2000–040), interview by author, Shanghai, China (2000).

113. *Ibid.*

114. Shortly after my interviews in 2000, the parent company was bought out and combined with its new owner's operations.

115. Most interviewees cited average labor turnover rates of 10–15 percent in their industry.

116. Chinese SOEs make less frequent use of migrant workers than collective, private, and foreign-owned factories, but a 1995 study by the Chinese Ministry of Labor estimated that seven percent of urban SOE employees were migrant workers. Cited in Loraine A. West, "Shifting Boundaries," *The China Business Review* (September–October, 1997), pp. 15–20. As early as 1987, Chinese newspapers reported on replacing released workers with contract and temporary workers in SOEs. Zhou Qiren, "It Is Necessary," p. 31.

117. Management consultant in an international consulting firm (C-2003–002), interview by author, Shanghai, China (2003).

118. Management consultant in an international consulting firm (C-2003–002), interview by author, Shanghai, China (2003).

119. Management consultant in an international consulting firm (C-2003–002), interview by author, Shanghai, China (2003).

120. Management consultant in an international consulting firm (C-2003–001), interview by author, Shanghai, China (2003).

121. Management consultant in an international consulting firm (C-2003–002), interview by author, Shanghai, China (2003).

122. Human resources manager in U.S. WFOE (C-2005–001), interview by author, Shanghai, China (2005).

123. Wang Ju, "A Preliminary Discussion of the Ideas Behind Wage Reform in China's State-Owned Enterprises and Their Theoretical Foundation," *Guangzhou Yanjiu*, no. 1 (1985) translated in *JPRS-CEA*, 86 (31 March 1986), pp. 130, 133.

124. Chinese management consultant in an international consulting firm (C-2003–002), interview by author, Shanghai, China (2003).

125. Chinese human resources manager in U.S. corporation (C-2005–01), interview by author, Shanghai, China (2005).

126. Chinese managerial consultant in an international consulting firm (C-2003–02), interview by author, Shanghai, China (2003).

127. Chinese human resources manager in U.S. corporation (C-2005–01), interview by author, Shanghai, China (2005).

128. Gallagher, *Contagious Capitalism;* Guthrie, *Dragon in a Three-Piece Suit;* Zaixin Ma, "What to Learn from the Japanese: The Process of Japanese-Style Management Transfer to China," in *Management in China: The Experience of Foreign Businesses,* ed. Roger Strange (London and Portland: Frank Cass, 1998), pp. 118–130.

129. Daniel H. Rosen, *Behind the Open Door: Foreign Enterprises in the Chinese Marketplace* (Washington, DC: Institute for International Economics, 1999); and Guthrie, *Dragon in a Three-Piece Suit.*

130. Paul Pierson, *Politics in Time: History, Institutions, and Social Analysis* (Princeton: Princeton University Press, 2004), pp. 17–22 and 153; Kathleen Thelen and Sven Steinmo, "Historical Institutionalism in Comparative Politics," in *Structuring Politics: Historical Institutionalism in Comparative Analysis,* eds. Sven Steinmo, Kathleen Thelen, and Frank Longstreth (Cambridge: Cambridge University Press, 1992), p. 17; and Douglass C. North, *Institutions, Institutional Change and Economic Performance* (Cambridge: Cambridge University Press, 1999), p. 33; and John L. Campbell, *Institutional Change and Globalization* (Princeton: Princeton University Press, 2004), pp. 13 and 33.

Chapter Six

1. China's SOEs allowed for intergenerational employment. Upon retirement, an SOE worker's child could replace the retiree in the enterprise, a process called *dingti* and *neizhao.* Luigi Tomba, *Paradoxes of Labour Reform: Chinese Labour Theory and Practice from Socialism to Market* (Abingdon, Oxford: RoutledgeCurzon, 2002), p. 59; and Andrew G. Walder, *Communist Neo-Traditionalism: Work and Authority in Chinese Industry* (Berkeley: University of California Press, 1988), p. 67.

2. Walder, *Communist Neo-Traditionalism,* pp. 69–71, notes that China had a low degree of labor turnover due to quits or dismissal in Chinese state owned enterprises prior to reforms. Tomba, *Paradoxes of Labour Reform,* p. 82, suggests that, prior to the labor contract system, labor turnover was close to zero.

3. For background on the concept of the "iron rice bowl," see Gordon White, "The Politics of Economic Reform in Chinese Industry: The Introduction of the Labour Contract System," *China Quarterly,* no. 111 (September 1987), pp. 365–389; Malcolm Warner, "Introduction: Whither the Iron Rice Bowl?" in *Changing Workplace Relations in the Chinese Economy,* ed. Malcolm Warner (Basingstoke, England: Macmillan, 2000), pp. 3–14; and Beijing Daily, "Should the 'Iron Rice Bowl' Be Smashed?" *Beijing Review,* no. 48 (30 November 1979), pp. 4–5.

4. Feng Chen, "Industrial Restructuring and Workers' Resistance in China," *Modern China* 29, no. 2 (April 2003), pp. 237–262, discusses labor protests that have occurred since the state forced collective layoffs beginning in 1992.

5. Paul Pierson, *Politics in Time: History, Institutions, and Social Analysis* (Princeton: Princeton University Press, 2004), pp. 160–162.

6. Anita Chan, "Chinese *Danwei* Reforms: Convergence with the Japanese Model?" in *Danwei: The Changing Chinese Workplace in Historical and Comparative Perspective,* eds. Xiaobo Lu and Elizabeth J. Perry (Armonk, NY: M.E. Sharpe, 1997), pp. 91–113; Ma Zaixin, "What To Learn from the Japanese: The Process of Japanese-Style Management Transfer to China," in *Management in China: The Experience of Foreign Businesses,* ed. Roger Strange (London and Portland: Frank Cass, 1998), pp. 118–131; and Malcolm Warner and Zhu Ying, "The Origins of Chinese 'Industrial Relations,'" in *Changing Workplace Relations in the Chinese Economy,* ed. Malcolm Warner (Basingstoke, England: Macmillan, 2000), pp. 28 and 30.

7. Michael Korzec, *Labour and the Failure of Reform in China* (New York: St. Martin's Press, 1992), p. 48.

8. Hillary Josephs, *Labor Law in China,* 2nd ed. (Huntington, NY: Juris Publishing, 2003), p. 13.

9. *Procedures for the Implementation of the Regulations on Labor Management in Joint Ventures Using Chinese and Foreign Investment,* issued and promulgated by the Ministry of Labor, (19 January 1984), article 7; *Labor Law of the People's Republic of China,* promulgated by the President of the People's Republic of China on 5 July 1994 and effective (1 January 1995), article 27.

10. Walder, *Communist Neo-Traditionalism,* pp. 59–67 and 71.

11. Korzec, *Labour and the Failure,* p. 45; Jamie P. Horsley, "The Chinese Workforce," *China Business Review* 15 (May-June 1988), p. 52.

12. "*Gongren Ribao* Comment," *FBIS-CHI* (16 February 1983), p. K12. "*Renmin Ribao* Promotes Foreseaking 'Iron Rice Bowl,'" *FBIS-CHI* (21 November 1986), p. K15, promotes the contract system as a way for enterprises to adjust their workforce based on changing staff requirements.

13. Cited in Horsley, "The Chinese Workforce," p. 51.

14. Hong Yung Lee, "Xiagang, the Chinese Style of Laying off Workers," *Asian Survey* XL, no. 6 (November–December 2000), p. 918.

15. *Notice of the Ministry of Labor and Personnel on Active Trial Implementation of the Contract Employment System* (1983), Article 4 in Josephs, *Labor Law,* p. 117.

16. Li Xingyuan, "Break Down the Prejudice against the Labor Contract System," *Gongren Ribao,* 11 August 1986, p. 4, translated in *FBIS-CHI* (27 August 1986), p. K6; "Speed up the Popularization of the Labor Contract System," *Gongren Ribao* (22 December 1984), translated in *FBIS-CHI* (15 January 1985), p. K18; and Yue Guangzhao, "*Shilun Laodong Hetongzhi,*" *Hongqi* (1983), no. 21, pp. 33–35, reprinted in Zhongguo, *Fuyin Baokan Ziliao,* 1983, no. 11 (*Laodong Jingji yu Renkou*) (Beijing Renmin Daxue Shubao Ziliao She,1983), pp. 6–7.

17. M. Francis Johnston, "Elites and Agencies: Forging Labor Policy at China's Central Level," *Modern China* 28, no. 2 (April, 2002), p. 153.

18. Josephs, *Labor Law,* p. 54.

19. "Shanghai Experiments with Labor Contract System," *Xinhua,* in *FBIS-CHI* (10 July 1986), p. 01.

20. Josephs, *Labor Law,* pp. 55–60.

21. "Ministry Gives Figures on Contract Labor System," *Xinhua* (26 July 1986), translated in *FBIS-CHI* (28 July 1986), p. K4; Xinhua, "Shanghai Experiments with Labor Contract System" (8 July 1986), translated in *FBIS-CHI* (10 July 1986), p. 01. On resistance to the contract labor system, see White, "Politics of Economic Reform," p. 378; W. Gary Vause and Georgia Bush Vrioni, "China's Labor Reform Challenge: Motivation of the Productive Forces," *Stanford Journal of International Law* 24 (Spring 1988), pp. 463–464; and Hillary Josephs, *Labor Law,* pp. 55–60.

22. Mary Gallagher, *Contagious Capitalism: Globalization and the Politics of Labor in China* (Princeton: Princeton University Press, 2005), pp. 173–174, refers to contracts in foreign invested enterprises as the dynamic element of labor reform in SOEs. Xiaobo Lu, "Transition, Globalization, and Changing Industrial Relations in China," in *Politics of Labor in a Global Age,* eds. Christopher Candland and Rudra Sil (Oxford: Oxford University Press, 2001), p. 194, asserts that foreign invested enterprises' labor reforms were particularly important in the early years of state-owned enterprise reforms. Tomba, *Paradoxes of Labour Reform,* p. 110, claims that the labor contract system was first mentioned in the 1980 regulations on equity JVs.

23. *The Regulations of the People's Republic of China on Labor Management in Joint Ventures Using Chinese and Foreign Investment* (1980), Article 2. The article also guarantees the right to dismiss employees in JVs.

24. *Procedures for the Implementation of the Regulations on Labor Management in Joint Ventures Using Chinese and Foreign Investment* (1983), Article 5. Such contracts typically were collective contracts that laid out basic terms of employment for all workers.

25. *Notice of the Ministry of Labor and Personnel on Active Trial Implementation of the Contract Employment System* (1983). The *Notice* does not specify Shenzhen as a model, but it does mention ongoing trials in several cities.

26. Edward X. Gu, "Guest Editor's Introduction," *Chinese Law and Government* 34, no. 1(January–February 2001), p. 6.

27. On the reduction of pay and benefits, see Han Jiyou, "Speed up the Popularization of the Labor Contract System," *Gongren Ribao* (Beijing), translated in *FBIS-CHI* (15 January 1985), pp. K18–K20; and Li Hong, "Employment Contract System to Expand," *China Daily* (28 March 1991), in *FBIS-CHI*, 91–060 (28 March 1991), p. 26; Cao Min, "Contract Labor in Effect This Year," *China Daily* (2 May 1996), in *FBIS-CHI*, 96–086 (2 May 1996), claims that such benefits eliminated by the contract labor system reduced state-owned enterprises' "efficiency and competitiveness."

28. For the appropriate legal passage, see *Provisional Regulations on the Implementation of the Contract Employment System in State Owned Enterprises* (1986), Article 18. Tomba, *Paradoxes of Labour Reform*, p. 113, argues that wages could be used to substitute for any diminution of benefits. This point is also noted by the former governor of Guangdong Province, Ye Xuanping, "Necessary Reforms Should Be Conscientiously Conducted in Coordination with the Labor Contract System," *Nanfang Ribao* (7 September 1986), pp. 1–2, translated in *FBIS-CHI* (16 September 1986), pp. P4–P7.

29. Josephs, *Labor Law*, p. 61, refers to the situation in Shenzhen as "greenfields," a term that evokes its undeveloped quality and receptivity to new institutions.

30. "Adoption of Labor Contract System Urged," *Xinhua* (4 January 1988), translated in *FBIS-CHI*, 88–001 (4 January 1988), p. 24.

31. Zhang Dawei and Ling Wancheng, "What Has the Contract System Brought to the People?" *Liaowang*, no. 37 (15 September 1986), pp. 16–17, translated in *FBIS-CHI* (26 September 1986), p. K16; "Labor Minister on Advantages of Contract System," *Xinhua*, translated in *FBIS-CHI* (21 June 1984), p. K12.

32. Ye Xuanping, "Necessary," p. P7. "Labor Minister on Advantages of Contract System," *Xinhua*, translated in *FBIS-CHI* (21 June 1984), p. K12.

33. *Provisional Regulations Governing [the] Labor Contract System for State-Owned Enterprises* (1986), Article 2, translated in Josephs, *Labor Law*, p. 121.

34. In 1991, state officials continued to allocate college graduates to state-owned work units. Such allocated workers were treated as permanent employees. "Urban Unemployment, 'Iron Rice Bowl' Jobs Viewed," *China Daily*, translated in *FBIS-CHI*, 91–216 (7 November 1991), p. 42. Edward X. Gu, "Forging a Labor Market in Urban China: The Legacies of the Past and the Dynamics of Institutional Transformation," *Asian Affairs* 28, no. 2 (2001), p. 109, argues that, in the 1990s, China's labor institutions were caught in a form of Soviet-style "institutional isomorphism" that kept contract system laborers working as permanent employees.

35. Feng Chen, "Industrial Restructuring and Workers' Resistance in China," *Modern China* 29, no. 2 (April 2003), pp. 237–262, analyzes protest by workers in state-owned enterprises who fear restructuring. Chen distinguishes such protests

from the numerous protests carried out by those workers who have already been laid off and workers who are subjected to illegal, abusive work conditions.

36. Jeanne Wilson, "Labor Policy in China: Reform and Retrogression," *Problems of Communism* (September–October 1990), pp. 63–65; and Josephs, *Labor Law*, p. 52.

37. Tomba, *Paradoxes of Labour Reform*, p. 103. Internal hiring practices violated the principle of open recruitment espoused in the *Provisional Regulations on the Implementation of the Contract Employment System in State Enterprises* (1986), Article 4. Ministry of Labor, "Notice on Continuing Implementation of 'Regulations on Hiring Workers for State Owned Enterprises,'" (1990) (at http://trs.molss.gov.cn/was40/mainframe.htm) calls for vigilance in getting rid of new forms of internal hiring and hiring of employees' children, some four years after the practice was banned.

38. Wilson, "Labor Policy," p. 50; and Xiaobo Lu, "Transition, Globalization, and Changing Industrial Relations in China," p. 195.

39. Diane Rosemary Sharpe, "Globalization and Change: Organizational Continuity and Change within a Japanese Multinational in the UK," in *The Multinational Firm Organizing Across Institutional and National Divides*, eds. Glenn Morgan, Peer Hull Kristensen, and Richard Whitley (Oxford: Oxford University Press, 2001), p. 211, makes a similar point with regard to brown-field and green-field Japanese investments in Great Britain.

40. Cherrie Jiuhua Zhu, *Human Resources Management in China: Past, Current, and Future HR Practices in the Industrial Sector* (London and New York: RoutledgeCurzon, 2005), p. 56.

41. *Provisional Regulations on the Hiring of Workers in State Enterprises* (1986), Article 2 states, "[an enterprise] must hire from society at large through a system of open recruitment and take those applicants who have scored highest on a comprehensive examination of their moral, intellectual, and physical qualifications."

42. Doug Guthrie, *Dragon in a Three-Piece Suit: The Emergence of Capitalism in China* (Princeton: Princeton University Press, 1999), pp. 52 and 63–66.

43. The term is a Chinese euphemism for mostly young people who have not yet found a job.

44. Tomba, *Paradoxes of Labour Reform*, p. 76, notes that Chinese documents first mentioned labor service companies in 1980. *Opinions on Issues Concerning Labor Service Companies* (1982), translated in *Chinese Law and Government* 34, no. 1 (January–February 2001), pp. 31–37, provides guidance on the duties and functions of labor service companies.

45. *Opinions on Issues Concerning Labor Service Companies*, Point 3, and *Regulations on the Management of Labor Employment Service Enterprises*, 1990, translated in *Chinese Law and Government* 34, no. 1 (January–February 2001), pp. 41–47; and Tomba, *Paradoxes of Labour Reform*, pp. 76–77.

46. *Decisions on Personnel Management of Foreign Investment Enterprises*, issued by the Ministry of Personnel and approved by the State Council (15 December 1988), Article 2, allows foreign invested enterprises to recruit from the public, i.e., labor market. Previous laws on labor relations in foreign invested enterprises did not specifically comment on hiring from the labor market.

47. Horsley, "The Chinese Workforce," p. 50.

48. State Council Administrative Office, *State Council Administrative Office's Circular on the Labor Ministry's and Personnel Ministry's Notice on Opinions to*

Advance the Autonomy of Existing Foreign Invested Enterprises (1988), Article 1 (author's translation).

49. On job seekers' use of *guanxi* to find jobs, see Yanjie Bian, "Institutional Holes and Job Mobility Processes: *Guanxi* Mechanisms in China's Emergent Labor Markets," in *Social Connections in China*, eds. Thomas Gold, Doug Guthrie, and David Wank (Cambridge: Cambridge University Press, 2002), pp. 119–126.

50. Cherrie Jiuhua Zhu, *Human Resource Management*, p. 134, notes the cost of such hiring was 10,000 *yuan* per graduate in 1994.

51. *Regulations of Shanghai Municipality Concerning Control of Resident Representative Offices of Foreign Enterprises* (1986) calls for representative offices to hire their local staff through the Shanghai Foreign Services Company. *Detailed Rules for Implementing the Law of the People's Republic of China on Enterprises Operating Exclusively with Foreign Capital,* approved by the State Council on 20 October 1990 and promulgated by the Ministry of Foreign Economic Relations and Trade (12 December 1990), Article 11, calls for WFOEs, in their applications, to include plans for staffing their enterprises without details on the mechanisms to do so. Moreover, FESCO rules did not call for fines of foreign invested enterprises that hired outside of FESCO. See "PRC: Foreign Firms To Hire Through State Approved Agencies," *China Daily, FBIS-CHI,* 96–105 (30 May 1996), p. 60.

52. Beginning in 1993, China allowed non-state-owned labor service companies to operate, although they were still required to register with the local labor department. See Edward X. Gu, "Guest Editor's Introduction: Labor Market Reforms," *Chinese Law and Government* 34, no. 1 (January–February 2001), p. 8). *Provisional Regulations on Labor Exchange,* (1990), Article 10; *Opinions on Issues Concerning Labor Service Companies* (1982), Article 1.

53. "PRC: Foreign Firms To Hire Through State-Approved Agencies," *China Daily, FBIS-CHI,* 96–105 (30 May 1996), p. 60.

54. *Labor Law,* Article 2.

55. *Labor Law,* Article 27.

56. *Regulations of the People's Republic of China on Labor Management in Joint Ventures Using Chinese and Foreign Investment* (1980), Article 4. For both SOEs and FIEs, dismissing an employee required the enterprise to discuss the matter with the trade union affiliate and report the dismissal to the local labor department. *Provisional Regulations on the Dismissal of Workers* (1986), Article 3. Workers who voluntarily transferred to another enterprise had to receive the approval of the "relevant labor administration authorities." *Provisional Regulations on the Implementation of the Contract Employment System* (1986), Article 11.

57. In the case of WFOEs, some staff chose to be hired by the FESCO and then to be transferred into WFOEs. Such workers returned to the FESCO if they were dismissed. Other workers could be hired without going through the FESCO and, if fired, they registered with the local labor department.

58. Ingmar Bjorkman and Yuan Lu, "Local or Global? HRM in International Joint Ventures in China" in *Changing Workplace Relations in the Chinese Economy,* ed. Malcolm Warner (Basingstoke, England: Macmillan, 2000), p. 120; White, "The Politics of Economic Reform," p. 373.

59. M. Francis Johnston, "Elites and Agencies," pp.159–162.

60. John Child, *Management in China during the Age of Reform* (Cambridge: Cambridge University Press, 1994), p. 170, notes that the 1986 temporary regulations did little to institute the practice of dismissal in state-owned enterprises.

61. Hong Yung Lee, "Xiagang," p. 915. Lee cites China's extraordinary figures on employment rates—59 percent, compared to just 41 percent in the United States—a product of China's attempt to spread work among a large population.

62. Guthrie, *Dragon in a Three-Piece Suit*, p. 92, quotes a manager of a state owned enterprise to the effect that state-owned enterprises, even after introducing labor contracts, "can't just let workers go or fire them." Gordon White, "The Politics of Economic Reform," p. 381, contends that young state managers were supportive of the labor contract system reform, but older managers had little interest in its implementation.

63. "Smashing 'Iron Rice Bowl' Necessary for Reform," *Shijie Jingji Daobao*, translated in *FBIS-CHI*, 88–196 (11 October 1988), p. 29.

64. Of course, dismissals did occur prior to 1994. For example, in 1987 a Sino-Hong Kong hotel JV fired 200 employees with the help of its trade union branch. The *Beijing Review* lauded this event as an example of cooperation between trade unions and management in the trade union's new role for the reform era. Yue Haitao, "Trade Union and Party Organizations," *Beijing Review* 30 (September 7, 1987), p. 26.

65. Expert on and consultant to SOEs' human resources management (C-2008–02), interview by author, Shanghai, China (2008); and Cherrie Jiuhua Zhu, *Human Resource Management*, p. 47.

66. Grace O. M. Lee and Malcolm Warner, "The Management of Human Resources in Shanghai: A Case Study of Policy Responses to Employment and Unemployment in the People's Republic of China," in *China's Business Reforms: Institutional Challenges in a Globalized Economy*, eds. Russell Smyth, On Kit Tam, Malcolm Warner, and Cherrie Jiuhua Zhu (London: RoutledgeCurzon, 2005), p. 128.

67. Zhu, *Human Resource Management*, p. 55; and expert on and consultant to SOEs' human resources management (C-2008–02), interview by author, Shanghai, China (2008).

68. *Regulations on the Placement of Surplus Staff and Workers of State-Owned Enterprises*, promulgated by State Council (20 April 1993).

69. *Labor Law* (1995), Article 16. Guthrie, *Dragon in a Three-Piece Suit*, p. 99, contends that the likelihood of a state-owned enterprise having adopted labor contracts by 1995 was a function of the enterprise's economic burdens. The greater an enterprise's burden, the more likely it was to have adopted labor contracts.

70. General manager of Japanese trading company (C-2000–029), interview by author, Shanghai, China (2000).

71. *The Labor Law* (1995), Article 30.

72. Sheila Oakley, *Labor Relations in China's Socialist Market Economy: Adapting to the Global Market* (Westport, CT: Quorum Books, 2002), pp. 76–83.

73. Cited by Lee and Warner, "The Management of Human Resources," p. 127. Fang Lee Cooke, *HRM, Work and Employment in China* (London and New York: Routledge, 2005), p. 47, cites a study that estimates 65 million workers were laid off during the period 1993–2000, although no re-employment figures were offered.

74. Cooke, *HRM, Work and Employment*, p. 48.

75. Expert on and consultant to SOEs' human resources management (C-2008–02), interview by author, Shanghai, China (2008), provided the information contained in this paragraph.

76. Zhu, *Human Resource Management in China*, p. 56; and Expert on and consultant to SOEs' human resources management (C-2008–02), interview by author, Shanghai, China (2008).

77. Ross Garnaut, Ligang Song, Stoyan Tenev, and Yang Yao, *China's Ownership Transformation: Process, Outcomes, and Prospects* (Washington, DC: International Finance Corporation, 2005), p. 93; and Zhu, *Human Resource Management in China*, p. 68. Mary Gallagher, *Contagious Capitalism: Globalization and the Politics of Labor in China* (Princeton: Princeton University Press, 2005), pp. 46–47, discusses the privatization of small- and medium-sized enterprises.

78. Expert on and consultant to SOEs' human resources management (C-2008–02), interview by author, Shanghai, China (2008).

79. *Regulation on the Placement of Surplus Staff* (1993).

80. *Procedures for the Implementation of the Regulations on Labor Management in Joint Ventures Using Chinese and Foreign Investment,* issued and promulgated by the Ministry of Labor and Personnel (19 January 1984), Article 7, calls for such compensation for dismissal in the middle or at the termination of a labor contract. Workers with more than ten years of experience who are dismissed were to receive 1.5 months' pay for every year of employment.

81. Japanese manager of trading company (C-2000–039), interview by author, Shanghai, China (2000).

82. U.S. manager of a WFOE (C-2000–061), interview by author, Shanghai, China (2000).

83. Japanese general manager of a Sino-Japanese cooperative venture (C-2000–048), interview by author, Shanghai, China (2000).

84. Anita Chan, "Labor Relations in Foreign-Funded Ventures," in *Adjusting to Capitalism: Chinese Workers and the State,* ed. Greg O'Leary (Armonk, NY: M. E. Sharpe, Inc., 1997), p. 124, suggests that Chinese authorities aspire to institute the Japanese style of consensual collective bargaining. She goes on to note that U.S. and Western firms are amenable to collective bargaining, but that most investors in China, especially those from Asian newly industrializing economies are unaccustomed to such labor practices (pp. 126 and 129–133).

85. Chinese human resources training program manager in U.S. WFOE (C-2000–063), interview by author, Shanghai, China (2000); Chinese general manager in Japanese WFOE (C-2000–046), interview by author, Shanghai, China (2000); Chinese human resources consultant (C-2003–02), interview by author, Shanghai, China (2003); and Chinese assistant general manager in Sino-Japanese JV (C-2000–015), interview by author, Shanghai, China (2000).

86. Hideshi Ito, "The Economics of the 'Company Man,'" *Japanese Economic Studies* 24, no. 6 (November–December 1996), pp. 41–42; Makoto Kumazawa, "Ability-Oriented Management in Japanese Firms," *The Japanese Economy* 25, no. 6 (November–December 1997), p. 6.

87. Mari Sako, "Introduction," in *Japanese Labour and Management in Transition,* eds. Mari Sako and Hiroki Sato (London: Routledge, 1997), pp. 4–8; Robert Cole, *Japanese Blue Collar: The Changing Tradition* (Berkeley: University of California Press, 1973).

88. For blue-collar positions, especially those in unionized firms, promotion and horizontal job transfer is more determined by seniority. For an excellent discussion of this practice, see Clair Brown et al., *Work and Pay in the United States and Japan* (New York: Oxford University Press, 1997) , p. 12.

89. Yoshio Higuchi, "Labor Turnover Behavior: Japan Versus the West," *Japanese Economic Studies* (Fall 1993), p. 67, shows that Japanese turnover rates are at

the lower end of the advanced capitalist economies of Europe, but U.S. turnover rates are roughly twice as high as Japan and European countries.

90. *Decisions on Personnel Management of Foreign Investment Enterprises,* issued by the Ministry of Labor and Personnel on 12 October 1988 and approved by the State Council (15 December 1988), Article 3, calls for government departments and Chinese enterprises "to support the transfer of their staff who have been recruited by foreign invested enterprises." *Regulations on Labor Management in Enterprises Involving Overseas Investment,* issued by the Ministry of Labor and Ministry of Foreign Trade and Economic Cooperation (11 August 1994), Article 5, states, "Enterprises must not recruit those who still hold a job at another work unit." Other regulations called for the hiring enterprise and staff member to compensate the enterprise from which the staff member departed. *Measures Governing Compensation for Losses Resulting from Violations of Labor Contract Stipulations of the Labor Law of the PRC* (10 May 1995), Article 6.

91. Margaret Pearson, *China's New Business Elite: The Political Consequences of Economic Reform* (Berkeley: University of California Press, 1997), p. 80, discusses early resistance (and its decline) to hiring staff away from state-owned enterprises. *Decisions on Personnel Management in Foreign Investment Enterprises* (1988), Article 3, calls on all administrative offices to support foreign invested enterprises' recruitment of Chinese staff from Chinese employers. Shanghai regulations create room for Chinese enterprises to seek compensation from the lost employee who is hired away and/or the foreign enterprise does the hiring. *Regulations of Shanghai Municipality on the Flow of Talented Personnel* (1996), Article 14 (at http://www.efesco.com/eng/wf/lp/lp_Labor_7.htm), allows a company to demand compensation for training and housing from the employee, if its worker is hired away in the middle of a contract. Often, such expenses are passed on to the new employer.

92. In 2000, Japanese labor turnover registered 5 percent as measured by a survey conducted by the Japanese Ministry of Labor. The turnover rate marked a high point since the Ministry began conducting the survey in 1984. Japnese Institute of Labor, *Working Conditions and the Labor Market* 40, no. 1 (January 1, 2001). http://www.jil.go.jp/bulletin/year/2001/v0140–01/02.htm.

93. Brown et al., *Work and Pay,* p. 111, argues that, despite attempts to decrease the importance of seniority in Japanese pay determinations, performance still "has little impact" on individual pay.

94. For a discussion of the economic rationale of the "late promotion" pattern in Japan, see Hideshi Ito, "The Economics of the 'Company Man,'"pp. 40–41.

95. Nailin Bu and Ji-Liang Xu, "Work-Related Attitudes among Chinese Employees *vis-à-vis* 'American' and 'Japanese' Management Models," in *Changing Workplace Relations in the Chinese Economy,* ed. Malcolm Warner (New York: St. Martin's Press, 2000), pp. 185–203.

96. Japanese general manager of a Sino-Japanese JV (C-2000–051), interview by author, Shanghai, China (2000). Manager of a Japanese WFOE (C-2000–033), interview by author, Shanghai, China (2000), echoed those comments.

97. Chinese human resources manager in a Sino-Japanese JV (C-2005–02), interview by author, Shanghai, China (2005).

98. Singaporean general manager of a Sino-Japanese JV (C-2000–032), interview by author, Shanghai, China (2000).

99. Nailin Bu and Ji-Liang Xu, "Work-Related Attitudes," p. 198, argues that Chinese workers' commitment to work organizations is "much weaker" than that of Japanese employees.

100. Leading Japanese human resource scholars at Tokyo University (J-2001–013), interview by author, Tokyo, Japan (2001).

101. Not all blue-collar workers were happy in Japanese-invested enterprises. In other locales, Chinese blue-collar workers complained about harsh working conditions in some Japanese-run factories. In the 1990s, a wave of strikes hit many foreign-invested factories, and several high-profile cases involved Japanese affiliates. In the wake of the June 4, 1989, massacre, strikes flourished in Shenzhen and Zhuhai, two special economic zones in Guangdong; 74 strikes involving 10,000 people broke out between June 1989 and December 1990. "Frequent Strikes Reported in Shenzhen," *Ming Pao* (Hong Kong), 30 January 1991, translated in *FBIS-CHI* (30 January 1991), p. 67. In Zhuhai in May 1993, 2,000 workers struck at a factory run by Mitsumi Electric. Agence France Presse, "Strike Reported at Japanese Plant in Zhuhai," translated in *FBIS-CHI*, 93–091 (13 May 1993), p. 32. In May 1994, a "massive strike" occurred against the Japanese Mabuchi Motor Co. plant in Dalian, resulting in a 45 percent wage hike. "Workers Get 45 Percent Wage Increase at Japanese Firm," *Kyodo* (14 May 1994), translated in *FBIS-CHI*, 94–096 (18 May 1994), p. 13. Again in Zhuhai Special Economic Zone, a factory run by Japan's National Panasonic faced a strike in January 1995. Harald Bruning, "Workers Strike at Japanese Factory in Zhuhai," *Eastern Express*, 17 January 1995, p. 8, translated in *FBIS-CHI*, 95–011 (18 January 1995), p. 23. Mary Gallagher, "Contagious Capitalism," pp. 178–180.

102. Rochelle Kopp, "The Rice Paper Ceiling in Japanese Companies: Why It Exists and Persists," in *Japanese Business*, Vol. IV, eds. Schon Beechler and Kristin Stucker (London and New York: Routledge, 1998).

103. Chinese human resources manager in a Sino-Japanese JV (C-2005–02), interview by author, Shanghai, China (2005).

104. Mitchell W. Sedgwick, "Do Japanese Business Practices Travel Well? Managerial Technology Transfer to Thailand," in *Japanese Multinationals*, ed. Dennis J. Encarnation (New York and Oxford: Oxford University Press, 1999), pp. 167, 168–169; H. Ishida, "Transferability of Japanese Human Resources Management Abroad," *Human Resources Management* 25, no. 1 (1986). Reprinted in *Japanese Business*, Vol. IV, eds. Schon Beechler and Kristin Stucker (London and New York: Routledge, 1998), pp. 81–83.

105. Chinese consultant for international human resources firm (C-2003–002), interview by author, Shanghai, China (2003), noted that Chinese workers prefer U.S. to Japanese firms, in part, due to better training opportunities in the former.

106. Personnel manager in Japanese parent company (J-2001–005), interview by author, Tokyo, Japan (2001) [emphasis added].

107. Senior director personnel for Japanese parent company (J-2001–004), interview by author, Tokyo, Japan (2001).

108. Brown et al., *Work and Pay*, p. 76, cites studies that U.S. firms offer training programs to professional, white-collar staff but not blue-collar employees.

109. Chinese human resources manager in Sino-Japanese JV (C-2005–02), interview by author, Shanghai, China (2005).

110. Expatriate director of research in a U.S.-invested high-tech firm (C-2000–042), interview by author, Shanghai, China (2000).

111. Chinese researcher in a U.S. high-tech company (C-2000–012), interview by author, Shanghai, China (2000). The researcher planned eventually to leave the U.S. firm in order to found his own company, thus spreading U.S.-inspired institutions.

112. Chinese human resources manager in a Sino-Japanese JV (C-2005–02), interview by author, Shanghai, China (2005).

113. Rochelle Kopp, "The Rice Paper Ceiling," p. 111; and H. Ishida, "Transferability of Japanese Human Resources Management Abroad," p. 85, found the same to be true of Japanese subsidiaries in Southeast Asia.

114. Chinese assistant general manager of a Sino-Japanese JV (C-2000–015), interview by author, Shanghai, China (2000).

115. Kazuo (John) Fukuda, "Japanese Companies in China: Problems of Human Resource Management," *Asia Pacific Business Review* 1, no. 4 (Summer 1995), p. 56, notes that Epson transferred such an approach with mixed results to its Chinese affiliates.

116. Chinese deputy general manager in Sino-Japanese JV (C-2000–059), interview by author, Shanghai, China (2000).

117. Japanese manager of Japanese trade representative office (C-2000–028), interview by author, Shanghai, China (2000).

118. Japanese president of Japanese WFOE (C-2000–062), interview by author, Shanghai, China (2000).

119. Japanese general manager in Sino-Japanese JV (C-2000–036), interview by author, Shanghai, China (2000).

120. "Job Hopping Rampant as Skilled Workers Chased," *China Daily* (14 November 2006) (http://www.chinadaily.com.cn/english/doc/2006–02/22/content_522975.htm), notes that in Shanghai and Guangzhou, some firms lose one third of their workforce each year.

121. Japanese general manager of a Sino-Japanese JV (C-2000–051), interview by author, Shanghai, China (2000).

122. Blue-collar workers rarely opted to leave Japanese factories due to a combination of limited job mobility for unskilled and semi-skilled Chinese workers and a flat pay scale in Japanese firms, which favors lower-rung employees.

123. Japanese general manager of a Sino-Japanese JV (C-2000–058), interview by author, Shanghai, China (2000).

124. President of Japanese WFOE (C-2000–062), interview by author, Shanghai, China (2000).

125. Human resources officer of Japanese parent company (J-2001–05), interview by author, Tokyo, Japan (2001).

126. Engineer in Sino-U.S. JV (C-2000–007), interview by author, Shanghai, China (2000).

127. Jim Mann, *Beijing Jeep: A Case Study of Western Business in China* (Boulder, CO: Westview Press, 1997),, pp. 201–202. Eventually, the U.S. managers became so frustrated that they abandoned the idea of disciplining workers.

128. General manager of Sino-U.S. JV (C-2000–040), interview by author, Shanghai, China (2000).

129. Managing director of U.S. WFOE (C-2000–006), interview by author, Shanghai, China (2000).

130. *Provisional Regulations Governing [the] Labor Contract System for State-Owned Enterprises,* 1986, Article 2. Translated in Josephs, *Labor Law,* p. 121.

131. U.S. regional manager for a U.S. corporation with several factories in China (C-2000–006), interview by author, Shanghai, China (2000).

132. U.S. assistant general manager in a Sino-U.S. JV (C-2000–054), interview by author, Shanghai, China (2000).

133. U.S. engineer at Sino-U.S. JV (C-2000–010), interview by author, Shanghai, China (2000) [emphasis added].

134. Chinese HR manager in Sino-Japanese JV (C-2000–055), interview by author, Shanghai, China (2000).

135. Japanese general manager in Sino-Japanese JV (C-2000–062), interview by author, Shanghai, China (2000).

136. Kazuo Koike, "White-Collar Workers in Japan and the United States: Which Are More Ability Oriented?" in *The Transformation of the Japanese Economy,* ed. Kazuo Sato (Armonk, NY: M. E. Sharpe, 1999), p. 185; and Chinese human resources manager in a Sino-U.S. JV (C-2005–01), interview by author, Shanghai, China (2005).

137. *Labor Law* (1995), Article 25, permits employers to dismiss hirees after a probationary period of observation of up to six months.

138. U.S. manager in U.S. WFOE (C-2000–061), interview by author, Shanghai, China (2000).

139. Chinese human resources manager in Sino-U.S. JV (C-2000–044), interview by author, Shanghai, China (2000).

140. Robert Cole, *Work, Mobility, Participation* (Berkeley: University of California Press, 1979), showed that his sample of workers in Detroit had a 16 percent annual quit rate, while workers in Yokohama had an annual quit rate of 8 percent. Jacob Mincer and Yoshio Higuchi, "Wage Structures and Labor Turnover in the United States and Japan," *NBER Working Paper* no. 2306, cites more starkly contrasting statistics, 16.6 percent quit rates in the United States and 4.9 percent in Japan. Both works cited in James Lincoln, "Commitment Quits and Work Organization in Japanese and US Plants," *Industrial and Labor Relations Review* 50 (October 1996), fn. 7.

141. Yoshio Higuchi, "Labor Turnover Behavior," p. 67, cites figures showing that the United States has a turnover rate that is twice that of Japan.

142. Chinese assistant general manager in a Sino-Japanese JV (C-2000–015), interview by author, Shanghai, China (2000); and Chinese human resources training program manager (C-2000–063) interview by author, Shanghai, China (2000). In a survey of Chinese employees, Ma Chengsan found high levels of satisfaction with both U.S. and Japanese employers, but 37.9 percent of employees in Japanese companies "occasionally" had trouble with their employers, slightly higher than the 24.5 percent figure in U.S. affiliates. Ma Chengsan, *Labor Disputes at Foreign Enterprises in China* (Tokyo: Fuji Research Institute Corporation, 1998), p. 26.

143. According to a Chinese Communist Party journal, only 17 percent of foreign invested enterprises had party cells. Cited in "The Withering Away of the Party," *The Economist* (30 May 2002). A Chinese article complains, "Party organizations share no power or position in solely foreign owned enterprises." So, even the presence of a party cell is no guarantee of shared control over a firm's operations. Peng Xin'an, "Strengthening the Party in Foreign-owned Enterprises," *Dangxiao Luntan,* no. 12 (5 December 1993), pp. 49–51, translated in *JPRS-CAR,* 94–018 (18 March 1994).

144. Pearson, *China's New Business Elite,* p. 74, suggests that foreign investment has weakened the dossier system of control.

145. Pearson, *China's New Business Elite*, pp. 87–95 and 137, argues that local managers in foreign invested enterprises have developed reformist views on the party and on China's economy, although those views do not necessarily lead to a democratic outlook.

146. Chinese general manager of a Sino-U.S. JV (C-2000–041), interview by author, Shanghai, China (2000).

147. *Ibid.*

148. Expert on and consultant to SOEs' human resources management (C-2008–02), interview by author, Shanghai, China (2008).

149. A consultant at Hewitt, an international human resources consulting firm, reported that by 2003 the pattern of foreign invested enterprises poaching from one another had shifted to SOEs poaching from foreign invested firms. U.S. consultant in international human resources and management firm (C-2003–001), interview by author, Shanghai, China (2003).

150. Anita Chan and Robert A. Senser, "China's Troubled Waters," *Foreign Affairs* 76, no. 2 (March–April 1997), pp. 104–117.

151. *Labor Contract Law of the People's Republic of China*, promulgated 29 June 2007 effective (1 January 2008), Articles 14 and 19.

152. Wei Jie, "Huawei Denies Circumventing New Labor Law," *Shenzhen Daily* (7 November 2007). http://paper.sznews.com/szdaily/20071107/ca2819038.htm.

153. Russell Flannery, "An Air of Mystery," *Forbes* (29 November 2004). http://www.forbes.com/global/2004/1129/030.html; and Brad Reese, "Cisco vs. Chinese Military Partner—Huawei Technologies," *Ciscosubnet* (21 January 2008). http://www.networkworld.com/community/node/24176, cites a Rand Report on Huawei's links to the Chinese government.

154. "Workers Protest over Job Losses before Labor Law," *Shanghai Daily* (December 10, 2007). http://www.civillaw.com.cn/english/article.asp?id=1282

155. "Union Warns Bosses over Moves to Terminate Contracts," *Shanghai Daily* (14 December 2007).

156. The US-China Business Council posted its detailed and constructive response to the second draft version of the Labor Contract Law on its website. US-China Business Council, "Comments on the Draft People's Republic of China Law on Employment Contracts (Draft of December 24, 2006)," letter dated 31 January 2007. http://uschina.org/public/documents/2007/01/comments-employment-contracts-english.pdf

157. The American Chamber of Commerce-Shanghai, "Response to China's New Labor Contract Law," letter dated (4 July 2007). http://www.amcham-shanghai.org/NR/rdonlyres/DE724602–2608–4FF5–94E2-DDD2805521C3/4492/AmChamShResponsetoLCLJuly2007.pdf

158. Jonathan Unger and Anita Chan, "China, Corporatism, and the East Asian Model," pp. 29–53; Malcolm Warner and Ying Zhu, "The Origins of Chinese 'Industrial Relations,'" pp. 28 and 30; and Hong Yung Lee, "Xiagang, the Chinese Style of Laying off Workers," *Asian Survey* XL, no. 6 (November–December 2000), pp. 936–937 claims that Japanese and European more than U.S. styles of handling layoffs are suitable for China.

159. My claim supports a similar assertion by Nailin Bu and Ji-Liang Xu, "Work-Related Attitudes," p. 185.

160. U.S. general manager of Sino-U.S. JV (C-2003–04), interview by author, Shanghai, China (2003).

161. U.S. consultant for international human resources and management consulting firm (C-2003–01), interview by author, Shanghai, China (2003).

162. Chinese consultant for international human resources and management consulting firm (C-2003–02), interview by author, Shanghai, China (2003).

Chapter Seven

1. John J. Mearsheimer, "China's Unpeaceful Rise," *Current History* (April 2006), p. 162; John J. Mearsheimer, "Better To Be Godzilla than Bambi," *Foreign Policy*, no. 146 (January/February 2005); Bates Gill, "China's Evolving Regional Security Strategy," in *Power Shift: China and Asia's New Dynamics*, ed. David Shambaugh (Berkeley: University of California Press, 2005), pp. 261–262; and David Shambaugh, "Containment or Engagement of China?" *International Security* 21, no. 2 (Fall 1996), p. 187.

2. Evan S. Medeiros, "Strategic Hedging and the Future of Asia-Pacific Stability," *The Washington Quarterly* 29, no. 1 (2005), pp. 145–167.

3. Randall L. Schweller, "Managing the Rise of Great Powers: History and Theory," in *Engaging China: The Management of an Emerging Power*, eds. Alastair Iain Johnston and Robert S. Ross (London and New York: Routledge, 1999), p. 14.

4. Zheng Yunling and Tang Shiping, "China's Regional Strategy," in *Power Shift: China and Asia's New Dynamics*, ed. David Shambaugh (Berkeley: University of California Press, 2005), pp. 50–59; and Jonathan D. Pollack, "The Transformation of the Asian Security Order: Assessing China's Impact," in *Power Shift*, p. 340.

5. Schweller, "Rise of Great Powers," pp. 2–3; Mearsheimer, "China's Unpeaceful Rise," pp. 159–161; and Mearsheimer, "Better To Be Godzilla."

6. Mearsheimer, "China's Unpeaceful Rise," pp. 159–161; Mearsheimer, "Better To Be Godzilla"; Richard Bernstein and Ross H. Munro, "The Coming Conflict with America," *Foreign Affairs* 76, no. 2 (March–April 1997), pp. 18–32; Aaron L. Friedberg, "The Future of U.S.-China Relations: Is Conflict Inevitable?" *International Security* 30, no. 2 (Fall 2005), p. 21; and Avery Goldstein, *Rising to the Challenge: China's Grand Strategy and International Security* (Stanford: Stanford University Press, 2005), p. 218, calls for a policy of "congagement," which blends elements of containment and engagement.

7. Anita Chan, "Labor Standards and Human Rights: The Case of Chinese Workers under Market Socialism," *Human Rights Quarterly* 20, no. 4 (1998), pp. 886–904; Robert E. Scott, "The Wal-Mart Effect: Its Chinese Imports Have Displaced Nearly 200,000 U.S. Jobs," *EPI Issue Brief*, no. 235 (26 June 2007) http://www.epi.org/content.cfm/ib235; Friedberg, "The Future of U.S.-China Relations," p. 18; and Shambaugh, "Containment or Engagement," pp. 180–209.

8. David Lampton, *Same Bed, Different Dreams: Managing US-China Relations 1989–2000* (Berkeley: University of California Press, 2000); Shambaugh, "Containment or Engagement of China?" pp. 180–209; and "A Risky Tilt in U.S. Foreign Policy," *BusinessWeek* (May 28, 2001), http://www.businessweek.com/magazine/content/01_22/b3734177.htm.

9. Adam Segal, "Practical Engagement: Drawing a Fine Line for U.S.-China Trade," *The Washington Quarterly* 27, no. 3 (Summer 2004), pp. 157–173.

10. Phillip C. Saunders, "Supping with a Long Spoon: Dependence and Interdependence in Sino-American Relations," *The China Journal*, no. 43 (January, 2000), pp. 55–81; and Lampton, *Same Bed, Different Dreams*.

11. Michael A. Santoro, *Profits and Principles: Global Capitalism and Human Rights in China* (Ithaca and London.: Cornell University Press, 2000).

12. Mary E. Gallagher, "'Reform and Openness': Why China's Economic Reforms Have Delayed Democracy," *World Politics* 54 (April 2002), pp. 338–372; Doug Guthrie, *China and Globalization: The Social, Economic and Political Transformation of Chinese Society* (London and New York Routledge, 2006); and Margaret Pearson, *China's New Business Elite: The Political Consequences of China's Economic Reforms* (Berkeley: University of California Press, 1997), analyze the affect of foreign direct investment on China's prospects for democracy; Yasheng Huang, *Selling China: Foreign Investment during the Reform Era* (New York: Cambridge University Press, 2003), discusses how China's restrictive policy on private enterprise left China prone to foreign investors; Hongying Wang, *Weak State, Strong Networks*; and Qunjian Tian, *Government, Business, and the Politics of Interdependence and Conflict across the Taiwan Strait* (New York: Palgrave-Macmillan, 2006), address the role of personal relations in facilitating foreign investment in China; Doug Guthrie, *Dragon in a Three-Piece Suit: The Emergence of Capitalism in China* (Princeton: Princeton University Press, 1999), links foreign investment to the diffusion of international business practices to SOEs; and Eric Thun, *Changing Lanes in China: Foreign Direct Investment, Local Governments, and Auto Sector Development* (Cambridge: Cambridge University Press, 2006); and Zheng Yongnian, *Globalization and State Transformation in China* (Cambridge: Cambridge University Press, 2004), relate foreign investment to changes in China's state structure.

13. Lampton, *Same Bed, Different Dreams*; and Saunders, "Supping with a Long Spoon," pp. 55–81, are exceptions.

14. Rosemary Foot, "Chinese Power and the Idea of a Responsible State," *The China Journal*, no. 45 (January, 2001), pp. 1–19.

15. David Lampton, "China's Rise in Asia Need Not Be at America's Expense," in *Power Shift*, p. 320; Susan Shirk, *China: Fragile Superpower* (New York: Oxford University Press, 2007), pp. 10–11, suggests that China displays status quo intentions, but those intentions could change in the context of a crisis; and Adam Segal, "Chinese Economic Statecraft and the Political Economy of Asian Security," in *China's Rise and the Balance of Influence in Asia*, eds. William W. Keller and Thomas G. Rawski (Pittsburgh: University of Pittsburgh Press, 2007), p. 153, calls "China a status quo power in Asia."

16. Pitman B. Potter, "China and the International Legal System: Challenges of Participation," *The China Quarterly*, no. 191 (September 2007), pp. 699–715.

17. Gill, "China's Evolving Regional Security Strategy," pp. 261–262; Robert S. Ross, "Beijing as a Conservative Power," *Foreign Policy* 76, no. 2 (March–April 1997), p. 35 and 37, argues that China is a revisionist power but will remain a status quo country for the present due to its relative weakness; and Thomas Christensen, "The Contemporary Security Dilemma: Deterring a Taiwan Conflict," *The Washington Quarterly* 25, no. 4 (2002), pp. 6–7.

18. Shambaugh, "Containment or Engagement?"; Mearsheimer, "China's Unpeaceful Rise"; and Gill, "China's Evolving Regional Security Strategy," pp. 261–262.

19. James V. Feinerman, "Chinese Participation in the International Legal Order: Rogue Elephant or Team Player?" *The China Quarterly*, no. 161 (March 2000), pp. 124–141; and Pitman B. Potter, "China and the International Legal System," pp. 699–715.

20. Foot, "Chinese Power," pp. 2–3 and 9–10; and Jack Donnelly, "Human Rights, Democracy, and Development," *Human Rights Quarterly* 21, no. 3 (1999), pp. 608–632.

21. Foot, "Chinese Power," p. 18.

22. Robert G. Sutter, *Chinese Foreign Relations: Power and Policy since the Cold War* (Lanham: Rowman and Littlefield, 2008), p. 117; and Alastair I. Johnston, "Is China a Status Quo Power?" *International Security* 27, no. 4 (Spring 2003), pp. 14–15.

23. Neil MacFarquhar, "2 Vetoes Quash U.N. Sanctions on Zimbabwe," *New York Times* (12 July 2008), http://www.nytimes.com/2008/07/12/world/africa/12zimbabwe.html?_r=1&scp=1&sq=2%20vetoes%20quash%20un%20sanctions&st=cse&oref=slogin, notes that China likely would not have vetoed Security Council sanctions against Zimbabwe had Russia not vetoed the measure as well; and Robert G. Sutter, *Chinese Foreign Relations*, pp. 117–118; and Yitzhak Shichor, "China's Voting Behavior in the Security Council," *China Brief* 6, no. 18 (6 September 2006). http://www.jamestown.org/publications_details.php?volume_id=415&issue_id=3845&article_id=2371415, notes that China, as of mid-2006, had only used its veto power twice since joining the Security Council in 1971—once in 1972, to block Bangladesh's admission as a member, and a second time in 1999, not to extend the deployment of UN troops to Macedonia. In contrast, the United States had cast 76 veto votes in the Security Council during the same period of time.

24. Yong Deng and Thomas G. Moore, "China Views Globalization: Toward a New Great-Power Politics," *The Washington Quarterly* 27, no. 3 (Summer 2004), p. 117. Sutter, *China's Foreign Relations*, p. 298, makes a similar point.

25. William R. Hawkins, "Competing Interests Divide U.S. Policy," *China Brief* 6, issue 13 (June 21, 2006), pp. 6–7 (http://www.jamestown.org/images/pdf/cb_006_013.pdf); Testimony of Representative Frank R. Wolf, House Committee on Ways and Means, Subcommittee on Trade, Permanent Normal Trade Relations for China, http://www.globalsecurity.org/wmd/library/news/china/2000/000503-prc-usia4.htm; Alastair I. Johnston, "Is China a Status Quo Power?" p. 56, argues against this position.

26. David Shambaugh, "China Engages Asia: Reshaping the Regional Order," *International Security* 29, no. 3 (Winter 2004–2005), pp. 64–99.

27. David Shambaugh, "China Engages Asia"; David C. Kang, "Getting Asia Wrong: The Need for New Analytical Frameworks," *International Security* 27, no. 4 (Spring 2003), pp. 57–85; Amitav Acharya, "Will Asia's Past Be Its Future," *International Security* 28, no. 3 (Winter 2003–2004), pp. 151–153, argues that Asian countries are not bandwagoning with China, according to accepted definitions of bandwagoning.

28. Shambaugh, "China Engages Asia," p. 73, claims that China suggests Asian multilateral organizations "may have some utility in constraining the United States in the region."

29. Sutter, *Chinese Foreign Relations*, pp. 11, 82, 404–408; Adam Segal, "Chinese Economic Statecraft," p. 159, also sees China's neighbors shaping the institutional context in which China is rising.

30. Zhang Yunling and Tang Shiping, "China's Regional Strategy," p. 56.

31. Yong Deng and Thomas G. Moore, "China Views Globalization," p. 126; David Shambaugh, "China Engages Asia," p. 74, also acknowledges this point.

32. Thomas J. Christensen, "Fostering Stability or Creating a Monster? The Rise of China and U.S. Policy toward East Asia," *International Security* 31, no. 1 (Summer 2006), pp. 81–126; and Aaron L. Friedberg, "The Future of U.S.-China Relations," pp. 7–45, discuss the divergent views that liberals and realists hold of China's position in these groups.

33. John J. Mersheimer, "False Promise of International Institutions," *International Security* 19, no. 3 (Winter 1994–1995), pp. 5–49, makes a general argument against the use of institutions to induce peace.

34. "Chinese Army Told to Shut up Shop," *BBC News* (23 July 1998), http://news.bbc.co.uk/2/hi/asia-pacific/137682.stm; Johnston, "Is China a Status Quo Power?" pp. 16–17, suggests that WMD proliferation improved around 1996.

35. Shiping Zheng, *Party vs. State in Post-1949 China: The Institutional Dilemma* (Cambridge: Cambridge University Press, 1997), p. 240.

36. Joby Warrick and Peter Slevin, "Libyan Arms Designs Traced back to China," *Washington Post* (15 February 2004), p. A01 (http://www.washingtonpost.com/ac2/wp-dyn/A42692–2004Feb14?language=printer); Bates Gill and Evan S. Medeiros, "Foreign and Domestic Influences on China's Arms Controls and Nonproliferation Policies," *The China Quarterly*, no. 161 (March 2000), pp. 77–81.

37. Carin Zissis, "Modernizing the People's Liberation Army of China," *Backgrounder* 5 (December 2006) (Council on Foreign Relations). http://www.cfr.org/publication/12174/

38. Ross, "Beijing as a Conservative Power," p. 41.

39. Gill and Medeiros, "Foreign and Domestic Influences," pp. 92–93.

40. Stephanie Lieggi, "China's New Export Controls," *CNS Web Report* (24 October 2002). http://cns.miis.edu/research/china/chiexp/chiexp.htm

41. Cited in Johnston, "Is China a Status Quo Power?" p. 18. Johnston goes on to note that China has complied with the Comprehensive Test Ban Treaty (CTBT).

42. Jeff Abramson and Jessica Lasky-Fink, "Chinese Arms Shipment Sparks Outrage," *Arms Control Today* (June 2008). http://www.armscontrol.org/act/2008_06/ChinaArms.asp

43. Carin Zissis, "Modernizing the People's Liberation Army," quotes Jonathan D. Pollack of the Naval War College who contends, against Department of Defense claims, that China's military budgets are now transparent.

44. Jim Garamone, "Gates Discusses Steps to Deepen Military Exchanges with China," *Armed Forces Press Service* (5 November 2007). http://www.defenselink.mil/news/newsarticle.aspx?id=48042

45. For a critical analysis of China's efforts to modernize its military, see David Shambaugh, *Modernizing China's Military: Progress, Problems, and Prospects* (Berkeley: University of California Press, 2004).

46. Joseph Kahn, "China Warmly Welcomes Taiwan Opposition Leader," *New York Times* (29 April 2005). http://www.nytimes.com/2005/04/29/international/asia/29cnd-taiw.html?_r=1&scp=2&sq=lien%20chan%20china&st=cse&oref=slogin

47. Robert S. Ross, "Balance of Power Politics and the Rise of China: Accommodation and Balancing in East Asia," in *China's Rise and the Balance of Influence in Asia*, eds. William W. Keller and Thomas G. Rawski (Pittsburgh: University of

Pittsburgh Press, 2007), pp. 128–129; Michael D. Swaine, "China's Regional Military Posture," in *Power Shift*, pp. 272–273; Avery Goldstein, *Rising to the Challenge: China's Grand Strategy and International Security* (Stanford: Stanford University Press, 2005), pp. 61–62; and Shambaugh, *Modernizing China's Military*, p. 270, notes that great powers project power with aircraft carriers, which China has not been able to purchase or produce on its own.

48. Friedberg, "The Future of US-China Relations," pp. 22–24.

49. Garamone, "Gates Discusses Steps."

50. United States Department of Defense, *Military Power of the People's Republic of China, Annual Report to Congress* (2008), p. 6. http://www.scribd.com/doc/3290889/China-Military-Report-08

51. Shambaugh, "China Engages Asia," pp. 64–99.

52. Sutter, *Chinese Foreign Relations*, pp. 401–408; Robert S. Ross, "Balance of Power Politics and the Rise of China: Accommodation and Balancing in East Asia," in *China's Rise and the Balance of Influence in Asia*, eds. William W. Keller and Thomas G. Rawski (Pittsburgh: University of Pittsburgh Press, 2007), pp. 133–143, codes a mixture of accommodating and balancing nations among China's neighbors.

53. Representative of international business association (C-2007–01), interview by author, Shanghai, China (2007); associate of international business association (C-2007–05), interview by author, Shanghai, China (2007); and director of Chinese NGO (C-2007–14), interview by author, Beijing, China (2007). Pitman B. Potter, "China and the International Legal System," pp. 704–705, argues that Chinese efforts to solicit societal input into drafting legislation has been uneven and that non-transparency remains a problem.

54. Calculated from National Bureau of Statistics of China, *China Statistical Yearbook* (Beijing: China Statistics Press, various years). http://www.stats.gov.cn/english/statisticaldata/yearlydata/

55. Avery Goldstein, "Great Expectations: Interpreting China's Arrival," *International Security* 22, no. 3 (Winter 1997–1998), pp. 54–55.

56. Office of the Secretary of Defense, *The Military Power of the People's Republic of China, 2005: A Report to Congress Pursuant to the National Defense Authorization Act Fiscal Year 2000* (Washington, DC: 2005), pp. 21–22.

57. Bernstein and Munro, "The Coming Conflict with America," p. 25.

58. Shambaugh, *Modernizing China's Military*.

59. Keith Crane, Roger Cliff, Evan Medeiros, James Mulvenon, and William Overholt, *Modernizing China's Military: Opportunities and Constraints* (Santa Monica: Rand Corporation, 2005), p. xxiv.

60. Saunders, "Supping with a Long Spoon," p. 81.

61. Dali Yang, "Trying to Stay in Control," *Current History* 106 (September 2007), pp. 249–251, uses the term, "GNPism"; and William W. Keller and Thomas G. Rawski, "China's Peaceful Rise: Road Map or Fantasy?" in *China's Rise*, pp. 194–195, note the "unspoken contract" for the CCP to provide for economic growth in exchange for continued rule.

62. Calculated from National Bureau of Statistics of China, *China Statistical Yearbook* (Beijing: China Statistics Press, various years). http://www.stats.gov.cn/english/statisticaldata/yearlydata/

63. David Barboza, "Some Assembly Needed: China as Asia's Factory," *New York Times* (9 February 2006). http://www.nytimes.com/2006/02/09/business/worldbusiness/09asia.html, quotes Yasheng Huang.

64. Johnston, "Is China a Status Quo Power?"

65. Shirk, *China: Fragile Superpower*, pp. 29–30.

66. John Giles, Albert Park, and Juwei Zhang, "What Is China's True Unemployment Rate," *China Economic Review* 16, no. 2 (2005), pp. 149–170, estimate the 2002 unemployment rate among permanent urban residents to be 14 percent. Charles Wolf, Jr., "China's Rising Unemployment Challenge," *Asian Wall Street Journal* (7 July 2004), estimates Chinese unemployment rate in 2003 was 23 percent. China's official unemployment rate has hovered around 4.5 percent in recent years.

67. The recalibration of PPP exchange rates across currencies was necessary because the Chinese yuan's value had not been recalculated since 1985, when most Chinese goods were subsidized and not exposed to market-based pricing. By 2005, most commodities' prices were marketized, so the gap between the stated and real purchasing power of the Chinese yuan (compared to the U.S. dollar) had narrowed significantly. Calculated from "Special Focus—New PPPs and China's Economy," *World Bank China Quarterly Update* (January 2008), for a discussion of the changes.

68. Sutter, *Chinese Foreign Relations*, p. 94.

69. Calculated from "Special Focus—New PPPs and China's Economy," *World Bank China Quarterly Update*, (January 2008). http://web.worldbank.org/WEBSITE/EXTERNAL/COUNTRIES/EASTASIAPACIFICEXT/CHINAEXTN/0,contentMDK:21639761~pagePK:141137~piPK:141127~theSitePK:318950,00.html

70. Selim Elekdag and Subir Lall, "Global Growth Estimates Trimmed after PPP Revisions," *IMF Survey Magazine: IMF Research* (8 January 2008). http://www.imf.org/external/pubs/ft/survey/so/2008/RES018A.htm

71. Zhang Yuling and Tang Shiping, "China's Regional Strategy," p. 48.

72. Anita Chan and Robert J. Ross, "Racing to the Bottom: International Trade without a Social Cause," *Third World Quarterly* 24, no. 6 (December 2003), pp. 1011–1028.

73. Ming Wan, "Human Rights Lawmaking in China: Domestic Politics, International Law, and International Politics," *Human Rights Quarterly* 29 (2007), pp. 727–753; Andrew J. Nathan and Robert S. Ross, *The Great Wall and the Empty Fortress: China's Search for Security* (New York and London: W. W. Norton, 1997), p. 234; Alan M. Wachman, "Does the Diplomacy of Shame Promote Human Rights in China?" *Third World Quarterly* 22, no. 2 (April 2001), pp. 257–281; and Michael A. Santoro, *Profits and Principles*, pp. 44–71.

74. Johnston, "Is China a Status Quo Power?" p. 20.

75. *UN Declaration of Human Rights*, adopted and proclaimed by General Assembly Resolution 217 A (III) of 10 December 1948.

76. *International Covenant on Civil and Political Rights*, adopted and open for signature, ratification, and accession by General Assembly resolution 2200A (XXI) of 16 December 1966, entry into force 23 March 1976.

77. *International Covenant on Economic, Social, and Cultural Rights*, adopted and open for signature, ratification, and accession by General Assembly resolution 2200A (XXI) of 16 December 1966, entry into force 3 January 1976.

78. United Nations General Assembly, *Vienna Declaration and Programme of Action*, adopted by World Conference on Human Rights (12 July 1993), articles 5 and 72.

79. *Vienna Declaration*, article 10.

80. Potter, "China and the International Legal System," p. 710; Johnston, "Is China a Status Quo Power?" p. 20; and Wachman, "Does the Diplomacy of Shame," p. 271.

81. Article 19 notes that poverty impedes attainment of other human rights.

82. Chinese lawyer and activist (C-2007–057), interview by author, Shanghai, China (2008); Ming Wan, "Human Rights Lawmaking in China," pp. 727–753; and Alan M. Wachman, "Does the Diplomacy of Shame," pp. 257–281.

83. Ming Wan, "Human Rights Lawmaking in China," p. 748. According to a report in the *China Daily*, the Supreme People's Court overturned 15 percent of all death sentences in the first half of 2008 and there had been a 30 percent drop in death sentences handed down in 2007 from the previous year. Xie Chuanjiao, "Top Court Overturns 15% Death Sentences in 1st Half Year," *China Daily* (27 June 2008). http://www.chinadaily.com.cn/china/2008–06/27/content_6798854.htm; "China Sees 30% Drop in Death Penalty," *Xinhua* (10 May 2008). http://www.chinadaily.com.cn/china/2008–05/10/content_6675006.htm Both reports cited in "Welcome Reduction in Use of Capital Punishment in China," *Dui Hua Human Right Journal* (27 June 2008). http://www.duihua.org/hrjournal/2008/06/welcome-reduction-in-use-of-capital.html.

84. Anita Chan, "Labor Relations in Foreign-funded Ventures, Chinese Trade Unions, and the Prospects for Collective Bargaining," in *Adjusting to Capitalism: Chinese Workers and the State*, ed. Greg O'Leary (Armonk, NY: M. E. Sharpe, 1998).

85. A highly publicized instance of such abusive labor conditions involves brick kiln factories in Shanxi and Henan Provinces, where local officials were investigated and arrested for their lack of oversight of the factories. In one instance, the factory owner's father was the local Communist Party secretary who was subsequently expelled from the party. "Chinese Brick Factory Faces Allegations," *Online Newshour* (25 June 2007). http://www.pbs.org/newshour/bb/asia/jan-june07/labor_06–25.html; Zhu Zhe, "More Than 460 Rescued from Brick Kiln Slavery," *China Daily* (15 June 2007). http://www.chinadaily.com.cn/china/2007–06/15/content_894802.htm; "95 Officials Punished in Slave-labor Scandal," *Shanghai Daily* (16 July 2007). http://www.china.org.cn/government/local_governments/2007–07/16/content_1217212.htm

86. Michael Santoro, *Profits and Principles*; Michael Santoro, "Beyond Codes of Conduct and Monitoring: An Organizational Approach to Global Labor Practices," *Human Rights Quarterly* 25, no. 2 (2003), pp. 407–424.

87. Santoro, *Profits and Principles*.

88. The argument can be made that foreign firms hire many migrant workers who are not under contract and whose wages are not included in the average wages of firms. That may be true, but there are two caveats to such a point. First, many domestic firms, including SOEs, now hire migrant workers, so the effect of migrant workers may not be significant. Second, most of the migrant workers come from much worse employment circumstances, so they are improving their wages as they enter into even low-paying jobs. FIEs are not making migrant workers worse off.

89. Chan, "Labor Relations in Foreign-funded Ventures," pp. 122–149; and Chan, "Labor Standards and Human Rights," p. 893.

90. Human resources officer in U.S. WFOE (C-2000–063), interview by author, Shanghai, China (2000).

91. Santoro, *Profits and Principles*.

92. Representative of foreign business organization (C-2007–01), interview by author, Shanghai, China (2007); and representative of foreign business organization (C-2007–05), interview by author, Shanghai, China (2007).

93. "China Faces Labor Shortage," *Asia Times* (16 May 2007). http://www.atimes.com/atimes/China_Business/IE16Cb01.html; David Barboza, "Labor Shortage in China May Lead to Trade Shift," *New York Times* (3 April 2006). http://www.nytimes.com/2006/04/03/business/03labor.html; and Keith Bradshear, "Investors Seek Asian Options to Costly China," *New York Times* (18 June 2008). http://www.nytimes.com/2008/06/18/business/worldbusiness/18invest.html?scp=1&sq=china+labor&st=nyt

94. Program manager of international NGO (C-2007–005), interview by author, Shanghai, China (2007); professors at Chinese university (C-2007–007), interview by author, Shanghai, China (2007); and officer of Chinese domestic NGO (C-2007–017), interview by author, Shanghai, China (2007).

95. "Going Global," *The Economist* (17 January 2008). http://www.economist.com/surveys/displaystory.cfm?story_id=10491136; Program Manager of International NGO (C-2007–005), interview by author, Shanghai, China (2007); and Nick Farrell, "iPod Maker Admits Breaking Chinese Labour Laws," *The Inquirer* (26 June 2006). http://www.theinquirer.net/en/inquirer/news/2006/06/26/ipod-maker-admits-breaking-chinese-labour-laws

96. 李晓艳, "社会责任认证考验中国出口企业," 南方周末 (24 June 2004). http://www.nanfangdaily.com.cn/ZM/20040624/jj/qs/200406240034.asp, calls for China to apply its Labor Law and SA8000 standards to improve labor conditions in domestic firms.

97. CSR associate in FIE (C-2007–13), interview by author, Shanghai, China (2007).

98. Program manager of international NGO (C-2007–005), interview by author, Shanghai, China (2007); and officer of Chinese domestic NGO (C-2007–017), interview by author, Shanghai, China (2007).

99. Jim Yardley and David Barboza, "Many Hands, Not Held by China, Aid in Quake," *New York Times* (20 May 2008). http://www.nytimes.com/2008/05/20/world/asia/20citizens.html?scp=1&sq=many+hands+not+held+by+china&st=nyt

100. Rujun Shen, "Foreign Firms in China 'Stint on Quake Aid,' " *The Australian* (20 May 2008). http://www.theaustralian.news.com.au/story/0,25197,23729926-12335,00.html

101. G. John Ikenberry, "The Rise of China and the Future of the West: Can the Liberal System Survive?" *Foreign Affairs* 87, no. 1 (January–February 2008), p. 37.

102. "Decision of the Standing Committee of the National People's Congress on Amending the Judges Law of the Peoples Republic of China," promulgated by the Standing Committee of the National People's Congress on 30 June 2001 and effective (1 January 2002). http://www.7139.com/enfl/fl/200707/16748.html

103. Randall Peerenboom, *China's Long March Toward Rule of Law* (Cambridge: Cambridge University Press, 2002), pp. 289–295, offers a critical discussion of China's attempts to improve the competence of judges with particular attention to the selection process.

104. Kevin J. O'Brien and Lianjiang Li, *Rightful Resistance in Rural China* (Cambridge and New York: Cambridge University Press, 2006).

105. Fu Hualing, *Creating a Support Structure for Rights: Legal Aid and the Rule of Law in China*, Report Prepared for the Asia Foundation (December 2005),

discusses the role of legal aid centers in helping to defend and to assert average citizens' rights.

106. Mary E. Gallagher, "'Use the Law as Your Weapon!' Institutional Change and Legal Mobilization in China," in *Engaging the Law in China: State, Society, and Possibilities for Justice*, eds. Neil J. Diamant, Stanley B. Lubman, and Kevin J. O'Brien (Stanford: Stanford University Press 2005), pp. 54–83.

107. "China's Legislature Approves New Contract Labor Law," *International Herald Tribune* (29 June 2007). http://www.iht.com/articles/ap/2007/06/29/asia/AS-GEN-China-Labor-Law.php

108. Dispute Settlement Body, "DSB Adopts Panel and Appellate Body Reports on US Steel Safeguards," *WTO News* (10 December 2003). http://www.wto.org/english/news_e/news_e.htm

109. "China Opposes US Ruling on Pipe Dumping Duties," *Ministry of Metalurgical Industries Daily News* (17 June 2008). http://www.mmi.gov.cn/mmi_en/submenu.htm

110. United States Trade Representative, *2006 Report to Congress on China's WTO Compliance*, (11 December 2006), pp. 3, 6, and 96–100. http://www.ustr.gov/assets/Document_Library/Reports_Publications/2006/asset_upload_file688_10223.pdf

111. Potter, "China and the International Legal System," pp. 707–708.

112. "Law Is the Basic Language with Which We Communicate with the World," *Chinacourt* (24 March 2004). http://www.chinacourt.org/public/detail.php?id=155574&k_author=&k_content=&k_title=

113. Kevin J. O'Brien and Lianjiang Li, *Rightful Resistance*.

114. Yong Deng and Thomas G. Moore, "China Views Globalization," p. 129.

115. John C. K. Daly, "Energy Concerns and China's Unresolved Territorial Pursuits," *China Brief* 4, no. 24 (7 December 2004). http://www.jamestown.org/terrorism/news/article.php?articleid=2372940

116. China has made progress with Japan on competing claims to offshore territories with mineral resources. Martin Fackler, "China and Japan in Deal over Contested Gas Fields," *New York Times* (19 June 2008). http://www.nytimes.com/2008/06/19/world/asia/19sea.html?_r=1&ref=world&oref=slogin

117. M. Taylor Fravel, "Power Shifts and Escalation: Explaining China's Use of Force in Territorial Disputes," *International Security* 32, no. 3 (2008), pp. 43–44.

118. Rosemary Foot, "Chinese Power," pp. 13–14, citing a study by Michael Swaine and Iain Johnston.

119. Nicholas R. Lardy, *Integrating China into the Global Economy* (Washington, DC: Brookings Institution Press, 2002), p. 104.

120. The US-China Business Council, "China's Implementation of Its World Trade Organization Commitments," Trade Policy Staff Committee Hearing (27 September 2007). http://www.uschina.org/public/documents/2007/09/uscbc-china-wto-implementation-testimony.pdf

121. Xiao Yang, who served as minister of justice (1993–1998) and president of the Chinese Supreme People's Court (1998–2008), was an important agent in the professionalization of the courts and the bench of judges. In addition to measures to increase upper courts monitoring of lower courts, Xiao Yang led the effort to create a qualifying exam for new judges, which China only adopted in 2001.

122. Sutter, *Chinese Foreign Relations*, p. 99.

123. U.S. Trade Representative, *2006 Report to Congress*, pp. 6–7.

124. Ann Kent, "States Monitoring States: The United States, Australia, and China's Human Rights, 1990–2001," *Human Rights Quarterly* 23 (2001), p. 618.

125. Fu Hualing, *Creating a Support Structure for Rights.*

126. Wan Ming, "Human Rights Lawmaking in China," p. 745, also asserts that engagement has altered China's value structure, leading to a convergence with U.S. values.

127. Researcher in U.S. R&D facility (C-2000–012), interview by author, Shanghai, China (2000); and human resources manager in U.S. WFOE (C-2005–01), interview by author, Shanghai, China (2005).

128. Human resources manager in U.S. WFOE (C-2000–063), interview by author, Shanghai, China (2000); and human resources manager in Sino-Japanese JV (C-2005–02), interview by author, Shanghai, China (2005).

129. Santoro, *Profits and Principles.*

130. Joshua Kurlantzick, *Charm Offensive: How China's Soft Power Is Transforming the World* (Princeton: Princeton University Press, 2007).

131. David Barboza, "China Still Lags Behind U.S. in Influence, Survey Shows," *New York Times* (17 June 2008), cites a study by the Chicago Council on Global Affairs and the East Asia Institute in South Korea that indicates a high level of U.S. "soft power" in China, Japan, South Korea, Vietnam, Indonesia, and the United States. Amitav Acharya, "Will Asia's Past Be Its Future," p. 152, suggests that Asian states look to maintain ties to China and the United States to moderate China's behavior, and Robert G. Sutter, *China's Foreign Relations*, pp. 401–404, describes how Asian states still look to the United States for leadership and are wary of China, suggestive of a continuation of U.S. soft power.

132. Acharya, "Will Asia's Past," p. 156.

133. Potter, "China and the International Legal System," refers to an "interpretive community" rather than a policy community, but the two overlap.

134. Kurlantzick, *Charm Offensive.*

135. R. Daniel Kelemen and Eric C. Sibbitt, "The Globalization of American Law," *International Organization* 58, no. 1 (Winter 2004), pp. 106–136.

136. Nicholas Lardy, *Integrating China*, p. 104.

137. An example of such changes in orthodoxy comes from the two most recent incidents of financial crises endured by Argentina. In 1991, Argentina pegged its peso to the U.S. dollar to provide stability to the peso, a policy that the IMF supported. While the pegged currency exchange regime did stabilize the Argentine peso, as the U.S. dollar's value rose against other currencies in the 1990s, the Argentine peso rose next to other local trading partner's currencies, which undermined Argentina's ability to export goods. The resulting imbalance in trade triggered a financial crisis to which the government and currency markets could not respond because of the pegged exchange rate mechanism. In 2001, the IMF reversed its earlier recommendation, calling for a free-floating currency exchange rate for the Argentine peso. Independent Evaluation Office of the IMF, "Report on the Evaluation of the Role of the IMF in Argentina, 1991–2001," *IEO Publications* (July 2004). http://www.imf.org/EXTERNAL/NP/IEO/2004/ARG/ENG/INDEX.HTM

138. Alice H. Amsden, *Asia's Next Giant: South Korea and Late Industrialization* (Oxford: Oxford University Press, 1989), pp. 94–96, and 113; Karl J. Fields, *Enterprise and the State in Korea and Taiwan* (Ithaca, NY: Cornell University Press, 1995), p. 107; and Russell Mardon, "The State and the Effective Control of Foreign Capital: The Case of South Korea," *World Politics* 43, no. 1 (October, 1990), pp. 115–117.

139. Fernando Henrique Cardoso and Enzo Faletto, *Dependency and Development in Latin America* (Berkeley: University of California Press, 1979), p. 175.

140. Lardy, *Integrating China*, pp. 66–72 and 110–111.

141. Barry Naughton, *Growing out of the Plan: Chinese Economic Reform, 1978–1993* (Cambridge and New York: Cambridge University Press, 1996). Deng Xiaoping first used the term to describe China's reform process.

142. Medeiros, "Strategic Hedging."

Index